# RECONSTRUCTING THE TALMUD

## VOLUME TWO

Joshua Kulp and Jason Rogoff

# RECONSTRUCTING THE TALMUD

VOLUME TWO

JOSHUA KULP AND JASON ROGOFF

HADAR PRESS

Reconstructing the Talmud: Volume Two

Design by Dov Abramson Studio, Jerusalem

**Hadar Press**
190 Amsterdam Avenue
New York, NY 10023
www.hadarpress.org

ISBN-10: 1-946611-03-4
ISBN-13: 978-1-946611-03-1

Printed in the United States of America
10 9 8 7 6 5 4 3 2 1

# TABLE OF CONTENTS

# FOREWORD

Since the nineteenth century, with the advent of the modern academic field of Religious Studies, scholars of rabbinics have developed new, critical methodologies for reading the Babylonian Talmud. These new approaches have provided innovative and exciting tools that have deepened our understanding of talmudic texts, including the examination of manuscript variants, the separation of linguistic strata, reading texts in light of their historical contexts, marking the historical development of halakhic concepts within the texts, and more. These texts, once understood by their late antique composers and contemporaneous audiences, had been subjected to the passing of more than a millennium, hiding their meaning under the weight of new contexts, theology, and linguistic changes. The new critical tools supplied ways to uncover the Talmud's original meanings and the ways in which the transmitters of the texts influenced their shape and content.

What distinguished the Babylonian Talmud from many other historical texts subjected to this new methodology was the rich interpretive tradition built up continuously by generations of students who studied and revered the Talmud, from the time of its composition to the present. These students built upon the signposts and interpretations of previous generations of readers, offering new understandings rooted in a long chain of transmission and interpretation. The number of such students varied from place to place and from generation to generation, but over time they cemented the long scholastic tradition of talmudic readership, which continues to this day.

In the introduction to Hayim Nahman Bialik and Yehoshua Rawnitzki's 1908 composition, *Sefer Ha-Agaddah*, Bialik described the motivation behind the monumental work as follows:

בימינו לא כל אדם מצוי אצל ספרים
עתיקים ולא כל אדם יכול ורוצה לחטט
בתוך תלי-תלים שנצברו כהררים במשך
כמה דורות – על מנת למצוא מרגליות
תחתם. וכל שכן שלא כל אדם יכול לצרף
קרעים וטלאים לטלית שלמה, ושברי
אבנים מפוזרות לבנין.

Nowadays not everyone is well-versed in ancient volumes and not everyone can or wants to rummage in piles accumulated like mountains over generations, in order to find the jewels hidden underneath. Not to mention that not everyone can assemble shreds and patches into a full garment or scattered fragments of stones into a building.

Bialik and Rawnitzki set out to make the riches of the rabbinic sources accessible to this audience by gathering selected traditions and organizing them by topic. Their creation became a best-selling work that had a profound influence on Jewish learning for decades to come. Unfortunately, they also chose to alter the rabbinic sources in various ways, from the selection process itself to omissions to actual revisions of the original language, in order to create a smoother and more palatable dish than the original.[1]

While more modest in its scale, this present volume by Joshua Kulp and Jason Rogoff, has a similar vision. It also makes accessible some of the unbelievably rich text of the Babylonian Talmud. However, in this case, it does so with the full weight of the critical, academic toolbox. The stated goal of the volume is "to demonstrate to the reader how modern, critical talmudic analysis is performed in order to enable the reader to do so independently." It refuses to compromise the critical method, but rather exemplifies it and demonstrates its value for every reader of the talmudic text.

The authors begin with a richly informed and clearly written introduction that highlights the work of the stammaim, drawing on the most current research (even engaging critically with the research itself at times). They define and demonstrate the three main aspects of stammaitic thinking—consistency, completeness, and formalism—before moving on

---

[1]  See David Stern's introduction to the English edition of *Sefer Ha-Aggadah*, and Haim Weiss, "The Book of Legends and the Study of 'Dead' Legend in Contemporary Israel," *ARV* (Nordic Yearbook of Folklore) 69 (2013): 188–91; "Rabah Bar-Bar-Hannah Tzizit: Between the Talmud and the Book of Legends," *Odot* 5 https://www.reviewbooks.co.il/.

to the individual chapters where the critical method is tested and explained.

The study in this volume does an exemplary job tracking the development of halakhic concepts, separating chronological layers within the text, and identifying the clear distinction between scholastic motivation behind the creation of the sugyot and the ramifications they have for the actual performance of the halakhah derived from each text. The authors do not shy away from pointing out "strained" talmudic logic or the use of "intentionally weak argumentation." They explore possible socioeconomic and historical backgrounds and even dive into topics of considerable scholarly debate, such as the dating of talmudic baraitot. They focus on both content and form, highlighting the terminology and aesthetic goals of the stammaim.

The elusive stammaim seem to come alive in these pages, and, most importantly, the authors give sufficient weight to the nature of these redactors' work proven to be critical to the core understanding of the texts themselves.

This book is a wonderful resource for readers of the Talmud, scholars and non-scholars alike. I congratulate both the authors and **us**—for finally having such an important resource for use both in and out of the academy.

**Dr. Michal Bar-Asher Siegal**
Associate Professor, The Goldstein-Goren Department of Jewish Thought
Ben-Gurion University of the Negev

# INTRODUCTION

## STAMMAITIC THINKING

Throughout the previous volume of *Reconstructing the Talmud*, we pointed to the pervasive and thorough work of the "stammaim," the anonymous Babylonian editors living in the fifth through seventh centuries who created the Bavli as we know it. "Stammaim" is the plural form of the Hebrew word "stam," meaning anonymous, and throughout this book we use the two terms interchangeably. Though we do not know the names of the stammaim, they left their mark on every page of the Talmud, and they are responsible for many of the features that are regarded as the hallmarks of talmudic discourse.

The stammaim operated on many levels. Much of their work was editorial: They rephrased the statements of amoraim, arranged these statements into cohesive and continuous discourse, and added questions and explanations to the tannaitic and amoraic tradition. The stammaim edited the Talmud in the sense that they gave it its final form. Proto-sugyot, brief discourses including arguments and resolutions, did exist in the amoraic era, and some statements that are "stammaitic"—in the sense that they were transmitted anonymously—surely existed, at least in concept, during the amoraic period. But the stammaim gave the Bavli its broader and more final contours.

Yet there seems to be more to stammaitic activity than just editing and redacting. Earlier rabbinic works—the Mishnah, the Tosefta, and the Yerushalmi—are also all redacted, to a lesser or greater extent. The editorial activity that occurs in the Bavli differs substantively from that characteristic of earlier rabbinic activity. The stammaim engage in a type of intellectual work that is distinct from the amoraim at least in degree, if not always in kind. In this introduction, we discuss the nature of stammaitic activity in the various sugyot we treat in the previous volume and in the present one. We will try to distill their unique contribution by describing the characteristics of stammaitic thinking and considering how and why it differs from that of the amoraim who preceded them.

Our main position in this introduction is that the two aspects of stammaitic activity we address in these books, stammaitic redaction and stammaitic thinking, are inextricably connected. The impulse to edit the

Talmud and create a cohesive and comprehensive work is the main factor that led to the rise of an intellectual openness that went beyond that exhibited by their amoraic predecessors.[1] In other words, in our presentation of stammaitic thinking, we will show how the goals of the "stammaim as editors" led to many of the innovations of the "stammaim as thinkers." After all, it seems unlikely that rabbis in the late fifth century (or perhaps even a bit later) woke up one day and began to think differently from their teachers.[2] But rabbis in this period did gradually, if not overnight, decide that the time had come to redact the talmudic oral traditions in a particular manner. We probably will never understand the reason why the choice to redact these traditions was made, but in all likelihood, it was related to the fact that the oral tradition had grown so large that it required a form to facilitate organization and memorization. This is a pattern which repeats itself throughout the long history of creation of rabbinic texts beginning with the Mishnah. The move to redact the rabbinic tradition led the stammaim to make certain editorial decisions. In turn, these editorial decisions led them to offer interpretations, difficulties, and resolutions that differ qualitatively from those of the amoraim.

We consider this chapter an early attempt at a broader taxonomy of the intellectual world of the stammaim. In order to limit the discussion of what is a vast subject, we focus on three main aspects of stammaitic thinking that we have found present in the sugyot that we write about in these two volumes: **consistency**, **completeness**, and **formalism**. To illustrate these features, we will draw on examples from this volume and the first volume of *Reconstructing the Talmud*. In the interest of brevity, we will not reference every source we mention. Such references can be found in the chapters on which the analysis here is based.

Twenty sugyot is an extremely small number of sugyot to analyze before coming to any conclusion as to the work of the editors of the entire Talmud, which contains thousands of sugyot. While we do consider this

---

[1]  Lieb Moscovitz, *Talmudic Reasoning* (Tubingen: Mohr Siebeck, 2002), offers several answers as to what led to the proliferation of the "explicit formulation of legal principles" during the post-amoraic period. Mostly he posits that this was an attempt to bring greater coherence to earlier halakhic literature. Of course, this is one of the primary aims of the stammaim. But we also must take into account why this push for clarity occurs in the post-amoraic period.

[2]  Ibid., 341, 350.

introduction to be representative of stammaitic activity in general, we also hope that the reader will compare the conclusions we have drawn with conclusions drawn from other material. After all, this is the goal of our work: to demonstrate to the reader how modern critical talmudic analysis is performed in order to enable the reader to do so independently. A characterization of stammaitic activity throughout the entire Talmud is a lifetime's worth of work. We hope that this introduction makes a modest contribution.

Finally, we should emphasize how significant this endeavor is in light of the history of Jewish intellectual engagement. The stammaim displayed a remarkable openness to interpretive possibilities that impacted rabbinic intellectual activity for the next 1500 years. The Tosafot, the Talmudic commentators who lived in Germany and France in the 11th through 13th centuries, whose intense analysis of the Talmud set the agenda for Jewish learning to this day, found their muses in these unnamed individuals.[3] The stammaitic style of thinking is found on every page of the commentaries of the Spanish rishonim from the school of the Ramban, including the Rashba, the Ritba, the Ran and many, many others.[4] Indeed, talmudic learning has become synonymous with this type of highly scholastic, theoretical, intellectual study. Studying its origins seems to us to be a search for the roots of Jewish intellectual identity itself.

## I. The Strive for Consistency

The stammaim are the final redactors of the Babylonian Talmud. While rudimentary passages certainly existed in an earlier period and some modifications were made to the Talmud during the lengthy period of oral and written transmission that followed its redaction, it was the stammaitic

---

3   See Haym Soloveitchik, "Dialectics, Scholasticism, and the Origin of the Tosafot," *Collected Essays vol. II* (Oxford: Littman Library of Jewish Civilization, 2014), 23-28; Ephraim Kanarfogel, "Ashkenazic Talmudic Interpretation and the Jewish-Christian Encounter," *Medieval Encounter 22* (2016), 72-94.

4   See Israel Ta-Shma, *Ha-Sifrut ha-Parshanit la-Talmud be-Eropa u-ve-Tzfon Afrika* (Jerusalem: Hebrew University Magnes Press, 1999) 2:38-45; Zvi Groner, "Darkei Hora'ah shel Rishonim u-Geonim" *Meah Shearim*, eds. Ezra Fleischer et. al. (Jerusalem: Hebrew University Magnes Press, 2001), 267-278; Talya Fishman, *Becoming the People of the Talmud* (Philadelphia: University of Pennsylvania Press, 2011), 155-181.

editors who radically transformed the raw material of the earlier period into what has become the cornerstone of Jewish intellectual tradition ever since. As editors tend to do, the stammaim strive for various manifestations of consistency throughout the multiple levels of their creation: the individual passage, the sugya, the chapter, the tractate, and the entire Babylonian composition.[5] Of course, amoraim aspire to consistency as well—often trying to reconcile contradictions between one field of halakhah and another or conflicting statements of earlier sages. But with the stammaim, this drive for consistency goes well beyond harmonizing halakhic opinions. In this section, we will consider various ways in which this striving for consistency is brought to fruition.

We should note that the other two aspects of stammaitic thinking we highlight in this introduction, completeness and formalism, are related to consistency. Completeness is essentially the consistent application of one principle to all aspects of a tradition or legal ruling. Formalism could also be characterized as the consistent imposition of formal literary characteristics on a given text. Thus, the strive for consistency should be viewed as the most significant aspect of stammaitic creation that we have noted throughout our analysis.

## Example 1: The Creation and Imposition of Consistent Halakhic Rules

As many scholars have noted, there is a trend in rabbinic literature to move from case law, rulings related to specific instances, to general principles, applicable to a broader range of situations.[6] The advantage of case law is that it takes into account the smallest of nuances that

---

[5]   From an early period, talmudic scholars noted the existence of five tractates that differ in language and technical terminology from the rest of the Bavli (Nedarim, Nazir, Karetot, Meilah, Tamid). Nevertheless, it is clear that they are still part and parcel of the same larger composition. See Yochanan Breuer, "The Babylonian Aramaic in Tractate Karetot According to MS Oxford," *Aramaic Studies 5:1* (2007), 1-45.

[6]   Lieb Moscovitz, *Talmudic Reasoning*. See also, Jeffrey Rubenstein, "On Some Abstract Concepts in Rabbinic Literature in Rabbinic Literature," *Jewish Studies Quarterly 4* (1997), 33-73; idem, "The Explanation of Tannaitic Sources by Abstract Concepts," *Net'itot le-David: Jubilee Volume for David Weiss Halivni*, eds. Yaakov Elman, et. al. (Jerusalem: Orhot, 2004), 275-304.

distinguish the case at hand from its precedents. However, on account of these nuances, a particular ruling might not be applicable in future cases, and thus case law can at times be a less useful and less precise tool for future halakhic decision makers dealing with cases slightly different from those dealt with in the past.

The drive for consistency leads to several phenomena, most notably the creation of broad rules and general concepts which govern wide ranges of halakhah. Examples of these rules and concepts abound ( מלאכה שאינה צריכה לגופה, מוקצה, עדי מסירה/כתיבה כרתי, דיחוי,סוכה דירת קבע/עראי בעינן, חיישינן למיעוטא, זה וזה גורם אסור/מותר, etc.).[7] Some of these halakhic categories were created by amoraim but they are most fully developed by the stammaim. Indeed, Leib Moscovitz, who has written a full-length book on the subject, goes so far as to assert that "the principle contribution of the anonymous stratum of [the Babyonlian Talmud] to the development of rabbinic conceptualization is the explicit formulation of broadly applicable, abstract concepts and legal principles."[8]

Having created these broad rules and general concepts, the stammaim then attempt to stamp them onto all previous literature and rework earlier material so that tannaim and amoraim rule in a more consistent manner. The stammaim also apply these concepts to areas of halakhah where they had not previously been applied. This, in turn, leads to a myriad of "strained" interpretations and resolutions in stammaitic composition.[9] Indeed, perhaps the most prominent feature of stammaitic thinking is the need to resolve all difficulties, even while resorting to extraordinary explanations. But here we are pointing out more than just a willingness to resolve all difficulties, or to be open to all possibilities. We are calling attention to the application of general concepts to multiple aspects of

---

[7]   Each of these is a broad concept that appears in multiple contexts in the Talmud. Prohibited labor performed on Shabbat not for the sake of the labor itself; witnesses to the writing/delivery of the divorce document sever the marriage; something that may not be manipulated on Shabbat (*muktzeh*); once something is set aside it cannot return; a sukkah needs to be a permanent/impermanent structure; we are concerned about a minority; multiple causation is forbidden. There are far too many such concepts to list here.

[8]   Moscovitz, ibid., 350.

[9]   These forced explanations play a critical role in David Weiss Halivni's theory of the role of the stam and his methodology of interpretation of the Bavli. See David Weiss Halivni, *The Formation of the Babylonian Talmud*, trans. Jeffrey Rubenstein (Oxford: Oxford University Press, 2013), 41-44.

halakhah to which they did not originally apply, which forces the stammaim to suggest resolutions for difficulties that the amoraim never faced.

One outstanding example of this phenomenon is the "resting of vessels" (Shabbat 18a-18b), which is the subject of chapter 2 in the present volume. In the Mishnah and Tosefta, Bet Shammai and Bet Hillel argue over whether one may start a process before Shabbat that will continue on Shabbat, even though that process could not be started on Shabbat itself. For instance, Bet Shammai prohibits one from beginning to soak cloth in dye unless it will have completed the absorption process before Shabbat begins; Bet Hillel permits one to do so (Mishnah Shabbat 1:8). In most cases, Bet Shammai rules stringently and Bet Hillel leniently, but there are exceptions. Both the Mishnah and the Tosefta note some explicit examples where each side admits that the other is correct. For instance, Bet Shammai agrees that one may begin the process of pressing olives or grapes before Shabbat even though the pressing will not be completed before Shabbat (Mishnah Shabbat 1:10). There are also obviously instances where it would be common—perhaps even mandated—for a Jew to set a process in motion before Shabbat that would continue on Shabbat. Thus, at the tannaitic level, both schools are inconsistent, allowing some such processes to be set in motion and prohibiting others. Amoraim address these inconsistencies, but tend to offer ad hoc solutions, explaining why Bet Hillel occasionally rules strictly and why Bet Shammai occasionally rules leniently. Amoraim do not formulate absolute rules that would explain either of the two schools of thought.

In contrast, the talmudic sugya attributes to Bet Shammai a comprehensive prohibition on setting in motion a process that will result in vessels performing work on Shabbat. This prohibition is given a name, שביתת כלים, the "resting of vessels" (Bavli Shabbat 18a) invoked to explain why Bet Shammai prohibits in all of the specific cases found in the Mishnah and Tosefta, and presumably also related cases that are not explicitly mentioned in tannaitic literature. Bet Shammai would argue, according to the sugya, that just as a Jew must rest on Shabbat, so too must his vessels.

Once named, however, the exceptions become problematic, for it would seem that Bet Shammai should prohibit the use of all vessels on Shabbat. The unlimited expansion of this prohibition creates the strange practical problem of how the students of Shammai would allow one, for instance, to light a lamp before Shabbat and let it remain in use on Shabbat, an action which all rabbis clearly permitted and even mandated (Mishnah Shabbat Chapter 2). The stammaim resolve the difficulty by suggesting that Bet Shammai and their followers would declare all of their vessels ownerless prior to every Shabbat in order to skirt the prohibition and make use of these essential vessels. In other words, the vessels indeed "work" but they're not "your vessels"!

This is a creative solution, but as we will argue, it was by no means a practical one. The students of Bet Shammai did not begin every Shabbat by declaring all of their vessels ownerless. Rather, this is a theoretically possible solution which is sufficient to deflect the objection to the inconsistency. The stammaim prefer an absurd resolution of the inconsistency rather than tolerate inconsistency within a given halakhic methodology. Here, as elsewhere, the creation of broad halakhic concepts in an attempt to collect and categorize disparate concrete rulings forces the stammaim to offer extremely strained solutions to prevent these rules from having any exceptions.

Another example of this phenomenon is found in volume one in our chapter on the stolen lulav (Sukkah 29b-30a).[10] In this sugya, R. Yohanan refers to a halakhic concept called "a commandment performed through a transgression (מצווה הבאה בעבירה)." This concept is used to explain why one cannot fulfill one's obligation on Sukkot with a stolen lulav. In our textual analysis of R. Yohanan's statement, we suggested that it might have been created by a redactor and not by R. Yohanan himself. Thus, despite being ascribed to an amora, the very formula may have been created by the stammaim. Furthermore, originally the scope of this concept was very limited—it applied only to the use of stolen goods in the performance of a mitzvah. Amoraim invoke the problem of a commandment performed through a transgression only in the case of one stealing a certain item and then using it to perform a commandment, an act already condemned in the Bible. While it is possible that the amoraim, or some post-R. Yohanan redactor, gave a name to this concept, there is no evidence that the amoraim applied it beyond the particular issue at hand.

---

[10] Kulp and Rogoff, *Reconstructing the Talmud*, 2nd ed. (New York: Hadar Press, 2016), 233-266.

Our interest here is in the subsequent history of this concept. Once a halakhic concept is created in a particular context, it can be invoked and used in other contexts as well. For example, on Gittin 38b, R. Yehudah rules that one who frees his slave transgresses a positive commandment. The Talmud raises a difficulty from a tannaitic story in which R. Eliezer frees a slave in order to complete a minyan for prayer. The Talmud resolves the difficulty by saying that one can free a slave in order to perform a mitzvah—in this case the mitzvah of forming a minyan. But in a parallel in Berakhot 47b, the stammaim go on to ask the question—how can one perform a mitzvah (making a minyan) through a transgression (freeing a slave)? This is an example of the expansion of the concept of מצווה הבאה בעבירה well beyond the notion of using stolen objects to perform a mitzvah. Henceforth, the concept can theoretically be applied to a broad range of situations, which indeed it is, at least in the medieval period, as we show in that chapter. Again, the stammaitic creation of named, broadly applicable concepts facilitates the application of specific rulings to areas of halakhah in which they had never previously been invoked.[11]

## Example 2: Consistency without Named Rules

The imposition of halakhic rules plays a factor even in cases where such rules are not named. Such is the case with regard to the blessing before and after rice, an issue we analyze in chapter one of the current volume. Tannaitic and some early amoraic sources rule that the proper blessing to be recited before eating rice is "*borei minei mezonot*" because rice—at least in the dishes described in these passages—serves as the main source of nourishment at a meal, the *mazon*. The same blessing would have been recited over any dish that was a cooked, substantive "dish." The ingredients, which could include any form of starch, mattered less than the function of the dish within the meal.

However, when those same sources relate to the blessing recited after the meal, it is the ingredients and not the function of the dish that

---

[11]  Moscovitz, ibid., 351, writes, "It seems that post-tannaitic legal principles, once formulated, sometimes took on a life of their own...even if this was not the intention of the scholars who originally formulated these principles."

determine the blessing. Unless the dish is made of one of the five grains[12] or the seven species native to the Land of Israel,[13] no concluding blessing is recited (according to tannaitic sources). Thus, different criteria were used in determining the blessing before the meal and the blessing after. The lack of consistency in the factors which determine the blessing would have led to a lack of a correlation between the blessing before and the blessing after the food. For example, one would recite *mezonot* before eating dishes consisting of either rice or grain, but one would offer a concluding blessing only after eating grain and not after rice. Indeed, this is stated explicitly in the Tosefta.

This begins to change in the amoraic period, in which there is a drive for greater consistency. A new ruling begins to take hold: If no blessing is recited after rice, then the blessing before rice should not be the same as that used for products made from the five grains, which **do** require a blessing after the meal. This process is initiated by the amoraim, but only the stammaim flesh out the full rule. They derive it from a redundancy in two statements attributed to the amoraim Rav and Shmuel, both of whom mandate the blessing of "*borei minei mezonot*" for products made from one of the five grains. However, Rav and Shmuel do not explicitly rule that *mezonot* is **not** recited over **non**-grain products; they formulate their ruling only in the positive. It is the stammaim who, noting that Rav and Shmuel's ruling is formed in two slightly different ways that seem redundant, read into this redundancy the negative rule: *Mezonot* is never recited over rice (or millet).

This rule completely contradicts tannaitic halakhah, a contradiction that the stammaim seem willing to overlook. What is important to the stammaim is to preface the entire sugya with a straightforward, consistent, and memorable halakhic rule: *Mezonot* is recited only over anything made from one of the five grains and is never recited over anything made from any other ingredient, even if it is part of a cooked dish. Furthermore, this results in complete consistency between the blessing before and after: If one blesses *mezonot* before, then one blessing will be recited after (or "one

---

[12]   Wheat, barley, spelt, rye or oats.
[13]   Wheat, barley, dates, figs, olives, pomegranates, and grapes.

blessing that is derived from three").[14] For rice and millet, since one does not bless *mezonot* before, one will not recite a blessing after. Just as the concluding blessing is ingredient-based, so is the preceding blessing.

## Example 3: Imposition of Tannaitic Rules on Amoraim

In order to better contextualize the phenomenon of strained interpretations and resolutions within talmudic history, it is worth considering the historical position of the stammaitic editors. The stammaim inherited a tradition that often led to the necessity of offering strained interpretations and resolutions in order to harmonize conflicting earlier positions, whereas their predecessors had far less of a need to do so. The rabbis of the mishnaic period, the tannaim, disagree with each other in nearly every chapter of the Mishnah and there is little hierarchy of authority between them. Amoraim, certainly by the later generations, already began to treat the Mishnah as canonical and the earlier tannaitic sources as authoritative.[15] The amoraim therefore challenge one another by citing opposing tannaitic material, on the assumption that an amora can never be contradicted by a tannaitic tradition.

However, when all is said and done, amoraim frequently act independently of tannaitic opinion. They contradict tannaitic opinion, and they do not always resolve the challenges raised against them from tannaitic sources. The stammaim, on the other hand, strive to impose consistency between amoraic legal rulings and tannaitic halakhah. According to the stammaim, amoraim do not share the authority of their predecessors and therefore are not allowed to disagree with them. When they seem to do so, the stammaim **must** resolve their opinions.

---

14  This refers to the abbreviated form of birkat hamazon recited after eating the five grains or seven species (see Mishnah Berakhot 6:8). The Mishnah, Tosefta, and Yerushalmi always refer to "one blessing" whereas the Bavli calls this blessing "one blessing that is derived from three."

15  R. Isaiah di-Trani (*Piksei Rid* Shabbat 22a) succinctly explains: "The Mishnah is to the Amoraim as the Torah is to the Tannaim." See also David Henshke, "*Abaye ve-Rava: Shtei Gishot la-Mishnah*," *Tarbiz 49* (1980), 187-193; Richard Kalmin, *Sages, Stories, Authors, and Editors in Rabbinic Babylonia* (Atlanta: Scholars Press, 1994), 43-59; Michael Berger, *Rabbinic Authority* (Oxford: Oxford University Press, 1998), 114-131.

The stammaim also strive to create far greater consistency within tannaitic and amoraic halakhah, identifying inconsistencies where none were previously thought to exist and resolving them. Again, this trend certainly exists during the amoraic period. But it plays a far greater role for the stammaim, owing to the editorial role they play, their function as the Talmud's final redactors, and the massive scope of the literary corpus they inherited and sought to harmonize.[16]

An example of this phenomenon is found in the sugya on lost objects (Bava Metzia 24a), which appears in chapter seven of this volume. Tannaitic halakhah allows a finder to keep all objects discovered in the public domain under the assumption that the one who lost the object will not hope to recover it. The finder need not declare such an item in an attempt to find its original owner. Babylonian amoraic halakhah, however, does not perceive this to be a general rule and requires the declaration of lost objects found in the public domain in a place where there is a Jewish majority. Amoraim assume that when a Jew finds something, he will strive to return it to its owner; therefore, Jews who lose items, even in the public domain, with a Jewish majority, will not lose hope of recovering them.

This is a case in which amoraim do not perceive themselves to be beholden to tannaitic halakhah in its entirety. But the notion that amoraic halakhah can contradict tannaitic tradition is not acceptable to the stammaim, and thus, in an effort to reconcile the later Babylonian halakhah with the earlier tannaitic sources, they offer extraordinarily strained resolutions of earlier sources. These strained resolutions reach a crescendo with the treatment of a baraita which states that objects found in a synagogue or a bet midrash may be kept without declaration. Since these are public places, tannaitic halakhah holds that any items found in them need not be declared. As the stammaim are quick to note, this baraita contradicts amoraic halakhah, for these are quite certainly places in which Jews are located. To resolve the difficulty, the stam is willing to posit that the baraita refers to non-Jewish synagogues or, at the very least, to synagogues and batei midrash frequented by many non-Jews.

This stammaitic resolution is not based on historical fact, and any historian who attempts to invoke this passage as evidence for the actual

---

[16] For a description of this editorial role see Shamma Friedman, *Sugyot be-Heker ha-Talmud ha-Bavli* (Jerusalem: Jewish Theological Seminary of America, 2010), 57-62.

presence of non-Jews in synagogues simply does not understand the nature of stammaitic resolutions.[17] Rather, it is a classic example of the stammaitic preference for any theoretically possible response, no matter how unrealistic, in order to avoid inconsistency.

## Example 4: Consistency within Tannaitic Sources

It is of course not surprising that stammaim search for consistent reasoning within mishnayot and baraitot. An example of this is found in our analysis of women and birkat hamazon in volume one.[18] The Mishnah and the Tosefta both rule that women and children are obligated to recite birkat hamazon, but the Tosefta adds that they should not perform this mitzvah on behalf of "the multitudes." We interpreted this to mean that it is not considered proper for women and children to publicly perform this mitzvah in order to exempt adult males of their obligation. Nevertheless, women and children may exempt others of their obligation in private, and indeed the Tosefta says so explicitly. Women and children are obligated to recite birkat hamazon and therefore they can facilitate the performance of the mitzvah for others.

The Talmud opens up the question of whether this obligation and the obligation to recite kiddush on Shabbat are from the Torah or from the rabbis. This question is asked and at least partially answered by amoraim. Rava seems to think that both of these obligations are from the Torah. This would explain, to Rava, why a woman can fulfill the mitzvah of birkat hamazon for her husband—both are biblically obligated in the mitzvah. However, this creates a problem for the stam who assumes that children are not obligated in any mitzvot until they reach majority age. This is a notion that develops only in the late talmudic period and does not accord with the tannaitic sources.[19] Thus there is a difficulty for the stam—how can children who are not obligated by the Torah exempt adult men who are obligated?

To solve this difficulty, the stam invents a notion not found anywhere else in rabbinic literature: Adult men who eat to less than their satisfaction

---

[17] See for example David Novak, *Law and Theology in Judaism: Second Series* (New York: Ktav Publishing House, 1976), 207 n. 46.

[18] Kulp and Rogoff, *Reconstructing the Talmud*, 2nd ed., 171-195.

[19] See Y.D. Gilat, *Perakim be-Hishtalshelut ha-Halakhah* (Ramat Gan: Bar Ilan University, 1992), 19-31.

are only rabbinically required to recite birkat hamazon. Their obligation is from the Torah only if they eat an amount that would satisfy their hunger. The baraita is now considered to be completely consistent. Both women and children have only a rabbinic obligation to recite birkat hamazon and can fulfill the obligation only for men when their obligation is also only rabbinic.

We should emphasize the difference between the amoraim and the stam in this sugya. The amoraim here seem to be guided by a socio-halakhic agenda. Earlier in the sugya Rav Ada bar Ahava had stated that women are obligated by the Torah to recite the kiddush. Abaye proposes that a woman's obligation in kiddush is only of rabbinic origin in order to harmonize this statement with the mishnah in Kiddushin which states that women are exempt from positive, time-bound commandments. Abaye, like many amoraim, is interested in harmonizing amoraic statements with tannaitic halakhah, but he is probably also motivated by a socio-halakhic agenda as well. For Abaye, the status of women vis a vis mitzvot is not equal to that of men. The same is true for Ravina, who asks whether a woman's obligation in birkat hamazon is biblical or rabbinic.[20] Both amoraim seem to view women as having lesser obligations in the performance of ritual commandments than do men, and this conception guides their halakhic reasoning. There is also a similar halakhic agenda underlying the trend to consider minors as only obligated by rabbinic law in the performance of mitzvot. The rabbis restrict obligation in ritual commandments to adult males. The rabbis who transform these halakhot do so partly in order to solve difficulties, but also in an attempt to bring halakhah into greater consistency with their own worldview.

The stam, on the other hand, is motivated entirely by a drive for consistency. The stam invents the notion that if men eat less than to their satisfaction, their obligation is only rabbinic and not biblical *solely* in order to provide consistency to the baraita. Since the stam understands the obligation of children as rabbinic, and yet the baraita rules that children may fulfill the mitzvah for adult men, men's obligation must also be rabbinic. Thus, to solve the problem of how someone obligated by rabbinic law can fulfill the obligation of a man, who would seem to be obligated by biblical law, the stam invents a completely novel halakhic idea. It is worth noting that this ruling would create considerable

---

[20]   See *Reconstructing the Talmud*, 2nd ed., 196-204.

difficulty for practical halakhah, since one would always need to check if someone ate to satisfaction before that person could "lead" birkat hamazon. It therefore seems very unlikely that the stam invents this notion in order to shape halakhah in a particular manner or even as a reflection of his understanding of the obligation to recite birkat hamazon. Rather, this is yet another instance of the stammaim resolving difficulties and reconciling inconsistent sources with one another.

## II. Completeness

One of the main features that distinguishes the Bavli from the Yerushalmi is its style of discourse. As a general rule, Yerushalmi sugyot are more concise, narrower in scope, and adhere more closely to the tannaitic sources than their Babylonian counterparts.[21] In contrast, Babylonian sugyot are characterized by their commitment to investigate every conceivable position (no matter how unlikely) and leave no question unanswered. The stammaim strive to create sugyot that cite as many sources as possible and that explore as many avenues of interpretation as possible. Some of the examples below could also be characterized under the rubric of consistency which we described above: Completeness and consistency go hand in hand, since one complements the other. The stammaim apply a consistent approach in commenting and interpreting earlier literature and they attempt to apply that approach to the full tannaitic and amoraic tradition. In the examples below, we will demonstrate cases where the extension of reason and interpretation leads again to the signature characteristic of the stammaim: the creation of passages whose logic is extraordinarily strained, and whose legal content is not reflective of opinions held by any sages.

---

[21]   This is especially true in regard to Yerushalmi sugyot from tractates Bava Kama, Bava Metzia, and Bava Batra. See Yaakov Sussman, "Ve-Shuv le-Yerushalmi Nezikin," *Mehqerei Talmud I* (Jerusalem: Hebrew University Magnes Press, 1990), 98-99.

## Example 1: Expanding Amoraic Interpretation to its (Il)logical Conclusion

A notable characteristic of stammaitic thinking is the tendency to apply earlier rabbinic statements made in specific contexts to a broad spectrum of cases. This interpretive maneuver allows the stammaim to test the limits of a given rabbinic interpretation and explore the full range of implications of a particular position. The stammaim fervently pursue these interpretative explorations even if they lead to absurdity. We find this, for instance, in a passage concerning the status after Pesah of hametz owned by a Jew on Pesah (for the sake of brevity we shall call this "hametz after Pesah"). This sugya (Pesahim 28a-29b) is particularly complicated and has a complex redactorial history. Here we offer only a brief sketch of the more consequential stammaitic activity that occurs within it.

Mishnah Pesahim 2:2 teaches two laws. First, a Jew may derive benefit after Pesah from hametz owned by a non-Jew on Pesah. Second, a Jew may not derive benefit after Pesah from hametz owned by a Jew on Pesah. The mishnah appends a midrash to this second halakhah, implying that this prohibition is biblical. These two tannaitic halakhot are universally agreed upon in tannaitic literature. All tannaim prohibit a Jew from deriving benefit from hametz owned by a Jew on Pesah, and all permit deriving benefit from hametz owned by a non-Jew on Pesah. Tannaitic literature contains, at most, a dispute over the severity of the prohibition—biblical or rabbinic.

The amoraim argue over the authorship of this mishnah, particularly its second half, concerning hametz owned by a Jew. The mishnah clearly agrees with R. Yehudah from the Tosefta, who holds that it is biblically prohibited to derive benefit from hametz owned by a Jew on Pesah. R. Aha b. Ya'akov indeed ascribes the mishnah to R. Yehudah. In contrast, Rava (according to our interpretation) suggests that the mishnah could even agree with R. Shimon. R. Shimon, according to Rava, agrees that such hametz is prohibited, just not by the Torah.

The stam makes two assumptions in interpreting each amora's words:

1) When an amora says that "R. So-and-so" is the author of the mishnah, he implies that the other tanna (here R. Shimon or R. Yehudah) disagrees with the mishnah;

2) The amoraim were ascribing the entire mishnah to one tanna, and not just the section about hametz owned by a Jew.

With these two assumptions in mind, the stam then fleshes out what each amora holds is the position of the tanna who is not the author of the mishnah. As stated above, R. Aha b. Ya'akov identifies the mishnah with R. Yehudah. R. Yehudah holds that hametz owned by a Jew is prohibited after Pesah, as is explicitly stated in the mishnah. The stam never says what R. Aha b. Ya'akov would consider to be R. Shimon's position on the issue. Rava, on the other hand, identifies the mishnah with R. Shimon—he too holds that hametz owned by a Jew is prohibited, although not by the Torah but rather by the rabbis. And if the mishnah follows R. Shimon, by implication R. Yehudah must rule more strictly across the board, given that he is stricter when it comes to hametz owned by a Jew. Therefore, according to Rava, R. Yehudah prohibits even hametz owned by a non-Jew on Pesah. The following chart summarizes the way the stam understands each amora:

|  | **R. Yehudah** | **R. Shimon** |
|---|---|---|
| **R. Aha b. Ya'akov** | Hametz owned by Jew—prohibited by the Torah<br><br>Hametz owned by non-Jew—permitted | Stam never discusses this issue |
| **Rava** | Hametz owned by Jew—prohibited by the Torah<br><br>Hametz owned by non-Jew—also prohibited by the Torah. | Hametz owned by Jew—prohibited by the rabbis.<br><br>Hametz owned by non-Jew—permitted |

However, the prohibition of hametz owned by a non-Jew on Pesah is a law not found anywhere in tannaitic literature, and it is downright absurd. Why should hametz owned by a non-Jew on Pesah be prohibited after Pesah? Is a non-Jew mandated to remove his hametz on Pesah? As a result of the quest for a complete explanation of the full range of tannaitic positions according to each amora, the stam creates an entirely new tannaitic position not found anywhere in tannaitic literature, and one that certainly does not reflect Jewish practice at any point in time.

The search for completeness and consistency has not yet come to its full realization. To explain R. Aha b. Ya'akov's position that the mishnah follows R. Yehudah, the stam creates a midrash for the first half of the mishnah explaining why hametz owned by a non-Jew on Pesah is permitted after Pesah. According to the midrash, just as a Jew can *see* the hametz of a non-Jew on Pesah, so too he can **eat** the hametz after Pesah. This itself is accurate and explains the simple reading of the mishnah. But once this midrash is created, the stam pushes it to an absurd limit—just as a Jew can see the hametz owned by a non-Jew on Pesah, so too a Jew can eat hametz owned by a non-Jew on Pesah! Of course, no sage ever actually thought that a Jew could eat hametz on Pesah no matter who owns it— the prohibition is universal and familiar to anyone who knows anything about Jewish law. But completeness and consistency take on a life of their own, and if R. Yehudah derives the laws of eating hametz from the laws of seeing hametz (as he does with regard to eating the hametz of a non-Jew after Pesah), so too he must derive the laws of eating hametz during Pesah from the laws of seeing hametz during Pesah. Thus the stam has undone, at least according to one position, one of the most serious prohibitions in the Torah.

## Example 2: Expanding Tannaitic Interpretation to its (Il)logical Conclusion

As in the above example with amoraic statements, the stam also seeks to flesh out the full implications of tannaitic positions, even if this leads to the attribution of statements to tannaim that seem fundamentally at odds with prevailing rabbinic tradition. We find this phenomenon as well in our sugya in Pesahim.

Tannaitic literature always assumes that during Pesah a Jew may not derive any benefit from hametz: One may not sell it to a non-Jew, nor feed it to one's animals. If one could, then there would be no reason to destroy all hametz before Pesah. In tannaitic compositions, no tanna ever says anything even remotely opposed to this rule. Amoraim, too, never hint that one can derive benefit from hametz during Pesah. However, in a baraita found only in the Bavli, R. Yose Hagalili indeed does rule that a Jew may derive benefit from hametz on Pesah. This opinion, which opposes the very foundations of large portions of Tractate Pesahim—the laws of checking for hametz and burning hametz are both based on the complete prohibition of hametz during Pesah—cries out for an explanation.

Shamma Friedman has suggested that this opinion was derived in a very stammaitic fashion from a statement of R. Yose Hagalili in the Mekhilta.[22] In this tannaitic midrash, two tannaim use a biblical verse in order to prove that one may not derive benefit from hametz. R. Yose Hagalili, in contrast, interprets the same verse in an entirely different manner. In the midrash, R. Yose Hagalili does not claim to be disagreeing with the halakhic content of the other derashot. He simply provides another interpretation of the verse. However, the Bavli (essentially the stam, according to Friedman) assumes that since R. Yose Hagalili disagrees with the exegesis of the verse, he must also disagree with the halakhah derived by others from the verse. With this assumption in mind, the stam creates an explicit statement attributed to R. Yose Hagalili permitting deriving benefit from hametz on Pesah. Here too, the drive for completeness and consistency leads the stam to insist that tannaitic exegesis correlates with tannaitic halakhic ruling.

A word is in order here as to the type of literary activity to which we are referring and its dating. The Bavli contains many baraitot that are parallel but not identical to those in earlier collections—the Tosefta, the halakhic midrashim, and the Yerushalmi.[23] The common assumption among talmudic scholars is that these baraitot were edited during their transmission from Eretz Yisrael to Babylonia. Many were edited by the amoraim themselves, but some—like the statement attributed to R. Yose Hagalili—seem to be stammaitic creations. But we do not ascribe all changes in tannaitic sources to late stammaitic activity. Each case must be treated on its own to see whether it is possible to determine when the change in the tannaitic source came into being.

In this case, there are several indications that R. Yose Hagalili's statement as found in this baraita is of stammaitic origin. First, no amoraim ever refer to it. It seems unlikely that such an anomalous tannaitic position would be completely ignored by the amoraim. Second, the logic lying behind its creation is distinctly stammaitic. According to stammaitic thought, tannaim who interpret verses differently from other

---

[22] Shamma Friedman, *Tosefta Atikta* (Ramat Gan: Bar Ilan University Press, 2002), 212-216.

[23] See *Reconstructing the Talmud* 2nd ed., 18-22.

tannaim must also have different corresponding halakhic positions. Thus, this line found in the baraita is most likely a stammaitic creation, not an amoraic emendation and certainly not a genuine tannaitic position.

## Example 3: Broadening the Scope of Amoraic Disputes

The drive for completeness can also manifest itself as a drive to expand the ramifications of tannaitic and amoraic law. The more specific the case which tannaim and amoraim discuss and dispute, the less useful it will be in adjudicating other situations. The stammaim will thus at times transform a limited dispute, one relevant only to a particular historical circumstance, into an expansive dispute with broad application.

An example of this is found in chapter nine of the current volume. Mishnah Avodah Zarah 1:4 prohibits a Jew from entering a store participating in an idolatrous fair or festival. The sign of such participation is decorations. In the Yerushalmi, R. Yohanan rules that only decorations of myrtle are a sign of participation in the fair, whereas Resh Lakish rules that any decoration put up specifically for the fair is a sign of participation. This dispute is of limited application. It would be relevant only to Jews living in the particular milieu where stores used certain decorations to denote their participation in the fair. Furthermore, the debate is limited to the specifics of a particular case law and does not represent a larger conceptual disagreement between the amoraim. The two amoraim argue whether other vegetation put up as decoration—pomegranates, for instance—are a sign of participation in the fair. But such realistic details could change from place to place (maybe some places do use pomegranates as idolatrous decorations) and thus the dispute is relevant only where these conditions reign. In fact, the amoraim seem to agree on the underlying principle—it is forbidden to enter a store whose decorations are put up in honor of the fair.

The Bavli slightly modifies the words of this dispute but radically broadens its scope. In the Bavli, Resh Lakish (parallel to R. Yohanan in the Yerushalmi) rules that it is forbidden to enter a store decorated with a myrtle **or a rose**. Adding the small detail of the rose changes the entire meaning of the statement. As the stam explains, the problem is not that these items are signs of participation in the fair. The problem is that they smell nice. A Jew who enters such a store will benefit from the smell. By implication, a Jew can enter any other store, even those participating in the idolatrous fair, as long as he does not derive benefit (for free) from the goods. He may even purchase items there, and thereby confer a benefit on the sellers who are participating in idolatry. This ruling is then broadened even further by a stammaitic comment positing that according to Resh Lakish, while it is prohibited for a Jew to derive benefit from idolatry, it is always permitted to confer benefit on idolatry. This law blatantly contradicts multiple tannaitic sources, is based on a midrash not found in any tannaitic or earlier amoraic source, and seems to completely oppose the general direction of the discourse. The creation of this position by the stammaitic editors is a result of their desire to take the limited position and dispute in the Yerushalmi and transform it into a broad conceptual position with application to nearly every interaction between Jew and non-Jew. Furthermore, Resh Lakish's view now serves as a foil to the view attributed here to R. Yohanan and found throughout the tractate—it is prohibited to confer benefit on idolatry. Through this process, the stam creates an amoraic (and tannaitic, as the continuation of the sugya shows) dispute on one of the broadest concerns of Tractate Avodah Zarah.

## Example 4: Creating a Dissenting Opinion

This last example, whereby the stammaim create dissent on a broad issue, segues into another manifestation of the stammaitic drive for completeness—the stammaitic idea that for any position, there must be a counter-position. As we also saw above, with regard to the issue of hametz after Pesah, the stam is willing to create dissenting opinions to the rabbinic consensus even if no rabbi ever actually held such positions. If a position is attributed to one rabbi, then the stam will often create a counter-position.

One such example which we discuss in this current volume concerns killing a "pursuer," one who eminently threatens the life of another human being (Sanhedrin 72b). Tannaitic law, and common sense, dictates that one is allowed to kill a pursuer in order to save the life of the pursued, despite the fact that in all other cases a trial based on evidence is required in order to execute a person. R. Huna rules that a minor, too, can legally constitute a pursuer. This means that if a minor pursues another person with the intent to kill, a bystander may preemptively kill the minor to protect the pursued. One might have thought that since a minor cannot be held accountable in a court of law, he also cannot be killed in order to save the life of one he is pursuing. Nevertheless, R. Huna rules that since the minor threatens the life of another, he may be preemptively killed.

The stam extrapolates from this specific teaching a much broader ruling concerning the law of killing a pursuer. In standard cases of rabbinic jurisprudence, a person cannot be convicted of a crime unless he was warned before he committed it. Witnesses must say to him, "Know that if you commit such-and-such a crime, you will be punished." However, a minor cannot comprehend the meaning of a warning, for he is not considered to have "דעת," which is best translated as understanding. From the fact that a minor pursuer need not be warned, the stam deduces that pursuers never need to be legally warned before they are preemptively killed. This interpretive maneuver is emblematic of the stammaitic desire to broaden the scope of amoraic statements to create sugyot with more expansive fields of inquiry. A rule that applied just to a minor is assumed to apply to all pursuers. This position is of course intuitive: A pursuer is not being punished for a crime, he is being killed to protect the life of another; therefore, a warning concerning punishment would be out of place and indeed dangerous to the pursued. It is also halakhically correct: There is no hint that any sage actually rules that a pursuer must be warned before he is killed.

But the creation of a rule, or perhaps the very notion that such a rule needs to be stated, opens up the possibility that the opposite position exists. If R. Huna holds that pursuers do not need to be warned, then there must be a halakhic authority who holds that a pursuer must be warned before he is killed. In the absence of an actual sage who would put forth such a counter-intuitive position, the stam attributes this notion to R. Hisda. The particular attribution is not what is critical here. What is critical—and emblematic of stammaitic thinking—is that for halakhic discourse to be complete, halakhic positions must have their counter-positions. What motivates the stam is not practicality, for this law is one of the more impractical (if not immoral) laws in the Talmud. Warning a pursuer may impede stopping him from committing his deadly intent, thereby threatening the life of the pursued. Nor is the stam merely interested in offering interpretations of earlier halakhah. Rather, the stam is motivated by the impulse to create an intellectual world that is complete with both position and counter-position.

## Example 5: Interpreting the Mishnah

Amoraic literary activity does not include a comprehensive interpretation of the entire Mishnah. The amoraim were of course intensely interested in the Mishnah and a large portion of their literary activity revolves around it. But one would look in vain in either Talmud for an amoraic commentary on every single line of the Mishnah.

The stammaim also do not offer a commentary on the entire Mishnah, but they do strive to offer a more complete interpretation of it than their amoraic predecessors. This is evident in our chapter on betrothal in this volume (Ketubot 57b-58b). The rabbis in this sugya consider the nature of betrothal: How strong a bond does it create between the man and woman? One of the main ways the tannaim express their view is through the rules of terumah, food that may be eaten only by priests and their immediate family, including their spouses. If betrothal is considered a strong bond, then an Israelite woman (of non-priestly descent) betrothed to a priest can eat terumah. If it is regarded as weak, then she must wait until marriage proper.

Mishnah Ketubot 5:2-3 offers two positions:

1) That an Israelite woman can begin to eat terumah when the time for marriage arrives (defined by the mishnah as no longer than twelve months after one of the already-betrothed partners demands that the other party complete the marriage); and

2) That she must wait until marriage (the huppah).

For reasons detailed in the chapter, the amoraim accept the premise that a woman is biblically permitted to eat terumah immediately after betrothal but the rabbis nevertheless prohibit her from doing so. Therefore, the amoraim focus on the question—if biblical law allows her to eat terumah at the point of betrothal, then why must she, in reality, wait until marriage? This question emerges out of their analysis of tannaitic midrashic and halakhic compositions. The amoraim did not grapple with this mishnah from Ketubot, and indeed we do not find any amoraic interpretation of this particular clause.

The stam, however, feels the impulse to interpret the mishnah, and not just the tannaitic midrashic tradition. As a result, the stam uses this amoraic material which engages the halakhic midrashim to offer a comprehensive interpretation of this mishnah from Ketubot, even though this material is particularly ill-suited to do so. For example, the amora Ulla succinctly explains the rabbinic stringency. While the Torah would allow a woman to eat terumah while she is betrothed and still living in her father's home, the rabbis disallow it lest she offer the terumah to her Israelite family. But to the stam, Ulla's statement serves an entirely different purpose: He explains why the mishnah allows her to begin eating terumah while living in her father's house after the time for marriage has elapsed. The raises an obvious question: Why are we not concerned lest she give terumah to her family? In an effort to avoid the problem, the stam posits that that the husband sets aside a place for his fiancée even before he marries her. Of course, we have no evidence that this ever occurred. Notably, the stammaim's primary goal of interpreting the mishnah with preexisting sources results in a difficulty of their own creation which they reconcile with the unintended side effect of rewriting social history.

## III. Formalism

Stammaitic literature is highly formulaic, often preferring form over content and privileging the structure of the argument over coherent interpretation. Indeed, one of the hallmarks of the Bavli, one which makes it an easier work to understand than the Yerushalmi, is the consistent use of technical terms. At times, this simply helps the argument flow and aids the reader in understanding the function of each line of the discourse. Technical terms also enable the reader to anticipate what to expect out of talmudic argumentation. This terminology, which recurs throughout the text, is easy to remember and may also have served a mnemonic function. But the style of stammaitic writing seems to be motivated by more than just didactic ease. Consistent, complete, and formal composition seems to be a goal in its own right, pleasing to the ear like the refrain of a song. And as we have seen time and time again, these aesthetic goals often lead to strained proposals and resolutions. Plausibility is, at least to a certain extent, sacrificed for the sake of literary quality.

### Example 1: Adherence to a Predetermined Formula

The stam's adherence to predetermined formulae at times leads to suggestions and interpretations that are not reflective of the actual sources being interpreted. An example of this is the phrase "learn from it three

(שמע מינה תלת)," which appears over 25 times in the Bavli. In each case it means "learn three things," usually three abstract legal principles, from a mishnah or other tannaitic source.[24] The phrase and its attendant explication is always stammaitic. While amoraim clearly derive laws from the Mishnah and other tannaitic sources, they do not adhere to any particular number of deductions. In contrast, when deriving multiple abstract legal principles from a tannaitic source, the stam never proposes that one can learn two or four principles—only three.

This adherence to a predetermined formula inevitably leads to derivations from the Mishnah that are not really derived from there at all. At times, we can sense that two principles can be derived from the Mishnah, but not three. Nevertheless, the stam will of necessity add in a third derivation. Such is the case in the *Benin Dikhrin* sugya (Ketubot 90b-91a), the passage concerning the inheritance of sons from their mothers, which we analyze in this volume. The Talmud opens its discussion of that mishnah by saying "learn from this three." The first two derivations lie at the heart of the amoraic core of the sugya and do seem to reflect the meaning of the mishnah, although this point is debated within the sugya. But the third issue is not related at all to what the mishnah specifically teaches. It is hard to see how this principle is derived from the mishnah—doing so requires very strained assumptions. Furthermore, the amoraim in this sugya do not at all deal with this third derivation—it is the subject of another passage altogether. In sum, this third teaching is not part of the larger discourse here and is only brought to fill in the requisite three.

Broadly speaking, the stammaim are willing to let predetermined literary formulae impact their halakhic conclusions, or at least their potential halakhic conclusions. If something is "learned from the mishnah" then it has, or at least should have, greater halakhic authority. For the simple reason that this formula dictates that three matters be derived, and not two, an additional halakhah is pegged on the mishnah and thereby invested with its authority.

---

[24] The phrase "learn from it two (שמע מינה תרתי)," which also appears frequently, might seem to be related, but it is not. This expression is used to mean that one can learn two halakhot from one phrase in the Torah (rather than a tannaitic source). In contrast, "learn from it three" always applies to a tannaitic source.

## Example 2: Adherence to the Form of Earlier Source Material

The stammaim often adapt preexisting source material to fit into new contexts and to create new discourse. Frequently, the stammaim remain faithful to the style and arrangement of earlier sources, even if this conservative tendency creates some dissonance in their compositions. For instance, if in an earlier composition two subjects are discussed in juxtaposition, these two subjects might remain juxtaposed, despite the fact that their original connection has been lost.[25]

One such example is found in our analysis of Ketubot 110a-b in this volume. At the core of the sugya lies an amoraic story of R. Zera avoiding his master, R. Yehudah, because of the latter's prohibition of moving to the Land of Israel. R. Yehudah offers a prooftext for his position. Nevertheless, R. Zera ignores R. Yehudah and ultimately abandons Babylonia for Israel. The amoraic source material never provides an explicit justification for R. Zera's brazen disregard of his master's prohibition. To balance R. Yehudah's argument, the stam creates a counterargument equally based in the biblical text. The stam argues in R. Zera's name that the prohibition is limited to a mass movement, whereas individuals are permitted to move to the Land of Israel.

The stam draws this distinction from an older midrash that is found in Song of Songs Rabbah 2:7. According to this earlier source, which is based on the verse, "I adjured you, O maidens of Jerusalem" (Song of Songs 2:7), when Israel was sent into exile, they were adjured at least two oaths by God. Two Eretz Yisraeli amoraim debate the number and nature of the oaths. According to R. Yose b. R. Hanina, a single set of reciprocal oaths was made by Israel and the nations of the world, namely that Israel was not to rebel, and the nations should not persecute Israel too much. Based on the fact that this same verse appears twice in Song of Songs (again in 3:5), R. Helbo doubles the number of oaths. In his version, all of the oaths were made by Israel. One of the oaths cited by R. Helbo is the promise to not move בחומה, which we have translated "en masse," to the Land of Israel.

Returning to the sugya in Ketubot, R. Zera first defends himself against R. Yehudah's initial attack, and then R. Yehudah invokes the oath

---

25   For examples see David Rosenthal, "Lo Itparesh Lan Mai Ba'ei Hakha: Al Gufim Zarim ba-Bavli," *Bar-Ilan* 18-19 (1981), 150-169.

from Song of Songs 2:7 that was the focus of the midrash mentioned above to prove that Jews may not move to Israel. R. Zera replies by interpreting the verse as prohibiting moving to Eretz Yisrael only en masse. Since he is acting as an individual, R. Zera claims that he may return.

R. Yehudah presses on, noting that the verse concerning the oaths appears twice—once to prohibit moving en masse and once to prohibit moving as individuals. R. Zera must again defend himself and now claims that the second occurrence of the verse refers to a midrash of three oaths. These three oaths consist of the one that the stam attributed earlier to R. Zera, "that they should not move en masse," and the two other reciprocal oaths spoken by Israel and the nations of the world. For R. Zera's argument, it is essential that he include the oath "not to move en masse" with the two other oaths. However, it completely disrupts the structure of the original midrash, for it throws off the reciprocity of the two original oaths. Furthermore, there is no explanation why there should be "three oaths." In contrast, in the original midrash we can sense that there are two oaths corresponding to two phrases that appear at the end the verse: "do not wake" and "do not rouse." The stam's fealty to the form of the earlier midrash leads to the multiple distortions found in this midrashic exchange. One who reads the Bavli without being familiar with the earlier source would have trouble understanding the dispute over the nature and number of the oaths.

This is a classic case where older material leaves its imprint on later versions. But such is the nature of tradition, and it is certainly not unique to the stam. Rather, the hallmark of the stammaim is their creativity in creating frameworks to adopt this material for their own editorial needs. "Stammaitic thinking," to use the term that heads this chapter, is not found merely in preservation of earlier material. It is found in stammaitic adherence to form—each amora must do something with the other's verse, each amora must have a verse to defend their position—and the adaptation of this earlier material in order to achieve formal ends.

## Example 3: Creating Formally Structured Sugyot

Another hallmark of stammaitic activity is the use of intentionally weak arguments in order to expand the discourse, cite more sources, and properly structure sugyot. Rishonim already recognized this tendency in many talmudic passages. For example, in the 12-13th century R. Isaiah di Trani writes: "The nature of the Talmud is to begin by proposing simple solutions that are rejected and only then to offer the primary solution, in order to expand the argumentation and demonstrate that this is the only way to resolve the issue."[26]

We find an example of this phenomenon in the sugya on Pesahim 102a, about blessings recited over cups of wine.[27] The sugya contrasts two baraitot. The first baraita requires one to have separate cups of wine for kiddush and birkat hamazon. The second assumes the use of a single cup for the recitation of havdalah and birkat hamazon. How could it be possible that one source requires two cups while the other permits just one? The first resolution offered by the stam is an obvious but weak answer: The second baraita refers to a case where the individual reciting the blessing has only one cup of wine, and therefore has no other choice. This explanation is easily refuted by means of another source (this time an amoraic statement) which calls for the recitation of kiddush and havdalah over the same cup. The stam again suggests the same resolution, namely that the statement refers to a case where one has run out of wine and there is only enough left for a single cup. Deflecting the first two difficulties allows the stam to cite a third and final source, an amoraic disagreement which clearly indicates that kiddush and havdalah can be combined over a single cup. The sugya concludes with the stammaitic resolution that kiddush and havdalah may be combined because they are "one thing," unlike birkat hamazon and kiddush which are "two things."

The stam could have easily suggested this resolution before offering two weak resolutions, but deliberately chose to extend the argumentation with resolutions that were obviously destined to be rejected. By offering weak resolutions, the stam allows the discourse to grow so that more sources can be cited, while also furnishing the sugya with a tripartite structure that is literarily appealing and easy to remember. Indeed, as with the example above in which the stam insisted on adhering to the formula

---

[26] *Tosafot ha-Rid* Pesahim 77a. See David Weiss Halivni, *The Formation of the Babylonian Talmud*, 17; Shamma Friedman, "Perek ha-Ishah Rabbah ba-Talmud ha-Bavli," *Mehkarim u-Mekorot*, ed. H. Z. Dimitrovski (New York: Jewish Theological Seminary, 1978), 385.

[27] *Reconstructing the Talmud*, 2nd ed., 149-170.

of "learn three from it," here too we see the adherence to a structure built on threes even if it is necessary to go to artificial lengths to achieve it.[28]

## Example 4: Creating an Integrated Sugya

The stam will frequently try to integrate different types of amoraic responses to a mishnah so that the sugya flows more smoothly. Generally speaking, there are at least two distinct ways in which amoraim respond to the Mishnah. One response might be categorized as interpretative: explaining the Mishnah's underlying reasoning. A second could be categorized as halakhic or informational: adding halakhic information into the context of the Mishnah. The attempt to integrate these two types of responses serves to structure a passage we analyzed in our first volume concerning the maximum height of a sukkah.[29]

Sukkah 2a begins with the attempts of three amoraim to provide the Scriptural basis for the prohibition on building a sukkah more than twenty cubits above the ground. Each amora cites a verse that embodies, to his mind, the essence of the act of sitting in a sukkah that might not be fulfilled if the sukkah is too high. If the essence of sitting in a sukkah is seeing the *skhakh*, then it will not be noticed if the *skhakh* is too high. If the essence is sitting in the shade of the *skhakh*, then, if the sukkah is too high, one will sit in the shade of the walls and not the *skhakh*. If the essence of a sukkah is that it be impermanent, then the sukkah will of necessity be permanent in a case where the *skhakh* is too high. These three amoraic opinions do not disagree halakhically with one another; they each simply provide a different justification for the tannaitic height limit of twenty cubits.

In the second half of the sugya, three other amoraim disagree about the scope of the mishnah's prohibition, offering various limitations to its applicability. Unlike in the first half of the sugya, their disagreement is halakhic rather than interpretive. On the amoraic level, there is no connection between the first two halves of the sugya. This bothers the stammaitic editors, who are not satisfied with a sugya that contains disparate amoraic sections that are not at all integrated. Such a style is

---

[28]  On numeric patterns in the construction of Bavli sugyot see Shamma Friedman, *Sugyot be-Heker ha-Talmud ha-Bavli*, 136-148.

[29]  *Reconstructing the Talmud*, 2nd ed., 75-98.

typical of the Yerushalmi, and indeed all the amoraic sections in this sugya have parallels in the Yerushalmi (Sukkah 1:1, 51d). But as we so often see in the Bavli, the stammaim wish to create a flow of discourse that moves from one amoraic discussion to another, allowing for a more integrated structure.

To achieve this aim, the stam takes each of the three opinions in the second half of the sugya and attempts to pair them with one of the opinions in the first half of the sugya using the terminology, "כמאן אזלא/according to whom does this go." This improves the flow of the sugya, but it also leads to some forced interpretations because the first set of amoraim—those who explained the mishnah—did not essentially disagree with one another, at least not halakhically, while the second set of amoraim clearly did. The literary impulse to pair each amora from the first half of the sugya with an amora from the second leads to some strained reasoning. For example, R. Yoshaya teaches that a sukkah may be larger than twenty cubits if the walls touch the *skhakh*. The stam connects this teaching with Rabbah's explanation of the mishnah, that a sukkah may not be taller than twenty cubits because one must notice the *skhakh*. But it is hard to see why these two positions are connected. Is one more likely to notice the *skhakh* because it is touching the walls? Even Rashi (s.v. משלט שלטא בה עינה) cannot come up with a substantive link between the two and suggests that the sugya connects them merely because R. Yoshaya's opinion cannot possibly correspond to those of the other two amoraim.

**Example 5: Categorical Explanations of Tannaitic Prohibitions**

There are many cases in which the logic that lies behind a tannaitic prohibition is relatively fuzzy and ill-defined. This is often the case when it comes to the laws of Shabbat and holidays. An act such as riding on a horse is prohibited because it is simply not something done on Shabbat.[30] Similarly, it was considered prohibited to "heal" on Shabbat, a prohibition with roots in the Second Temple, as evidenced by various disputes

---

[30] See Aharon Shemesh, *Halakhah in the Making: The Development of Jewish Law from Qumran to the Rabbis* (Berkeley: University of California Press, 2009), 96-97.

between the Pharisees and Jesus in the New Testament.[31] The amoraim begin to look for the reason underlying these prohibitions in an attempt to impose stricter logic. But this process is brought to its greatest expression at the stammaitic level, in which a far broader range of prohibitions must be categorized under the rubric of "X is prohibited lest one come to perform Y."[32] Riding an animal is prohibited not because it is simply something one should not do on Shabbat, but, as the stam explains, "lest one break a branch off a tree" (Betzah 36b). Swimming is prohibited, so the stam proposes, "lest one make a flotation device" (ibid.). The closest we came to analyzing such an example in our two volumes is in our analysis of "the resting of vessels," where we see that setting up meat on a pit to roast before Shabbat is prohibited lest one turn over the meat or rake the coals (Shabbat 18b).

But perhaps the shift from ill-defined reasoning to concrete formalistic thought may be best demonstrated in our chapter in this volume on "the dust of Avodah Zarah." The first mishnah in Avodah Zarah prohibits engaging in business with non-Jews three days before their holidays. This mishnah also prohibits borrowing or lending things to or from them, borrowing or lending them money, and paying them back or being paid back. In our reconstruction, the original meaning is that it is simply prohibited to engage in any type of business with non-Jews while they are in the midst of their holiday season. Commerce and religion were intertwined, and participation in the former was regarded as tacit participation in the latter.

Amoraim begin the process of formalizing the interpretation of this mishnah, shifting from the fuzzy logic of "just stay away from them" to trying to understand exactly what the particular problem is. They try to understand what exactly is so bad about engaging economically with non-Jews around their festivals. After all, formally speaking, the Jew would know that he is not participating in the pagan religion. His intention is

---

[31] Gospel of Mark 3:1-6; Gospel of John 5:5-11. See Aharon Shemesh, "*Pikuah Nefesh Doheh Shabbat*," *Tarbiz 80:4* (2012), 481-505; Lutz Doering, "Much Ado About Nothing?: Jesus' Sabbath Healings and their Halakhic Implications Revisited," *Judaistik und Neutestamentliche Wissenschaft*, eds. Lutz Doering, et. al. (Göttingen: Vandenhoeck et Ruprecht, 2008) 217-241.

[32] See Avraham Goldberg, "Le-Hitpathut ha-Sugya ba-Talmud ha-Bavli" *Sefer ha-Yovel le-Rabbi Hanokh Albeck* eds. Y.L. Maimon et. al. (Jeruslaem: Mossad ha-rav Kook, 1963), 101-113; Y.D. Gilat, *Perakim be-Hishtalshelut ha-Halakhah*, 89-99.

merely to engage economically, so why should he not be permitted to do so?

This question leads the Yerushalmi and Babylonian amoraim to shift the focus from the Jew to the non-Jew. Rava states the problem clearest— "lest he (the idolater) thank [his God]," an interpretation that we maintain originally related to only one clause of the mishnah, the prohibition of paying back loans. The stam takes this statement and applies it to the full array of prohibitions in the mishnah. Here we see two quintessential stammaitic phenomena in progress. First, the search for more formal reasons for prohibitions. And second, the drive for consistency. Once the stam develops a formal interpretation, it is assumed that all of the prohibitions in the mishnah should have the same underlying logic.

The stammaitic insistence on a formal and consistent explanation of the mishnah leads to the application of the same reasoning to other related sources, again at the expense of cogency. This is evident in the amoraic story which immediately precedes the explanation of the clauses of this mishnah in Avodah Zarah. This story appears in both the Yerushalmi and the Bavli, and the differences between the two versions serve to highlight the changes made by the stam. In the Yerushalmi version, R. Yehudah Nesiah receives a gift of coins from a non-Jew in honor of the pagan festival. He immediately sends back most of the money, but assumedly out of courtesy, holds on to one dinar. Resh Lakish hears of it and demands that he destroy the remaining dinar to ensure that R. Yehudah Nesiah does not even tacitly participate in the non-Jewish festival. It is clear that the concern is for R. Yehudah Nesiah's behavior, not the non-Jew's reaction.

In the Bavli version, however, the stam adheres to the explanation offered elsewhere, namely that the concern is lest the non-Jew thank his god for his interaction with the Jew. Therefore, the story is entirely recast with the exchange between R. Yehudah Nesiah and Resh Lakish taking place in front of the non-Jewish gift-giver. In order to preclude any possibility that the non-Jew might thank his god, Resh Lakish demands that the dinar be destroyed while the non-Jew watches, which implies that this whole interchange must occur with the non-Jew in close proximity. The Bavli then expresses concern that this interaction might lead to enmity, and resolves the problem by suggesting that Resh Lakish advised R. Yehudah Nesiah to make it look like an accident.

The notion that R. Yehudah Nesiah could throw away the gift in front of the non-Jew and yet make it look like an accident is obviously not plausible. But because the stam had to shift the setting of the story so as to remain faithful to a consistent interpretation of the mishnah, the stam also had to come up with a strained interpretation in order to make the story work. In sum, this brief comparison between the versions of the stories underscores how the stam's editorial search for consistency is the source of characteristically strained stammaitic explanations.

## Conclusion: The Tomb of the Unknown Stam

Atop a hill overlooking Washington, D.C. in the Arlington National Cemetery lies the Tomb of the Unknown Soldier, a monument to US soldiers who fell in battle and were never identified. The Tomb was created in the aftermath of World War I and is visited by over three million people a year. It is considered one of the highest honors to be a guard at the Tomb, and fewer than twenty percent of applicants are accepted. Indeed, it is one of the least-awarded qualification badges in the US Military, second only to the astronaut badge. Upon visiting the Tomb, one sees a soldier holding a rifle walking a pattern of precisely twenty-one steps, waiting twenty-one seconds, and then turning around and repeating that same number of steps in a different direction. Every half hour during the summer, every hour during the winter, and every two hours when the cemetery is closed, a formal changing of the guard occurs.

The stammaim, those who composed the discourse of the Talmud as we are familiar with it today, would have identified with this American ritual. They would have found aesthetic pleasure in the repeating pattern and in the formality of the ritual, which almost seems like a talmudic sugya walked out on pavement by men wearing shiny polished boots. The remains of these soldiers were found, but we do not know their names. In this sense they resemble the talmudic editors, the stammaim, whose names have been entirely lost to history but whose remains, the Bavli, we do possess. The stammaim are memorialized not by their names or their graves, as are some other famous rabbis, but by the tremendous contribution they made to Jewish intellectual and legal history.

For over 1500 years, from the Babylonian period onward, there have been few, if any, successful attempts to unseat the Babylonian Talmud from its perch atop the heap of Jewish books studied by Jews on a daily basis. We know the names of the hundreds of rabbis whose statements contributed to the discussions, the rulings, the legends, the interpretations, and the narratives, that fill the Bavli's pages. But the people who put this puzzle altogether, who wove what is surely one of the most intricate literary tapestries the world has ever known, will have to remain anonymous. Much like those soldiers who pace back and forth in front of the Tomb in honor of those heroic soldiers who sacrificed their lives for their country, so too do we consider it an honor to spend our days paging our way back and forth to uncover the secrets of those who put together the work that is at the center of Jewish life—the Babylonian Talmud.

# CHAPTER ONE

## AGAINST THE GRAIN:
## THE HISTORY OF A RABBINIC BLESSING

## BERAKHOT 36B-37A

## Introduction

In this chapter we will consider the blessing *borei minei mezonot* ("Who creates various kinds of foods"), which is typically recited over non-bread products made from the five grains (usually identified as wheat, barley, rye, spelt and oats). This blessing is also recited over rice, though as we will demonstrate, this was not always the case. This chapter will trace the development of the application of the *mezonot* blessing over the course of the tannaitic, amoraic, and stammaitic periods in an effort to provide an example of the evolution of rabbinic blessings from their creation in the tannaitic period through their final standardization in the Babylonian Talmud. Our analysis highlights the rabbis' varying attempts to properly categorize foods, formulate standard language of blessing, and create uniform rules for the recitation of blessings before and after food.

As we will discover, there is a shift in the application of the *mezonot* blessing between the tannaitic and amoraic periods. In the tannaitic period, *mezonot* was a blessing over cooked dishes, which usually had a grain or a rice/millet base. Even though the rabbis did not conceive of rice as a grain, it was a common ingredient in cooked dishes, and so *mezonot* was recited over cooked dishes with rice. Notably the blessing was related to the function of the food and not to its ingredients: A cooked dish functioned as *"mazon"*—the main source of nourishment of the meal—and thus the *mezonot* blessing was recited over it.[1]

In the early amoraic period, *mezonot* began to serve as a blessing for all non-bread products that include one of the five grains. This is the beginning of a more ingredient-based understanding of the blessing. However, during the amoraic period *mezonot* was still recited over rice, at least under certain circumstances. During this period, it retained, to a certain extent, its function-based origins. In contrast with the amoraim, the stammaim attempt to transform the *mezonot* blessing into one exclusively used for one of the five grains, thereby excluding rice. This seems to have been motivated, at least partially, by the stammaitic focus on ingredients—*mezonot* is recited only when the ingredients are one of the five grains. Since rice is not considered a grain, a different blessing must be recited.

## Bavli Berakhot 36b-37b

AMORAIC STATEMENT OF RAV AND SHMUEL

| | |
|---|---|
| (1a) רב ושמואל דאמרי תרוייהו: כל שיש בו מחמשת המינין מברכין עליו בורא מיני מזונות. | (1a) Rav and Shmuel both said: Anything that contains an ingredient from the five species [of grains], we bless, *"borei minei mezonot."* |

A SECOND STATEMENT BY THE SAME RABBIS ON THE SAME SUBJECT

| | |
|---|---|
| (1b) ואיתמר נמי, רב ושמואל דאמרי תרוייהו: כל שהוא מחמשת המינין מברכין עליו בורא מיני מזונות. | (1b) And it has also been stated, Rav and Shmuel both said: Anything made of the five species [of grains] we bless, *"borei minei mezonot."* |

---

| Tannaitic Source | Amoraic Source | Stammaitic Source |
|---|---|---|

---

[1]  See Meir Lichtenstein, *Toward a History of Blessings Recited Before Eating Food in Rabbinic Literature* (PhD Dissertation: Bar Ilan University, 2017), 157-158.

## STAMMAITIC EXPLANATION OF THE NECESSITY OF BOTH STATEMENTS

(1c) וצריכא: דאי אשמעינן כל שהוא - הוה אמינא משום דאיתיה בעיניה, אבל על ידי תערובות - לא, קא משמע לן, כל שיש בו.

(1c) Now both statements are necessary. For if it had taught us "anything made of," I might have said this is because it is still distinguishable, but if it is mixed with something else it would not [receive this blessing]. Therefore, it teaches us, "anything that contains."

(1d) ואי אשמעינן כל שיש בו, הוה אמינא כל שיש בו חמשת המינים - אין, אבל אורז ודוחן - לא, משום דעל ידי תערובת; אבל איתיה בעיניה - נימא אפילו אורז ודוחן נמי מברכין עליו בורא מיני מזונות. קמשמע לן: כל שהוא מחמשת המינים הוא דמברכין עליו בורא מיני מזונות; לאפוקי אורז ודוחן, דאפילו איתיה בעיניה - לא מברכין בורא מיני מזונות.

(1d) And if it had taught only "anything that contains," I might have said that this applies to the five species [of grains], but not to rice and millet when they are mixed with other things; but when they are distinguishable we might say that even over rice and millet the blessing is "*borei minei mezonot.*" Therefore, it teaches us that over "anything made of the five species" we bless, "*borei minei mezonot,*" which excludes rice and millet, over which we do not bless, "*borei minei mezonot*" even when they are distinguishable.

## DIFFICULTY RAISED ON RAV AND SHMUEL FROM TWO BARAITOT

(2a) ואורז ודוחן לא מברכינן בורא מיני מזונות?

**והתניא: הביאו לפניו פת אורז ופת דוחן - מברך עליו תחלה וסוף כמעשה קדרה;**

(2a) And over rice and millet do we not bless, "*borei minei mezonot*"?

Has it not been taught: **If they brought in front of him rice bread or millet bread, he blesses before and after it as for a cooked dish;**

(2b) וגבי מעשה קדרה תניא: **בתחלה מברך עליו בורא מיני מזונות ולבסוף מברך עליו ברכה אחת מעין שלש.**

(2b) And with regard to a cooked dish, it has been taught: **Before [eating] he blesses, "*borei minei mezonot,*" and afterwards, he recites one blessing derived from three.**

| Tannaitic Source | Amoraic Source | Stammaitic Source |
|---|---|---|

45

### STAMMAITIC RESOLUTION TO THE DIFFICULTY

(2c) כמעשה קדרה, ולא כמעשה קדרה. כמעשה קדרה - דמברכין עליו תחלה וסוף; ולא כמעשה קדרה, דאילו במעשה קדרה - בתחלה בורא מיני מזונות ולבסוף ברכה אחת מעין שלש, ואילו הכא, בתחלה מברך עליו שהכל נהיה בדברו, ולבסוף בורא נפשות רבות וחסרונן על כל מה שבראת.

(2c) It is like a cooked dish but not like a cooked dish. It is like a cooked dish in that it requires a blessing before and after; but it is not like a cooked dish, for when it comes to a cooked dish, beforehand [he blesses], "*borei minei mezonot*" and afterwards he recites one blessing derived from three, whereas in this case [of rice] he blesses beforehand, "*shehakol nehiyah bidvaro*," and afterwards, "*borei nefashot rabot.*"

### OBJECTION TO THE STAMMAITIC RESOLUTION

(3a) ואורז לאו מעשה קדרה הוא? והתניא, אלו הן מעשה קדרה: חילקא, טרגיס, סולת, זריז, וערסן, ואורז!

(3a) But is rice not a cooked dish? Has it not been taught: The following count as a cooked dish: ground wheat groats, wheat groats, semolina, split grain, barley groats, and rice!

### RESOLUTION

(3b) הא מני? רבי יוחנן בן נורי היא; דתניא: רבי יוחנן בן נורי אומר: אורז מין דגן הוא, וחייבין על חמוצו כרת, ואדם יוצא בו ידי חובתו בפסח; אבל רבנן לא.

(3b) Whose opinion is this? That of R. Yohanan b. Nuri for it has been taught: R. Yohanan b. Nuri says: Rice is a kind of grain, and when leavened [one who eats it] is liable for *karet* and it can be used to fulfill the obligation of [matzah] on Pesah. But the [other] rabbis do not [agree].

### OBJECTION TO PREVIOUS RESOLUTION

(4a) ורבנן לא? והתניא: הכוסס את החטה מברך עליה בורא פרי האדמה.

(4a) But do the other rabbis not agree? Has it not been taught: One who chews wheat blesses, "*borei peri ha'adamah.*"

טחנה אפאה ובשלה, בזמן שהפרוסות קיימות - בתחלה מברך עליה המוציא לחם מן הארץ ולבסוף מברך עליה שלש ברכות.

If he grinds it and bakes it and then cooks it [in liquid], so long as the pieces are still whole, he blesses beforehand, "*hamotzi lehem min ha'aretz*" and afterwards three blessings.

אם אין הפרוסות קיימות - בתחלה מברך עליה בורא מיני מזונות ולבסוף מברך עליה ברכה אחת מעין שלש. הכוסס את האורז מברך עליו בורא פרי האדמה.

If the pieces are no longer whole, he blesses beforehand, "*borei minei mezonot*," and afterwards recites one blessing derived from three.
One who chews rice blesses, "*borei peri ha'adamah.*"

טחנו אפאו ובשלו, אף על פי שהפרוסות קיימות - בתחלה מברך עליו בורא מיני מזונות, ולבסוף מברך עליו ברכה אחת מעין שלש.

If he grinds it and bakes it and then cooks it, even if the pieces are still whole, he blesses beforehand, "*borei minei mezonot*," and afterwards recites one blessing derived from three.

CONCLUSION AND REJECTION OF ORIGINAL STATEMENT OF RAV AND SHMUEL

(4b) מני? אילימא רבי יוחנן בן נורי היא, דאמר אורז מין דגן הוא - המוציא לחם מן הארץ ושלש ברכות בעי ברוכי! אלא לאו - רבנן היא,

(4b) Whose opinion is this? If one were to say it is R. Yohanan b. Nuri's, who said that rice is a kind of grain, he should bless, "*hamotzi lehem min ha'aretz*" and [afterward] the three blessings! It must therefore be the rabbis' opinion.

ותיובתא דרב ושמואל! תיובתא...

This is a refutation of Rav and Shmuel, it is a refutation...[2]

QUOTE OF BARAITA FROM ABOVE

(5a) אמר מר: הכוסס את האורז - מברך עליו בורא פרי האדמה, טחנו אפאו ובשלו, אף על פי שהפרוסות קיימות - בתחלה מברך עליו בורא

(5a) The Master said: One who chews rice blesses, "*borei peri ha'adamah.*" If he grinds it and bakes it and then cooks it, even if the pieces are still whole, he

---

2    We have skipped over a section of text here that discusses the discrepancy between the Babylonian version of the toseftan baraita which reads, "בורא פרי האדמה" and the Tosefta itself which reads, "בורא מיני זרעים." See Moshe Benovitz, *Berakhot Chapter VI with Comprehensive Commentary* (Jerusalem: ha-Igud le-Farshanut ha-Talmud, 2015), 175-180.

מיני מזונות, ולבסוף ברכה אחת מעין שלש.

blesses beforehand, "*borei minei mezonot*," and afterwards recites one blessing derived from three.

## CONTRADICTORY BARAITA

(5b) והתניא: לבסוף ולא כלום.

(5b) But has it not been taught After he need not bless at all?

## AMORAIC RESOLUTION

(5c) אמר רב ששת: לא קשיא: הא רבן גמליאל והא רבנן.

(5c) R. Sheshet said: There is no difficulty—the one statement expresses the view of R. Gamliel, the other that of the rabbis.

## BARAITA SUPPORTING R. SHESHET'S RESOLUTION

(5d) דתניא: זה הכלל: כל שהוא משבעת המינים, רבן גמליאל אומר: שלש ברכות.

(5d) As it has been taught: This is the general rule: [After] anything that belongs to the seven species—R. Gamliel says: Three blessings.

וחכמים אומרים: ברכה אחת מעין שלש.

But the sages say: One blessing derived from three.

ומעשה ברבן גמליאל והזקנים שהיו מסובין בעלייה ביריחו, והביאו לפניהם כותבות ואכלו, ונתן רבן גמליאל רשות לרבי עקיבא לברך.

It happened that R. Gamliel and the elders were reclining in an upper chamber in Jericho, and dates were brought in and they ate them, and R. Gamliel gave permission to R. Akiva to bless.

קפץ וברך רבי עקיבא ברכה אחת מעין שלש.

R. Akiva jumped in and said one blessing derived from three.

אמר ליה רבן גמליאל: עקיבא, עד מתי אתה מכניס ראשך בין המחלוקת!

R. Gamliel said to him: Akiva, how long will you stick your head into disputes!

אמר לו: רבינו, אף על פי שאתה אומר כן וחבריך אומרים כן, למדתנו רבינו: יחיד ורבים הלכה כרבים.

He replied: Our master, although you say this way and your colleagues say the other way, you have taught us, master: When an individual disputes with the majority, the halakhah is determined by the majority.

רבי יהודה אומר משמו: כל שהוא משבעת המינים ולא מין דגן הוא, או מין דגן ולא עשאו פת:

R. Yehudah said in his [R. Gamliel's] name: [After] any food from the seven species that is not a type of grain or is a kind of grain but has not been made into bread:

רבן גמליאל אומר: שלש ברכות, וחכמים אומרים: ברכה אחת. כל שאינו לא משבעת המינין ולא מין דגן, כגון פת אורז ודוחן:

R. Gamliel says: Three blessings, But the sages say: One blessing. [After] any food which belongs neither to the seven species nor is a type of grain, for instance rice bread or millet bread— R. Gamliel says: One blessing derived from three. But the sages say: No [blessing] at all.

רבן גמליאל אומר: ברכה אחת מעין שלש. וחכמים אומרים: ולא כלום.

## REJECTION OF AMORAIC RESOLUTION

(5e) במאי אוקימתא?

(5e) To whom did you attribute this baraita?

כרבן גמליאל, אימא סיפא דרישא: אם אין הפרוסות קיימות - בתחלה מברך עליה בורא מיני מזונות, ולבסוף מברך עליה ברכה אחת מעין שלש.

If it is R. Gamliel, look now at the second half of the first statement, "If the pieces are no longer whole, beforehand he blesses, '*borei minei mezonot*,' and afterwards one blessing derived from three."

מני? אי רבן גמליאל - השתא אכותבות ואדייסא אמר רבן גמליאל שלש ברכות, אם אין הפרוסות קיימות מיבעיא?

Whose opinion is this? If it is R. Gamliel, since R. Gamliel requires the three blessings after dates and pounded grain, is there any question that he should require it if the pieces are no longer whole?

אלא פשיטא - רבנן.

Rather it is obviously the view of the sages.

## CONTRADICTION BETWEEN TWO BARAITOT

(5f) אי הכי קשיא דרבנן אדרבנן?

(5f) If that is the case, there is a contradiction between two statements of the sages?

| | |
|---|---|
| (5g) אלא, לעולם רבנן, ותני גבי אורז: ולבסוף אינו מברך עליו ולא כלום. | (5g) No; it is actually the view of the sages; and in connection with rice you should read: At the end he does not recite any blessing. |

| Tannaitic Source | Amoraic Source | Stammaitic Source |
|---|---|---|

## Bread, Rice, and Cooked Dishes

The Bavli sugya begins with two related amoraic statements which require the *mezonot* blessing over foods that include grain. The stam introduces the liminal case of rice, which is not normally identified as a grain, reading the amoraim as if they intend to exclude rice from the *mezonot* blessing. In contrast, the sugya cites multiple baraitot which seem to indicate that *mezonot* is recited over rice when included in a cooked dish. After failing to ascribe the baraitot to the minority opinion of R. Yohanan b. Nuri, who treats rice as a grain, the Talmud concludes by rejecting the validity of the original amoraic statements. The second half of the sugya explores the rulings of the sages and R. Gamliel regarding blessings recited after eating the seven species, grains, and rice. The sugya concludes with the resolution that the sages do not require a blessing after eating rice.

The baraita (sections 4a and 5a), which appears at the heart of the Bavli's sugya and is found in both the Tosefta (4:6-7) and in the Yerushalmi (6:1, 10b) is the earliest source, and indeed the only source in a tannaitic composition, that mentions *mezonot*. Thus, any discussion of the function of the blessing *mezonot* must begin here.

| תוספתא ברכות ד:ו-ז | Tosefta Berakhot 4:6-7 |
|---|---|
| הכוסס את החטין מברך עליהן בורא מיני זרעים. | One who chews wheat blesses, "*borei minei zeraim.*"[3] |
| אפאן, בשלן - אם היו פרוסות קיימות מברך עליהן המוציא לחם מן הארץ, ומברך אחריהן שלש ברכות. | If he bakes it [and then] cooks it [in liquid], if there are whole pieces he blesses, "*hamotzi lehem min ha'aretz*" and after [eating] them he recites the three blessings. |

---

[3]   See above n. 2.

| | |
|---|---|
| אין הפרוסות קיימות, מברך עליהן בורא מיני מזונות. ומברך אחריהן ברכה אחת. | If the pieces are no longer whole, he blesses, "*borei minei mezonot*," and after [eating] them he recites one blessing. |
| הכוסס את האורז מברך עליו בורא פרי האדמה. | One who chews rice blesses, "*borei peri ha'adamah*." |
| אפאן, בשלן - אף על פי שהפרוסות קיימות מברך עליהן בורא מיני מזונות, ואין מברך אחריהן כלום. | If he bakes it [and then] cooks it [in liquid], even if the pieces are still whole, he blesses "*borei minei mezonot*," and after [eating] them he does not bless at all. |

Each half of the baraita addresses two distinct ways of eating: 1) chewing the wheat/rice in its raw form; 2) baking the wheat/rice into bread and then cooking it into a dish. In the first case, the blessing is *borei minei zera'im*, the "natural" blessing, for both wheat and rice which are chewed in seed form. In the second case the "natural" blessing is not recited because the food has been included as an ingredient in a cooked dish, which requires a distinct blessing. There are two possibilities for which blessing is recited. If the bread is still recognizable as such, then this dish retains the status of bread, and *hamotzi* is recited. However, if the bread is no longer recognizable, or one of the five grains was not used, then the blessing is *mezonot*.

This baraita suggests that there is a fundamental difference between the blessings over wheat (or any of the five grains) and rice. In the case of a dish made from any of the five grains, the blessing depends on whether the dish contains recognizable bread: If the bread retains its form, the blessing is *hamotzi*; but if not, the blessing is *mezonot*. Since bread is no longer present, this is considered a "cooked dish." Rice, the baraita teaches, is not considered a grain and thus can never trigger the *hamotzi* blessing, even if baked into the form of bread. Once rice has been cooked, the blessing is always *mezonot*.

This distinction between the five grains and rice is also alluded to in another baraita from the Tosefta that is quoted in section 5d of the Bavli:

| תוספתא ברכות ד:טו | **Tosefta Berakhot 4:15** |
|---|---|
| ר' יהודה אומר משמו: כל שהוא ממין שבעה ולא ממין דגן או דגן ולא עשאו פת: | R. Yehudah said in his [R. Gamliel's] name: Any food from the seven species that is not a type of grain or which is a type of grain but he did not make it into bread— |

| | |
|---|---|
| רבן גמליאל אומר: מברך אחריו שלש ברכות. | R. Gamliel says: One recites after [eating] the three blessings. |
| וחכמים אומרים: ברכה אחת. | But the sages say: One blessing. |
| וכל שאינו לא ממין שבעה ולא ממין דגן: | [After] anything which belongs neither to the seven species nor is a type of of grain— |
| רבן גמליאל אומר: מברך אחריו ברכה אחת. | R. Gamliel says: One recites after [eating] one blessing. |
| וחכמים אומרים: ולא כלום. | But the sages say: No [blessing] at all. |

According to R. Yehudah, the sages rule that after eating anything made of the five grains that has not been made into bread, one recites only one blessing. But after eating any other food, including rice or millet, neither of which is one of the seven species or a grain (this is made explicit in many tannaitic sources)[4] one would not recite any blessing (according to the sages). R. Gamliel, in contrast, would require one blessing after rice or millet, despite the fact that they are not one of the five grains. As we will see below, the Yerushalmi debates the identity of this concluding blessing, while the Bavli assumes it is an abbreviated form of *birkat hamazon*. In any case, while not stated explicitly, we can assume that both the sages and R. Gamliel distinguish between rice and the other five grains, as do all sources found in the Mishnah and Tosefta. Nevertheless, this baraita has no bearing on whether one recites *mezonot* before a cooked dish based on rice. This baraita is only about the concluding blessing.

To summarize, these are the main points made in the tannaitic sources embedded in this sugya:

1) There is a distinction in the blessing recited before eating grain and rice in their raw form and when they are part of cooked dishes.

2) When one of the five grains is baked into bread, as long as the form of the bread is still recognizable, *hamotzi* is recited before and three blessings are recited after. Rice is not considered one of the five grains and, therefore, even if it is formed into bread it will not receive the *hamotzi* blessing before nor will it entail the recitation of the three blessings after. The blessing over rice in a cooked dish will always be *mezonot* and no blessing is recited after.

---

4    See Mishnah Pesahim 2:5; Mishnah Hallah 1:1; Mishnah Menahot 10:7.

3) The sages and R. Gamliel dispute whether the full, three blessing version of birkat hamazon is recited only over bread made from one of the five grains (the sages) or over any dish made from one of the five grains or seven species (R. Gamliel).

4) These two parties also dispute whether any concluding blessing at all is recited over foods not consisting of one of the five grains or seven species. The sages say no blessing is recited and R. Gamliel says that one blessing is recited.

## *Borei Minei Mezonot* in Tannaitic Literature

As we stated above, the only mention of *mezonot* in tannaitic compositions is the baraita from the Tosefta (4:6-7) examined above. While the baraita mentions only cases in which the wheat/rice had been first cooked into bread, it seems that the same blessing would have been recited over a cooked dish with a cereal base even if the grain had not first been baked.[5] Cooked dishes based on various grains were a main staple in the Mediterranean diet for a variety of reasons, including taste, caloric efficiency, cost, and ease of cooking.[6] *Borei minei mezonot* is an appropriate blessing for such a dish, for "*mazon*" or "*mezonot*" is the word typically used in rabbinic literature for food.[7] To emphasize: *Borei minei mezonot* was not originally conceived to be a blessing for non-bread products made of the five grains, as it is conceived of today. It was originally a blessing created **specifically for cooked dishes**, most of which would have included some type of grain.

While the blessing is not mentioned explicitly anywhere else in tannaitic compositions, the notion that a cooked dish has a unique blessing is alluded to in Mishnah Berakhot 6:5:

---

[5] This is our main disagreement with Moshe Benovitz. Benovitz suggests that, originally, this baraita referred only to bread placed into a cooked dish. Had the grains been ground into meal and then cooked into a dish, the blessing would have originally been *ha'adamah*. He posits that the notion that all cooked dishes using grain receive *mezonot* is an amoraic innovation. See Benovitz, ibid., 153-171.

[6] Our thanks to Dr. Tova Dickstein for conveying this to us by electronic communication. For more on food in the talmudic period see Dickstein, *Food in Roman-Byzantine Palestine* (PhD. Dissertation, Bar Ilan University, 2011).

[7] See for instance Mishnah Peah 8:5, 7; Mishnah Ma'asrot 3:1-2; Mishnah Ketubot 12:2-3. There are many more such examples.

| משנה ברכות ו:ה | **Mishnah Berakhot 6:5** |
|---|---|
| בֵּרַךְ עַל הַפַּת פָּטַר אֶת הַפַּרְפֶּרֶת, עַל הַפַּרְפֶּרֶת לֹא פָּטַר אֶת הַפַּת. | If he blessed over the bread, he has exempted the accompanying appetizer course. [But if he blessed] over the accompanying appetizer course, he has not exempted the bread. |
| בֵּית שַׁמַּאי אוֹמְרִים: אַף לֹא מַעֲשֵׂה קְדֵרָה. | Bet Shammai say: Not even a cooked dish. |

This is an unusual case in which Bet Shammai's opinion is found in the Mishnah without the corresponding dispute with Bet Hillel. It is not even clear if there is a dispute in this mishnah.[8] Whether or not any sage disputes, according to Bet Shammai if one blesses over an appetizer, a separate blessing is still required over the cooked dish.[9] Appetizers usually consisted of vegetables, fruits, or soft meat, whereas a cooked dish, as we have seen, consists of a starchy base. This is clearly evidenced by the fact that starch is the common property of the foods listed in the baraita in section 3a in the Bavli.[10] Bet Shammai seems to assume that since these foods both have different blessings and distinct functions, blessing one would not exempt the other.

Three baraitot in our sugya in the Bavli do not have any parallels in tannaitic literature. Taken together, they seem to assume that *mezonot* is recited over any cooked dish, even if the base is not one of the five grains. The baraita in section 2a issues a ruling concerning rice and millet bread, comparing both to a cooked dish. The baraita assumes that the blessing over a cooked dish is known. This blessing is explicitly stated in the baraita in section 2b—one recites *mezonot* over any cooked dish. The baraita in section 3a lists various forms of cooked dishes and does not distinguish between those made of the five grains and those made using

---

[8] Both Talmuds have difficulty with this mishnah because of the assumption that Bet Shammai disputes the opinion of Bet Hillel. See Yerushalmi Berakhot 6:5, 10c; Bavli Berakhot 42b.

[9] This interpretation best fits the second interpretation of the mishnah in the Bavli. See Benovitz, ibid., 519.

[10] See Dickstein, ibid., 77-83.

other starches as a base.[11] A cooked dish must have a starchy base, but that base can come from one of the five grains, from rice or millet or perhaps even from other sources. Indeed, according to Mishnah Tevul Yom 2:5, "A cooked dish and beans: When they are separated, they are not considered to be connected [for matters of purity]; but when they are one solid mass, they are connected," a cooked dish seemingly can be based, at least partially, on beans.

The tannaitic use of *mezonot* as a blessing before eating a cooked dish continues to echo throughout the Talmuds. We shall now turn our attention to those sugyot.

## Yerushalmi Berakhot I: *Borei Minei Mezonot* and Rice

The parallel sugya in Yerushalmi Berakhot (6:1, 10b) contains some of the material found in the Bavli and it too discusses the twin issues of rice and *borei minei mezonot*.

BARAITA CONCERNING BLESSING OVER RICE

**Yerushalmi Berakhot 6:1, 10b**

(1) One who chews rice says over it "*borei minei zeraim*." If he bakes it and then cooks it, even if the pieces are still whole, he says over it, "*borei minei mezonot*." And he does not need to bless afterwards.

**ירושלמי ברכות ו:א (י, ב)**
(1) הכוסס את האורז אומר עליו בורא מיני זרעונים. אפייו ובישלו, אף על פי שהפרוסות קיימות, אומר עליו בורא מיני מזונות ואינו צריך אחריו לברך.

THREE VARIANT AMORAIC OPINIONS CONCERNING THE BLESSING OVER RICE

(2) R. Yirmiyah said, "*borei peri ha'adamah*."

**(2) רבי ירמיה אמר: בורא פרי האדמה.**

(3) The son of Marina blessed in front of R. Ze'era and in front of R. Hiyya b. Ba, "*shehakol nehiyah bidvaro*."

**(3) בר מרינה בריך קומי רבי זעירא וקומי רבי חייא בר ווא: שהכל נהיה בדברו.**

(4) R. Shimon Hasida says, "*borei minei ma'adanim*."

**(4) רבי שמעון חסידא אומר: בורא מיני מעדנים.**

---

[11] Benovitz, ibid., 168, notes that the original context of this baraita is Tractate Nedarim, chapter six. For a parallel see Yerushalmi Nedarim 6:1, 39c.

HARMONIZATION OF THE FOUR VARIOUS OPINIONS

| | |
|---|---|
| (5) אמר רבי יוסי בי ר' אבון ולא פליגין: | (5) R. Yose b. R. Abun said: They do not disagree: |
| (5a) מאן דמר בורא מיני מזונות: בההיא דעביד בול. | (5a) The one who said, "*borei minei mezonot*," refers to a case where it is made into a clump. |
| (5b) מאן דמר בורא פרי האדמה: בההוא דבריר. | (5b) The one who said, "*borei peri ha'adamah*," refers to a case where he sifted it. |
| (5c) מאן דמר שהכל נהיה בדברו: בההוא דשליק. | (5c) The one who said, "*shehakol nehiyah bidvaro*," refers to a case where it was partially cooked. |
| (5d) ומאן דמר בורא מיני מעדנים: בההוא דטריף. | (5d) And the one who said, "*borei minei ma'adanim*," refers to a case where it is chopped up.[12] |

The Yerushalmi contains four opinions as to the blessing recited over a cooked dish containing rice: 1) *mezonot*; 2) *ha'adamah*; 3) *shehakol*; 4) *minei ma'adanim*. The question we must ask is why three amoraim (in sections 2-4) were so adamantly opposed to the simple reading of the baraita, according to which *mezonot* is recited over a cooked dish based on rice. It is possible that these opinions have been influenced by the tannaitic distinction between rice and the five grains and have applied that distinction even to a cooked dish that is based on rice. These amoraim reason that just as the concluding blessing for a cooked dish based on rice (no blessing is recited, according to the Tosefta and Yerushalmi) differs from a cooked dish based on one of the five grains (one blessing in the Tosefta and Yerushalmi, one blessing derived from three in the Bavli), so too the opening blessing should differ. Furthermore, rice and wheat have different opening berakhot when baked into bread, as we know from the Tosefta examined above. *Hamotzi* is reserved for bread made from the five

---

[12] This translation is based on Michael Sokoloff, *Dictionary of Palestinian Aramaic* (Ramat Gan: Bar Ilan University, 2003), 232. Lichtenstein, *History of Blessings*, 168 n. 31, interprets the word to mean "mixed up with fruits" which would offer a better explanation for why the blessing is *ma'adanim* - "delights."

grains.[13] Thus, most amoraim in this sugya posit that *mezonot* should not be said over a cooked dish based on rice. As we shall see, this will eventually lead to the positive position that *mezonot* is recited exclusively over dishes consisting one of the five grains. However, this is not stated directly in the Yerushalmi.

To a certain extent, R. Yose b. R. Abun reverses this trend by claiming that there is no real dispute between the four earlier opinions for they all apply to diverse ways in which the rice has been prepared. To accomplish this, he maintains the simple reading of the baraita, but limits it. A cooked dish that is based on rice can receive *mezonot*, but only if the rice has been made into a clump. Such a clump is similar to the consistency of grains or bread that have broken apart in a cooked dish and therefore receives the same blessing. If the rice grains have not been ground up and remain separated and whole such that they can be seen, then the blessing is *ha'adamah*. In other words, the "natural" blessing for rice, which is normally eaten cooked, is *ha'adamah*. If the rice is partially cooked in a process described using the verb של״ק, which is interpreted by scholars in a variety of different ways, then its blessing is *shehakol*.[14] If the rice is chopped up, the blessing is *borei minei ma'adanim* (Who creates a variety of delights). This blessing appears only here in the Yerushalmi and

---

[13] It is not clear whether the Tosefta would prescribe *mezonot* for bread made from rice. The Tosefta says that if one bakes bread from rice and puts it into a cooked dish, *mezonot* is recited, even if the pieces of bread remain distinct. It may be that *mezonot* would also be recited over plain rice bread outside of a cooked dish. But equally possible is that *mezonot* was recited only because this was a cooked dish. Over rice bread outside of the cooked dish one might recite a different blessing. This point is clarified in the Bavli's baraita (section 2a) which states explicitly that one recites *mezonot* over rice or millet bread.

[14] Saul Lieberman, *Tosefta Kifshuta: Zera'im* (New York: Jewish Theological Seminary of America, 1955), 1:693, explains that in Palestinian sources שליק means to be partially cooked, not over-cooked as it is usually interpreted according to the Bavli. Shmuel Safrai, et. al, *Mishnat Eretz Yisrael: Berakhot* (Jerusalem: Mikhlelet Lifshitz, 2010), 227-229, concludes that שלק refers to a type of cooking in which there is some additional processing and taste added to the cooked item. Yehudah Felix, "Rice in Rabbinic Literature," *Bar Ilan 1* (1973), 184, interprets that this is when the rice has been cooked to the point of turning into cereal. Since the grains are no longer identifiable the appropriate blessing is *shehakol*.

nowhere in the Bavli, and seems to refer to a sweet or particularly tasty way of eating rice, perhaps with fruit or honey.[15]

Rabbi Yose b. R. Abun may simply be trying to limit the dispute among the various opinions by showing that each blessing has its place. But his resolution also serves to limit the applicability of the *mezonot* blessing to only a specific way of preparing rice, suggesting that perhaps he preferred that the *mezonot* blessing not be recited over rice.

## Yerushalmi Berakhot II: *Borei Minei Mezonot* over Non-Grain Products

After a short passage discussing the blessing before and after meat and eggs (cited below, p. 77), the Yerushalmi returns to discussing *borei minei mezonot*:

| ירושלמי ברכות ו:א (י, ב) | Yerushalmi Berakhot 6:1, 10b |
|---|---|
| (1) זה הכלל שהיה רבי יהודה אומר משום רבן גמליאל: כל שהוא ממין שבעה ואינו ממין דגן, מין דגן ולא אפאו פת: | (1) This is the general rule that R. Yehudah would say in the name of R. Gamliel: Anything that is one of the seven species but is not a type of grain [or] is a type of grain but was not baked into bread— |
| רבן גמליאל אומר: מברך לאחריו שלש ברכות. | R. Gamliel says: He recites after it the three blessings. |
| וחכמים אומרים: ברכה אחת. | But the sages say: One blessing. |
| וכל שאינו ממין שבעה ולא ממין דגן: | And anything that is not of the seven species and is not a grain— |
| רבן גמליאל אומר מברך לפניו ולאחריו. | R. Gamliel says: He blesses before and after it. |
| וחכמים אומרים: לפניה ולא לאחריה. | But the sages say: [He blesses] before but not after. |
| (2) רבי יעקב בר אידי בשם רבי חנינא: כל שהוא כעין סולת וכעין חליטה ומחמשת המינין, אומר עליו בורא מיני | (2) R. Yaakov b. Idi said in the name of R. Hanina: Anything that is like semolina, or like boiled [flour], and is |

---

[15] Lichtenstein, ibid., 168 n. 31, interprets the word to mean "mixed up with fruits" which would explain the choice of blessing. The *ma'adanim* blessing also appears in ancient Eretz Yisraeli Haggadot. See Joshua Kulp, *The Schechter Haggadah* (Jerusalem: The Schechter Institute of Jewish Studies, 2009), 185.

מזונות ומברך לאחריה ברכה אחת מעין שלש. | from the five grains, one says over it "*borei minei mezonot*" and one recites after it one blessing derived from three.

(3) וכל שהוא כעין סולת וכעין חליטה ואינו מחמשת המנין? | (3) [And what about] something that is like semolina and like boiled [flour] but is not from one of the five grains?

(4) אמר ר' יונה: שלח רב זעורא גב אילין דבית ר' ינאי ואמרון לי לית אנא ידע מה אמרון לי. | (4) R. Yonah said: R. Ze'ora sent me to those from the house of R. Yanai and they said [something] to me, but I don't know what they said to me.

(5) מי כדון? אמר רבי יוסי: מסתברא שהכל נהיה בדברו. | (5) What is the law? R. Yose said: It makes sense [that it should be] "*shehakol nehiyah bidvaro.*"

In section 2, R. Yaakov b. Idi clarifies the lacunae in the dispute between R. Gamliel and the sages which appears in section 1 (=Tosefta 4:15 and section 5d of the Bavli sugya). While the baraita focuses on the concluding blessing, it does not discuss the blessing recited before eating. It does say that if one of the five grains has not been made into bread, the sages rule that only one concluding blessing is recited. R. Yaakov b. Idi identifies this as the abbreviated *birkat hamazon*, one blessing derived from three. Additionally, according to the sages if the food is not made of the five grains (or of the seven species) there is no concluding blessing. Food made from the five grains is considered more significant than other foods and thus it warrants a concluding blessing. R. Yaakov b. Idi deduces from here that grain's elevated status mandates not only a blessing afterwards, but also a special blessing **beforehand**. If the grains were processed but not made into bread, rather they were ground and then boiled into some sort of dish, the blessing before is *mezonot*.[16] This also helps clarify the earlier baraita about chewing wheat (section 1 of the Yerushalmi, section 4d of the Bavli and the parallel in the Tosefta). That baraita only discussed wheat consumed in two manners: 1) chewing raw

---

[16] According to Benovitz, ibid., 148, סולת is the hard part of the grain that remains after sifting the flour. In English this is called semolina. It is not, as is commonly thought, finely sifted flour, which would not be an appropriate base for a cooked dish. Concerning חליטה see Tosefta Hallah 1:1, which defines it as "putting flour in boiling water." In Mishnah Hallah 1:6, Bet Hillel exempts it from hallah.

wheat; 2) baking it into bread and then putting it into a cooked dish. R. Yaakov b. Idi emphasizes that a cooked dish with grain flour in it is treated the same as a cooked dish with dissolved slices of bread—*mezonot* is recited over both.[17]

Section 3 of this passage is extremely pertinent, for it explicitly asks about a cooked dish based on something besides one of the five grains. Although rice is not specifically mentioned, clearly rice and millet are two main candidates for the ingredients in this dish, which is described as ground and then boiled. While the earlier baraita stated that one recites *mezonot* over rice when it has been made into bread and then cooked in a dish, it is still unclear if one recites *mezonot* over rice when it has been ground and then cooked in a dish. In section 4, a few amoraim fail to answer this question. This is significant. In the early amoraic period, rabbis had yet to determine whether *mezonot* would be recited over all cooked dishes, including those based on rice, or whether the fact that one of the five grains was not used implied that a different blessing must be recited. In section 5, an answer is provided—the blessing is *shehakol*. In other words, there is another distinction between rice and the five grains—when the substance is ground and then boiled in a cooked dish, the former receives *shehakol* whereas the latter receive *mezonot*.

We should carefully note what we learn from this section and what we do not. First, with regard to *borei minei mezonot*, this blessing is still reserved for cooked dishes. There is no place in this sugya where it is extended to other sorts of foods made from the five grains, such as various forms of cakes or fried doughs. Second, rice is clearly not considered one of the five grains.

Overall, taking into account both of the sugyot in the Yerushalmi, the possibility of blessing *mezonot* over rice is extremely limited when compared to the five grains. As we learned in the previous sugya, for this blessing to be recited over rice it must first be made into bread, or at least into a clump, and then cooked in a dish (section 1a of the previous sugya). If it is ground, *shehakol* is recited, as we learn in this sugya. We should note that the relationship that this sugya has with the Yerushalmi's

---

17   This is not to say that prior to R. Ya'akov b. Idi, *mezonot* was not recited over cooked dishes based on grain. It is our opinion that *mezonot* was originally created for such a purpose. R. Ya'akov b. Idi is simply clarifying the issue and connecting it with the other baraita from the Tosefta (the dispute between R. Gamliel and the sages) as well as the issue of the concluding blessing.

previous sugya is difficult to determine. There, according to the conclusion, *shehakol* was recited over rice that was "partially cooked" (שליק), but whether this is the same form of preparation as "like semolina or like boiled flour" (כעין סולת or כעין חליטה) is unclear. According to the first sugya, if the rice was made into a clump (בול), *mezonot* is recited. It is unclear if this disagrees with sections 3-5 in this sugya. In any case, what is clear is that most amoraim hold the blessing recited before rice is usually different from the blessing before grain.

## Yerushalmi Hallah: Blessing Over Grain Products that are not Bread

There is yet another sugya in the Yerushalmi that discusses the blessing recited over non-bread grain products. As we shall see, in this sugya *borei minei mezonot* is not mentioned.

### Yerushalmi Hallah 1:3, 57d

(1a) R. Yohanan said: *Trakta*[18] is liable for hallah and one says over it "*hamotzi lehem min ha'aretz*" and one can use it to fulfill one's obligation [to eat matzah] on Pesah.

(1b) R. Shimon b. Lakish says: *Trakta* is not liable for hallah, and one does not say "*hamotzi lehem min ha'aretz*" and one cannot use it to fulfill one's obligation on Pesah...

(2a) R. Yose said in the name of R. Yohanan: Anything for which the fire is beneath it is liable for hallah, and one says over it "*hamotzi lehem min ha'aretz*," and one can use it to fulfill one's obligation on Pesah.

(2b) R. Shimon b. Lakish said: Anything for which the fire is beneath it is not liable for hallah, and one does not

ירושלמי חלה א:ג (נז, ד)

(1a) רבי יוחנן אמר: טריקטא חייבת בחלה ואומר עליו המוציא לחם מן הארץ ואדם יוצא בה ידי חובתו בפסח.

(1b) רבי שמעון בן לקיש אמר: טריקטא אינה חייבת בחלה ואין אומרים עליו המוציא לחם מן הארץ ואין אדם יוצא בה ידי חובתו בפסח...

(2a) רבי יוסי אמר רבי יוחנן: כל שהאור מהלך תחתיו חייב בחלה ואומרים עליו המוציא לחם מן הארץ ויוצא בה ידי חובתו בפסח.

(2b) רבי שמעון בן לקיש אומר: כל שהאור מהלך תחתיו אינו חייב בחלה ואין אומרים עליו המוציא לחם מן

---

18 This is how the word is vocalized in Sokoloff, ibid., 232.

61

| | |
|---|---|
| הארץ ואין אדם יוצא בה ידי חובתו | say over it "*hamotzi lehem min ha'aretz*," |
| בפסח. | and one cannot use it to fulfill one's obligation on Pesah. |
| (2c) אמר ליה רבי יוחנן: ובלבד על | (2c) R. Yohanan said to him: Only if it |
| ידי משקה. | contains liquid. |

This sugya discusses *trakta*, a Greek word whose Aramaic cognate is *sufganim*. The term refers to unleavened dough dried in the sun or cooked in a pan at a low heat. After the baking process, the dough could be soaked with liquids or sometimes boiled. Mishnah Uktzin 2:8 describes *sufganim* as formed in the shape of a hollow tube similar to onion shoots. Scholars suggest that the baked dough which was then boiled is an early form of pasta.[19] R. Yohanan and R. Shimon b. Lakish debate the status of this *trakta*: Should it be halakhically categorized as bread? If so, as R. Yohanan rules, one would be required to take the dough offering and recite *hamotzi* and one could use it to fulfill the commandment of eating matzah on Pesah.

The second half of this sugya contains a more generalized version of this dispute between R. Yohanan and R. Shimon b. Lakish. R. Yohanan considers dough cooked in a pan ("anything for which the fire is beneath it") to be bread, and therefore all the rules governing bread apply. R. Shimon b. Lakish disagrees and says that dough that is not baked in the standard method of preparing bread is not halakhically considered to be bread. Significant for our discussion is that R. Shimon b. Lakish does not say what blessing is supposed to be recited. We know only that he holds that *hamotzi* is not recited and that the product does not count as bread. Perhaps this sugya may be regarded as evidence that the recitation of *mezonot* over non-bread grain products had not yet been standardized. Had it been the standard blessing, perhaps R. Shimon b. Lakish would have made reference to it. While we cannot draw much of a conclusion from this silence, the comparison of this sugya with the Bavli's version will be significant, as we shall see below.

---

[19] Susan Weingarten, "The Debate About Ancient *Tracta*: Evidence from the Talmud," *Food History* 2/1 (2004), 21-40.

## *Borei Minei Mezonot*—The Two Versions of Rav and Shmuel

In the opening lines of our sugya in Bavli 36a, Rav and Shmuel introduce a new application to the blessing *borei minei mezonot*. As we have seen, in the tannaitic period, for the most part, *mezonot* was a function-based blessing. It was to be recited over cooked dishes that frequently would have served as the basis of the meal. An apt term for such a cooked dish is "*mazon*," and therefore this blessing was created. Generally, these cooked dishes included a source high in starch such as grain or rice, but the specific ingredients mattered less than the fact that the food was in the form of a cooked dish.

Rav and Shmuel, both early amoraim, begin to think of *mezonot* as an ingredient-based blessing—one that is stated over **anything** which contains one of the five species of grain. Their intention is presumably to include foods made from grain but not baked into bread, such as those found in Tosefta Pesahim 2:20 or something like the *trakta* discussed above. In so doing, they broadened the applicability of the blessing and shifted the significance of the word *mazon* from its original reference point. If *mazon* originally applied to the typical main dish of a meal, in Rav and Shmuel's thinking, the word must be thought of differently.

Rav and Shmuel may have derived the notion that grains always have their own blessing from the baraita (section 5d in the Bavli; Tosefta 4:15) in which R. Gamliel and the sages disagree with regard to the **concluding** blessing over non-bread products from the five grains. It seems likely that Rav and Shmuel reason that just as there is a special concluding blessing for non-bread grain products, so too non-bread grain products have their own unique opening blessing. In other words, there is a category of food which can be described as "something made from grain but not baked into bread." The sages in the Tosefta ruled that this substance merits its own concluding blessing, different from that recited over bread, and these early Babylonian amoraim add that it merits its own opening blessing as well, one which they borrowed from the context of the cooked dish. Note that this statement does not necessarily imply its inverse. Rav and Shmuel affirm that one says *mezonot* over products from the five grains that are not made into bread. They do not explicitly state that one does not recite *mezonot* over anything else that is not made from the five grains. As we shall see, such a claim is made only by the stam.

As we saw in the opening of our sugya, Rav and Shmuel's statement has been preserved in two versions, "anything made of" and "anything that contains." The former implies that the grains are a key ingredient, whereas the latter implies that the grains are merely one ingredient among others. Moshe Benovitz, in his commentary on Berakhot chapter six, convincingly demonstrates that the statement worded as "anything that contains" was originally Shmuel's opinion and was not shared by Rav.[20] Rav held that in order to require *mezonot*, the main component of the food had to be one of the five grains, an opinion widespread among other early amoraim. Shmuel held that even if a small amount of the five grains was used, *mezonot* must be recited. In other words, there was no dispute that if grain was the main ingredient, then *mezonot* was recited; the dispute related only to the case when the grains were merely one ingredient among many.

Benovitz proves this by pointing to evidence in several other sugyot that Rav did not rule that *mezonot* is recited over anything that contains even a small amount of one of the five grains. For example, on Berakhot 38a the following dispute exists with regard to שתיתא, which according to Benovitz, refers to a very thin mixture of flour made from roasted grain and water or vinegar.[21] In other words, it contains only a small amount of flour.

| בבלי ברכות לח ע״א | Bavli Berakhot 38a |
|---|---|
| שתיתא, רב אמר: שהכל נהיה בדברו. | *Shatita*: Rav said, "*shehakol nehiyah bidvaro.*" |
| ושמואל אמר: בורא מיני מזונות. | But Shmuel said, "*borei minei mezonot.*" |
| אמר רב חסדא: ולא פליגי, הא בעבה הא ברכה; עבה - לאכילה עבדי לה, רכה - לרפואה קא עבדי לה. | R. Hisda said: But they do not dispute, for one refers to a thick mixture and one to a thin mixture. A thick mixture was made for eating; a thin mixture was made for medicinal purposes. |

---

20  Benovitz, ibid., 155-157.
21  Ibid. 258-260.

Rav's own opinion is that despite the presence of grain, the blessing is *shehakol* due to the watery nature of the dish.[22] Shmuel rules that the blessing is *mezonot*. From here we can see that only Shmuel holds that even a small amount of grain in a dish mandates that *mezonot* be recited. Rav would assumedly hold that in order for *mezonot* to be recited, the majority of the dish must consist of grain. Subsequently, R. Hisda, a third-generation amora, limits Rav's statement to a case where the *shatita* was made thin and for medicinal purposes. If the *shatita* was intended to be food, Rav too would rule that the blessing is *mezonot*.

It is obvious here that Rav did not rule according to the statement attributed to both him and Shmuel on 36b ("anything that contains"). Rather, it is the later amora, R. Hisda, who takes this statement into consideration and interprets Rav's ruling about the *shatita* accordingly. Thus, by the third generation of Babylonian amoraim, Rav's opinion had been rendered consistent with Shmuel's: Both amoraim were considered to hold that even if the smallest part of the dish is grain, *mezonot* is recited. The only reason not to recite *mezonot* would be if the mixture was imbibed as medicine and not food.

A similar phenomenon occurs in the following sugya on Bavli Berakhot 36b:

| בבלי ברכות לו ע"ב | Bavli Berakhot 36b |
|---|---|
| (1) חביץ קדרה, וכן דייסא: | (1) Over a dish made of breadcrumbs [and honey] or porridge [mixed with honey]:[23] |
| רב יהודה אמר: שהכל נהיה בדברו. | R. Yehudah said, "*shehakol nehiyah bidvaro.*" |
| רב כהנא אמר: בורא מיני מזונות. | R. Kahana said, "*borei minei mezonot.*" |
| (2) בדייסא גרידא כולי עלמא לא פליגי דבורא מיני מזונות, כי פליגי - בדייסא כעין חביץ קדרה: | (2) If the porridge is alone no one disagrees that "*borei minei mezonot*" is recited. They disagree over porridge that is like a dish made of breadcrumbs [and honey]: |
| רב יהודה אמר: שהכל - סבר דובשא | R. Yehudah said, "*shehakol,*" for he holds |

---

22 This accords with R. Huna in Yerushalmi Berakhot 6:1, 10a-b who says that one recites *shehakol* over *shatita*. In the Yerushalmi there is no opinion according to which *mezonot* is recited.

23 Concerning the definition of these foods see, Benovitz, ibid., 145-149.

עיקר. that the honey is the main ingredient.

רב כהנא אמר: בורא מיני מזונות - R. Kahana said, "*borei minei mezonot*,"
סבר סמידא עיקר. for he holds that the ground grain is the main ingredient.

(3) אמר רב יוסף: כותיה דרב כהנא (3) R. Yosef said: R. Kahana's ruling is
מסתברא, דרב ושמואל דאמרי more reasonable, for Rav and Shmuel
תרוייהו: both say:

כל שיש בו מחמשת המינין מברכין Anything that contains one of the five
עליו בורא מיני מזונות. grains, they bless over it, "*borei minei mezonot*."

In section 1, R. Yehudah prescribes *shehakol* over these dishes despite the fact that they both include grain. The stam explains that R. Yehudah identifies honey as the main ingredient in the dish which mandates the *shehakol* blessing. However, it is possible to interpret R. Yehudah's statement without assuming the stammaitic explanation of the amoraic dispute. Rather, R. Yehudah may prescribe *shehakol* for the same reason that Rav did for the case of "*shatita*"—the mixture is too watery to justify *mezonot*. R. Kahana disagrees and prescribes *mezonot*, which, as the stam explains, is because of the presence of even a small amount of grain.

Thus, R. Yehudah seems to agree with his teacher Rav, that only if the main ingredient is grain is *mezonot* recited ("anything made of"), whereas R. Kahana agrees with Shmuel, that as long as any grain is present, *mezonot* is recited ("anything that contains").

The stam in the middle section, in essence, transforms this debate into one over the nature of the dish—what is the main ingredient: honey or grain? Similar to R. Hisda in the *shatita* passage, the stam here erases any principled dispute between the amoraim. All would agree that if grain is considered the main ingredient, *mezonot* is recited; and that if honey is the main ingredient, *shehakol* is recited. They only differ in their assessment of the dish itself—what is considered the main ingredient? The stam here does not seem to take into account Shmuel's teaching "anything that contains one of the five grains." In contrast to that statement, R. Yehudah would prescribe *shehakol* for a dish that includes grain as long as the grain is not the main ingredient.

At the end of the sugya, R. Yosef rules like R. Kahana and explicitly credits his own ruling to the influence of the first statement attributed to

Rav and Shmuel (originally held only by Shmuel), that anything which contains one of the five grains receives *mezonot*. Thus, while R. Yehudah, a second generation amora, seems to rule against the first of the statements attributed to Rav and Shmuel ("anything that contains") or to not have been familiar with it, R. Yosef, a third generation amora, is clearly familiar with this statement and rules accordingly. Nevertheless, according to this sugya, and even according to the stammaitic layer embedded in it, not all amoraim agree with this statement.

The following sugya on 37b provides further evidence that the teaching "anything that contains" was either not known or not observed by early amoraim but went on to become more dominant in later halakhic development:[24]

| בבלי ברכות לז ע"ב | **Bavli Berakhot 37b** |
|---|---|
| אמר רבא: האי ריהטא דחקלאי דמפשי ביה קמחא - מברך בורא מיני מזונות. | Rava said: This dish made of flour and honey of the farmers, in which they put a lot of flour, he blesses "*borei minei mezonot*." |
| מאי טעמא? דסמידא עיקר. | What is the reason? The flour is the main ingredient. |
| דמחוזא דלא מפשי ביה קמחא - מברך עליו שהכל נהיה בדברו. | Over the dish made of flour and honey of the townspeople in which they do not put so much flour, he blesses, "*shehakol nehiyah bidvaro.*" |
| מאי טעמא? דובשא עיקר. | What is the reason? The main ingredient is the honey. |
| והדר אמר רבא: | Rava went back and said:[25] |
| אידי ואידי בורא מיני מזונות; דרב ושמואל דאמרי תרוייהו: כל שיש בו מחמשת המינים מברכין עליו בורא מיני מזונות. | Over both the blessing is, "*borei minei mezonot*," for Rav and Shmuel both said: Anything that contains one of the five species [of grain], the blessing is "*borei minei mezonot*."[26] |

---

[24] See Benovitz, ibid., 156.

[25] Other manuscripts read "ולא היא." Rava did not change his mind. Rather, the stam notes that the halakhah does not accord with the above statements. See Benovitz, ibid., 193-194.

[26] Although it seems to be a later addition, both the Paris and Munich manuscripts conclude with "דקיימא לן כרב ושמואל." See *Dikdukei Soferim: Berakhot* 204 n. 200.

The original statement of Rava, where he distinguished between the dish as made by the townspeople and that made by the farmers, accords well with the second statement attributed to Rav and Shmuel—anything made of the five grains. One recites *mezonot* over the dish made by the farmers because it consists mostly of grain. One recites *shehakol* over the dish made by the townspeople because the grain is not the main ingredient. Only Rava's retraction (or the stammaitic rejection of Rava's statement[27]) accounts for the ruling "anything that contains." Regardless of whether it was Rava or the stam who was responsible for this retraction, it is certainly later than Rava's original statement. Again, we see a progression—the earlier stratum holds that *mezonot* is recited only if the dish is mostly grain (in accordance with Rav's original position), while the later level holds that even a small amount of grain requires *mezonot*.

Further evidence of this development is found on Bavli Berakhot 39a:

### Bavli Berakhot 39a

R. Ashi said: When we were in the house of R. Kahana he said to us: [Over] a dish of beets that did not have a lot of flour in it, [one blesses] "*borei peri ha'adamah.*"

Over turnips that have a lot of flour in it "*borei minei mezonot.*"

He went back and said: Both are "*borei peri ha'adamah,*" and the reason he put a lot of flour in it was just to get it to stick together.

### בבלי ברכות לט ע"א

אמר רב אשי: כי הוינן בי רב כהנא אמר לן: תבשילא דסלקא דלא מפשו בה קמחא - בורא פרי האדמה.

דלפתא, דמפשו בה קמחא טפי - בורא מיני מזונות.

והדר אמר: אידי ואידי בורא פרי האדמה, והאי דשדי בה קמחא טפי - לדבוקי בעלמא עבדי לה.

In this sugya, R. Kahana does not seem to be influenced by the ruling "anything that contains." Therefore, *ha'adamah* may be recited over a dish of beets even though it contains flour. *Mezonot* is recited only if there is a significant amount of flour in it. At the end of the sugya, R. Ashi changes his mind and now challenges R. Kahana's halakhah, likely under the influence of the ruling "anything that contains." R. Ashi simultaneously disagrees with the second half of R. Kahana's statement, concerning turnips, and explains the first half. Despite the ruling that one says

---

[27] See n. 25

*mezonot* over any product that contains one of the five grains, if the flour was put into the dish only to improve the consistency, then *mezonot* is not recited. This seems to be an attempt to bring R. Kahana's first statement (beets) in line with the "anything that contains" statement: Although one usually does say *mezonot* over a dish with any flour in it, if the flour is there only to thicken the dish, another blessing can be said.

Finally, we should add that the ruling "anything made of" was used as a blueprint for a modification made to R. Hanina's statement from the Yerushalmi concerning cooked dishes. This becomes apparent when we line the two versions up into parallel columns:

| Yerushalmi Berakhot 6:1 (10b) | Bavli Berakhot 44a |
|---|---|
| רבי יעקב בר אידי בשם רבי חנינא: כל שהוא כעין סולת וכעין חליטה ומחמשת המינין, אומר עליו בורא מיני מזונות ומברך לאחריה ברכה אחת מעין שלש. | אמר רבי יעקב בר אידי אמר רבי חנינא: כל שהוא מחמשת המינין - בתחלה מברך עליו בורא מיני מזונות, ולבסוף ברכה אחת מעין שלש. |
| R. Yaakov b. Idi said in the name of R. Hanina: Anything that is like ground [grain], or like boiled [flour] and is from the five grains, one says over it "*borei minei mezonot*"and one recites after it one blessing derived from three. | R. Yaakov b. Idi said in the name of R. Hanina: Anything that is made of the five grains, before he blesses "*borei minei mezonot*,"and after he recites one blessing derived from three. |

In the Eretz Yisraeli version on the left, R. Hanina offers a definition of a cooked dish over which one recites *mezonot* and the abbreviated one-blessing version of *birkat hamazon*. In the Yerushalmi, at least at this early point in its development, *mezonot* is reserved for cooked dishes. In contrast, the Babylonian version has been expanded. The Bavli replaces the ground grains and boiling with the same language attributed to Rav and Shmuel in our sugya, emphasizing the dish's ingredients and not its function or preparation. Even if the food is not part of a cooked dish, if it is based on one of the five grains, both Rav and Shmuel agree *mezonot* is recited beforehand.

## Pat HaBa'ah Bekisanin

There is another sugya on Bavli Berakhot 42a which reveals the influence of Rav and Shmuel's statement on the blessing to be recited over non-bread grain products. To demonstrate this point of influence, we need to begin by looking at the parallels to this sugya that appear in the Tosefta (5:12-13) and in the Yerushalmi (6:5, 10c). The issue at hand is whether food eaten for dessert at the end of a meal requires a separate blessing. The Tosefta reads:

| תוספתא ברכות ה:יב-יג | Tosefta Berakhot 5:12-13 |
|---|---|
| באת להם מתיקה בתוך המזון מברך על המזון ופוטר את המתיקה. | If sweets are served during the meal, he blesses over the meal and exempts the sweets. |
| ר' מונא או' משם ר' יהודה: פת הבאה בכיסנין לאחר המזון טעונה ברכה לפניה ולאחריה. | R. Muna says in the name of R. Yehudah: *Pat haba'ah bekisanin* after the meal requires a blessing before and after. |

According to the first halakhah, if sweets are served during the meal, they do not require a separate blessing, but are covered by *birkat hamazon*. By extension, if the sweets were brought following the conclusion of the meal, they would require an independent blessing, even if *birkat hamazon* has not yet been recited. Similarly, R. Muna rules that *pat haba'ah bekisanin*, which is brought at the end of the meal but before *birkat hamazon*, requires its own set of blessings.[28]

*Pat haba'ah bekisanin* refers to some sort of dessert. *Kisanin* is understood as a reference to a sweet biscuit or cake customarily served at the end of the meal. *Pat haba'ah bekisanin* should thus best be understood as a food which contains the same basic ingredients as bread, *pat*, but is sweet and is served as dessert.[29] R. Muna rules that this "dessert bread" requires its own set of blessings, but he does not clarify what these blessings are. But a chapter earlier, Tosefta Berakhot 4:4 provides the answer, at least with regard to the blessing beforehand:

| תוספתא ברכות ד:ד | Tosefta Berakhot 4:4 |
|---|---|
| הביאו לפניו מיני תרגימא מברך עליהן בורא מיני כיסנין. | They brought before him types of *tragma*—he recites *borei minei kisanin*. |

---

28 Lieberman, *Tosefta Kifshuta: Zeraim*, 1:80.
29 Lichtenstein, *History of Blessings*, 190-195.

*Tragma* is Greek for dessert and is thus synonymous with the Semitic *kisanin*.[30] The blessing over this course is extremely specific to the food: *borei minei kisanin*. While the Yerushalmi sugya (Yerushalmi Berakhot 6:5) on this toseftan baraita questions whether the halakhah follows R. Muna, there is no further discussion of what blessing is recited.

In contrast, the Bavli inquires as to what blessing is recited over *pat haba'ah bekisanin*.

| בבלי ברכות מב ע״א | Bavli Berakhot 42a |
|---|---|
| רב יהודה הוה עסיק ליה לבריה בי רב יהודה בר חביבא. | Rav Yehudah gave a wedding feast for his son in the house of R. Yehudah b. Habiba. |
| אייתו לקמייהו פת הבאה בכסנין. כי אתא, שמעינהו דקא מברכי המוציא. | They brought before them *pat haba'ah bekisanin*. He came in and heard them saying *hamotzi*. |
| אמר להו: מאי ציצי דקא שמענא? דילמא המוציא לחם מן הארץ קא מברכיתו? | He said to them: "What is this *tzitzi* that I hear? Are you saying, '*hamotzi lehem min ha'aretz*?'" |
| אמרי ליה: אין; דתניא רבי מונא אמר משום רבי יהודה: פת הבאה בכסנין מברכין עליה המוציא. | They replied: "We are, for it has been taught: R. Muna said in the name of Rabbi Yehudah: Over *pat haba'ah bekisanin* one blesses '*hamotzi lehem min ha'aretz*.'" |
| ואמר שמואל: הלכה כרבי מונא. | And Shmuel said that the halakhah follows R. Muna. |
| אמר להו: אין הלכה כרבי מונא אתמר. | He said to them: It has been stated that the halakhah does not follow R. Muna. |
| אמרי ליה: והא מר הוא דאמר משמיה דשמואל, לחמניות - מערבין בהן ומברכין עליהן המוציא! | They said to him: Is it not the Master himself who has said in the name of Shmuel that bread wafers may be used for an eruv and the blessing said over them is "*hamotzi lehem min ha'aretz*"? |

---

[30] The Greek and its Semitic cognate are both derived from roots meaning "to chew." See Lichtenstein, ibid., 190.

שאני התם דקבע סעודתיה עלייהו, אבל [Rav Yehudah said to them:] That is a
היכא דלא קבע סעודתיה עלייהו - לא. different case, where they are made the
basis of the meal; but if they are not the
basis of the meal, this does not apply.

From Rav Yehudah's words at the end of the passage, we can see that these
guests are eating *pat haba'ah bekisanin* independent of a meal, and not at
the end, as in the Tosefta.[31] Rav Yehudah (a second generation
Babylonian amora) criticizes them for blessing *hamotzi*. In their defense,
they reply with a reworked version of the toseftan baraita. According to
this version, R. Muna in the name of Rabbi Yehudah (the fourth
generation tanna) explicitly requires *hamotzi* over *pat haba'ah bekisanin*.
The topic of the baraita has thus shifted, from **whether** a blessing is
required, to **which** blessing is required. As support, the guests also cite a
statement attributed to Shmuel.

Rav Yehudah's opposition is clearly not to the fact that they are
reciting a blessing at all. Since they are eating this food independent of the
meal, they must recite some sort of blessing. Rather, Rav Yehudah is
opposed to their choice of blessing. He does not explicitly state what
blessing they should have recited, but *mezonot* would seem to be the most
likely candidate. The guests appeal to Shmuel's statement about bread
wafers, which are made from grain but not made into regular bread. They
argue that if this food receives *hamotzi*, so too should *pat haba'ah
bekisanin*. In contrast, we must assume that Rav Yehudah, influenced by
the rulings of Rav and Shmuel, would assign *mezonot*. In so doing, Rav
Yehudah harmonizes Shmuel's statement here—that bread wafers require
*hamotzi*—with the statements attributed to Rav and Shmuel in our sugya:
"Anything that contains/is made of one of the five grains, they bless over it
*mezonot*." He explains that the blessing recited depends upon the context
in which the food is consumed.

## *Mezonot* in Later Babylonian Usage

Later Babylonian amoraim continue this usage of *borei minei mezonot* as a
blessing for products that include any of the five grains, even if they are
not part of a cooked dish. This is evident when we look at the Babylonian
version of the discussion concerning *trakta,* the baked dough from the

---

[31]  Ibid., 196.

Yerushalmi that we discussed above, referred to in the Bavli as *teruknin*. In the Yerushalmi sugya, there are two options over what to say over this product: *hamotzi* or not *hamotzi*. The Yerushalmi never specifies what the other option is. In contrast, in the Bavli the dispute is over whether *hamotzi* or *mezonot* is recited.

| | |
|---|---|
| **בבלי ברכות לז ע״ב-לח ע״א** | **Bavli Berakhot 37b-38a** |
| טרוקנין חייבין בחלה. | *Teruknin* is liable for hallah. |
| וכי אתא רבין אמר רבי יוחנן: טרוקנין פטורין מן החלה. | When Rabin came, he said in the name of R. Yohanan: *Teruknin* is exempt from the dough offering. |
| מאי טרוקנין? אמר אביי: כובא דארעא... | What is *teruknin*? Abbaye says: A loaf baked on the ground...[32] |
| אמר ליה אביי לרב יוסף: האי כובא דארעא מאי מברכין עלויה? | Abbaye said to R. Yosef: That loaf baked on the ground, what do we bless over it? |
| אמר ליה: מי סברת נהמא הוא? גובלא בעלמא הוא ומברכין עלויה בורא מיני מזונות. | He said to him: Do you hold that that is bread? It is simply dough and we recite over it "*borei minei mezonot.*" |

This passage is parallel to the Yerushalmi above—it discusses the same unleavened dough, there is a similar debate over whether it is liable for the dough offering, and it too features R. Yohanan. But, in the Bavli's version, those who hold that *teruknin* is not bread rule that one recites *mezonot* over it. As this sugya indicates, by R. Yosef's time (third generation Babylonia), *mezonot* has been instituted for non-bread grain products, even those not part of a cooked dish. The critical issue for our purpose is that in the Yerushalmi's sugya when R. Shimon b. Lakish states that one does not recite *hamotzi* over this type of dough, he does not correspondingly say that one does recite *mezonot*. In contrast, in the parallel in the Bavli, *mezonot* is the clear alternative when *hamotzi* is not recited.[33]

R. Yosef issues a similar halakhah elsewhere in the chapter:

---

[32] The unleavened dough was either cooked on low burning coals on the ground or out in the sun.

[33] There are opinions in the Bavli that one recites *hamotzi* over *trakta*. But the issue we are discussing is what blessing is recited for those who do not identify this as bread. Those who identity it as bread will always prescribe *hamotzi*.

בבלי ברכות לז ע"ב | **Bavli Berakhot 37b**

אמר רב יוסף: האי חביצא דאית ביה
פרורין כזית - בתחלה מברך עליו
המוציא לחם מן הארץ ולבסוף מברך
עליו שלש ברכות.

R. Yosef said: These breadcrumbs (*havitza*), if the crumbs are the size of an olive, he blesses beforehand, "*hamotzi lehem min ha'aretz*" and he recites afterwards three blessings.

דלית ביה פרורין כזית - בתחלה מברך
עליו בורא מיני מזונות, ולבסוף ברכה
אחת מעין שלש.

If the crumbs are not the size of an olive, beforehand he blesses, "*borei minei mezonot*" and afterwards one blessing derived from three.

According to Benovitz, *havitza* refers to breadcrumbs, often thrown into a cooked dish.[34] The issue at hand here is therefore not the blessing over a cooked dish, but over the breadcrumbs themselves. If the breadcrumbs are the size of an olive, then they retain the status of bread. But, as R. Yosef explains, if the crumbs are smaller than the size of an olive, one recites *mezonot*. The most important issue here is if *hamotzi* is not recited, the blessing becomes *mezonot*. Clearly R. Yosef is influenced by Rav and Shmuel who both rule that *mezonot* is recited over anything made of one of the five grains. In the continuation of this sugya, later amoraim vehemently disagree with R. Yosef over the second half of his statement, holding that breadcrumbs still require *hamotzi*. But regardless of the subsequent unfolding of the halakhic conversation, it is significant for our purposes that R. Yosef considers *mezonot* the appropriate blessing for anything made of the five grains and not considered bread.

## The Blessing after Rice

To recall, there are two toseftan halakhot that lie at the heart of our sugya. The first, Tosefta Berakhot 4:6-7 (sections 4a and 5a in Bavli 36a), which we have analyzed in depth above, concerns what we call "function-based" blessings. The same ingredients receive a different blessing based on the way they are prepared and eaten. A cooked dish consisting of either wheat or rice bread receives an opening blessing of *mezonot* (unless the wheat bread still retains its form), which differs from the blessing which is recited over the food in its raw form. The ingredients matter less than the processing and manner of consumption. In contrast, Tosefta Berakhot

---

34    Benovitz, ibid., 212.

4:15 (section 5d in Bavli 36a), in which R. Gamliel and the sages debate which concluding blessing is recited, is basically ingredient-oriented, again with the exception of bread. According to R. Gamliel, if one of the seven species or one of the five grains is the main ingredient, the full *birkat hamazon* (three blessings) is recited. If not, one blessing (or one blessing derived from three) is sufficient. According to the sages, *birkat hamazon* is recited only over bread. If one of the seven species or five species of grain is the main ingredient, one blessing is recited; if not, no blessing at all. The blessing (with the exception of bread) is determined based on ingredients alone.

R. Gamliel's requirement for *birkat hamazon* is clearly based on his interpretation of Deuteronomy 8:10, "And you shall eat and you shall be satisfied and you shall bless." Verse eight mentions the seven species and verse nine mentions bread; hence he concludes that ingredients determine the choice of concluding blessing.[35] In contrast, according to the sages, the blessing before is not determined by a verse of the Torah and therefore can be function-based.[36]

Turning our attention to the blessing recited after rice, the main complication in tracing the history of this issue is the singular version of the baraita that appears in the Bavli.

| Tosefta 4:15 | Yerushalmi | Bavli (section 5b) | Bavli (section 5a) |
|---|---|---|---|
| וחכמים אומרים: ולא כלום. | וחכמים אומרים: לפניה ולא לאחריה. | לבסוף ולא כלום. | ולבסוף ברכה אחת מעין שלש. |
| But the sages say: No [blessing] at all. | And the sages say: [He blesses] before but not after. | After it he need not bless at all. | And after one blessing derived from three. |

35  As is stated explicitly on Bavli Berakhot 44a. In tannaitic halakhah, blessing before the food allows that food to be consumed. Before the blessing, the food belongs to God and only the blessing allows the person to consume what was created by God (see Benovitz, ibid., 645). This may be connected to the overt connection that opening blessings have with creation, using words such as "עץ" "פרי" "בורא" and "אדמה" all of which feature in the opening chapters of Genesis. In contrast, concluding blessings relate to Deuteronomy 8 which refers to satisfaction and sustenance. Thus, there may be a lack of consistency in terms of the origins of opening and concluding berakhot.

36  See Bavli Berakhot 35a.

The baraita that appears in the Bavli (section 5a) states that after a cooked dish with rice one recites the abbreviated *birkat hamazon*: "one blessing derived from three."[37] In contrast, the Tosefta, the Yerushalmi, and the baraita in section 5b state that no blessing at all is recited. In the end (section 5g) the Bavli emends its own sui generis baraita so that all versions essentially agree—there is no blessing recited after a cooked dish based on rice. What is left to be accounted for is how the Bavli's unique baraita which assigns "one blessing derived from three" to rice, developed in the first place.

It is unlikely that this baraita is simply an error in transmission, an error in which the halakhah from the end of the first section (section 4a) was mistakenly copied into the concluding section.[38] This baraita in its Babylonian version seems to have already been known to R. Sheshet, a third generation amora (section 5c).[39] It seems more likely that the baraita was intentionally altered from its original form. Perhaps the reasoning behind this emendation was to make rice consistent with the five grains for the concluding blessing, just as it is consistent in terms of the blessing recited before. If *mezonot* is recited before eating a cooked dish based on either grain or rice, then the blessing after the cooked dish should remain standard for both grain and rice, "one blessing derived from three." Thus, the last clause of the baraita was emended before the baraita reached the third generation of Babylonian amoraim (R. Sheshet).[40] However, the Bavli still retained the original version from the Tosefta (section 5b), thereby creating the discrepancy between the baraitot.

R. Sheshet solves the difficulty by attributing this baraita (Tosefta 4:6-7) to R. Gamliel (5c), an attribution that seems glaringly erroneous. While it is obvious that R. Gamliel would indeed have prescribed "one blessing derived from three" (or just "one blessing") for a cooked dish based on rice, R. Gamliel is clearly not the source of the entire baraita which begins

---

[37] We should note that the blessing recited today "*borei nefashot rabot*" is not found in the Tosefta (or anywhere else in tannaitic literature) as a concluding blessing.

[38] Benovitz, ibid.., 185-186, notes this possibility, but also does not seem to find it likely.

[39] R. Sheshet's statement in the Bavli is extremely difficult—how could he not have noted that the baraita in section 5a accords with the sages and not R. Gamliel? See below.

[40] Benovitz, ibid., 186, posits that this change occurred already during the tannaitic period. This is possible, but we should note that there is no record of such a baraita in the Yerushalmi.

with the rule that "one blessing" is recited over a cooked dish with dissolved slices of bread. After all, this same R. Gamliel explicitly mandates in the other toseftan baraita (4:15) that full *birkat hamazon* (three blessings) is recited for any dish based on grain (as the stam notes in 5e). One solution as to how R. Sheshet could issue such a seemingly erroneous statement might be that he was originally referring only to the end of this baraita in isolation, the section that deals with rice. This section of the baraita, according to which a concluding blessing is recited over rice, accords with R. Gamliel, but this does not mean that he is the source of the entire baraita.

Benovitz offers a somewhat comparable solution to the problem of R. Sheshet's statement, noting that it is similar to an anonymous remark in Yerushalmi Berakhot 6:1, 10b.[41] The section we have quoted here opens by asking what concluding blessing is recited over various dishes composed of rice (cited above):

**Yerushalmi Berakhot 6:1, 10b**

**ירושלמי ברכות ו:א (י ע"ב)**

(1) This refers only to the beginning [blessing]. What about the concluding [blessing]?

(1) עד כדון בתחילה, בסוף?

(2) R. Yonah said in the name of R. Shimon Hasida: "Who created all sorts of delights to delight through them all living things. Blessed are You, for the land and its delights."

(2) רבי יונה בשם רבי שמעון חסידא: אשר ברא מיני מעדנים לעדן בהן נפש כל חי ברוך אתה ה' על הארץ ועל מעדניה.

(3) R. Abba b. Ya'akov in the name of R. Yitzhak the Great: Rabbi [Yehudah Hanasi] when he would eat meat or eggs would say: "Who created many living things to sustain the life of all living things. Blessed are You, one who lives eternally..."

(3) רבי אבא בר יעקב בשם רבי יצחק רובה: רבי כשהיה אוכל בשר או ביצה היה אומר: אשר ברא נפשות רבות להחיות בהן נפש כל חי ברוך אתה ה' חי העולמים...

(4) R. Shimon Hasida agrees with Rabbi and both of them agree with R. Gamliel, as it is taught: This is the general rule that R. Yehudah would

(4) אתיא דרבי שמעון חסידא כרבי ודברי שניהן כרבן גמליאל דתני: זה הכלל שהיה רבי יהודה אומר משום רבן גמליאל...

41   Ibid., 186-187.

say in the name of R. Gamliel...

וכל שאינו ממין שבעה ולא ממין דגן: And anything that is not one of the seven species and is not a species of grain—

רבן גמליאל אומר: מברך לפניו ולאחריו. R. Gamliel says: One blesses before and after.

וחכמים אומרים: לפניה ולא לאחריה. But the sages say: Before, but not after.

In the Yerushalmi, amoraim prescribe a concluding blessing for various types of foods. Section 2 discusses the blessing recited after eating rice and section 3 the blessing after meat or eggs. These concluding blessings relate to the type of food consumed. R. Shimon Hasida considers rice a "delight" while Rabbi [Yehudah Hanasi] references the fact that the meat and eggs both come from living creatures. The anonymous voice (section 4) remarks that these opinions agree with R. Gamliel, who also prescribes a concluding blessing for all foods even if they are not from the seven species or five grains. In contrast, the sages rule that no blessing is recited after eating any foods in that category. This passage is consistent with the Yerushalmi's understanding that "one blessing" is not the same as "one blessing derived from three." "One blessing" is open to interpretation, and here in this passage it appears in two different forms, dependent upon the type of food consumed, neither of which is synonymous with "one blessing derived from three."[42] Thus, in this passage R. Shimon Hasida identifies which blessing R. Gamliel would have recited after a dish based on rice. R. Sheshet's statement in the Bavli is similar to the anonymous voice in the Yerushalmi—according to both, amoraim that posit that a blessing is recited after rice rule in accordance with R. Gamliel. The Babylonian editor shifted the context of R. Sheshet's statement from its original reference point—amoraim who rule in accordance with R. Gamliel—to baraitot or parts thereof that accord with him.

Despite their similar function, the statement in the Bavli may go one step further than the statement in the Yerushalmi by directly emphasizing that the sages would hold that no blessing whatsoever is recited after rice. While this is implied in the Yerushalmi, R. Sheshet makes the point more explicit. By ascribing this baraita to R. Gamliel, a minority opinion, R.

---

[42]    See Benovitz, ibid., 631-632.

Sheshet seems to be rejecting it as halakhah. And if it is at all uncertain whether this is R. Sheshet's intent, it is clearly the goal of the stam at the end of the sugya, who entirely emends the baraita (5g). The amoraic opinion in the Yerushalmi that a concluding blessing is recited over rice is thus completely rejected by this sugya in the Bavli.

The Bavli's rejection of the ruling that a concluding blessing is recited over rice may be related to the difference between "one blessing" in the Tosefta/Yerushalmi and "one blessing derived from three" in the Bavli. The anonymous voice of the Yerushalmi may be willing to tolerate that "one blessing" should recited after rice, meat and eggs, even though this opinion disagrees with the sages. After all, there would still be a distinction between seven species/grain and other products, for each food type would receive a distinct type of concluding blessing, a shortened *birkat hamazon* for the former and a unique blessing for the latter. In contrast, the Bavli cannot tolerate "one blessing derived from three" for rice, for this would be identical with the blessing recited over seven species/grain products.[43] Thus, while both Talmuds may ascribe the blessing to R. Gamliel, only the Yerushalmi can accept it is as observed halakhah.

While the stam eventually rejects R. Sheshet's ascription of the first baraita to R. Gamliel, (section 5e), it is not because the stam is bothered by the halakhic implications of R. Sheshet's relegation of the requirement to bless after rice to a minority opinion. Indeed, the opposite is true: The stam is so adamant about distinguishing between rice and the five grains that it emends this baraita out of existence (section 5g). At the conclusion of the sugya, both baraitot read that after a cooked dish including rice, one does not recite any concluding blessing. This ruling would disagree with all the amoraim in the Yerushalmi who recited a blessing after rice, meat, and eggs.

---

43  Benovitz, ibid., 644, offers a similar comment but from a different angle. If, according to the Bavli, R. Gamliel ruled that "one blessing derived from three" should be recited over foods that are not of the seven species or five grains, then *borei nefashot* and the other blessings in the Yerushalmi would not accord with him. Thus, these blessings must accord with the sages, and "no blessing" is interpreted as "one does not recite 'one blessing derived from three.'"

## The Stam's Interpretation of Rav and Shmuel

Returning to the main sugya on 36b-37a, we find the opinion that even Rav agrees that a dish with the smallest amount of the five grains in it receives *mezonot*. As we demonstrated above, by the third generation of amoraim, Rav's name was included in a statement that originally was issued only by Shmuel. But if so, then Rav's original statement—the second statement attributed to Rav and Shmuel in our sugya—is rendered superfluous. If even the smallest amount of grain causes the dish to be liable for *mezonot*, then clearly one in which most of the dish consists of grain requires *mezonot*. The stam picks up on this superfluity and claims that the point of the second statement ("anything made of") is to **limit** *mezonot* to dishes that include one of the five grains. If we only knew of the first statement, we might have thought that if the dish was mostly based on rice or millet, *mezonot* could still be recited. The second statement, "anything that contains," teaches, according to its stammaitic reading, that the food must contain one of the five grains for *mezonot* to be recited. In other words, while Rav and Shmuel originally issued statements concerning when one **does** recite *mezonot*, the stam reads their statements as also **excluding certain foods from the *mezonot* blessing.** The stam thus uses the explanation of the redundancy as an opportunity to specifically disagree with the Tosefta (section 4a of the Bavli) which states unequivocally that a cooked dish with rice receives *mezonot*.

The stam is probably influenced by the debate found elsewhere in rabbinic literature concerning the status of rice. The debate over whether rice is grain is quoted later in the passage (section 3b). Clearly, Rav and Shmuel think that rice is not a grain, as do the sages in their dispute with R. Yohanan b. Nuri.[44] There are five species of grain, not six or seven (rice and millet). Similarly, the sages in the baraita in section 5d limit "one blessing derived from three" to foods that have one of the five grains (or one of the seven species). Thus, according to the stam, there should be full consistency between opening and concluding blessings.

Furthermore, since the distinction between rice and grain is drawn in all other sources in this sugya (except for R. Yohanan b. Nuri's opinion),

---

[44] Benovitz, ibid., 170-171, points out that this is the Babylonian version of this dispute. In Tosefta Hallah 1:1 and Tosefta Pesahim 2:17, R. Yohanan ben Nuri refers only to "*karmit*"—a grass that grows with wheat and according to some can become hametz.

the stam assumes that Rav and Shmuel must also exclude rice. However, this is not necessarily the correct interpretation of Rav and Shmuel. There is no reason to assume that Rav and Shmuel intended to rule that *mezonot* could not be recited over rice—clearly the Tosefta (and parallels) say otherwise. Rather, their ruling was simply that one **does** say *mezonot* over the five grains even if they are not part of a cooked dish, such as *trakta* or other such foods. Nevertheless, according to these two amoraim **as portrayed by the stam**, rice is never eligible for the blessing of *mezonot*.

## The Halakhic Impact of the Stam

In our historical exploration above, we claimed that the stam was the first to ascribe to Rav and Shmuel the position that rice cannot receive *mezonot*. Despite the stam's insistence on this reading of Rav and Shmuel, this position was eventually refuted—the sugya ends with a refutation of Rav and Shmuel, and along with them, the stammaitic understanding of their statements. *Mezonot*, the Bavli concludes, can be recited over rice. However, this does not mean that the stam did not have halakhic impact on post-talmudic authorities. The tannaim did not state any position with regards to a blessing recited before rice when not eaten in a cooked dish. According to our reconstruction, Rav and Shmuel also did not discuss the blessing over rice. But when the stam reads Rav and Shmuel as claiming that one **never** recites *mezonot* over rice, the tannaitic opinion—which is understood as the opposite of Rav and Shmuel—could become that one **always** recites *mezonot* over rice (unless chewed raw). Thus, according to some post-talmudic halakhic authorities, if one makes plain cooked rice (what the Yerushalmi calls דבריר), *mezonot* is recited.[45]

Even though the stam ends up rejecting Rav and Shmuel, the stam's own interpretation of their statements still has halakhic impact. Put another way, rice needs to fit into a system of ingredient-based opening

---

45   This is the position found in the Shulkhan Arukh Orah Hayyim 208:7. For an extended discussion, see the Bet Yosef. There are medieval authorities who hold that if the rice is not cooked into a sort of porridge, then the blessing is, "*borei peri ha'adamah*" in accordance with the Yerushalmi, where we saw that when rice was sifted (1b)—which probably means that it was served somewhat like it is often served today—it receives *ha'adamah*.

blessings.[46] If *mezonot* is sometimes recited before rice, then it must always be recited before rice (unless eaten raw, a highly unusual way to eat rice). This removes the possibility for the blessing over rice to be dependent upon the manner in which it was prepared or its function in the dish. In modern halakhah, which tends to regard most blessings, both opening and concluding, as being ingredient-based, rice is sui generis in nature. One blesses *mezonot* over rice, as if it were a grain, but one concludes with *borei nefashot* because, in reality, it is not a grain. A classic stumper in any berakhah bee!

---

[46] There is a geonic halakhic tradition (see *Otzar ha-Geonim, Berakhot: Responsa*, no. 240) which rejects the stammaitic ruling that *mezonot* is recited over rice, and instead rules like Rav and Shmuel according to whom *mezonot* is reserved for one of the five grains. This tradition notes that in the sugya concerning ריהטא (Berakhot 37b), Rava explicitly states that he rules according to Rav and Shmuel. Assumedly, they rule in accordance with Rava because he is the last named amora. See Robert Brody, *Teshuvot Rav Natronai Bar Hilai Gaon* (Cleveland: Ofeq Institute, 2011), 83-84.

# CHAPTER TWO

## THE RESTING OF VESSELS ON SHABBAT

### SHABBAT 18A-18B

## Introduction

The first chapter of Massekhet Shabbat contains a well-known debate between Bet Shammai and Bet Hillel concerning whether it is permissible to begin a process involving labor on erev Shabbat (Friday afternoon, before dark) that will continue on Shabbat. For instance, is it permissible to place wool in a vat of dye so that it continues to soak on Shabbat, or must our vessels rest as well? Would it be permissible to turn on a dishwasher on erev Shabbat, or must our machines also desist from labor? In our analysis of this material, we will proceed chronologically from the earliest texts (the Mishnah, the Tosefta, and the tannaitic midrashim) through the Yerushalmi, and conclude with an analysis of two sugyot in the Bavli. This inquiry will illuminate how the understanding of this debate developed over the mishnaic and talmudic periods.

This chapter is an excellent example of how an issue can sometimes be better understood when the earlier material is examined closely, without taking the Bavli's interpretations at face value. The Bavli attempts to offer one broad explanation for all particular manifestations of this debate, but the explanation encounters difficulty in explaining every detail, and eventually leads to certain halakhic and interpretive shifts found only in the Bavli. In addition, the Bavli's analysis of the resting of vessels includes examples of several phenomena that we have seen elsewhere, including the tendency of the Bavli to create names for broad legal categories and the tendency to join together smaller independent sugyot into longer, more intricate dialectics. Finally, the Talmud's analysis of this aspect of Shabbat observance is an excellent illustration of the impact of late stammaitic interpretations on normative halakhic practice.

## Mishnah and Tosefta

The first chapter of Mishnah and Tosefta Shabbat contain parallel sources which cite the following dispute between Bet Shammai and Bet Hillel:

| | |
|---|---|
| **משנה שבת א:ה** | **Mishnah Shabbat 1:5** |
| בית שמאי אומרים אין שורין דיו וסממנים וכרשינים אלא כדי שישורו מבעוד יום, | Bet Shammai says: One may not soak ink, dyes, and vetch[1] [on Friday afternoon] unless they can be fully soaked while it is yet day; |
| ובית הלל מתירין. | But Bet Hillel permits it. |
| **משנה שבת א:ו** | **Mishnah Shabbat 1:6** |
| בית שמאי אומרים אין נותנין אונין של פשתן לתוך התנור אלא כדי שיהבילו מבעוד יום ולא את הצמר ליורה אלא כדי שיקלוט העין. | Bet Shammai says: One may not place bundles of wet flax in an oven unless they can be steamed while it is still day, nor wool in the dyer's kettle unless it can [absorb the color] such that [the color] is visible. |
| ובית הלל מתירין. | But Bet Hillel permits it. |
| בין שמאי אומרים אין פורשין מצודות חיה ועופות ודגים אלא כדי שיצודו מבעוד יום; | Bet Shammai says: One may not spread traps for wild beasts, fowl, and fish unless they can be caught while it is still day; |
| ובית הלל מתירין. | But Bet Hillel permits it. |

**תוספתא שבת א:כ-כא**

אמרו בית שמיי לבית הלל: אין אתם מודין שאין צולין בשר בצל וביצה בערב שבת עם חשיכה אלא כדי שיצולו, אף דיו סמנין וכרשנין כיוצא בהן. אמרו להן בית הלל אי אתם מודין שטוענין קורות בית הבד ותולין עגולי הגת ערב שבת עם חשיכה אף דיו סמנין וכרשנין כיוצא בהן.

**משנה שבת א:ט-י**

ושוין אלו ואלו שטוענים קורות בית הבד ועגולי הגת.
אין צולין בשר בצל וביצה אלא כדי שיצולו מבעוד יום. אין נותנין פת לתנור עם חשכה ולא חררה על גבי גחלים אלא כדי שיקרמו פניה מבעוד יום.

---

[1]  An animal food.

אילו עמדו בתשובתן ואילו עמדו
בתשובתן אלא שבית שמיי אומרים: *שֵשֶׁת*
*יָמִים תַּעֲבוֹד וְעָשִׂיתָ כָּל מְלַאכְתֶּךָ* (שמות
כ:ח)—שתהא כל מלאכתך גמורה מערב
שבת. ובית הלל אומרים: *שֵשֶׁת יָמִים*
*תַּעֲבֹד*—מלאכה עושה אתה כל ששה.

## Tosefta Shabbat 1:20

Bet Shammai said to Bet Hillel: Don't you agree that one may not roast meat, onion or egg on Friday afternoon as it gets dark unless they are roasted [before Shabbat]? So too ink, dyes and vetch should be the same.

Bet Hillel said to them: Don't you agree that one may lay down olive press beams and suspend wine press rollers Friday afternoon as it gets dark. So too ink, dyes and vetch should be the same.

These stood by their arguments and these stood by their arguments, for Bet Shammai says: *Six days you shall work and perform all your labor* (Exodus 20:8)—[meaning] all your labor should be completed by Friday afternoon. And Bet Hillel says: *Six days you shall work*—[meaning] you may work all six days.

## Mishnah Shabbat 1:9-10

And they [both Bet Shammai and Bet Hillel] agree that one may lay down olive press beams and wine press rollers.

One may not roast meat, onion, or egg unless they can be [fully] roasted while it is still day.

One may not put bread into an oven just before nightfall, nor a cake upon coals, unless its surface can form a crust while it is still day.

## משנה שבת א:יא

משלשלין את הפסח בתנור עם חשכה

ומאחיזין את האור במדורת בית המוקד.

## Mishnah Shabbat 1:11

One may lower the Passover sacrifice into the oven just before nightfall;

And one may light the fire in the fireplace of the Chamber of Fire.

ובגבולין כדי שתאחוז האור ברובן.

But in the provinces, there must be time for the fire to take hold of its greater part.

רבי יהודה אומר בפחמין כל שהוא.

Rabbi Yehudah says: In the case of charcoal, just a little [is sufficient].

**תוספתא שבת א:כג**

פותקין מים לגנה בערב שבת עם חשיכה
והיא שותה והולכת בשבת.

**Tosefta Shabbat 1:23**

One may conduct water into a garden on Friday afternoon just before dark, and it may continue being filled the whole day.

נותנין קילור לעין ואספלנית למכה בערב
שבת עם חשיכה והן מתרפין והולכין כל
השבת כולה.

And one may place an eye salve on the eye and a plaster on a wound on Friday afternoon just before dark and it will continue healing all day.

נותנין גפרית תחת הכלים בערב שבת עם
חשיכה והן מתגפרין והולכין בשבת.

And one may place sulfur under [silver] vessels on Friday afternoon just before dark and it may continue making sulfurous odor all day;

נותנין מגמר על גבי גחלים בערב שבת
עם חשכה.

And one may place incense on top of coals on Friday afternoon just before dark.

ואין נותנין חטים לרחים של מים אלא
כדי שייטחנו.

But one may not place wheat in a water mill unless it can be ground [when it is still day.]

## Analysis of the Mishnah and Tosefta

Both tannaitic corpuses contain a series of disputes and debates between Bet Hillel and Bet Shammai concerning whether it is permitted to initiate an activity on erev Shabbat that is prohibited on Shabbat if that activity will continue on its own without human intervention on Shabbat. In both corpuses, there are multiple points of disagreement between the two schools (in each of these cases Bet Shammai prohibits the activity and Bet Hillel permits it) and at least one point of agreement. Since this material was first studied, talmudic sages, commentators, and modern academic scholars have struggled to find an organizing principle that will explain all of these cases. That is to say, why does Bet Shammai usually prohibit a given activity, and what distinguishes the cases when this school rules permissively? Likewise, why does Bet Hillel usually permit these actions, and what distinguishes the cases in which they agree that the activity is prohibited?

The following chart lists the points of agreement and disagreement in the Mishnah and Tosefta:

| | **Disputes** | **Agreement concerning prohibited activities** | **Agreement concerning permitted activities** |
|---|---|---|---|
| **Mishnah** | Soaking inks, dyes and vetch. | Roasting meat, onion and eggs. | Laying olive press beams and wine press rollers. |
| | Putting flax into the oven. | Baking bread. | Putting the pesah into the oven, lighting a fire. |
| | Putting wool into a dyers pot. Spreading out traps. | | |
| **Tosefta** | Soaking inks, dyes and vetch. | Roasting meat, onion and eggs. | Laying olive press beams and wine press rollers. |
| | | Placing wheat in water mill. | Conducting water into garden. Placing salve on eye and plaster on wound. Placing sulfur under vessels. Placing incense on top of coals. |

In an effort to systematize the various opinions, we will first consider the points of disagreement. As we can see from the Tosefta, the paradigmatic activity over which the two schools argue is soaking inks, dyes, and vetch (animal food). These are all activities which involve initiating a process that will render various items ready for use by the next day, i.e. on Shabbat. However, the person processing these items probably did not intend to use them on Shabbat, because their use on Shabbat is prohibited. Inks and dyes may not be used on Shabbat because their use is considered a violation of the prohibition on writing. Animals may be fed on Shabbat (under certain circumstances) but using vetch for animal feed will require separating the inedible waste from the edible feed, which is considered a violation of the prohibition on separating the inedible from the edible.[2]

Each school formulates a consistent stance. Bet Shammai maintains that one is not allowed to process any object on Shabbat if that object will be ready for use and might potentially be used on Shabbat. It does not matter to Bet Shammai that the person is not actively performing work with his hands on Shabbat, nor does it matter that the object probably will not be used because its use is considered a Shabbat violation. Bet Hillel rules that as long as one is not performing the work with his hands, and he will likely not use the item on Shabbat, it is permitted to set the process in motion before Shabbat.

Trapping animals also seems to fit well into this paradigm. The animal that is trapped will be ready for slaughter on Shabbat although it is prohibited to slaughter it, just as the dye will be ready for use on Shabbat even though it is prohibited to use it. Therefore, Bet Shammai prohibits setting traps on erev Shabbat and Bet Hillel permits it.

The points of agreement are basically the opposite. The paradigmatic activity which both schools prohibit is starting to roast meat, onion, or eggs before Shabbat. Clearly, the point of initiating such an activity on erev Shabbat would be to eat the meat, onion, or eggs on Shabbat itself. Thus, the individual will benefit on Shabbat from work done after Shabbat has started, and Bet Hillel agrees that such an action is

---

2   See Mishnah Shabbat 24:2; Saul Lieberman, *Tosefta Kifshuta: Zeraim* (New York: Jewish Theological Seminary of America, 1955), 1:731.

forbidden.[3] Note that the permission to put the pesah sacrifice in the oven on erev Pesah which falls on erev Shabbat is an exception for both schools because there is no other option. One must eat the pesah sacrifice that night and there is not enough time to fully roast it from the time of its sacrifice until Shabbat begins. Furthermore, allowing one to light a fire to keep warm or for light is not an exception to the general rule because this is not considered "processing" the wood or oil. "Processing" is transforming something from an undesirable state—such as raw meat— into a desirable state—cooked meat. In contrast, lighting a fire from wood or oil is not transforming the wood or oil, it is consuming them. This is not considered a violation of Shabbat because prohibited labors are generally constructive, not destructive.[4]

The paradigm for activities that both schools permit is laying olive press beams and wine press rollers. There are several reasons to rule permissively in this case. Unlike the roasted meat, onion, and eggs, which will be ready for use on Shabbat, the grapes and olives will only be available for consumption in the long term.[5] So while one is in some sense benefiting from work performed on Shabbat, the intention is likely not to use these items on that very Shabbat. Moreoever, unlike the dyes, flax, and vetch that are transformed from an unusable state to a usable one, the olives have already been crushed before they are placed in the press and the grapes have already been trodden. Pressing the olives and grapes is simply a way of more quickly and efficiently extracting what has already begun to ooze out. We will encounter this latter explanation in both Talmuds.

The Tosefta concludes with a list of activities of a different nature concerning which both schools would seem to agree: placing a salve on the eye or a plaster on a wound, placing sulfur under silver vessels, placing incense on top of coals (all of which are permitted), and placing wheat in

---

[3]   Stephen Wald, "For He Has Benefited from the Holy Sabbath: Restrictions on the Preparation of Food for the Sabbath," *Sidra* 19 (2004) 47–75, demonstrates that this is certainly R. Yehudah's interpretation of Bet Hillel. R. Yehudah holds (Tosefta Shabbat 2:14) that putting a dish in the oven before Shabbat so that it will cook on Shabbat is equivalent to actively cooking on Shabbat and therefore the dish cannot be eaten until after Shabbat.

[4]   See Mishnah Shabbat 13:3; cf. Tosefta Shabbat 8:4.

[5]   See Wald, ibid., 49. This is the same reason that Bet Shammai allows the beer-making process to continue on Shabbat, as is stated in the Bavli, section 7c (see below).

a water wheel (which is forbidden). There are grounds to suspect that this halakhah was not originally part of the literary unit containing the debate between the two schools. First, it is not found or referenced in the Mishnah. Second, it appears in the Tosefta after the dispute between the two schools seems to have concluded. In the Tosefta, the two schools argue with each other and then each presents a midrash to support its position. At this point, at the end of halakhah 21, the literary unit seems to be complete. Halakhah 22 deals with the issue of giving items to a non-Jew on Shabbat and it is not part of the same literary unit as 20-21, as we will discuss below. Halakhah 23 then returns to the subject of processes set in motion on erev Shabbat and allowed to continue throughout Shabbat. This is strong evidence that this halakhah was originally part of a separate tradition. Nevertheless, since it is analyzed in both Talmuds in light of the schools' debate, we shall try to offer an explanation which accords with the explanation above.

In all the permitted activities listed in this final halakhah in the Tosefta, nothing is being processed. The intention is not to transform the water, sulfur, salve, bandage, or incense. Rather, each of these items serves to aid or improve something else, namely the garden, vessel, eye, wound, or clothes. Since there is no processing involved, even Bet Shammai would permit these activities. Put another way, most of these substances are used up in the process they undergo, much in the same way that oil is used up by a lamp and wood is used up by a burning fire—both of which are activities that Bet Shammai permits setting in motion on Friday before Shabbat.

However, when it comes to grinding wheat, an item is being processed, and since it is a food item that potentially could be eaten on Shabbat, even Bet Hillel would agree that it is prohibited. In other words, grinding wheat is somewhat similar to cooking meat, onions, and eggs, and therefore all agree that it is prohibited.

Taken together, the examples in the Mishnah and Tosefta suggest that the original difference between the opinions of Bet Shammai and Bet Hillel is that Bet Shammai prohibits beginning to process an item before Shabbat if that item could be used on Shabbat, even if it likely will not, such as vetch; whereas Bet Hillel only prohibits if that item will likely be used on Shabbat.[6] This is a cogent, relatively consistent explanation that leads to a coherent elucidation of each school's opinion.

However, the midrashim in Tosefta 1:21 might be read as allowing for a more all-inclusive reading of the opinions of both schools. Bet Shammai says, "All your labor should be completed by Friday afternoon." This could mean that Bet Shammai does not allow any of the activities listed as permitted in Tosefta 1:23. It also might cause us to wonder if Bet Shammai would allow the laying of olive beams or wine presses, despite the fact that Bet Hillel assumes in their rhetorical argument that they do agree that such actions are permitted. Along similar lines, Bet Hillel says: "You can do work all six days," meaning, as long as you are not actively performing work on Shabbat, anything can be done on Friday until Shabbat begins. Perhaps this means that Bet Hillel would allow grinding wheat if the process is set in motion before Shabbat. Furthermore, the midrash attributed to Bet Hillel causes us to question why—or even if— they would prohibit one from beginning to roast meat, onion, or eggs on erev Shabbat, again despite the fact that Bet Shammai assumes that Bet Hillel does indeed prohibit these activities.

On the other hand, these midrashim may just be a secondary explanation of the debate. The disagreement between the two schools may have originated in particular disputes over what actions may be performed on erev Shabbat. While there assumedly were principles that guided each of these rulings, and we have tried to surmise these principles above, the dispute may have originally manifested in details and not principles. According to this understanding, at a later stage in the tannaitic period, there was an attempt to create a midrash to defend each school's position. But this midrash may have "overshot the mark" and created the impression that both schools' positions are absolute. Overarching principles will often result in the loss of nuance.

With all of this in mind, we can now begin to analyze the later material to see how it makes sense of the particular tannaitic disputes. Specifically, we will look for attempts to offer overarching explanations of this dispute. These explanations will cause forced justifications for why Bet Shammai occasionally permits and Bet Hillel occasionally prohibits.

---

[6]  For a somewhat different explanation see Saul Lieberman, *Ha-Yerushalmi Kifshuto* (New York: Jewish Theological Seminary, 1994), 52.

However, first we will briefly examine one issue we have excluded from our discussion until this point.

## Causing a non-Jew to Work on Shabbat

Mishnah Shabbat 1:7-9, a section which lies between the mishnayot we quoted above, contains two disputes between the schools about causing a non-Jew to work on Shabbat. In the first Mishnah, the prohibited labor is carrying, and in the second, it is processing hides and laundering.[7] As we will explain, this subject, while similar to the larger subject at hand, is not the same issue as that found in the other mishnayot of this chapter.

| משנה שבת א:ז-ט (כ"י קופמן) | Mishnah Shabbat 1:7-9 (MS Kaufmann) |
|---|---|
| בית שמאי אומרין: אין מוכרין לנכרי ולא טוענין עמו ולא מגביהין עליו אלא כדי שיגיע למקום קרוב. ובית הלל מתירין. | Bet Shammai says: One may not sell to a non-Jew, load [a donkey] with him, or lift up onto his back, unless he can arrive somewhere close [before Shabbat]. But Bet Hillel permits [this]. |
| בית שמאי אומרין: אין נותנין עורות לעובדן ולא כלים לכובס נכרי אלא כדי שיעשו מבעוד יום. ובכולם בית הלל מתירין עם השמש. | Bet Shammai says: One may not give hides to a tanner to process or clothes to a non-Jewish launderer to wash, unless they may be done while it is still day. And in all of these cases, Bet Hillel permits [the act as long as he does it] while the sun is still up. |
| אמר רבן שמעון בן גמליאל: נוהגין היו בית אבא שהיו נותנין כלי לבן שלהן לכובס נכרי שלשה ימים קודם לשבת. | R. Shimon b. Gamliel said: In father's house, they used to give their white garments to a non-Jewish launderer three days before Shabbat. |

In all of these cases, Bet Shammai prohibits giving a non-Jew something that he may either carry or process on Shabbat, and Bet Hillel permits it. The difference between this issue and the issues discussed in the rest of

---

7  The issue is also discussed in Tosefta Shabbat 1:22 and 13:10-11. This latter chapter does not present the issue as a dispute between the schools, causing both Talmuds to ponder the relationship between this material and that in chapter one. See Yerushalmi Shabbat 1:8, 4a; Bavli Shabbat 19a.

this chapter is that there is a separate prohibition on causing a non-Jew to work on Shabbat.[8] Regarding this issue, Bet Shammai rules even more stringently than in the case of work involving a Jew's vessels. To recall, in the Mishnah and Tosefta, Bet Shammai allows one to start a process before Shabbat if the items being processed will not be used on Shabbat (i.e. the olive press and wine press). But Beit Shammai prohibits giving an item to a non-Jew, regardless of whether that item (e.g. clothes to be laundered or skins to be tanned) will not be used on Shabbat. Indeed, even if the item has been sold to a non-Jew or never even belonged to a Jew, Bet Shammai still prohibits entrusting it to a non-Jew because the Jew will be directly abetting work performed by a non-Jew on the Shabbat immediately following the sale or other interaction. The issue here is not the items being used or processed; it is the fact that a person will be performing the forbidden labor, and a Jew is not allowed to directly cause a non-Jew to do work on Shabbat.

In contrast to Bet Shammai, Bet Hillel rules permissively as long as the Jew is not performing work on erev Shabbat that the Jew himself (or other Jews) will benefit from on this Shabbat, or telling a non-Jew to perform a forbidden labor that will certainly be performed on Shabbat. Note that Bet Hillel's position concerning interaction with non-Jews is consistent with the school's position concerning a Jew's vessels. Bet Hillel would not allow a Jew to tell a non-Jew before Shabbat to cook for her on Shabbat because the food will be eaten by the Jew on Shabbat. But Bet Hillel does allow giving clothes to a launderer because the clothes will (presumably) not be used on that Shabbat.

We should note that neither Bet Shammai nor Bet Hillel seems to hold the maximalist position that a Jew is responsible to prevent non-Jews from ever transgressing Shabbat. The issue, for Bet Shammai, is direct causation. A Jew may not directly cause a non-Jew to perform forbidden labor on Shabbat, as would be the case if a Jew sells a donkey to a non-Jew right before the onset of Shabbat. But if the non-Jew can arrive at a reasonably close destination before Shabbat, then Bet Shammai permits the sale, even though he will almost certainly ride that donkey on Shabbat in the future. Similarly, Bet Shammai rules in Tosefta Pesahim 1:7 that a Jew selling his hametz to a non-Jew must sell it early enough so that the

---

[8]    See Mekhilta De-R. Yishmael Pasha parashah 9.

non-Jew could consume it before Pesah. Again, Bet Shammai is interested in direct causation.

The interpolation of the discussion about interactions with a non-Jew on erev Shabbat reflects a certain similarity between this issue and the main dispute between Beit Shammai and Beit Hillel: Both are about initiating a process on erev Shabbat that will continue on Shabbat. Furthermore, while for Bet Shammai these may be two different issues (processing material on Shabbat and causing a non-Jew to work on Shabbat), for Bet Hillel the same reason allows both actions to be permitted—the Jew is not doing anything on Shabbat or benefitting on Shabbat from work performed that day. Thus, while these may have originally been two different issues, the editor of the Mishnah, and in his wake the editor of the Tosefta, included them both here.[9]

## Mekhilta De-R. Shimon B. Yohai: An Attempt at Harmonization

Mekhilta de-R. Shimon b. Yohai (MDRSBY) contains a passage that deals directly with our issues and shares material with the Mishnah and Tosefta. Although MDRSBY is a tannaitic text, it did not survive in its entirety but was reconstructed by later scholars.[10] The textual history of this reconstructed document is relevant to our discussion, since below we will question the tannaitic authenticity of this passage.

Mekhilta de-R. Shimon b. Yohai was first reconstructed by David Tzvi Hoffmann in Germany and published in 1905, based mostly on quotes found in the Midrash Hagadol, a medieval collection of midrashim compiled in the fourteenth century by R. David ben-Avraham Ha'adani. In 1955, J.N. Epstein and E.Z. Melamed published an edition of MDRSBY based on manuscripts as well as fragments found in the Cairo Geniza. These manuscripts and fragments do not cover the entire original MDRSBY and, therefore, the remainder of the Epstein/Melamed edition is based on Midrash Hagadol. Scholars have noted that whereas the material found in the manuscripts and Cairo Geniza fragments is to be treated as authentic tannaitic material, the material reconstructed based on Midrash Hagadol must be treated with greater caution, for it is possible, and at times likely, to have originated in the post-tannaitic—and perhaps

[9] See Tosefta Shabbat 1:22; 13:10-11.
[10] See Menahem Kahana, "The Halakhic Midrashim," *The Literature of the Sages. Second Part*, eds. Shmuel Safrai, et. al. (Philadelphia: Fortress Press, 2006), 72-78.

even post-talmudic—period. The passage below was reconstructed in the Epstein/Melamed edition based on Midrash Hagadol.[11] It is not found in any actual MDRSBY manuscript or geniza fragment.

| מכילתא דרבי שמעון בר יוחאי כ:ח | Mekhilta de-R. Shimon b. Yohai 20:8 |
|---|---|
| *ששת ימים תעבד ועשית כל מלאכתך:* | *Six days you shall work and perform all your labors:* |
| (1) זו היא שבית שמאי אומרין אין שורין דיו וסמנין וכרשינין אלא כדי שישורו מבעוד יום. | (1) This is what Bet Shammai says: One may not soak ink, dyes, and vetch [on Friday afternoon] unless they can be fully soaked while it is yet day. |
| (2) ואין פורשין מצודות חיות ועופות אלא כדי שיצודו מבעוד יום. | (2) One may not spread traps for wild beasts, fowl, and fish unless they can be caught while it is still day. |
| (3) ואין טוענין בקורת בית הבד ובעיגולי הגת אלא כדי שיזובו מבעוד יום. | (3) One may not lay down olive press beams and wine press rollers unless the [liquid] oozes out while it is still day. |
| (4) ואין פותקין מים לגנות אלא כדי שתתמלא מבעוד יום. | (4) One may not conduct water into a garden unless it can be filled while it still day. |
| (5) ואין נותנין בשר בצל וביצה על גבי האש ולא תבשיל לתוך התנור אלא כדי שיצלו מבעוד יום. | (5) One may not roast meat, onion, or egg on a fire, nor [may one place] a cooked dish in an oven, unless they can be [fully] roasted while it is still day. |
| ובית הלל מתירין בכולן. | But Bet Hillel allows all of these. |
| אלא שבית שמאי אומרין: *ששת ימים תעבד ועשית כל מלאכתך* שתהא מלאכתך גמורה מערב שבת. | Rather Bet Shammai says: *Six days you shall work and perform all your labors*—that your labor should be completed by Friday afternoon. |
| ובית הלל אומרין: *ששת ימים תעבד* עושה אתה כל ששה ושאר מלאכתך היא נעשית מאיליה בשבת. | But Bet Hillel says: *Six days you shall work*—you can work all six days, and the rest of your labor can be done on its own on Shabbat. |

[11] There is a midrash which references our subject that appears in the Horowitz edition of Mekhilta de-R. Yishmael (p. 332), but it is based on a medieval collection and not found in any manuscript.

This midrash contains five points of dispute between Bet Shammai and Bet Hillel, two of which (1 and 2) are consistent with our Mishnah. However, in case 3, the Mishnah specifically states that Bet Shammai agrees that it is permitted to lay olive beams and wine press rollers on erev Shabbat, and in the Tosefta Bet Hillel assumes that Bet Shammai agrees on this point. Case 4, the prohibition on opening an irrigation line on erev Shabbat, is found in the Tosefta, but there the action is permitted, and there is no mention of a dispute between the schools. Case 5, the prohibition of beginning to roast meat, onion, or egg, is presented in the Mishnah as a point on which both schools agree, and in the Tosefta as well Bet Shammai assumes that Bet Hillel agrees.

In short, in this midrash Bet Shammai and Bet Hillel have no points of agreement. All of the points upon which they agree in the Mishnah and the Tosefta are presented here as disagreements. The main question we need to ask is whether or not this is an authentic tannaitic tradition, or whether this version of the material is one that was created at a later stage by scholars/copyists interested in harmonizing the earlier material. Saul Lieberman, in his commentary on the Tosefta, posits that this is an authentic tannaitic tradition, despite the fact that it was not found in any text prior to the medieval Midrash Hagadol. Second, he goes a step further and posits that it represents an actual moment in history in which the two schools were entirely consistent in their prohibitions/permissions and disagreed on each and every issue. [12]

Lieberman begins by noting that there is evidence, mostly among the geonim and rishonim, of a tradition whereby Bet Hillel allowed even the roasting of meat, onions, and eggs on erev Shabbat (Mishnah 1:10). Indeed, he cites one geniza fragment of the Mishnah itself (Canterbury BE 2) which reads: "One may not roast meat... But Bet Hillel permits." Lieberman proceeds to demonstrate that some Karaitic polemicists (9th-12th centuries) were familiar with a text according to which Bet Shammai prohibited laying olive press beams and prohibited conducting water into a garden on erev Shabbat. This testimony affirms the accuracy of the version of the midrash preserved in Midrash Hagadol. In other words, there is clear evidence that the Midrash Hagadol accurately drew its material from an earlier tradition.

---

[12] See Saul Lieberman, *Tosefta Kifshuta: Moed* (New York: Jewish Theological Seminary of America, 1962), 17-19.

Lieberman then suggests that this version is also alluded to in the following statement in the Bavli referring to a series of disputes between Bet Shammai and Bet Hillel (Shabbat 15a): "R. Yehudah said in the name of Shmuel: They made eighteen decrees and on eighteen they disagreed." Lieberman explains that the eighteen on which they disagreed are the eighteen issues listed in mishnayot 5-10 of our chapter. In the Mishnah as we know it, the two schools do not disagree on all of these issues. Lieberman maintains that the MDRSBY reflects this Babylonian tradition, referred to by R. Yehudah and Shmuel, according to which the two schools did indeed disagree on all of the issues in the Mishnah. Finally, Lieberman concludes based on this Babylonian passage that initially the two schools disagreed on all of these cases. This is the tradition preserved in the MDRSBY. They later came to agreement on certain issues (roasting meat, laying olive beams and wine presses, conducting water) and that agreement is reflected in the Mishnah, Tosefta, and both Talmuds.

Lieberman's evidence proves sufficiently that such a version of the Mishnah, and a midrash that reflects it, existed by the geonic period. Midrash Hagadol consistently copies from earlier sources and does not invent them whole cloth, thus rendering it likely that this text existed prior to its inclusion in this late midrashic collection. However, Lieberman's evidence as to the tannaitic authenticity of this midrash is scant and cannot stand against the version preserved in all manuscripts of the Mishnah (except for the one cited above) and in all manuscripts of the Tosefta, and which clearly served as the basis for the sugyot in both Talmuds. Furthermore, Yaakov Sussmann, the world's foremost scholar in talmudic manuscripts in the generation following Lieberman and Epstein, has demonstrated that the Mishnah manuscript which states that Bet Hillel permits roasting meat etc., is not a manuscript of the Mishnah but rather a Bavli manuscript which begins with all of the mishnayot of the chapter before recording the talmudic discussion.[13] Indeed, the same tradition may be alluded to in a quote from the Mishnah that appears in the Munich manuscript of the Bavli: "Bet Shammai says one may not roast meat..." By attributing the prohibition to Bet Shammai, the

---

[13] Yaakov Sussmann, "Kitvei Yad u-Mesorot Nusah shel ha-Mishnah," *Proceedings of the Seventh World Congress of Jewish Studies, vol 3, Studies in Talmud, Halakhah, and Midrash* (Jerusalem: World Union of Jewish Studies, 1981), 248-249.

implication is that Bet Hillel would permit. But these are Babylonian traditions of the Mishnah, which often preserve variant readings that are not authentic tannaitic traditions. As Sussmann has proven conclusively, the most original and pristine readings of the Mishnah are found in manuscripts of Eretz Yisraeli origin, for the most part MSS Kaufmann and Parma.[14]

It is possible to surmise the reason that someone would have added into a copy of the Mishnah that Bet Hillel permits roasting. Bavli Shabbat 20a asks "How much [must the meat be roasted before Shabbat]?" and answers, "So that it is roasted enough while it is still day like the food of Ben Drosai." This term connotes meat that is minimally roasted.[15] Thus, the Bavli seems to say that while the Mishnah prohibits roasting meat on Shabbat, the meat may continue to roast over an open flame on Shabbat as long as it has been lightly cooked before Shabbat. But, in essence, it seems that the Talmud contradicts the Mishnah—the latter prohibits roasting meat and the former basically permits it. We will return to this issue below. It is possible that someone at some point added into the Mishnah that Bet Hillel permits, and then understood the Talmud to be a slight restriction on Bet Hillel. The meat may be roasted on Shabbat as long as it was slightly roasted before.

To return to the midrash preserved in Midrash Hagadol, it is far more likely that this is a secondary version of the material, one that was familiar to the Babylonian geonim and to some medieval Karaites. This version partially reflects—and may have been influenced by—late Babylonian traditions of the Mishnah, but it does not accurately represent the material as it existed in its earliest form during the tannaitic period. In this reworked midrash we can see, as we shall see in both Talmuds, just how problematic the lack of consistency in the tannaitic material was in the eyes of later sages. The editors of this midrash, whenever and wherever they may have lived, chose to deal with their material by harmonizing it and denying that such a lack of consistency ever existed.

---

[14]   Ibid., 215-250.

[15]   For suggestions regarding the identity of Ben Drosai see Shamma Friedman, "Mi Hayah Ben D'rosai" *Sidra 14* (1998), 77-91; Shlomy Raiskin, "She'elat Zekhuto shel Ben Drusai" *Sidra 22* (2007), 177-184.

## The Yerushalmi

There are two sugyot that address this material in the Yerushalmi. We will consider both sources, noting how the apparent inconsistencies in the tannaitic material are dealt with.

### Yerushalmi Shabbat 1:5, 3d

(1) What is the reasoning for Bet Shammai? *Six days you shall work and perform all your labor* (Exodus 20:8): All your labor—finish it while it is still day.

And what is the reason for Bet Hillel? *Six days you shall do your actions, and on the [seventh] day* (Exodus 23:12).

(2) How would Bet Hillel deal with the reasoning of Bet Shammai [who said], *Six days you shall work and perform all your labor*? [This refers] to those who work actively [on Shabbat].

(3) How does Bet Shammai deal with the reasoning of Bet Hillel [who said] *Six days you shall do your actions, and on the [seventh] day*?

It is like that which is taught: One may conduct water into a garden on Friday afternoon, and it will continue being filled on Shabbat.

One may place an eye salve on the eye on Friday afternoon and it will heal on Shabbat.

One may place a plaster on a wound on Friday afternoon and it will continue healing on Shabbat.

One may place incense underneath clothing on Friday afternoon and it may continue emitting smoke on Shabbat.

One may place sulfur under [silver] vessels on Friday afternoon and it may

### ירושלמי שבת א:ה (ג, ד)

(1) ומה טעמהון דבית שמאי? *ששת ימים תעבוד ועשית כל מלאכתך* (שמות כ:ח) כל מלאכתך גומרה מבעוד יום.

ומה טעמהון דבית הלל? *ששת ימים תעשה מעשיך וביום* (שמות כג:יב).

(2) מה מקיימין בית הלל טעמון דבית שמאי *ששת ימים תעבוד ועשית כל מלאכתך*? בעובדי ביידן.

(3) ומה מקיימין בית שמאי טעמון דבית הלל *ששת ימים תעשה מעשיך וביום?*

כהדא דתני: פותקין אמת המים לגינה מערב שבת והיא שותה והולכת בשבת.

נותנין קילורית על גבי העין מערב שבת והוא מתרפא והולכת בשבת.

נותנין רטייה על גבי מכה מערב שבת והיא מתרפא והולכת בשבת.

נותנין מגמר תחת הכלים מערב שבת והן מתעשנין והולכין בשבת.

נותנין גפרית תחת הכלים מערב שבת והן מתגפרין והולכין בשבת.

אין נותנין חיטים לריחים של מים אלא
כדי שיטחנו כל צורכן מבעוד יום.

(4) אמר רבי חגיי: מפני שהן
משמיעות את הקול.

(5) אמר ליה רבי יוסי: יאות רבי סבר
כרבי יהודה, ברם כרבנין כמה דאינון
אמרין תמן, משום לא הותחל בכל
טיפה וטיפה כן אינון אמרין הכא
משום לא הותחל בכל חיטה וחיטה.

(6) אמר רבי יוסי בי רבי בון: מפני
שהוא שכח ותוקע את היתד.

(7) בית שמאי אמרו לבית הלל דבר
אחד ולא יכלו להשיבן,
בית הלל אמרו לבית שמאי דבר אחד
ולא יכלו להשיבן.
אמרו להן בית הלל לבית שמאי: אין
אתם מודין לנו שטוענין קורת בית
הבד ובעיגולי הגת עם חשיכה ולא
יכלו להשיבן.

אמר רבי זעירא: אילולא דלא מעלה
רישי ביני אריוותא הוינא אמר טעמא
תמן כבר נעקרה כל טיפה וטיפה
ממקומה, הכא מה אית לך מימר?

(8) בית שמאי אמרו לבית הלל דבר
אחד ולא יכלו להשיבן. אמרו בית
שמאי לבית הלל: אין אתם מודין לנו
שאין צולין בשר בצל וביצה אלא כדי
שיצולו כל צורכן מבעוד יום ולא יכלו
להשיבן.

אמר רבי זעירא: אילולי דלא מעלה
רישי ביני אריוותא הוינא אמ' טעמא

continue making sulfurous odor all day;
One may not place wheat in a watermill
unless it can be fully ground when it is
still day.

(4) R. Haggai said: Because they make a
sound.

(5) R. Yose said to him: What you say is
true, Rabbi, if you hold like R. Yehudah.
But according to the other rabbis, it is
like we said there, for each drop has not
yet begun [to drip into the lamp]. So too
we say here that [the grinding] has not
begun with each piece of wheat.

(6) R. Yose b. R. Bun said: Because he
will forget and he will put in the peg.

(7) Bet Shammai said to Bet Hillel one
matter and they couldn't respond.

Bet Hillel said to Bet Shammai one
matter and they couldn't respond.

Bet Hillel said to Bet Shammai: Don't
you agree with us that it is permitted to
lay olive press beams and wine press
rollers right before it gets dark? And they
[Bet Shammai] couldn't respond.

R. Zera said: If I did not want to put my
head between the lions, I would have
said that the reason is that [in that case]
every drop has already been moved from
its place. But what can you say here?

(8) Bet Shammai said to Bet Hillel one
matter and they couldn't respond. Bet
Shammai said to Bet Hillel: Don't you
agree that one does not roast meat,
onion, or egg unless they can be fully
roasted while it is still day? And they
couldn't respond.

R. Zera said: Had I wanted to to put my
head between the lions, I would have said

תמן בצל בשר וביצה דרכן להתהפך.    that the reason is that in that case it is

הכא מה אית לך מימר?    customary to turn over onion, meat, and
egg. But what can you say here?

## Analysis of the Yerushalmi

The Yerushalmi opens with an echo of the midrash that we saw above in the Tosefta. According to Bet Shammai, one must complete all work by erev Shabbat, even if the work will be done on its own, without human intervention, on Shabbat. Bet Hillel partially quotes a different verse so that it reads, "Six days you shall work and on the [seventh] day." It seems that this midrash is a secondary version—perhaps even a tertiary version—of the Tosefta. The original debate between the schools probably did not stem from any midrash but rather from concepts and ideas, as we have suggested above. The Tosefta searched for a midrashic reading of the verses in which to anchor the debate, and the Yerushalmi's midrash develops this a step further.

The fact that the Yerushalmi's midrash is a further development of an earlier source can be sensed from the intentional misreading attributed to Bet Hillel, appending the word "and on the [seventh] day" to the previous clause, as opposed to its simple meaning in the context of the verse, "and on the seventh day you shall rest." This type of midrash, in which words are read out of context, is not typical of the earliest strata of tannaitic midrash.[16] Bet Hillel's midrash in the Yerushalmi succeeds in conveying Bet Hillel's halakhic position better than the midrash in the Tosefta. In the earlier text, the Tosefta, Bet Hillel emphasizes that one may work all day on Friday. But this is not Bet Hillel's precise argument with Bet Shammai; the latter would agree that one can work all day Friday as long as that work is completed before Shabbat. By using a tendentious reading of another verse, Bet Hillel goes so far as to claim that one can even work, in a sense, on Shabbat.

Section 2 contains Bet Hillel's response to Bet Shammai. Bet Hillel says that the work prohibition in the Torah applies only to work done with one's actual hands. Work done "on its own" on Shabbat, without

---

[16]   See Yohanan Breuer, "Veshuv le-Mikraot she-Ein Lahem Hekhre'a" *Israel: Linguistic Studies in Memory of Israel Yeivin* (Jerusalem: Mandel Institute of Jewish Studies, 2011), 53-63; Aharon Glatzer, *Ha-Basis ha-Leshoni shel ha-Midrash lefi Midrash Sifre Bamidbar* (M.A. Thesis: Hebrew University, 2015), 42-45.

human intervention, would be permitted. We should note that this explanation of Bet Hillel does not in any way explain Beit Hillel's occasional prohibitions. If all work that is done on its own is permitted, why can't one begin, for example, to roast food?

Section 3, Bet Shammai's response to Bet Hillel, further complicates matters. Bet Shammai admits to Bet Hillel that there are some "labors" which one can begin late Friday afternoon and allow them to continue through Shabbat. These are the labors mentioned in Tosefta 1:23. There are two important points here. First, the Yerushalmi attributes this baraita to Bet Shammai—that is, even to Bet Shammai. Bet Shammai's dispute with Bet Hillel is not absolute (as it is in the MDRSBY). Second, there is no explanation in the Yerushalmi as to why Bet Shammai permits these activities.

In section 4, R. Haggai explains why placing wheat in a mill is prohibited. Unlike the processes in the first half of the baraita, which are relatively silent, the grinding of wheat will make noise. The prohibition of creating a noise on Shabbat is well-documented in both Talmuds.[17] From the opening of section 3, where we learned that this baraita contains points where Bet Shammai would agree with Bet Hillel, the implication is that Bet Hillel agrees with Bet Shammai that putting wheat in the watermill is prohibited. The fact that Bet Hillel agrees is probably why the amoraim were more interested in this section of the baraita than the others.

In section 5, R. Yose provides an alternative explanation for the prohibition of putting wheat in a watermill before Shabbat. R. Yose compares the issue of putting wheat in a mill to the issue of putting oil in a vessel so that it can drip into a lamp on Shabbat. Mishnah Shabbat 2:4 reads, "One may not pierce an eggshell, fill it with oil, and place it over the mouth of a lamp, in order that it should drip, and even if it is of clay. But R. Yehudah permits." The Yerushalmi (2:4, 5a) comments on this mishnah: "Why? Is it because [the burning] has not started with every drop or [is it] lest he forget and pour it out?" R. Yose says that if one holds like R. Yehudah in that mishnah, then we would require the reason of

---

[17] Yerushalmi Betzah 5:2, 63a; Bavli Eruvin 104a. See Yitzhak Gilat, *Perakim be-Hishtalshelut ha-Halakhah* (Ramat-Gan: Bar Ilan University, 1992), 89. See also Tosefta Eruvin 8:21; Aviad Stollman, *Ha-Motzei Tefillin: Eruvin Perek Asiri min ha-Talmud ha-Bavli* (Jerusalem: Ha-Igud le-Farshanut ha-Talmud, 2008), 375-391.

"because it makes a noise" to prohibit placing wheat in a mill. But if we hold like the majority of sages in that mishnah, that putting oil in the egg is prohibited because "the burning has not started with every drop," then the same reason could apply here to grinding wheat. Each piece of wheat begins to be ground on Shabbat, and therefore this is not a case of work that began before Shabbat, but work that begins on Shabbat itself.

Section 6 contains a third amoraic explanation for why grinding wheat in a watermill is prohibited: "Because he will forget and he will put in the peg." This refers to an action undertaken to fix the mill or to stop it from grinding. We should note that this reason is qualitatively different from those found in earlier sections. According to the reasoning provided in sections 4 and 5, Bet Hillel prohibits putting wheat in a watermill because this will lead to a violation of Shabbat, either through the production of a sound or the grinding of each individual grain of wheat. In contrast, R. Yose b. R. Bun's explanation is based on a concern about potential future violations. Putting wheat in the watermill does not in and of itself constitute a violation of Shabbat, but it might lead to a person performing a prohibited action. This notion is one that is open to expansion, and indeed it is refined and elaborated upon at length in the Bavli.

Sections 7 and 8 contain R. Zera's response to Tosefta Shabbat 1:20-21, where Bet Shammai attacks Bet Hillel and vice versa. In the Tosefta, neither school responds, which leaves an opening for R. Zera "to put his head in between the lions." In section 7 he explains how Bet Shammai could differentiate between laying olive press beams and soaking flax, dye, and vetch. In the former case, the beams are laid only once the olives have already been crushed. Since the actual forbidden labor is to squeeze the oil out, the labor is completed before Shabbat, and therefore laying the beams before Shabbat is permitted. In essence, the process is not pressing oil out of olives, rather it is moving oil that has already been released from the olives.

In section 8, R. Zera explains how Bet Hillel could differentiate between roasting meat (forbidden) and soaking dye (permitted). When it comes to meat, eggs, or onions, which a person would want to eat on Shabbat, he may come to turn over the food in the process of its cooking. This would violate the prohibition of cooking. However, there is no reason that one would want to turn over or stir dyes on Shabbat, and therefore there is no reason to prohibit. This reasoning is similar in essence to section 6: Roasting food on Shabbat should be in principle permitted but is forbidden lest one come to perform a forbidden labor on Shabbat.

The second relevant sugya in the Yerushalmi addresses the Mishnah's case of initiating the dying process before the onset of Shabbat.

| ירושלמי שבת א:ו (ד, א) | Yerushalmi Shabbat 1:6, 4a |
|---|---|
| רב יהודה בשם שמואל: והיא | R. Yehudah said in the name of Shmuel: And |
| שתהא היורה עקורה. אבל אם | that is only if the cauldron is removed [from |
| היתה היורה קבועה אסורה מפני | the fire]. But if the cauldron is set [on the |
| שהוא מתיירא שמא מתאכל ציבעו | fire], it is forbidden, because he fears that the |
| והוא מוסיף מוי. | dye will be consumed, and he will add water. |

According to the mishnah, Bet Hillel permits putting wool into a cauldron containing dye sitting on a fire on erev Shabbat. R. Yehudah in the name of Shmuel limits this allowance to a case where the cauldron has already been removed from the fire, such that there is no concern that he will add water to the cauldron for fear that liquid will evaporate. Note that this limitation does not seem to accord with the simple reading of the mishnah. First of all, how effective will a cauldron removed from the fire be in processing the wool on Shabbat? In all likelihood, the heat will dissipate quickly. Second, would Bet Shammai prohibit leaving the dye in the cauldron when the cauldron is not even on the fire?

Shmuel's ruling here is part of a broader transformation with regard to the rules of initiating of a process of cooking before Shabbat. The history of this prohibition, which was traced by Stephen Wald in a comprehensive analysis, is beyond the scope of this paper, so we will merely summarize some of his conclusions.[18]

As we have seen, originally Bet Hillel allowed cooking dyes because they would not be used on Shabbat, whereas Bet Hillel prohibited roasting meat because the intention would be to eat it on Shabbat. The underlying logic is that one is not allowed to derive benefit on Shabbat from work performed on Shabbat. But amoraim in the Yerushalmi already begin to put forth the notion that as long as the process began before Shabbat, it cannot be a biblical prohibition of Shabbat. So why then does Bet Hillel prohibit roasting meat? R. Zera's answer in the Yerushalmi was "it is customary to turn over onion, meat, and egg." In other words, the

---

18  See above n. 3.

fear is of possible human interaction with the fire, food, or other substance on Shabbat. A similar shift in the interpretation of Bet Hillel leads to a stringency in the case of dye in the cauldron. Bet Hillel should be concerned lest the dyer intervene by adding water. Thus, Shmuel limits Bet Hillel's allowance to a case where the cauldron has already been removed from the fire and there is no concern that the water will entirely evaporate, and hence no concern that water might be added.

## Bavli Shabbat 18a-18b

The Bavli contains an extended sugya dealing with the debates between the two schools. This is the first place where the notion of the "resting of vessels" is formed into a named halakhic concept. It is a difficult sugya to follow, but we shall try to explain how it developed and why in its present form it appears so convoluted:

BARAITA

(1) ת"ר פותקין מים לגינה ערב שבת עם חשיכה ומתמלאת והולכת כל היום כולו ומניחין מוגמר תחת הכלים ומתגמרין והולכין כל היום כולו ומניחין גפרית תחת הכלים ומתגפרין והולכין כל השבת כולה. ומניחין קילור על גבי העין ואיספלנית על גבי מכה ומתרפאת והולכת כל היום כולו.

אבל אין נותנין חטין לתוך הריחים של מים אלא בכדי שיטחנו מבעוד יום.

(1) Our rabbis taught: One may conduct water into a garden on the eve of Shabbat just before dark, and it may continue being filled the whole day. And one may place incense under garments and it may continue making smoke the whole day. And one may place sulfur under vessels and it may continue making sulfurous odor all day. And one may place an eye salve on the eye and a plaster on a wound and it will continue healing all day.

But one may not place wheat in a watermill unless it can be ground when it is still day.

### FIRST AMORAIC INTERPRETATION OF BARAITA

מפני :אמר רבא ?מאי טעמא (2)
.שמשמעת קול

(2) What is the reason? Rava[19] said: Because it makes a noise.

### DIFFICULTY RAISED BY AMORA BASED ON BARAITA

אמר ליה רב יוסף: ולימא מר משום (3)
:שביתת כלים דתניא

*ובכל אשר אמרתי אליכם תשמרו* (שמות
.כג, יג) לרבות שביתת כלים

(3) R. Yosef said to him: Let the Master say it is on account of the resting of vessels? For it was taught: *And in everything that I have said to you take heed* (Exodus 23:13)—this includes the resting of vessels.

### SECOND AMORAIC INTERPRETATION OF BARAITA

אלא אמר רב יוסף: משום שביתת (4)
.כלים

(4) Rather R. Yosef said: It is on account of the resting of vessels.

### STAMMAITIC INTERPRETATION OF BARAITA IN LIGHT OF R. YOSEF

והשתא דאמרת לבית הלל אית להו (5a)
שביתת כלים דאורייתא גפרית ומוגמר
?מאי טעמא שרו

(5a) Now that you say that Bet Hillel holds that the resting of vessels is a biblical commandment, why did they permit sulfur and incense?

.משום דלא קעביד מעשה (5b)

(5b) Because it [the vessel in which they lie] performs no action.

?אונין של פשתן מאי טעמא שרו (5c)

(5c) Why did they permit wet bundles of flax?

משום דלא עביד מעשה ומינח (5d)
.נייחא

(5d) Because it [the oven in which they lie] performs no action and is motionless.

מצודת חיה ועוף ודגים דקא עביד (5e)
?מעשה מאי טעמא שרו

(5e) But why did they permit traps for wild beasts, fowl, and fish, which

---

[19] All textual witnesses of our sugya, including geniza fragments, manuscripts, and most printed editions, attribute this statement to Rava. The Vilna printed edition, influenced by the emendation of R. Solomon Luria (16th century), reads Rabbah. The early medieval commentators also attribute this statement to Rabbah because of the direct engagement with R. Yosef, his colleague. We will see below, however, that Rav Yosef's comment was not originally a response to Rava. On the difficulty of determining the attribution of statements to Rava/Rabbah see Shamma Friedman, "Orthography of the names Rabbah and Rava," *Sinai* 110 (1992), 140-164.

(5f) התם נמי בלחי וקוקרי דלא קעביד מעשה.

(5f) There too [it refers to] a fishhook and a trap made with little joists, so that no action is performed.

(6) והשתא דאמר רב אושעיא אמר רב אסי: מאן תנא שביתת כלים דאורייתא? בית שמאי היא ולא בית הלל.

(6) Now, however, that R. Oshaya said in the name of R. Asi: Which tanna [holds that] the resting of vessels is from the Torah? It is Bet Shammai and not Bet Hillel.

לבית שמאי בין קעביד מעשה בין דלא קעביד מעשה אסור, לבית הלל אף על גב דקעביד מעשה שרי.

Then according to Bet Shammai, whether it [the utensil] performs an action or not, it is forbidden; while according to Bet Hillel even if it performs an action, it is permitted.

(7a) והשתא דאמרת דלבית שמאי אף על גב דלא עביד מעשה אסור אי הכי מוגמר וגפרית, מאי טעמא שרו בית שמאי?

(7a) And now that you say that according to Bet Shammai, even if it performs no action, it is prohibited, why do they permit incense and sulfur?

(7b) התם מנח אארעא.

(7b) In that case it is placed on the ground.

(7c) גיגית ונר וקדרה ושפוד מאי טעמא שרו בית שמאי?

(7c) Why do Bet Shammai permit a basin, lamp, pot, and skewer?

(7d) דמפקר להו אפקורי.

(7d) That is in a case where he made the vessels ownerless.

(8a) מאן תנא להא דתנו רבנן: לא תמלא אשה קדרה עססיות ותורמסין ותניח לתוך התנור ערב שבת עם חשכה ואם נתן למוצאי שבת אסורין בכדי שיעשו.

(8a) Who is the author of the following which our rabbis taught?: A woman must not fill a pot with pounded wheat and lupines and place it in the oven on the eve of Shabbat shortly before nightfall; and if she

107

does put them [there], they are forbidden at the conclusion of Shabbat for as long as they take to prepare.

כיוצא בו לא ימלא נחתום חבית של מים ויניח לתוך התנור ערב שבת עם חשכה ואם עשה כן למוצאי שבת אסורין בכדי שיעשו.

Similarly, a baker must not fill a barrel of water and place it in the oven on the eve of Shabbat shortly before nightfall; and if he does, it [the water] is forbidden at the conclusion of Shabbat for as long as it takes to prepare [i.e. boil].

### QUESTION

(8b) לימא בית שמאי היא ולא בית הלל?

(8b) Shall we say that this agrees with Bet Shammai and not Bet Hillel?

### ANSWER

(8c) אפילו תימא בית הלל גזירה שמא יחתה בגחלים.

(8c) You may even say that it agrees with Bet Hillel: It is a preventive measure, lest he stir the coals.

### DIFFICULTY

(8d) אי הכי מוגמר וגפרית נמי לגזור?

(8d) If so, let us decree [likewise] with respect to incense and sulfur?

### RESOLUTION

(8e) התם לא מחתי להו דאי מחתי סליק בהו קוטרא וקשי להו.

(8e) There he will not stir them, for if he does, the smoke will enter and harm them.

### DIFFICULTY

(8f) אונין של פשתן נמי ליגזור?

(8f) Let us decree with respect to wet bundles of flax too?

### RESOLUTION

(8g) התם כיון דקשי להו זיקא לא מגלו ליה.

(8g) There, since a draft is injurious to them, he will not uncover it.

### DIFFICULTY

(8h) צמר ליורה ליגזור?

(8h) Let us decree with respect to wool in the dye kettle?

AMORAIC RESOLUTION

(8i) אמר שמואל: ביורה עקורה    (8i) Shmuel said: This refers to a kettle removed [from the fire].

DIFFICULTY

(8j) וניחוש שמא מגיס בה.    (8j) But let us fear that he may stir it?

RESOLUTION

(8k) בעקורה וטוחה.    (8k) This refers to [a kettle] removed from [the fire] and sealed.

---

| Tannaitic Source | Amoraic Source | Stammaitic Source |

## Analysis of the Bavli

The sugya opens by quoting the baraita from the Tosefta. Thereupon Rava immediately explains why the final example in the baraita, putting wheat into a watermill on erev Shabbat, is prohibited: because it makes a noise. This is the same reason provided in section 4 of the Yerushalmi. The other two reasons found in the Yerushalmi for prohibiting placing wheat in the watermill. Although the baraita does not mention either Bet Hillel or Bet Shammai, it seems likely that Rava would have understood all these laws as being a point of agreement between the two schools, as it is explained in the Yerushalmi. We will return to this part of the sugya (sections 1-2) and refer to it as **sub-sugya 1**, for reasons that will be apparent below.

The turning point in our sugya in the Bavli occurs in section 3 with R. Yosef's difficulty on Rava and his alternative explanation of the toseftan baraita. First, R. Yosef asks why Rava did not explain that the prohibition was "because of the resting of vessels." R. Yosef then cites a midrashic baraita[20] supporting the idea that one is commanded to allow one's vessels to "rest" on Shabbat, and then, in section 4, he replaces Rava's answer with his own: "because of the resting of vessels."

The great difficulty here is that according to the arrangement of the sugya which assumes that the baraita is agreed upon by both schools, R.

---

[20]    This baraita is not found in tannaitic midrashim, but it was included in the printed edition of Mekhilta de-R. Yishmael. See above n. 12.

Yosef is supposed to be explaining Bet Hillel **and** Bet Shammai. R. Yosef seems to posit that Bet Hillel prohibits using a watermill not because of a specific problem with the equipment, but due to a larger category of prohibitions which he terms "the resting of vessels." This creates all of the difficulties found in section 5—how can Bet Hillel hold that one's vessels must rest when they permit nearly all the other activities discussed in the Mishnah, as well as those in the baraita and elsewhere? "Resting of vessels" can explain why Bet Hillel prohibits the grinding of wheat in a watermill only if we completely ignore Bet Hillel's overall system of what is permitted and what is not. Indeed, the Tosafists ask nearly the same question (s.v. "*ve-leima mar*"):

> And if one were to ask, in light of what we conclude, that Bet Shammai is the one who holds that the Torah mandates the resting of vessels, what kind of a difficulty did R. Yosef raise? Wouldn't it be better to agree with Rabbah[21] who explains that [grinding wheat] is prohibited because it makes a noise, and this would accord with Bet Hillel?

We need to ask why R. Yosef would offer such a tenuous explanation for the baraita's prohibition when, as the Tosafot note, a perfectly cogent explanation had just been given. Indeed, it is exceedingly difficult to imagine that the unfolding of the amoraic discourse occurred in the way it is presented in this sugya.

A more plausible explanation of the baraita is found in R. Oshaya's statement in section 6. R. Oshaya explains that it is Bet Shammai, and not Bet Hillel, who maintains that vessels must rest on Shabbat. Why does the sugya then not begin with R. Oshaya's statement? Indeed, we would argue that R. Oshaya's statement originally preceded R. Yosef's statement, and that R. Oshaya's statement was based on the baraita quoted above, "*And in everything that I have said to you take heed*—this includes the resting of vessels." R. Oshaya identified this baraita with Bet Shammai's position in the Mishnah. The words "from the Torah" strongly imply that R. Oshaya is referring to a source that reads "the resting of vessels" into the Torah— and that can only be the midrashic baraita (section 3). The toseftan

---

110

baraita (section 1) does not in any way imply that the prohibition is from the Torah. Subsequently, R. Yosef, who lived after R. Oshaya, affirmed this and explained that Bet Shammai prohibits putting wheat in the watermill, the topic of the end of the toseftan baraita, because of "the resting of vessels." Note that according to this reconstruction, R. Yosef never engages with Rava's explanation of the reason for the prohibition of the watermill.

Based on this understanding, we can tentatively reconstruct an original brief sugya that related to the mishnah and the baraita from the Tosefta, which looked something like this (we will refer to it as **sub-sugya 2**, for reasons which will become apparent):

## Sub-Sugya 2

| | |
|---|---|
| וּבכל אשר אמרתי אליכם תשמרו (שמות כג, יג) לרבות שביתת כלים. | *And in everything that I have said to you take heed* (Exodus 23:13)—this includes the resting of vessels. |
| אמר רב אושעיא אמר רב אסי: מאן תנא שביתת כלים דאורייתא? בית שמאי היא ולא בית הלל. | R. Oshaya said in the name of R. Asi: Which tanna [holds that] the resting of vessels is from the Torah? It is Bet Shammai and not Bet Hillel. |
| תנו רבנן: פותקין מים לגינה ערב שבת עם חשיכה ומתמלאת והולכת כל היום כולו ומניחין מוגמר תחת הכלים ומתגמרין והולכין כל היום כולו ומניחין גפרית תחת הכלים ומתגפרין והולכין כל השבת כולה. ומניחין קילור על גבי העין ואיספלנית על גבי מכה ומתרפאת והולכת כל היום כולו. | Our rabbis taught: One may conduct water into a garden on the eve of Shabbat just before dark, and it may continue being filled the whole day. And one may place incense under garments and it may continue making smoke the whole day. And one may place sulfur under vessels and it may continue making sulfurous odor all day. And one may place an eye salve on the eye and a plaster on a wound and it will continue healing all day. |
| אבל אין נותנין חטין לתוך הריחים של מים אלא בכדי שיטחנו מבעוד יום. אמר רב יוסף: משום שביתת כלים. | But one may not place wheat in a watermill unless it can be ground when it is still day. R. Yosef said: Because of the resting of vessels. |

Since, according to our chronological reconstruction of the sugya, this baraita and R. Oshaya are the earliest mentions of "resting of vessels," we will begin by explaining how this halakhic concept "resting of vessels" can be understood as it directly relates to the tannaitic dispute between the two schools. The Bavli's understanding of "resting of vessels," that one's vessels may not perform any work on Shabbat, leads to forced answers as to why Bet Shammai sometimes permits (section 7). In order for Bet Shammai to permit the lighting of a lamp on Shabbat, one must make his lamp ownerless! However, this difficulty can be avoided if "resting of vessels" is interpreted as signifying that one may not use **vessels to process products on Shabbat**, as we suggested above. Literally, one's vessels must take a "shabbat." This is true of the dyer's cauldron and the soaking pool. It is even true of the traps, which in a sense process the animal by changing it from free to trapped. As we stated above, Bet Shammai allows one to open a water conduct because no material is being processed. Similarly, the salve and bandage are not really vessels and they are not "working," in the sense that they are not processing anything else. In other words, "resting of vessels" is not a restriction on starting any process on erev Shabbat that will continue on Shabbat; it is a restriction on starting a process using one's **vessels** on erev Shabbat if that activity will cause the **vessel itself** to do its intended processing work on Shabbat. This is how R. Oshaya explained Bet Shammai's prohibitions in the Mishnah.

Once the concept of "resting of vessels" has been applied to the Mishnah, R. Yosef can use it to explain the prohibition of placing wheat in the watermill on erev Shabbat. According to his reasoning, this too is a case of a vessel performing work on Shabbat, and therefore Bet Shammai would prohibit it. The result of R. Yosef's explanation of the baraita would be that Bet Hillel would permit such an activity. It is possible that R. Yosef does not find the noise of the watermill problematic because of a shift in understanding the prohibition of making a noise on Shabbat. The Yerushalmi rules that creating any loud noise is prohibited. This would include the wheat grinding in the watermill. But the Bavli limits the prohibition to creating music.[22]

The rest of the sugya is best analyzed in the chronological order in which it became part of the talmudic discussion. The earliest amoraic engagement with this dispute between the schools is Shmuel's opinion in section 8i. Shmuel limits Bet Hillel's opinion in mishnah six (that one is allowed to put dye into a kettle) to a case where the kettle has already been

---

22   See Bavli Eruvin 104a.

removed from the fire. The same comment is attributed to Shmuel in the second passage from the Yerushalmi quoted above. It is clear that this statement was originally made directly on the mishnah and not in the context of any discussion, as it appears in the Bavli. This also explains how Shmuel could respond to a stammaitic question, likely composed long after Shmuel's lifetime.

The baraita in section 8a is taken from Tosefta Shabbat 3:1. The main subject of these halakhot is cooking or heating processes set up on erev Shabbat with the express purpose of deriving benefit **after the conclusion of Shabbat**. This is clearest from the case of the baker. Assuming that a Jewish baker is not intending to bake bread on Shabbat, the only reason he would heat up water erev Shabbat is to use it immediately after Shabbat has ended. So too with regard to the woman cooking lupines in the first half of the halakhah: It can be assumed that these types of beans take a long time to cook, and therefore there is no intent to eat them on Shabbat.[23] This is different from the prohibition of cooking meat, egg, or onion where the intent was to benefit from the food **on Shabbat** itself. Thus, the baraita addresses deriving benefit from these products after Shabbat if they were cooked or heated over Shabbat. The baraita demands a waiting a period after Shabbat equivalent to the time needed to cook the food or heat the water.[24] The waiting period after Shabbat nullifies the benefit gained by using Shabbat to cook.

In any case, the baraita seems to have been brought to our sugya specifically to demonstrate that Bet Hillel agrees that certain actions may not be initiated on erev Shabbat. The explanation for Bet Hillel's stringency hinges on what we described above as a shift in the conception of cooking on Shabbat. To reiterate, originally Bet Hillel conceived of a process of cooking food/water that was set on the fire on erev Shabbat as a transgression of the prohibition of cooking on Shabbat. This is the simple meaning of the mishnah that begins the third chapter of Shabbat. According to that mishnah (and the parallels in the Tosefta), one cannot

---

[23] This explanation follows Rashi. Other medieval commentators suggest that the legumes cook quickly and will be ready for consumption on Shabbat. See Lieberman, *Tosefta Kifshuta: Moed,* 44.

[24] This accords well with what Stephen Wald has described as R. Yehudah's reading of Bet Hillel concerning setting up a cooking process on erev Shabbat (see Tosefta Shabbat 2:13-15). One may not derive benefit from a forbidden act performed on Shabbat, even an act performed passively such as cooking. See above nn. 3, 56-59.

leave uncooked food on a stove on erev Shabbat unless the stove's source of fire has been removed or covered and there are no coals to stoke. Leaving food on erev Shabbat on an active fire is prohibited because this is considered cooking on Shabbat, even though no act was performed on Shabbat. The assumption is that the food or water will certainly be consumed on Shabbat.

Already in the Yerushalmi, there is a shift in understanding this prohibition. Some amoraim seem to feel that simply leaving something on an active fire before Shabbat is not a transgression of Shabbat because the person did not perform any forbidden act on Shabbat itself. Rather, the concern about cooking relates to forbidden activities that might potentially be performed on Shabbat: The roaster might turn over the meat (R. Zera), and the dyer might add water to the cauldron (Shmuel). In each case the prohibition is understood to be grounded in a fear that someone will manipulate the food or the fire on Shabbat itself.

The Bavli unifies what in the Yerushalmi were two different concerns, turning over the meat and adding water, into a single concern—"lest he stoke the coals."[25] According to this line of thought, Bet Hillel prohibits only those activities in which a Jew might intervene in the cooking process. This leads to stringencies such as Shmuel's interpretation that the dyer's cauldron must be removed from the oven, as well as the leniencies found in the continuation of this section of the Bavli (sections 8d-8k). As long as there is no fear that one will stoke the coals or stir the contents of the pot, a Jew may indeed, in essence, cook on Shabbat, at least according to how Bet Hillel would have originally defined the prohibition. These are also the guiding principles throughout the late amoraic sugya that

---

[25] The fear of stoking coals is first raised by Abaye on Shabbat 34b regarding covering food on erev Shabbat and not concerning leaving it on the fire. Abaye explains that one cannot leave food covered in something that increases the heat (following Rashi's reading; see the Rif for an alternative reading) lest one come to stoke coals on Shabbat. This makes eminent sense with regard to the case at hand—one may want to increase the heat so that the food stays hotter—but it makes less sense in the case of the beans left before Shabbat, because there is no intent to eat the food on Shabbat. Later the sugya says that leaving raw meat is permitted because one will not stoke the coals, since the food is not meant to be eaten until the next day. For a discussion of this contradiction, see the Rashba. For our purpose we should note that the difficulties with this statement are the typical result of a secondary usage of material, a phenomenon that occurs frequently in the Bavli.

immediately follows the sugya we are dealing with here. According to this sugya, one can, for instance, put raw meat into a pot in an oven; since it is raw and will not be cooked anyway until tomorrow, he will not stoke the coals.

We would tentatively suggest that this section of the sugya originally looked roughly like this. We will refer to it as **sub-sugya 3**:

## Sub-Sugya 3

בית שמאי אומרים אין נותנין אונין של פשתן לתוך התנור אלא כדי שיהבילו מבעוד יום ולא את הצמר ליורה אלא כדי שיקלוט העין.

Bet Shammai says: one may not place bundles of wet flax in an oven unless they can be steamed while it is still day, nor wool in the dyer's kettle unless it can [absorb the color] such that [the color] is visible.

ובית הלל מתירין.

But Bet Hillel permits it.

אמר שמואל: ביורה עקורה.

Shmuel said: This refers to a kettle removed from the fire.

מאן תנא להא דתנו רבנן: לא תמלא אשה קדרה עססיות ותורמסין ותניח לתוך התנור ערב שבת עם חשכה; ואם נתנן - למוצאי שבת אסורין בכדי שיעשו. כיוצא בו, לא ימלא נחתום חבית של מים ויניח לתוך התנור ערב שבת עם חשכה, ואם עשה כן - למוצאי שבת אסורין בכדי שיעשו.

Who is the author of the following which our rabbis taught? A woman must not fill a pot with pounded wheat and lupines and place it in the oven on the eve of Shabbat shortly before nightfall; and if she does put them [there], they are forbidden at the conclusion of Shabbat for as long as they take to prepare. Similarly, a baker must not fill a barrel of water and place it in the oven on the eve of Shabbat shortly before nightfall; and if he does, it [the water] is forbidden at the conclusion of Shabbath for as long as it takes to prepare [boil].

לימא בית שמאי היא ולא בית הלל?

Shall we say that this agrees with Bet Shammai and not Bet Hillel?

אפילו תימא בית הלל.
מאי טעמא? גזירה שמא יחתה בגחלים.

You can even say that it is Bet Hillel. What is the reason? Lest he rake the coals.

אי הכי, מוגמר וגפרית נמי לגזור.

If so, let him decree also about incense

115

|  | and sulfur. |
| הַתָם לא מַחֲתֵי לְהוּ, דְּאִי מַחֲתֵי - סָלִיק | In that case he won't rake the coals, for |
| בְּהוּ קוּטְרָא, וְקַשֵׁי לְהוּ. | if he does smoke will rise and cause damage. |
| אוֹנִין שֶׁל פִּשְׁתָּן נַמִי לִיגְזוֹר. | Let him also decree concerning bundles of wet flax. |
| הַתָם, כֵּיוָן דְּקַשֵׁי לְהוּ זִיקָא - לא מְגַלֵּי | There, since the wind is damaging, he |
| לֵיהּ. | won't uncover it. |

---

| Tannaitic Source | Amoraic Source | Stammaitic Source |

The amoraic material in this sugya was reworked and augmented by the stam. Shmuel's comment on the mishnah is integrated into the broader discussion of why Bet Hillel permits processes involving fire to be set in motion erev Shabbat despite the fear of stoking the coals. But we should note the artificiality of some of these reasons. From the toseftan baraita (section 1 of the larger sugya), the stam knows that Bet Hillel permits incense to be burned on erev Shabbat and continue through Shabbat, but has to explain why. The stam invents the notion that stoking the coals is bad for incense and wind is bad for flax. These are not even contextualizations such as that of Shmuel; they are simply strained ad hoc justifications for why Bet Hillel permits these activities.

Now that we have accounted for sub-sugyot 2 and 3, we can conclude our reconstruction by noting that sub-sugya 1 is quite simply the toseftan baraita with Rava's comment:

## Sub-Suya 1

| תָּנוּ רַבָּנַן: פּוֹתְקִין מַיִם לַגִּנָּה עֶרֶב שַׁבָּת עִם חֲשֵׁכָה וּמִתְמַלֵּאת וְהוֹלֶכֶת כָּל הַיּוֹם כֻּלּוֹ. | Our rabbis taught: One may conduct water into a garden on the eve of Shabbat just before dark, and it may continue being filled the whole day. |
| וּמַנִּיחִין מוּגְמָר תַּחַת הַכֵּלִים וּמִתְגַּמְּרִין וְהוֹלְכִין כָּל הַיּוֹם כֻּלּוֹ. | And one may place incense under garments and it may continue making smoke the whole day. |
| וּמַנִּיחִין גָּפְרִית תַּחַת הַכֵּלִים וּמִתְגַּפְּרִין וְהוֹלְכִין כָּל הַשַּׁבָּת כֻּלָּהּ. | And one may place sulfur under vessels and it may continue making sulfurous odor all day. |

| | |
|---|---|
| ומניחין קילור על גבי העין ואיספלנית על גבי מכה ומתרפאת והולכת כל היום כולו אבל אין נותנין חטין לתוך הריחים של מים אלא בכדי שיטחנו מבעוד יום. | And one may place an eye salve on the eye and a plaster on a wound and it will continue healing all day. But one may not place wheat in a watermill unless it can be ground when it is still day. |
| מאי טעמא? אמר רבא: מפני שמשמעת קול. | What is the reason? Rava said: Because it makes a noise. |

Let's now review the three separate sub-sugyot that the Bavli seems to contain concerning the disputes between Bet Shammai and Bet Hillel:

| Sub-Sugya 1 | Toseftan baraita—one may conduct water... Rava's explanation—why placing wheat in the mill is prohibited whereas the other actions are not. |
|---|---|
| Sub-Sugya 2 | Midrashic baraita—"resting of vessels" R. Oshaya—in light of the Mishnah, he ascribes this baraita to Bet Shammai. Toseftan baraita (same as above)—one may conduct water... R. Yosef—reason that Bet Shammai prohibits putting wheat in the watermill is the "resting of vessels." |
| Sub-Sugya 3 | Mishnah—Bet Hillel allows one to place wool in a dyer's kettle. Shmuel—contextualization of Bet Hillel—kettle has been removed from fire. Baraita—a woman should not fill up a pot... Stammaitic explanation of the prohibition in this baraita in light of Shmuel's comment. |

Together, these sugyot would offer a comprehensive Babylonian explanation for the positions of both schools. Bet Shammai generally prohibits activities involving labor on Shabbat because of the concept of "resting of vessels" (sub-sugya 2). Bet Hillel prohibits these activities only when there is some fear that work will be done on Shabbat (sub-sugya 3) or when there is an ancillary problem such as making a noise (sub-sugya 1). None of these sugyot contradict each other, nor do the amoraim who operate within each sugya (Rava, R. Oshaya, R. Yosef, and Shmuel) seem to argue at all with one another.[26]

We now must account for how the final editors of the sugya reworked this material. How did three relatively comprehensible sugyot develop into the convoluted sugya, with its strained interpretations, that we find in the Bavli as we know it?

Sub-sugyot 1 and 2 both contain the baraita "one may conduct water..." That is to say, Rava and R. Yosef both originally commented on this baraita, although, according to our reconstruction, it is not certain that they were arguing with each other. It seems that the editors wished to combine these two sugyot. In order to do so, they manufactured a debate between the two amoraim, adding in the comment from R. Yosef to Rava, "Let the master say because of the resting of vessels."[27] As the rishonim noted (see above), and indeed as can be detected in the continuation of the sugya itself, this comment is almost impossible to understand. Why should Rava have explained why even Bet Hillel prohibits by invoking "because of the resting of vessels" when it seems abundantly clear that Bet Hillel does not demand any sort of "resting of vessels?" Even if Rava knew the midrashic baraita in section 3, why would he have used it to explain Bet Hillel's agreement that putting wheat in the watermill is prohibited? And why would "resting of vessels" be a better explanation for Bet Hillel than "because they make a sound?" Rather, this artificially contrived dialogue was fabricated by the editors of the sugya in order to unify these two sugyot and to create dialogue between the two amoraim.

As a consequence of unifying the two sugyot, R. Yosef is understood, at least at the outset, as referring also to Bet Hillel. After all, Rava clearly was explaining why even Bet Hillel prohibits placing wheat in a watermill. If R. Yosef was responding to him, then R. Yosef must have been explaining Bet Hillel's position as well—Bet Hillel shares the prohibition of "resting of vessels." While the stam eventually corrects this impression in section 6 with the introduction "now that R. Oshaya has said...," the

---

[26]   It is possible that R. Yosef disagreed with Rava over whether the noise is sufficient reason to prohibit grinding wheat with a watermill. However, when it comes to the main issues at hand concerning "resting of vessels," there do not seem to be any amoraic disputes in this sugya.

[27]   Had R. Yosef originally responded to Rava and disagreed with him concerning the production of sound, we would have expected a line referring to this issue.

mere fact that the assumption exists, at least for a short time, is a telltale sign of editorial intervention in the original amoraic layer.

Section 6 is structured on R. Oshaya's original statement that only Bet Shammai demands the "resting of vessels." The stam then fleshes out the ramifications of this statement within the larger sugya. Bet Hillel can now permit processes set in motion on erev Shabbat, even if the forbidden labor will be performed in an active manner (such as a trap) on Shabbat. In section 5, putting flax into an oven was considered a case of "not performing an action." Prior to R. Oshaya's attribution of the resting of vessels to Bet Shammai alone, this allowed Bet Hillel to permit it. Now that it is Bet Shammai who maintains that the resting of vessels is mandated, we must conclude that Bet Shammai prohibits in all cases, even when the vessel does not perform an action on Shabbat.

In section 7, the stam is forced to explain how Bet Shammai could agree in cases where the accepted halakhah allows for a process to be set in motion on erev Shabbat, such as placing incense under garments or sulfur under vessels. We should also note that the stam assumes that all of these activities are permitted without even citing any evidence. While Rashi (s.v. גיגית) relates the skewer to the pesah offering, it seems more likely that the stam simply chose household items that we know can be set before Shabbat and let to run on Shabbat. The pot and the skewer probably refer to heating food under conditions that the stam believes are permitted— for instance, when the food was already cooked. These concepts come mostly from the third chapter of the tractate. But there remains a problem: Even if there is no fear that one will intervene on Shabbat with the process, the vessels are still working merely by sitting on the fire. Bet Shammai should prohibit. This leads to the extremely strained answer that Bet Shammai permits these cases only if the vessel has been made ownerless. Since they are no longer "his vessels," he can set them up so that he will benefit from their work on Shabbat.

In sum, the difficulties found in our sugya can be attributed to a well-documented tendency among the editors of the Bavli to combine small, distinct sugyot into larger, more comprehensive analyses. This literary process necessitates the addition of transitions between the component sugyot, some of which are strained or forced. Indeed, scholars have noted that this is one of the key differences between the Bavli and the Yerushalmi. The Yerushalmi is far "choppier," with smaller sugyot or even straight amoraic commentary on tannaitic sources following one after the other.[28] However, the Bavli's combination of small pieces into extended discourse often leaves traces at the seams. The strained words of R. Yosef to Rava and the forced interpretation of Bet Hillel in section 5 and Bet Shammai in section 7 are the frayed ends where the stammaitic stitching has left its trace.

## Bavli Shabbat 19a: An Alternative Explanation for Bet Shammai

There is another passage in the Bavli that deals directly with these debates between Bet Shammai and Bet Hillel. This passage is essentially distinct from the sugya on Bavli 18a-b. That is to say, the authors or sages who participate in one discussion are not familiar with the contents of the other. And perhaps most notably, this second sugya makes no mention of the "resting of vessels":

| | |
|---|---|
| ושוין אלו ואלו שטוענים קורות בית הבד ועגולי הגת. | And they [both Bet Shammai and Bet Hillel] agree that one may lay down olive press beams and wine press rollers. |
| מאי שנא כולהו דגזרו בהו בית שמאי, ומאי שנא קורות בית הבד ועיגולי הגת דלא גזרו? | What is the difference between all of these that Bet Shammai decree against them, and the olive press beams and wine press rollers, that Bet Shammai did not forbid them? |
| הנך דאי עביד להו בשבת מיחייב חטאת - גזרו בהו בית שמאי ערב שבת עם חשכה, קורות בית הבד ועיגולי הגת דאי עביד להו בשבת לא מיחייב חטאת - לא גזרו. | Those other [acts] which, if done on Shabbat one would be liable for a *hatat* offering, Bet Shammai decree on erev Shabbat just before nightfall; [but laying down] olive oil beams and wine press rollers, which if done on Shabbat one does not incur a *hatat*, they did not decree. |

This sugya, which explains why Bet Shammai permits laying olive press beams and wine press rollers, does not seem to be at all aware of the

---

28  See Yaakov Sussmann, "Ve-Shuv le-Yerushalmi Nezikin," *Mehqerei Talmud 1*, ed. Y. Sussman and D. Rosenthal (Jerusalem: Magnes Press, 1990), 96-99.

120

concept of "resting of vessels."[29] According to this sugya, Bet Shammai does not permit these activities because they are not a violation of the demand for the "resting of vessels." Rather, Bet Shammai permits initiating any activity on erev Shabbat which, if performed on Shabbat, would not cause one to be liable for a *hatat*, a sin-offering—the punishment for an unintentional transgression of a biblical Shabbat prohibition. This sugya also does not seem to be aware of the stammaitic comments on 18b, which explain that when Bet Shammai permits a given action it is because it does not involve a vessel (section 7b), or because the vessel has been declared ownerless (section 7d). In almost all of the other passages we have seen, Bet Shammai is assumed to have prohibited an activity because of a principled objection, either based on midrash (Yerushalmi and Tosefta) or based on a conception of the Shabbat prohibitions ("resting of vessels"). Only in this sugya is the suggestion offered that Bet Shammai's prohibitions stem from rabbinic decrees. According to this sugya, Bet Shammai decrees that any process that would incur biblical liability if begun on Shabbat cannot be started erev Shabbat and continued through Shabbat.

The sugya is related to—and perhaps even based on—R. Zera's explanation in section 7 of the Yerushalmi: "[In that case] every drop has already been moved from its place." R. Zera explained that Bet Shammai allows one to lay olive press beams because his vessels will not be squeezing out the oil on Shabbat, for the oil was already removed from the olives on erev Shabbat. The stam in our sugya picks up on the consequence of this explanation—if one were to lay olive press beams on Shabbat, one would not have transgressed a biblical law; therefore, one can do so on erev Shabbat, even according to Bet Shammai. It is possible that R. Zera's comments in the Yerushalmi, which refer specifically to laying olive press beams and wine rollers, have been generalized in the Bavli and formed into a rule—Bet Shammai prohibits performing any action on erev Shabbat that will continue on Shabbat only if that action would make one liable for a *hatat* if performed on Shabbat. The expansion of a particular interpretation into a general principle is a common phenomenon between Yerushalmi and Bavli parallels.[30]

---

[29] This was already noted by the Tosafot s.v. ולימא מר משום שביתת כלים.

[30] See, for example, Shamma Friedman, *Tosefta Atikta* (Ramat Gan: Bar Ilan University, 2003), 434-435 n. 52.

## The Halakhic Impact of the Sugya

The baraita "one may conduct water" is transmitted anonymously in the Tosefta. The Yerushalmi already assumed that even Bet Shammai would agree that the activities in the first part of the baraita are permitted and that Bet Hillel would agree that putting wheat in a watermill is prohibited. According to our reconstruction of the Bavli, Rava explained why even Bet Hillel would have prohibited putting the wheat into a watermill and R. Yosef explained why Bet Shammai would have prohibited it. In other words, it seems that according to amoraim, the activities in this baraita were not disputed by the two schools—both schools permitted the activities in the beginning and prohibited putting wheat in the watermill.

However, the stam's creation of the dialogue in sections 3-4 of the Bavli and the reversal of R. Yosef's opinion in section 6 definitively indicate that R. Yosef attributes the baraita to Bet Shammai **exclusively**, and not to Bet Hillel. And since the halakhah does not follow Bet Shammai, placing the wheat in the watermill should be permitted. Thus, Rabbenu Tam (referenced in Tosafot s.v. והשתא דאמר רב אושעיא) states: "The halakhah is according to R. Yosef who attributes the baraita to Bet Shammai, for R. Oshaya holds like him. And according to this, putting the [wheat] in the mill is permitted, for to him [R. Yosef], Bet Hillel permits, even if the [mill] performs an action, and he is not concerned with creating a sound."[31] In this case, Rabbenu Tam rules in accordance with the editing of the passage, even though no amora actually states conclusively that it is permitted to put wheat into the watermill.

In contrast, most rishonim, including other Tosafists, ruled that placing wheat in the watermill was prohibited. Interestingly, the author of the Tosafot who references Rabbenu Tam even engages in a bit of talmudic criticism in order to justify ruling against him:

> ...it appears to me that R. Oshaya does not attribute the baraita to Bet Shammai. Rather, it is the anonymous voice who states: "Who is this? It is Bet Shammai," according to R. Yosef who says the problem is the "resting of vessels." However, it is possible to say that R. Oshaya

---

[31] The Rif also rules that putting wheat in the watermill is permitted, although he notes that there are those who prohibit. See the comments of the Baal ha-Meor who also rules that this is permitted.

attributes it to Bet Hillel, and he holds [there is concern] of producing noise, as does Rabbah [Rava]. [32] This is also the ruling of R. Hannanel: The reason the case of the mill is prohibited is because of producing noise and it is according to Bet Hillel.

Furthermore, the later sugya (19a) can only be established according to Rabbah [Rava], as I have explained previously. We rule like R. Oshaya that the tanna who holds of the "resting of vessels" is Bet Shammai.

The author of the Tosafot disagrees with Rabbenu Tam's reading of the sugya. He provides two justifications for ruling according to Rava, that the watermill is prohibited because of the noise. First, he demonstrates that the sugya takes R. Oshaya's words out of context. R. Oshaya originally states that only Bet Shammai, and not Bet Hillel, mandates "resting of vessels." R. Oshaya clarifies that the midrashic baraita should be ascribed to Bet Shammai and not Bet Hillel. R. Oshaya was not referring to the baraita concerning the watermill. It is only the context of the sugya, where R. Oshaya's statement follows the debate between R. Yosef and Rava, that makes it seem as if R. Oshaya is siding with R. Yosef, who explains the prohibition as the result of "resting of vessels" and not due to the problem of making noise. It is the editors who lead us to believe that Bet Hillel would allow putting wheat into the watermill. Second, the anonymous sugya that appears on 19a agrees only with Rava and not with R. Yosef, for the latter holds that Bet Shammai's prohibition is "resting of vessels" and not a decree lest one come to transgress a biblical violation on Shabbat.

This passage is an excellent example of the sensitivity of the Tosafot to separating the editorial layer from the words of the amoraim themselves.[33] The Tosafist separates R. Oshaya's statement from its context in the sugya and arrives at his halakhic conclusion by focusing on the original intent of the amoraic material. He finds further support in the sugya on 19a, which prohibits initiating any activity before Shabbat which if done on Shabbat would cause one to be liable for a *hatat*. As we explained above, this implies that even Bet Shammai would not require the "resting of vessels," a total rejection of R. Yosef's explanation of the prohibition of the

---

[32] See above n. 19.

[33] See Shamma Friedman, "A Critical Study of Yevamot X with a Methodological Introduction," *Texts and Studies: Analecta Judaica I*, ed. H. Z. Dimitrovsky (New York: Jewish Theological Seminary, 1977), 283-300.

watermill. Therefore, the Tosafist argues that the halakhah must follow Rava.

The later halakhic authorities debate the merits of each interpretation of the sugya. The Shulkhan Arukh ultimately rules in favor of Rabbenu Tam, permitting the watermill, while R. Moshe Isserles rules that the watermill is prohibited (see Orah Hayyim 252:5). This debate becomes extremely significant in modern halakhic rulings concerning the validity of initiating automated electronic processes before candlelighting which will continue into Shabbat.[34]

---

[34] For more on this topic see Joshua Kulp and Jason Rogoff, "*Mar'it Ozen:* From the Ancient Water-Mill to Automated Electronic Devices," *Hakol Kol Yaakov: The Joel Roth Jubilee Volume* (Leiden: Brill, forthcoming).

# CHAPTER THREE

## SOURDOUGH, SOLDIERS, AND SANCTIFIED FOOD: HAMETZ ON PESAH

### PESAHIM 28A-29B

## Introduction

The Torah is extraordinarily stringent when it comes to the prohibition of hametz (leavened bread) and *se'or* (the leavening agent) on Pesah. Any Jew who eats hametz on Pesah is liable for the penalty of "being cut off (*karet*)" from Israel (Exodus 12:15). But it is not just eating hametz that is prohibited. Leaven may not be found in one's home throughout the festival (v. 19). Exodus 13:7 prohibits one from even seeing hametz or *se'or* "in all of your territory." The Torah forbids the consumption of many substances, some of which—such as blood and forbidden fat—are punishable by *karet*. But hametz is the only food that a Jew must remove from her home. It is so forbidden that it may not even be seen or found in one's possession.

And yet, the day after Pesah, hametz returns to being completely permitted. Just as no other food is treated as stringently as hametz, no other prohibited food has a time limit to its prohibition. Obviously hametz can be eaten during the rest of the year; it is prohibited only on Pesah itself. But does hametz really automatically change its status from prohibited to permitted once Pesah is over? Is there a difference if the hametz is owned by a Jew or a non-Jew during the holiday? If it was owned by a Jew who did not observe the biblical commandment to remove the hametz from her home, does such hametz go from being prohibited on Pesah to being fully permitted after? Or, once prohibited, does it remain prohibited forever?

Beyond discussing the history of the rabbinic discussion of this issue, we will discuss some sui generis halakhic positions that are entertained within the discourse of the sugya that we focus on below. At its most extreme, the sugya offers one of the most outlandish claims in the entire talmudic record: On Pesah, a Jew may eat hametz owned by a non-Jew! How could the Talmud entertain such a counterintuitive notion, one that flies in the face of the Torah's explicit prohibition? Other strange notions that arise in this sugya include the idea that hametz owned by a non-Jew on Pesah is prohibited after Pesah, a notion not found in any other source and countered by the common practice of selling hametz to a non-Jew before Pesah so that a Jew can recover it after. The suyga also raises the possibility that hametz is not prohibited on the second half of the day before Pesah, again a notion countered by all tannaitic opinion. Indeed, one of the main characteristics of this sugya is its willingness to entertain positions that clearly are not halakhically correct.

This chapter will demonstrate how these positions are the result of literary and interpretive impulses and do not reflect any fundamental change in the halakhot of hametz on or after Pesah. The Bavli's most radical assertion, that a tannaitic sage would allow one to eat on Pesah hametz owned by a non-Jew, is not reflective of the opinion of any sage, early or late. Rather it, along with many of the other strange and sui generis positions found in this passage, is the result of a chain of literary processes. This sequence began with the editing of the Mishnah and culminated in the formation of the Bavli's literary discourse, woven together by a late Babylonian redactor from distinct tannaitic and amoraic sources related to the prohibitions of hametz before and after Pesah.

## Mishnah and Tosefta: Hametz Before and After Pesah

We will begin with a discussion of several halakhot in the Tosefta, and then will we go on to consider their parallels in the Mishnah. Tosefta Pesahim begins with laws relating to the search for hametz on the eve of Pesah and continues with a discussion of the status of hametz immediately prior to the onset of the festival.

## Tosefta Pesahim 1:8 | תוספתא פסחים א:ח

האוכל חמץ אחר חצות וחמץ שעבר עליו
הפסח הרי זה בלא תעשה ואין בו כרת,
דברי ר' יהודה.

וחכמים אומרים: כל שאין בו כרת אין בו
בלא תעשה.

One who eats hametz after midday [on the fourteenth of Nissan] and [one who eats after Pesah] hametz owned on Pesah has transgressed a negative commandment, but there is no penalty of *karet*. [These are] the words of R. Yehudah.

But the sages say: Anything not punished with *karet* is not a negative commandment.

This halakhah delineates the severity of the prohibition on eating hametz owned by a Jew before and after Pesah. R. Yehudah holds that hametz after midday on erev Pesah and hametz after Pesah are prohibited by the Torah, despite the fact that the transgressor is not subject to *karet*. The anonymous sages maintain that only hametz during Pesah is prohibited by the Torah (and penalized by *karet*). Hametz before Pesah (after midday on the day before Pesah) and hametz after Pesah are not prohibited by the Torah. As they put it, if it is not punishable by *karet*, then it is not biblically prohibited.

We should note that the sages do not say that it is permitted to eat hametz owned by a Jew after Pesah; they state only that such hametz is not prohibited by the Torah. Just as we can assume that the sages agree that it is prohibited to eat hametz during the second half of the day on the fourteenth of Nissan—a prohibition made explicit in Mishnah Pesahim 2:1 and taken for granted in many other halakhot in the Mishnah and Tosefta—so too we can assume that the sages agree that hametz owned by a Jew is prohibited after Pesah—another halakhah on which there is no disagreement in the Mishnah or Tosefta. The disagreement is only over the level of its prohibition: biblical or not.

The nature of this prohibition is discussed in a parallel dispute concerning hametz after midday found in Sifre Deuteronomy. Here, R. Yehudah maintains the same position as in the Tosefta, while the position attributed to the sages in the Tosefta is attributed instead to R. Shimon.

## ספרי דברים פיסקא קל

*לא תאכל עליו חמץ* (דברים טז:ג), רבי
יהודה אומר: מנין לאוכל חמץ משש
שעות ולמעלה שעובר בלא תעשה?
תלמוד לומר: *לא תאכל עליו חמץ.*

אמר רבי שמעון: יכול כן הוא הדבר?
תלמוד לומר: *לא תאכל עליו חמץ שבעת
ימים תאכל עליו מצות* (שם) את שהוא
בקום אכול מצה, הרי הוא בבל תאכל
חמץ. את שאינו בקום אכול מצה, אינו
בבל תאכל חמץ.

## Sifre Deuteronomy piska 130

*Do not eat with it hametz*
(Deuteronomy 16:3)—R. Yehudah
says: From where do we know that
one who eats hametz after the sixth
hour (midday) transgresses a negative
commandment? Scripture states: *Do
not eat with it hametz.*

R. Shimon said: Is this possible?
Scripture states: *Do not eat with it
hametz, for seven days eat with it
matzot* (ibid)—When there is a
commandment to eat matzah, there is
a prohibition on eating hametz; when
there is no commandment to eat
matzah, there is no prohibition on
eating hametz.

R. Yehudah opens the midrash by quoting a verse regarding the laws of
consumption of the pesah sacrifice. The Torah teaches that the pesah
sacrifice may not be eaten with hametz. R. Yehudah reads the words "with
it" as signifying that the biblical prohibition on eating hametz begins at
the earliest time that one can offer the pesah sacrifice (see Mishnah
Pesahim 5:1). Hametz may not be eaten "with it," and so any time that
one could potentially offer the sacrifice, one cannot at the same time be
eating hametz. In contrast, R. Shimon argues that the prohibition on
eating hametz applies only when there is a positive commandment to eat
matzah, i.e. during the seven days of Pesah. R. Shimon anchors his
halakhah in a typical midrashic reading whereby he equates the first half
of a verse (the prohibition on eating hametz) with its second half (the
commandment to eat matzah). The juxtaposition creates a rule: The
biblical prohibition of hametz exists only when there is a mitzvah to eat
matzah. Thus, for R. Shimon, there is no biblical prohibition on eating
hametz after the sixth hour on the day before Pesah.

In the Sifre, R. Shimon's midrash focuses exclusively on hametz before
Pesah. Since the commandment to eat matzah does not yet apply, the
biblical prohibition on eating hametz also does not yet apply. The Sifre
does not provide any information as to R. Shimon's position on hametz

after Pesah. However, there is some evidence elsewhere in the Tosefta that R. Shimon agrees that hametz owned by a Jew is prohibited after Pesah. Tosefta Pesahim 2:1 rules that a Jew may use the hametz of a Samaritan baker after Pesah as long as the Samaritan has baked three ovens full, an amount sufficient to use up any leaven that had been in his possession on Pesah. On this halakhah R. Shimon comments:

| תוספתא פסחים ב:ב | Tosefta Pesahim 2:2 |
|---|---|
| ר' שמעון אומר אף כשאמרו של נחתומין בכרכים עד שלשה תנורים אסור עד שלשה ימים שמשחרית היה בודה לו שאר כל אותו היום. | R. Shimon says: When they said that [hametz of Samaritan] bakers in cities is prohibited until [he has baked] three ovens full, [the meaning is that it is prohibited] for three days, for in the morning he sets aside enough leaven for the entire day. |

Before, we analyze this source, a note about the Samaritans. The origins of this group are obscure and probably lie somewhere in the First Temple period. By the Second Temple period and throughout rabbinic times, they are related to as an ethnically distinct group, who share many of the same commandments as Jews, but have a different center of worship.[1] Rabbis often seem interested in the Samaritans not so much as a group they frequently encounter, but as an idea that interrupts the binary of Jew/non-Jew, and therefore can serve as a test-case to better elucidate particular issues. The most important issue at hand in this halakhah is the rabbinic assumption that while the Samaritans adhere to the laws of removal of hametz on Pesah, they might differ in calculating the calendar date of Pesah. This might lead to a situation wherein a Samaritan would remove hametz from his home during Pesah according to his calculation, but might be in possession of hametz on the dates when Pesah falls out according to the rabbinic calculation.

This halakhah treats the Samaritan as a Jew. Therefore, if the date on which he observed Pesah differs from the rabbinic date, his hametz would

---

[1] For more on the status of Samaritans in rabbinic Judaism, see Yair Furstenburg, "The Rabbis and the Roman Citizenship Model: The Case of the Samaritans," *Citizenship(s) and Self- Definition(s) in the Roman Empire: Roman, Greek, Jewish and Christian Perspectives*, eds. K. Berthelot and J. Price (Leuven: Peeters) 2019, 181-216.

need to be considered hametz owned by a Jew on Pesah. R. Shimon explains that although the bread of the Samaritan is freshly baked, the leaven used to ferment the dough may have been in his possession for as long as three days. Therefore, after Pesah, one must wait three days before consuming bread baked by a Samaritan. From here we can see that R. Shimon agrees that hametz owned by a Jew on Pesah is prohibited after Pesah.

To return to the Sifre, it seems that this source is chronologically earlier than the Tosefta and served as the basis for its halakhah concerning hametz owned by a Jew on Pesah.[2] In this case, it seems that the editor of the Tosefta (1:8) detached the rule concerning hametz before Pesah from its midrashic origins and applied it more broadly to hametz after Pesah as well. The attribution of this halakhah to R. Shimon was shifted to the anonymous sages, a common phenomenon when material is transferred from one tannaitic composition to the other. The Toseftan editor would argue that to the sages, just as hametz before Pesah is not prohibited by the Torah, so too hametz after Pesah is not prohibited by the Torah. Hametz is prohibited by the Torah only on Pesah itself, for only on Pesah itself is one commanded to eat matzah. At the same time, the editor of the Tosefta has expanded R. Yehudah's position as well. Whereas R. Yehudah in the Sifre holds that hametz before Pesah is prohibited by the Torah, R. Yehudah in the Tosefta holds that hametz is prohibited **by the Torah** after Pesah as well. We should note that while the rule concerning hametz before Pesah is rooted in midrash, there is no midrash in the Tosefta supporting the argument that hametz is prohibited by the Torah after Pesah. We will return to this point below.

Importantly, neither of these sources refers to hametz owned by a non-Jew, nor are they found in the context of a discussion about hametz owned by a non-Jew: The Samaritan is considered a Jew. Throughout Massekhet Pesahim, we can assume that whenever hametz on or after Pesah is discussed, it refers to the hametz of a Jew unless otherwise specified. This halakhah in the Tosefta is no exception.

The Tosefta addresses the issue of hametz owned by a non-Jew at the end of the first chapter:

---

[2]    This understanding is consistent with Shamma Friedman's claim that midrashic texts often predate their parallels in the Tosefta and the Mishnah. See Friedman, *Tosefta Atikta* (Ramat Gan: Bar Ilan University Press, 2002), 75-77.

| תוספתא פסחים א:יב | **Tosefta Pesahim 1:12** |
|---|---|
| חמץ של נכרי מותר אחר הפסח מיד. | Hametz owned by a non-Jew—it is permitted after Pesah immediately. |
| רבן שמעון בן גמליאל ור' ישמעאל בי | R. Shimon b. Gamliel and R. Yishmael |
| ר' יוחנן בן ברוקה אומרים: אף של | b. R. Yohanan b. Berokah say: Even that |
| הקדש מותר אחר הפסח מיד. | belonging to the Temple—it is permitted after Pesah immediately. |

The halakhah teaches that hametz owned by a non-Jew can be consumed immediately after Pesah. Two tannaim add that one can eat hametz owned by the Temple immediately after Pesah (once it has been desanctified). Indeed, this is made clear in a series of halakhot (2:5-9), all of which can be summarized as ruling that if the hametz can be assumed to have been owned by a non-Jew during Pesah, it is permitted to eat it immediately after Pesah.

One final relevant toseftan halakhah for our discussion concerns hametz owned by Jews who intentionally transgress the laws of Pesah:

| תוספתא פסחים ב:ד | **Tosefta Pesahim 2:4** |
|---|---|
| חמיצן של עוברי עבירה מותר אחר הפסח מיד מפני שמחליפין את השאר. | The hametz of transgressors is permitted immediately after Pesah because they exchange their leaven. |

The Tosefta rules that, after Pesah, hametz owned by Jews who are lax in their observance of Pesah is permitted, because we can assume that the leaven they use after Pesah was possessed by non-Jews during Pesah.[3] In sum, these halakhot all assume that hametz owned by a Jew on Pesah is prohibited after Pesah; the only question remains is how certain we are that the hametz was actually owned by the Jew/Samaritan on Pesah. There is no question that hametz owned on Pesah by non-Jews or by the Temple is permitted after Pesah immediately without reservation.

We turn now to the Mishnah. Our analysis will be guided by a theory advanced by Shamma Friedman in his book *Tosefta Atikta*, an analysis of the parallel passages in Mishnah and Tosefta of Massekhet Pesahim. Friedman demonstrates that the Mishnah, at times, consists of an

---

[3]   For an analysis of this halakhah, see below in the appendix to this chapter.

abbreviated form of parallel tannaitic material found in the Tosefta.[4] In these cases, the Mishnah is thus a summary of material found in the Tosefta. Friedman's analysis serves as an important correction to scholars who assume that the entirety of the Tosefta postdates the Mishnah and is in its essence a commentary on the Mishnah. As in the other examples in his book, a comparison between the mishnaic and toseftan passages concerning the status of hametz after Pesah reveals that the mishnaic material is an abbreviated form of earlier sources found in the Tosefta.

Here, we will list two relevant halakhot from the toseftan material discussed above, along with their mishnaic parallels. We list the two halakhot from the Tosefta in the reverse order to which they are found in the Tosefta in order to compare them to their mishnaic parallels.

| Tosefta Pesahim 1:12, 1:8 | Mishnah Pesahim 2:2 |
|---|---|
| חמץ של נכרי מותר אחר הפסח מיד. רבן שמעון בן גמליאל ור' ישמעאל בי ר' יוחנן בן ברוקה אומרים: אף של הקדש מותר אחר הפסח מיד. | חמץ של נכרי שעבר עליו הפסח - מותר בהנאה, |
| Hametz owned by a non-Jew—it is permitted after Pesah immediately. R. Shimon b. Gamliel and R. Yishmael b. R. Yohanan b. Berokah say: Even that belonging to the Temple—it is permitted after Pesah immediately. | Hametz owned by a non-Jew on Pesah—it is permitted to derive benefit from it [after Pesah]. |
| האוכל חמץ אחר חצות וחמץ שעבר עליו הפסח הרי זה בלא תעשה ואין בו כרת, דברי ר' יהודה. וחכמים אומרים: כל שאין בו כרת אין בו בלא תעשה. | ושל ישראל אסור בהנאה שנאמר: *לא יראה לך שאר* (שמות יג:ז). |

---

4    Shamma Friedman, *Tosefta Atikta* (Ramat Gan: Bar Ilan University Press, 2002).

132

One who eats hametz after midday [on the fourteenth of Nissan] and [one who eats after Pesah] hametz owned on Pesah has transgressed a negative commandment, but there is no penalty of *karet*. [These are] the words of R. Yehudah.

And the sages say: Anything not punished with *karet* is not a negative commandment.

But that owned by a Jew [on Pesah], it is prohibited to derive benefit from it [after Pesah] as it says: *You shall not see any leaven* (Exodus 13:7).

When the editor of the Mishnah reworked the toseftan source, he omitted the halakhah regarding the level of the hametz prohibition after midday on the day before Pesah. This halakhah was dealt with in the first chapter of the Mishnah and need not be repeated here. For instance, in Mishnah Pesahim 1:4-5, R. Meir and R. Yehudah dispute what time one must finish eating hametz on erev Pesah, but both agree that it must be destroyed by midday.

The mishnah we are dealing with in the second chapter is concerned only with hametz after Pesah. This mishnah clearly rules according to R. Yehudah from the Tosefta that such hametz is prohibited. Indeed, the second clause quotes a midrash in order to back up the idea that such hametz is prohibited by the Torah, an idea first expressed in the Tosefta, but absent in the Sifre. Friedman posits that this midrash is the Mishnah's attempt to provide biblical support for a halakhah that in the Tosefta has no midrashic basis: Hametz owned by a Jew during Pesah remains prohibited after Pesah. According to Friedman's explanation of the midrash, the prohibition on eating hametz owned by a Jew during Pesah is a result of the transgression of "you shall not see" (Exodus 13:7; Deuteronomy 16:4). Since a Jew transgressed by owning the hametz over Pesah, it remains prohibited forever. We can summarize the history of this halakhah in tannaitic literature by noting that the scope of a midrashic dispute in the Sifre over hametz on the day before Pesah was expanded in the Tosefta into a dispute concerning the level of prohibition of hametz after Pesah. The mishnah then provides midrashic support for R. Yehudah's claim that the prohibition is biblical.

In addition, the tanna of the mishnah used this opportunity to directly juxtapose hametz owned by a non-Jew and hametz owned by a Jew.

Indeed, the very next mishnah deals with another comparative halakhah involving Jews and non-Jews, in this case concerning a Jew who used his hametz as a pledge to secure a loan from a non-Jew and a non-Jew who used his hametz to secure a loan from a Jew. Thus, the Tosefta teaches two separate laws about hametz after Pesah:

[A] If it was owned by a non-Jew, it is permitted immediately after Pesah;

[B] If it was owned by a Jew during Pesah, it is prohibited even after Pesah.

In contrast, the mishnah combines these two separate halakhot into a single two-part law. According to the mishnah:

1) It is permitted to benefit from hametz owned by a non-Jew during Pesah after Pesah (parallels Tosefta 1:12).

2) Jewish-owned hametz during Pesah is biblically prohibited after Pesah (accords with R. Yehudah's position in Tosefta 1:8).

However, upon conjoining these originally disparate halakhot, the mishnah shifts the language of the Tosefta's first ruling, stating that it is permitted to derive **benefit** from hametz owned by a non-Jew, in contrast with the Tosefta's formulation that after Pesah such hametz is simply permitted. The Tosefta implies (and elsewhere states clearly) that one may not only derive benefit from such hamtz, but one may also **consume** such hametz. Presumably, the Mishnah makes this change in order to parallel the formulation of the second half of the mishnah, which prohibits even the derivation of benefit from hametz and not merely its consumption. It is not unusual for the Mishnah to abbreviate earlier sources in order to preserve literally parallelism.[5]

This is an excellent example of the different literary styles of the Mishnah and Tosefta. Tosefta Pesahim 2:5-8 repeats each of the following phrases twice: "And they found there [i.e. in a store] hametz after Pesah, it is forbidden to derive benefit from it, and it is not even necessary to state [that it is forbidden] to eat it;" or "And they found there hametz after Pesah it is permitted to eat it, and it is not even necessary to state that one may derive benefit from it." The Tosefta sacrifices brevity for clarity; the

---

5   See Joshua Kulp, "Organisational Patterns in the Mishnah in Light of their Toseftan Parallels," *JJS* 58, 1 (2007), 52-78.

Mishnah is brief and more artfully constructed, but it may be susceptible to misinterpretation due to its lack of clarity.

Finally, we should add a word about the origin of the prohibition of hametz after Pesah in light of the reconstruction of the development of this law. The fact that the earlier tannaitic texts, the Sifre and the Tosefta, do not provide a midrashic explanation for why hametz is prohibited after Pesah may indicate that the origins of the prohibition lie not in midrash, as the Mishnah implies, but rather in reason. How, the sages may have asked, could a food spontaneously change from prohibited to permitted? As we discussed in the introduction, there is no other example of such a phenomenon in halakhah. It is indeed possible to locate a reason why hametz owned on Pesah would have been universally considered prohibited after Pesah. Bread in mishnaic times was generally made with sourdough (leaven), which was more effective when aged. Were a Jew to hold on to leaven during Pesah and then use it after Pesah, he would derive direct benefit from the fact that he had possessed hametz during Pesah. Using leaven owned during Pesah would thus have clearly been a case of benefiting from a transgression. As we shall see, this consideration is reflected in some passages that appear in the Tosefta and the Bavli.

Whatever the origin (midrashic or a reasoned penalty on a transgressing Jew) all tannaitic halakhot assume that hametz owned by a Jew on Pesah is prohibited after Pesah. The opinion attributed to the sages in the Tosefta that such hametz is not prohibited by the Torah was likely fashioned by the editor of the Tosefta based on the Sifre, patterned after their opinion concerning hametz after midday on the day before Pesah. It is impossible to prove that there were tannaim who held that such hametz was not prohibited by the Torah. But what seems to be clear is that no one ever held that such hametz was in practice permitted.

## Babylonian Baraita: Hametz Before and After Pesah

We have now surveyed the tannaitic material concerning the topic of hametz after Pesah. But there is a baraita in the Bavli that deals with the topic as well. This extraordinarily long baraita was analyzed by Friedman, who demonstrated that it is composed of five parts, some of which are later adaptations of authentic tannaitic material, and some of which are post-tannaitic creations.[6] The baraita appears below, as divided by Friedman:

**Bavli Pesahim 28a-b**

**בבלי פסחים כח ע"א-כח ע"ב**

(1) חמץ בין לפני זמנו בין לאחר זמנו - עובר עליו בלאו.

(1) Hametz before its time [of prohibition] or after its time—[one who eats it] has transgressed a negative commandment.

תוך זמנו - עובר עליו בלאו וכרת, דברי רבי יהודה.

[If he ate it] during its time—he transgresses a negative commandment punishable by ~~*karet.* [These are] the words of R. Yehudah.~~

רבי שמעון אומר: חמץ לפני זמנו ולאחר זמנו - אינו עובר עליו בלא כלום, תוך זמנו - עובר עליו בכרת ובלאו.

R. Shimon says: Hametz before the time [of its prohibition] and after its time—[one who eats it] does not transgress anything; during its time [of prohibition] he transgresses a negative commandment punishable by *karet*.

(2) ומשעה שאסור באכילה אסור בהנאה.

(2) From the time when it is prohibited to eat, it is prohibited to derive benefit [from it].

(3) אתאן לתנא קמא.

(3) This relates to the first opinion [R. Yehudah].

(4) רבי יוסי הגלילי אומר: תמה על עצמך, היאך חמץ אסור בהנאה כל שבעה?

(4) R. Yose Hagalili said: You should be surprised! Is it really prohibited to derive benefit from hametz all seven days?

(5) ומנין לאוכל חמץ משש שעות ולמעלה שהוא עובר בלא תעשה - שנאמר: *לא תאכל עליו חמץ* (דברים טז:ג), דברי רבי יהודה.

(5) And from where do we know that one who eats hametz after the sixth hour (midday) transgresses a negative commandment? As it says: *Do not eat hametz with it* (Deuteronomy 16:3)—the words of R. Yehudah.

אמר לו רבי שמעון: וכי אפשר לומר כן? והלא כבר נאמר: *לא תאכל עליו חמץ שבעת ימים תאכל עליו מצות.*

R. Shimon said to him: Is it possible to say this? But has it not already stated: *Do not eat hametz with it, for seven days*

---

6   *Tosefta Atikta*, 212-216.

eat with it matzot.

אם כן מה תלמוד לומר: *לא תאכל*
*עליו חמץ* - בשעה שישנו בקום אכול
מצה - ישנו בבל תאכל חמץ.

If so, what does it mean *Do not eat hametz with it?* When there is a positive commandment to eat matzah, there is a prohibition on eating hametz.

ובשעה שאינו בקום אכול מצה - אינו
בבל תאכל חמץ.

And when there is no commandment to eat matzah, there is no prohibition on eating hametz.

Section 1 corresponds to the halakhah from Tosefta Pesahim 1:8 analyzed above. While there are a few differences in wording, it clearly is the same baraita that has merely undergone the changes typical of baraitot adapted from the Tosefta into the Bavli. For instance, the words "after midday" and "owned on Pesah" have been changed to "before its time" and "after its time." The phrase "before its time" is probably meant to avoid the tannaitic debate over whether hametz is prohibited after midday or an hour earlier. The use of "after its time" serves merely to parallel "before its time." The Babylonian baraita adds the clarification that, during Pesah, hametz is prohibited by the Torah and punishable by *karet*. The phrase "has transgressed a negative commandment" and its opposite, "there is no negative commandment," have been stylistically changed. Finally, the attribution to the sages has been changed to R. Shimon, presumably to accord with section 5 of the baraita, whose roots are in the Sifre.

Section 1 is the only section of this larger baraita whose content relates directly to the mishnah. All amoraic sections of the sugya that we shall analyze below relate solely to this first section of the baraita and to the mishnah. Nowhere do we find amoraim relating to the other sections of the baraita, which suggests that sections 2 through 5 were originally not part of one long baraita. Rather, they were relatively late additions to this sugya, probably not part of the baraita until after the amoraic period. We will need to ask, then, why the editor of the baraita decided to augment the original baraita so substantially.

Before considering the rest of the baraita, we will skip ahead to section 5, which also has clear tannaitic precedent. This section is drawn from Sifre Deuteronomy piska 130, the midrash we analyzed above. The topic of the midrash is the prohibition on eating hametz on the day before Pesah, a topic not discussed by the amoraim in our sugya. However, it is clear why the editor would incorporate this baraita into our sugya: It provides midrashic basis for the tannaitic dispute in section 1. The baraita answers the question of what prohibition one transgresses by eating hametz after the sixth hour on the day before Pesah. While there are sources in both Mekhiltot on Exodus that address this prohibition (Mekhilta de-R. Yishmael, Pasha 17; Mekhilta de-R. Shimon b. Yohai 13:7), neither of these sources contain a dispute between R. Yehudah and R. Shimon. By bringing this particular baraita, drawn from the Sifre, into the sugya, the editor offers a fitting midrashic explanation for the baraita in section 1.

Section 2 is a paraphrase of Mishnah Pesahim 2:1:

| משנה פסחים ב:א | Mishnah Pesahim 2:1 |
|---|---|
| כל שעה שמותר לאכול, מאכיל לבהמה לחיה ולעופות, ומוכרו לנכרי, ומותר בהנאתו. | The entire time that one is allowed to eat [hametz], one may feed it to a domesticated animal, to a wild animal, and to birds, or sell it to a non-Jew, and it is permitted to derive benefit from it. |
| עבר זמנו, אסור בהנאתו. | Once this time has passed, it is prohibited to derive benefit from it. |

Presumably this line was introduced by the author of the baraita into this long composite source to teach that just as after Pesah the halakhah is stringent and prohibits one from even deriving benefit, as was stated in the mishnah, so too before Pesah, after the sixth hour, it is prohibited to derive benefit from hametz. The Tosefta never stated that it was prohibited to derive benefit from hametz after the sixth hour; it stated only that it was prohibited to **eat** hametz. Thus, this additional line in the Babylonian baraita serves to equate the two time periods, before and after Pesah, which are also equated in the Tosefta itself. Furthermore, the addition of this section aids in the transition to section 4, which contains the puzzling words of R. Yose Hagalili.

Section 3 is in Aramaic, which indicates that is a late stammaitic insertion. According to this section, it is only R. Yehudah who holds that it is forbidden to derive benefit from hametz from the hour when it is forbidden to eat it, that is, after the sixth hour. In other words, R. Shimon would allow one to derive benefit from hametz after the sixth hour, although eating is clearly prohibited. There is no echo of such a halakhah anywhere in tannaitic or amoraic literature, much to the bafflement of medieval commentators.

With this comment in section 3, the stammaitic editor proposes practical ramifications to the dispute in the Tosefta. If R. Yehudah holds that after the sixth hour hametz is prohibited by the Torah, then the disputing position—that hametz is not prohibited by the Torah until nightfall—must be practically more lenient. The stam locates that practical distinction in the issue of deriving benefit. This also allows for a graduated dispute, from the most stringent opinion attributed to R. Yehudah (it is prohibited to derive benefit from hametz after the sixth hour), to a middle ground attributed to R. Shimon (it is prohibited to derive benefit only on Pesah), to the most lenient opinion, R. Yose Hagalili (it is permitted to derive benefit from hametz even on Pesah, as we shall discuss below). To emphasize: There is no evidence that R. Shimon or any other tanna actually allowed one to derive benefit from hametz after the sixth hour. Only here, in this late stammaitic comment, inserted forcefully into a baraita, is such an opinion countenanced.

R. Yose Hagalili's position in section 4, that one may derive benefit from hametz even on Pesah, is among the most puzzling points in this sugya. The Torah is adamant that hametz may not be seen or possessed on Pesah and that one must destroy it (Exodus 12:15-19; 13:7). How then is it possible that one could continue to derive benefit from it during the festival? Commentators and scholars viewed the entire baraita (except section 3, obviously a later insertion) as one literary source. Thus, even if some of its elements were not known from other compositions, the entire baraita was considered one authentic tannaitic source, all of whose elements were thought to be reflective of tannaitic thought. By dividing the baraita into its component parts, Friedman demonstrates that not all of the baraita is authentically tannaitic. Section 4, as we shall now demonstrate (based on Friedman), is clearly not.

## R. Yose Hagalili: It is Permitted to Derive Benefit from Hametz on Pesah

As stated, R. Yose Hagalili's opinion in the baraita is one of the more surprising opinions in the entire tractate, and perhaps in the entire talmudic corpus. The Torah explicitly commands the children of Israel to destroy hametz. An Israelite is prohibited even from seeing hametz or having it in his possession. Granted, the tannaim in both Mekhiltot limit the hametz that a Jew must destroy to hametz fully owned by a Jew that is found solely in his possession. Nevertheless, there is no doubt whatsoever that a Jew may not retain possession of hametz on Pesah, let alone derive any benefit from it. The entire strict and rigorous system of checking for hametz and destroying it before Pesah is predicated on the simple and obvious fact that one cannot derive any benefit from it on Pesah.

Nevertheless, the baraita in the Bavli contains an explicit opinion attributed to R. Yose Hagalili that it is in fact permitted for a Jew to derive benefit from hametz on Pesah. Due to the notable absence of such an opinion in all tannaitic compositions and from early amoraic discussions which would surely have cited this opinion had they been familiar with it, Friedman concludes that this baraita is fictitious and is not representative of this tanna's or any tanna's actual belief. Friedman even suggests how this opinion could have been deduced from the following passage in Mekhilta de-R. Yishmael:

### Mekhilta de-R. Yishmael, Pasha 16

(1) *Hametz may not be eaten* (Exodus 13:3): This equates the one who feeds another with one who eats. Or does it forbid deriving benefit from hametz?

When it says: *Do not eat hametz with it* (Deuteronomy 16:3) we learn that it is prohibited to derive benefit from it. Then why does Scripture state: *Do not eat hametz*? This equates one who feeds another with one who eats. [These are] the words of R. Yoshiyah.

(2) R. Yitzhak said: This is not necessary. For with regard to creepy-crawlers, with which the law is lenient, one who feeds another is equated with one who eats. And so when it comes to hametz, which is treated stringently, is it not logical that one who feeds another is equated with one who eats? Then why does Scripture state: *Hametz may not be eaten*? The verse

### מכילתא דרבי ישמעאל פסחא טז

(1) *לא יאכל חמץ* (שמות יג:ג) לעשות את המאכיל כאוכל. או אינו אלא לאסרו בהנאה?

כשהוא אומר: *לא תאכל עליו חמץ* (דברים טז:ג) למדנו שאסור בהנאה. הא מה ת"ל: *לא יאכל חמץ*? לעשות את המאכיל כאוכל, דברי רבי יאשיה.

(2) רבי יצחק אומר: אינו צריך. ומה אם שרצים קלים עשה בהם את המאכיל כאוכל, חמץ חמור אינו דין שנעשה בו את המאכיל כאוכל. הא מה ת"ל *לא יאכל חמץ*? לא בא הכתוב אלא לאסרו בהנאה.

רבי יוסי הגלילי אומר: לא יאכל (3)
חמץ היום (שמות יג:ג-ד) מגיד שלא
אכלו ישראל מצה במצרים אלא יום
אחד בלבד.

prohibits one from deriving benefit from it.
(3) R. Yose Hagalili says: *Hametz may not be eaten today* (Exodus 13:3-4). This teaches that Israel ate matzah in Egypt for only one day.

In sections 1 and 2, R. Yoshiyah and R. Yitzhak, two tannaim who appear frequently in the Mekhilta, argue about the source for two halakhot whose content they both agree upon:

1) That one who feeds another person hametz has transgressed the biblical laws of Pesah;
2) That it is prohibited to derive benefit from hametz on Pesah.

R. Yose Hagalili's exegesis in section 3 is independent of the previous two midrashim. R. Yose Hagalili is not a frequent disputant with these two other tannaim, and clearly the content of his exegesis has nothing to do with either of the subjects discussed by R. Yoshiyah and R. Yitzhak. Nevertheless, if R. Yose Hagalili uses the verse "hametz may not be eaten" as a source for his assertion that Israel ate matzah for only one day when leaving Egypt, it might be possible to deduce (in a very Babylonian-stammaitic fashion) that he disagrees with these other sages' use of this verse, since he uses it for another midrash. According to Friedman, this supposition is the source of R. Yose Hagalili's "baraita" in the Bavli. R. Yose Hagalili disgrees with R. Yitzhak's reading that one is prohibited from deriving benefit from hametz.

Friedman suggests that the creation of the baraita attributed to R. Yose Hagalili was meant to strengthen the difficulty the Talmud wishes to raise on the mishnah. The main question the Talmud asks about the mishnah concerns the first clause: "It is permitted to derive benefit [after Pesah] from hametz owned by a non-Jew during Pesah." The fact that the mishnah permits deriving benefit leads the Talmud to deduce that while benefit is permitted, eating is not. That is, **eating** hametz owned by a non-Jew on Pesah is prohibited after Pesah. This mishnah seems overly stringent—why should it be prohibited to eat hametz owned by a non-Jew on Pesah after the holiday has elapsed? Friedman proposes that the Talmud wished to balance this difficulty by positing the existence of a diametrically opposed position: The mishnah seems even more stringent in light of a tanna who allows one to derive benefit on Pesah from hametz, even if is owned by a Jew!

R. Yose Hagalili's statement in the Mekhilta that the Israelites leaving Egypt ate hametz for only one day is also included in a section of this sugya that we have not analyzed here. There, it appears as part of a stammatic dialogue concerning how R. Shimon understands the biblical verses that R. Yehudah uses as proof that hametz is biblically prohibited before and after Pesah.[7] R. Yehudah uses three verses (Exodus 12:20,13:3; Deuteronomy 16:3)—one for before Pesah, one for during, and one for after. R. Shimon uses one of these verses (Exodus 13:3) to derive the same midrash as does R. Yose Hagalili in the Mekhilta—in the wilderness, Israel observed Pesah for only one day. It is common for editors to create new material derived from other material found in close literary proximity. The presence of R. Yose Hagalili's statement about the one-day observance of Pesah in Egypt in our sugya implies that the original context of his words in the Mekhilta may have influenced the Babylonian editors who created his opinion that it is not prohibited to derive benefit from hametz on Pesah, despite the fact that the midrash from the Mekhilta is not quoted in its entirety here in the Bavli (the opinions of R. Yoshiyah and R. Yitzhak are absent).

## The Talmud's Rereading of the Tannaim: Who is the Author of the Mishnah?

We shall now deal with the Bavli's sugya on this mishnah. We have skipped over the section consisting of typical stammaitic questions—how does each tanna derive his halakhah, and what does each tanna do with the opposing tanna's verse? This section is not relevant for our analysis of

---

[7] In the Bavli, R. Yose Hagalili says that when leaving Egypt, hametz was prohibited for only one day, the flipside to his statement in the Mekhilta that they ate matzah for only one day. His statement is also found in the context of our mishnah in Yerushalmi Pesahim 2:2, 29b. Both the Bavli and Yerushalmi posit that R. Shimon reads the verse "Do not eat hametz with it" as does R. Yose Hagalili and not R. Yehudah—the verse teaches that the Pesah observed in Egypt was for one day and does not mean that hametz is prohibited after the sixth hour. This would not be sufficient, however, to conclude the R. Yose Hagalili allows one to benefit from hametz **on** Pesah. It would at most imply that he does not hold that hametz is prohibited by the Torah after the sixth hour, with R. Shimon and contra R. Yehudah.

the Bavli. We have also skipped over the baraita, which appears in its entirety above.

## Bavli Pesahim 28b-29a

MISHNAH

משנה: חמץ של נכרי שעבר עליו הפסח - מותר בהנאה.

ושל ישראל אסור בהנאה שנאמר: *לא יראה לך שאר* (שמות יג:ז).

Mishnah: Hametz owned by a non-Jew on Pesah—it is permitted to derive benefit from it [after Pesah]. But that owned by a Jew [on Pesah], it is prohibited to derive benefit from it [after Pesah] as it says: *You shall not see any leaven* (Exodus 13:7).

STAMMAITIC COMMENT

מני מתניתין? אי רבי יהודה - חמץ סתמא קאמר, אפילו דנכרי.

Who is the author of our mishnah? If it is R. Yehudah, he said hametz in general, and even that of a non-Jew [is prohibited].

ואי רבי שמעון –דישראל נמי מישרא קא שרי.

And if it is R. Shimon, he permitted even the hametz of a Jew.

ואי רבי יוסי הגלילי - אפילו תוך זמנו נמי מישרא קא שרי בהנאה...

And if it is R. Yose Hagalili, even during its time he permits one to derive benefit from it... [BARAITA FROM ABOVE]

SUGYA 1, ANSWER 1

(1a) אמר רב אחא בר יעקב: לעולם רבי יהודה היא, ויליף שאור דאכילה משאור דראייה. מה שאור דראייה - שלך אי אתה רואה, אבל אתה רואה של אחרים ושל גבוה - אף שאור דאכילה: שלך אי אתה אוכל, אבל אתה אוכל של אחרים ושל גבוה.

(1a) R. Aha b. Yaakov said: [The mishnah] follows R. Yehudah, who derives eating leaven from seeing leaven. Just as with seeing leaven— you may not see your own leaven, but you may see leaven belonging to non-Jews and to the Temple; so too with eating leaven—you may not eat your own leaven, but you may eat leaven belonging to others or to the Temple.

143

(1b) ובדין הוא דאיבעי ליה למיתנא דאפילו באכילה נמי שרי, ואיידי דתנא דישראל אסור בהנאה - תנא נמי דנכרי מותר בהנאה.

(1b) And it should have taught that even eating [such hametz] is permitted, but since it taught that it is forbidden to derive benefit from [hametz] belonging to a Jew, it also taught that it is permitted to derive benefit from [hametz] belonging to a non-Jew.

(1c) ובדין הוא דאיבעי ליה למיתנא דאפילו בתוך זמנו מותר בהנאה, ואיידי דתנא דישראל לאחר זמנו תנא נמי דנכרי לאחר זמנו.

(1c) And it should have taught that it is permitted even during Pesah, but since it taught after Pesah concerning hametz owned by a Jew, it taught after Pesah concerning hametz owned by a non-Jew.

SUGYA 1, ANSWER 2

(1d) רבא אמר: לעולם רבי שמעון היא, ורבי שמעון קנסא קניס הואיל ועבר עליה בבל יראה ובל ימצא.

(1d) Rava said: It follows R. Shimon, and R. Shimon penalizes him for transgressing the prohibition on seeing and possessing hametz.

(1e) בשלמא לרבא היינו דקתני של ישראל אסור, משום שנאמר: *לא יראה*.

(1e) The mishnah accords well with Rava—that is why it teaches that [hametz] belonging to a Jew is prohibited, as it says, *You shall not see.* But to R. Aha b. Yaakov, it should have stated, hametz may not be eaten!

אלא לרב אחא בר יעקב משום לא יאכל חמץ מיבעי ליה.

(1f) מי סברת אסיפא קאי? ארישא קאי, והכי קאמר: חמץ של נכרי שעבר עליו הפסח מותר בהנאה, משום שנאמר: *לא יראה לך* שלך אי אתה רואה, אבל אתה רואה של אחרים ושל גבוה. ויליף שאור דאכילה משאור דראייה.

(1f) Do you really think it refers to the second clause? It refers to the first clause and this is what it means to say: Hametz owned by a non-Jew on Pesah—it is permitted to derive benefit from it after Pesah, as it says, *You shall not see.* You may not see your own, but you may see that belonging to a non-Jew or to the Temple. And he derives eating leaven from seeing leaven.

| Tannaitic Source | Amoraic Source | Stammaitic Source |

## SUGYA 2

(2a) ואזדו לטעמייהו: דאיתמר, האוכל שאור של נכרי שעבר עליו הפסח, לדברי רבי יהודה,

(2a) And they follow their own reasoning: As it was said: One who eats after Pesah leaven owned by a non-Jew on Pesah, according to R. Yehudah—

רבא אמר: לוקה, ורב אחא בר יעקב אמר: אינו לוקה.

Rava said: He is lashed. But R. Aha b. Yaakov said: He is not lashed.

(2b) רבא אמר: לוקה, לא יליף רבי יהודה שאור דאכילה משאור דראייה.

(2b) Rava said: He is lashed, for R. Yehudah does not derive eating leaven from seeing leaven.

ורב אחא בר יעקב אמר: אינו לוקה, יליף שאור דאכילה משאור דראייה.

But R. Aha b. Yaakov said: He is not lashed, for he does derive eating leaven from seeing leaven.

## SUGYA 3, BARAITA

(3a) והדר ביה רב אחא בר יעקב, מההיא דתניא: האוכל חמץ של הקדש במועד - מעל, ויש אומרים: לא מעל.

(3a) But R. Aha b. Yaakov retracted that statement as it has been taught: One who eats sanctified hametz on the festival has trespassed. But there are those who say he has not trespassed.

(3b) מאן יש אומרים? אמר רבי יוחנן: רבי נחוניא בן הקנה היא. דתניא: רבי נחוניא בן הקנה היה עושה את יום הכפורים כשבת לתשלומין. מה שבת, מתחייב בנפשו ופטור מן התשלומין - אף יום הכפורים מתחייב בנפשו ופטור מתשלומין.

(3b) Who are "those who say"? R. Yohanan said: It is R. Nehuniah b. Hakaneh, as it has been taught: R. Nehuniah b. Hakaneh would make Yom Kippur like Shabbat in terms of monetary payments. Just as Shabbat [one who transgresses] is liable for death and exempt from monetary payments, so too Yom Kippur [one who transgresses] is liable for death and is exempt from monetary payments.

### SUGYA 3, INTERPRETATION 1

**(3c)** רב יוסף אמר: בפודין את הקדשים
להאכילן לכלבים קמיפלגי. מאן דאמר
מעל, קסבר: פודין את הקדשים להאכילן
לכלבים. ומאן דאמר לא מעל - קסבר:
אין פודין.

(3c) R. Yosef said: They disagree over whether one can redeem sanctified food in order to feed it to the dogs. The one who says he has trespassed reasons that one can redeem sanctified food in order to feed it to the dogs. And the one who says he has not transgressed reasons one cannot redeem.

### SUGYA 3, INTERPRETATION 2

**(3d)** רב אחא בר רבא תנא לה להא
שמעתא משמיה דרב יוסף בהא לישנא:
דכולי עלמא אין פודין את הקדשים
להאכילן לכלבים, והכא בהא קמיפלגי:
בדבר הגורם לממון, כממון דמי. מאן
דאמר מעל - קסבר: דבר הגורם לממון -
כממון דמי.

(3d) R. Aha b. Rava taught this teaching in the name of R. Yosef in the following version: Everyone holds that one may not redeem sanctified food in order to feed it to the dogs, but here they disagree about the following: Whether something that causes monetary loss counts as money. The one who says that he has transgressed holds that something that causes monetary loss counts as money.

ומאן דאמר לא מעל - קסבר: דבר הגורם
לממון - לאו כממון דמי.

Whereas the one who says that he has not transgressed holds that something that causes monetary loss does not count as money.

### SUGYA 3, INTERPRETATION 3

**(3e)** רב אחא בר יעקב אמר: דכולי
עלמא דבר הגורם לממון - כממון דמי.
והכא בפלוגתא דרבי יהודה ורבי שמעון
קמיפלגי. מאן דאמר לא מעל - כרבי
יהודה, ומאן דאמר מעל - כרבי שמעון.

(3e) R. Aha b. Yaakov said: All hold that something that causes monetary loss counts as money. But here they disagree about the same dispute between R. Yehudah and R. Shimon. The one who said that he has not trespassed is like R. Yehudah. And the one who said that he has trespassed is like R. Shimon.

(3f) והא רב אחא בר יעקב הוא דאמר דרבי יהודה יליף שאור דאכילה משאור דראייה! אלא: הדר ביה רב אחא בר יעקב מההיא.

(3f) But was it not R. Aha b. Yaakov who said that R. Yehudah derives eating leaven from seeing leaven! Therefore, R. Aha b. Yaakov retracted his earlier statement.

SUGYA 3, INTERPRETATION 4

(3g) רב אשי אמר: דכולי עלמא אין פודין, ודבר הגורם לממון לאו כממון דמי.

(3g) R. Ashi said: All hold that one does not redeem [sanctified food in order to feed it to the dogs], and that something that causes monetary loss does not count as money.

והכא בפלוגתא דרבי יוסי הגלילי ורבנן קמיפלגי. מאן דאמר מעל - כרבי יוסי, ומאן דאמר לא מעל - כרבנן.

But here they disagree about the same dispute between R. Yose Hagalili and the rabbis. The one who said he did trespass is like R. Yose, and the one who said he did not trespass is like the rabbis.

---

| Tannaitic Source | Amoraic Source | Stammaitic Source |

## The Babylonian Amoraic Layer

This sugya in the Bavli consists of three independent amoraic sugyot that the talmudic editor has woven into one extended passage. The first sugya deals with the identification of the author of the mishnah in light of the baraita. The second sugya deals with the case of a Jew who, after Pesah, ate hametz owned by a non-Jew during Pesah. The third sugya is an explanation of a baraita concerning a Jew who, on Pesah, ate hametz belonging to the Temple (i.e. it was dedicated to the Temple before Pesah). We will first examine each of these sugyot independent of their context in the composite Babylonian sugya.

Our goal in this section will be to explain the halakhic, editorial, and literary processes that led to the far-fetched reasoning that is found in this complex sugya (especially sections 1b-1c). This sugya is an excellent example of a two-part methodology commonly used by talmudic scholars: first to separate the amoraic layer from the stammaitic layer, and second to compare the amoraic statements in the Bavli with their parallels in the Yerushalmi. Both of these methodologies help unravel this sugya, showing how reasonable amoraic assertions can yield very difficult stammaitic explanations.

## Sugya 1: Who is the Author of the Mishnah?

| | |
|---|---|
| (1a) אמר רב אחא בר יעקב: לעולם רבי יהודה היא. | (1a) R. Aha b. Yaakov said: [The mishnah] follows R. Yehudah. |
| (1d) רבא אמר: לעולם רבי שמעון היא, ורבי שמעון קנסא קניס הואיל ועבר עליה בבל יראה ובל ימצא. | (1d) Rava said: It follows R. Shimon, and R. Shimon penalizes him for transgressing the prohibition on seeing and possessing hametz. |

Two amoraim, R. Aha b. Yaakov and Rava, answer the question posed twice in our sugya: Who is the author of the mishnah? That is, who is it that held that hametz owned by a Jew is prohibited after Pesah? R. Yehudah or R. Shimon? Despite the possibility that the mishnah accords with R. Yose Hagalili brought up in the stammaitic comment that immediately follows the mishnah, neither amora mentions his name. As we have argued, his opinion was not an authentic tannaitic opinion known to early amoraim.

The first opinion, that of R. Aha b. Yaakov, remains faithful to the historical antecedent of this mishnah found in the Tosefta. The simple interpretation of the mishnah accords with R. Yehudah, for R. Yehudah is the tanna in the Tosefta who rules that hametz owned by a Jew on Pesah is prohibited **by the Torah** after Pesah. R. Aha b. Yaakov's statement relates primarily to the second part of the mishnah, concerning hametz owned by a Jew on Pesah, and less (if at all) to the first part, hametz owned by a non-Jew. R. Yehudah in the Tosefta never offered any statement concerning hametz owned by a non-Jew on Pesah, and there is no reason for him to have done so: In the tannaitic period, no authority prohibited eating after Pesah hametz owned by a non-Jew on Pesah. We can assume that, to R. Aha b. Yaakov, it was obvious that R. Yehudah would allow one to eat such hametz after Pesah, an opinion that does not disagree with the mishnah.

Rava's opinion is more puzzling. Why would he say that the mishnah accords with R. Shimon when it so obviously fits R. Yehudah? The answer may be found by considering a parallel source in the Yerushalmi:

## Yerushalmi Pesahim 2:2, 28d

**ירושלמי פסחים ב:ב (כח, ד)**

(1) מאן תנא *לא יראה לך* ? ר' יודה.

(1) Who is the tanna [who taught] *You shall not see*? It is R. Y[eh]udah.

(2) דתני האוכל חמץ משש שעות ולמעלה וכן חמץ שעבר עליו הפסח הרי זה בלא תעשה ואין בו כרת דברי ר' יודה. רבי שמעון אומר כל שאין בו כרת אין בו בלא תעשה.

(2) As it is taught: One who eats hametz after the sixth hour, and similarly hametz that was owned on Pesah, has transgressed a negative commandment but is not liable for *karet*, these are the words of R. Y[eh]udah. R. Shimon says: Anything for which one is not liable for *karet*, is not a negative commandment.

(3) מודה רבי שמעון באסור שהוא אסור.

(3) R. Shimon agrees that it is prohibited.

(4) איסורו מהו?

(4) What is its prohibition?

ר' ירמיה אמר איסורו דבר תורה.

R. Yirmiyah says: It is prohibited by the Torah.

רבי יונה ורבי יוסה תריהון אמרין איסורו מדבריהן.

R. Yonah and R. Yose both say it is prohibited by the rabbis.

The Yerushalmi opens with the same question as the Bavli: Who is the author of the mishnah? The mishnah is referred to using the shorthand "You shall not see," a reference to the midrash quoted at the end of the mishnah. The answer is the same as that offered by R. Aha b. Yaakov in the Bavli—the author of the mishnah is R. Yehudah. The passage proves this in section 2 with the same baraita found in Tosefta Pesahim 1:8, and in the long composite baraita in the Bavli. Section 3 is not found in the baraita, and it is difficult to determine whether it is part of a revised version of the baraita or whether it is an anonymous amoraic statement appended to it. In any case, according to this section, R. Shimon agrees with R. Yehudah that during these times (after the sixth hour on the day before Pesah and after Pesah) hametz is prohibited. As we have seen, this is a faithful portrayal of tannaitic opinion—all tannaim agree that hametz is prohibited during these times. The only disagreement is over the level of the prohibition (section 4): R. Yehudah holds, according to all opinions, that it is prohibited by the Torah as a negative commandment. The amoraim differ on the level of prohibition according to R. Shimon. R. Yirmiyah maintains that while the prohibition is not explicitly expressed as a negative commandment, R. Shimon still grants it the status of a biblical prohibition. R. Yonah and R. Yose argue that R. Shimon believes the prohibition is only rabbinic.

Based on the Yerushalmi, we can surmise that Rava in the Bavli posits that the mishnah accords **even** with R. Shimon and is not exclusively R. Yehudah's opinion.[8] Of course the tendency in disputes like these is to interpret that if one Rabbi says it is X and means "only X," when the other rabbis says "it is Y" he means "only Y" and not "even Y" as we are suggesting here. Nevertheless, it is possible that the creation of diametrically opposite positions is a result of the Bavli being a later literary revision of the earlier version in the Yerushalmi. As so often happens in such cases, the nuances of the earlier sources are lost.

In sum, R. Aha b. Yaakov and Rava address the post-Pesah status of hametz **owned by a Jew** during Pesah. R. Aha b. Yaakov attributes the prohibition in the mishnah to R. Yehudah, and Rava, according to our interpretation, argues that the prohibition is shared by both R. Yehudah and R. Shimon. There is no reason to assume that they were addressing the issue of hametz owned by a non-Jew during or after Pesah, as the stam later interprets their statements.

## Sugya 2: Hametz of a Non-Jew After Pesah

The second amoraic sugya involves another dispute between R. Aha b. Yaakov and Rava, this time about the status after Pesah of hametz owned by a non-Jew on Pesah:

| | |
|---|---|
| איתמר: האוכל שאור של נכרי שעבר עליו הפסח, לדברי רבי יהודה: | As it was said: One who eats after Pesah leaven owned by a non-Jew on Pesah, according to R. Yehudah— |
| רבא אמר: לוקה, | Rava said: He is lashed. |
| ורב אחא בר יעקב אמר: אינו לוקה. | But R. Aha b. Yaakov said: He is not lashed. |

According to Rava, R. Yehudah holds that one who eats after Pesah hametz owned by a non-Jew during Pesah has transgressed biblical law

---

8    *Tosefta Atikta*, 164, n. 36.

and therefore is punished by lashes. In contrast, R. Aha b. Yaakov holds that this is not a biblical transgression.

Here too, R. Aha b. Yaakov maintains the more straightforward reading of the tannaitic sources: Such a person is not lashed because hametz owned by a non-Jew on Pesah is completely permitted after Pesah. As we saw above, while the mishnah states only that it is permitted **to benefit** after Pesah from hametz owned by a non-Jew during Pesah, the Tosefta clearly held that it was permitted **to eat** such hametz immediately upon the festival's end. There is no hint of any disputing opinion in any tannaitic source.

Rava's position, as above, is problematic. We should emphasize here that the issue with Rava's opinion is not its lack of practicality. Perhaps it would have been possible in the ancient world for a Jew to avoid consuming hametz that had been owned by a non-Jew on Pesah. After all, they did not live in a world with Twinkies—hametz that could be preserved on a supermarket shelf for all eternity. The problem is that the entire corpus of tannaitic literature presupposes that one can eat, immediately after Pesah, hametz that was owned by a non-Jew during Pesah. Did Rava really think that any tanna, even the stricter R. Yehudah, would maintain that eating hametz owned by a non-Jew after Pesah is prohibited by the Torah?

Here too, Friedman suggests that the dispute between R. Aha b. Yaakov and Rava is not authentic; rather, it was invented by the editors of the sugya in light of their understanding of the first half of the mishnah, about hametz owned by a Jew. As we saw in amoraic sugya 1, Rava attributed the first half of the mishnah to R. Shimon. We should reemphasize that in our historical reading of Rava's words, we posited that he referred only to the second half of the mishnah and meant to say that it accords **even** with R. Shimon. The stam, however, does not read Rava in that way. Rather, he assumes that Rava in fact attributed the whole mishnah to R. Shimon, and only to R. Shimon. By extension, we would need to posit that R. Yehudah would disagree with the whole mishnah.[9] Thus, if R. Shimon holds along with the mishnah that hametz belonging to a non-Jew is permitted after Pesah, R. Yehudah must hold that it is prohibited. As a balance to the first sugya which dealt with the second

---

[9]    Ibid.

clause of the mishnah, the editors created this pseudepigraphical dispute that is related to the first clause of the mishnah.[10]

## Sugya 3: Sanctified Hametz during Pesah

תניא: האוכל חמץ של הקדש במועד - מעל, ויש אומרים: לא מעל.

It was taught: One who eats sanctified hametz on the festival has trespassed. But there are those who say he has not trespassed.

(1) מאן יש אומרים? אמר רבי יוחנן: רבי נחוניא בן הקנה היא. דתניא: רבי נחוניא בן הקנה היה עושה את יום הכפורים כשבת לתשלומין. מה שבת, מתחייב בנפשו ופטור מן התשלומין - אף יום הכפורים מתחייב בנפשו ופטור מתשלומין.

(1) Who are "those who say"? R. Yohanan said: It is R. Nehuniah b. Hakaneh, as it has been taught: R. Nehuniah b. Hakaneh would make Yom Kippur like Shabbat in terms of monetary payments. Just as Shabbat [one who transgresses] is liable for death and exempt from monetary payments, so too Yom Kippur [one who transgresses] is liable for death and is exempt from monetary payments.

(2) רב יוסף אמר: בפודין את הקדשים להאכילן לכלבים קמיפלגי. מאן דאמר מעל, קסבר: פודין את הקדשים להאכילן לכלבים. ומאן דאמר לא מעל - קסבר: אין פודין.

(2) R. Yosef said: They disagree over whether one can redeem sanctified food in order to feed it to the dogs. The one who says he has trespassed reasons that one can redeem sanctified food in order to feed it to the dogs. And the one who says he has not transgressed reasons that one cannot redeem.

---

[10]  The major difficulty with Friedman's understanding of the sugya is that it seems a particularly unusual and convoluted type of literary activity for the stammaim—to create an entire amoraic dispute to summarize the consequences of another dispute between the same two amoraim. Friedman cites this example in his article concerning amoraic statements that were actually the creation of the stam. See Shamma Friedman, *Sugyot Beheker Hatalmud Habavli* (New York: JTS Press, 2010), 68.

(3) רב אחא בר רבא תנא לה להא שמעתא משמיה דרב יוסף בהא לישנא: דכולי עלמא אין פודין את הקדשים להאכילן לכלבים, והכא בהא קמיפלגי: בדבר הגורם לממון, כממון דמי.

מאן דאמר מעל - קסבר: דבר הגורם לממון - כממון דמי. ומאן דאמר לא מעל - קסבר: דבר הגורם לממון - לאו כממון דמי.

(4) רב אחא בר יעקב אמר: דכולי עלמא דבר הגורם לממון - כממון דמי. והכא בפלוגתא דרבי יהודה ורבי שמעון קמיפלגי. מאן דאמר לא מעל - כרבי יהודה, ומאן דאמר מעל - כרבי שמעון.

(5) רב אשי אמר: דכולי עלמא אין פודין, ודבר הגורם לממון לאו כממון דמי.

והכא בפלוגתא דרבי יוסי הגלילי ורבנן קמיפלגי. מאן דאמר מעל - כרבי יוסי, ומאן דאמר לא מעל - כרבנן.

(3) R. Aha b. Rava taught this teaching in the name of R. Yosef in the following version: Everyone holds that one may not redeem sanctified food in order to feed it to the dogs, but here they disagree about the following: Whether something that causes monetary loss counts as money. The one who says that he has transgressed holds that something that causes monetary loss counts as money. Whereas the one who says that he has not transgressed holds that something that causes monetary loss does not count as money.

(4) R. Aha b. Yaakov said: All hold that something that causes monetary loss counts as money. But here they disagree about the same dispute between R. Yehudah and R. Shimon. The one who said that he has not trespassed is like R. Yehudah. And the one who said that he has trespassed is like R. Shimon.

(5) R. Ashi said: All hold that one does not redeem [sanctified food in order to feed it to the dogs], and that something that causes monetary loss does not count as money. But here they disagree about the same dispute between R. Yose Hagalili and the rabbis. The one who said he did trespass is like R. Yose, and the one who said he did not trespass is like the rabbis.

The third sugya consists of five amoraic interpretations of a baraita dealing with a Jew who eats, on Pesah, sanctified hametz—that is, hametz that has been dedicated to the Temple. It does not seem that this issue has anything to do with whether or not the person has transgressed the laws of Pesah—clearly he has. The issue is whether a person who eats such hametz has transgressed the prohibition on using Temple property (*me'ilah*). For such a transgression, one incurs a monetary fine to atone for the misuse of sanctified items. This question is related to the question of whether hametz owned by the Temple during Pesah can be considered as having any value whatsoever, since one trespasses Temple property only when using an article of value and hametz during Pesah is forbidden from benefit.

The first two amoraim do not connect this baraita with the issue of deriving benefit from hametz during or after Pesah. In the first amoraic interpretation, R. Yohanan explains the dispute in the baraita as dependent on the question of whether an individual can incur a financial penalty for *me'ilah* at the same time he incurs the penalty of *karet*, the punishment for eating hametz on Pesah. The issue here is the rabbinic principle that when performing one act that is a violation of two prohibitions for which one is punished in two different ways, one only incurs the more severe penalty (Bavli Ketubot 37b). R. Nehuniah b. Hakaneh says that just as one cannot incur a financial penalty while at the same time incurring the death penalty, so too one cannot incur a financial penalty while at the same time incurring *karet*. Since he is liable for *karet* for eating hametz on Pesah, he is exempt from the monetary penalty. In contrast, the other sages say that one may be liable for *karet* and pay a financial penalty for the same crime, and therefore one who eats sanctified hametz on Pesah is liable for *me'ilah*.

In the second amoraic interpretation, R. Yosef correlates the baraita with an ancillary dispute about whether one can redeem sanctified food to feed it to dogs. The one who holds that he has trespassed by eating sanctified hametz would say that one can redeem sanctified food in order to feed it to dogs. Rashi interprets this opinion as correlating with R. Yose Hagalili's dispensation to derive benefit from hametz on Pesah. One could have redeemed the hametz on Pesah and derived benefit from it by giving it to dogs, who are not prohibited from eating hametz on Pesah. However, as we have noted, R. Yose Hagalili's opinion is a later creation, and therefore could not have been known to R. Yosef, a third generation amora. Also, if R. Yosef was interpreting the baraita concerning sanctified hametz based on sources found earlier in our sugya, we would have expected him to make explicit note of those sources.

In contrast, R. Hananel interprets more simply that one opinion in the baraita holds that hametz could be redeemed during or after Pesah in order to feed it to dogs. While it is prohibited to derive benefit from hametz on Pesah, this does not change the fact that one who nevertheless transgresses and does derive benefit from sanctified hametz would still have to repay the Temple. There is no problem of double penalty involved, since one who benefits from hametz is not liable for *karet*. Therefore, according to this opinion, sanctified hametz has potential value and one who eats it has trespassed by depriving the Temple of its value. The other opinion would hold that it is not possible to redeem sanctified food in order to feed it to the dogs and therefore it has no value on Pesah. Thus, according to R. Hananel, there is no need to link R. Yosef's interpretation to R. Yose Hagalili's statement in the baraita.

R. Aha b. Rava offers a third interpretation of the baraita, attributing it to the same amora, R. Yosef, who offered the second interpretation. According to R. Aha b. Rava, R. Yosef makes the dispute dependent on the question of whether an individual who destroys something worthless is nonetheless liable to repay the owner for that which he destroyed. In his explanation of this passage, R. Hananel cites a case in which Reuven eats hametz that was in the possession of Shimon during Pesah.[11] Such hametz has no value to Shimon, for no Jew can ever derive any benefit from it. Thus, we might have thought that Reuven need not compensate Shimon. Nevertheless, that hametz might have value to Shimon, for if Shimon had stolen it from a third party or if it had been dedicated to the Temple, he could have given the hametz back to the thief or the Temple and thus be spared the payment for the item he stole. If Shimon were to eat hametz dedicated to the Temple on Pesah, he would have to pay the Temple back, thus causing himself a loss. This is "something that causes a monetary loss."

According to R. Aha bar Rava, this issue of "something that causes monetary loss" is the focal point of the dispute in the baraita. The one who held that the individual who eats sanctified hametz has trespassed would hold that even though the hametz has no value, he has caused

---

[11]  See Bava Kamma 66a and 105a.

himself a monetary loss, because he will now have to pay out of pocket to the Temple. In contrast, the one who holds that such an individual has not trespassed holds that a future monetary loss is not sufficient to render an individual liable for trespassing Temple property.

The fourth amoraic explanation, attributed to R. Aha b. Yaakov, is the first to connect the dispute about sanctified hametz with the dispute between R. Yehudah and R. Shimon. This is not surprising, for R. Aha bar Yaakov related to the baraita earlier in the sugya concerning which tanna is the author of the mishnah (amoraic sugya 1). Here, R. Aha b. Yaakov posits that the two opinions in the baraita are a direct outgrowth of the foundational dispute between R. Yehudah and R. Shimon concerning the status of hametz owned by a Jew on Pesah—is it prohibited by the Torah or not. If, as R. Yehudah states, hametz owned by a Jew is prohibited by the Torah, then sanctified hametz will never have value and one who eats it on Pesah has not transgressed the laws of *me'ilah*. In contrast, according to R. Shimon, he has transgressed the laws of *me'ilah*, for such hametz is permitted after Pesah, at least by the Torah, and therefore has value. We will return to some of the problems with this interpretation when we examine the stammaitic commentary below.

The fifth and final amoraic interpretation of the baraita is attributed to the late amora, R. Ashi. Clearly by R. Ashi's time R. Yose Hagalili's opinion was known to the amoraim, and perhaps had been incorporated into the composite baraita. In any case, R. Ashi states that those who hold that he has committed *me'ilah* accord with R. Yose Hagalili, who allows one to derive benefit from hametz even during Pesah. Certainly, according to such a position one who eats sanctified hametz on Pesah has transgressed *me'ilah*, for the Temple could sell the hametz to a Jew on Pesah itself. We should also note that R. Ashi is the only amora in the entire Bavli who cites this specific opinion of R. Yose Hagalili. If we can trust the attribution of these words to R. Ashi, we have a relatively precise date for the invention of such a tannaitic opinion: somewhere during the fifth or sixth generation of amoraim.

## The Stammaitic Layer of the Sugya

There are substantial stammaitic additions to this sugya that yield some extraordinarily strange notions which Rashi highlights. For instance, Rashi writes in his commentary on this sugya that "hametz owned by a non-Jew is permitted even for consumption, and even on Pesah itself, at least according to the Torah." The idea that the Torah would allow a Jew to eat **hametz on Pesah** as long as it is owned by a non-Jew is the reductio ad absurdum of a halakhah found in many tannaitic sources, namely that a Jew can see the hametz of a non-Jew on Pesah, or that the hametz of a non-Jew can be present (under certain circumstances) in a Jew's house. As we will demonstrate, these rather absurd conclusions are a product of the stammaitic process of expanding rabbinic statements made in specific contexts to a broad spectrum of possibilities in order to test the limits of their validity.

Our analysis focuses on the increasing complexity or, to put it bluntly, absurdity of the stammaitic additions to the sugya. In other words, at what point do simple, reasonable explanations that would largely accord with earlier law end, and strange halakhot, which do not accord at all with tannaitic halakhah, begin to arise? As we have noted, all tannaim and amoraim hold that hametz is forbidden after the sixth hour on the day before Pesah. All tannaim and amoraim hold that it is prohibited to derive benefit from hametz during Pesah. And all tannaim and amoraim hold that only hametz owned by a Jew during Pesah is prohibited after Pesah. But the stam invents opposing views to all of these universally accepted halakhot. We maintain that all of these stammaitic assertions are the result of protracted literary and interpretive impulses, which carry unintended, and in this case, extreme, consequences. They do not reflect any fundamental change in the halakhot of hametz on or after Pesah. Rather, the stam's goals are editorial, literary, and interpretive—to weave together an extended literary discourse on the prohibitions of hametz before and after Pesah. We begin our analysis with what we have termed sugya 2.

## SUGYA 2

(2a) ואזדו לטעמייהו: דאיתמר, האוכל שאור של נכרי שעבר עליו הפסח, לדברי רבי יהודה:

(2a) And they follow their own reasoning: As it was said: One who eats after Pesah leaven owned by a non-Jew on Pesah, according to R. Yehudah—

רבא אמר: לוקה, ורב אחא בר יעקב אמר: אינו לוקה.

Rava said: He is lashed. But R. Aha b. Yaakov said: He is not lashed.

(2b) רבא אמר: לוקה, לא יליף רבי יהודה שאור דאכילה משאור דראייה.

(2b) Rava said: He is lashed, for R. Yehudah does not derive eating

157

leaven from seeing leaven.

ורב אחא בר יעקב אמר: אינו לוקה, יליף
שאור דאכילה משאור דראייה.

But R. Aha b. Yaakov said: He is not lashed, for he does derive eating leaven from seeing leaven.

In our discussion above, we posited, following Friedman, that this dispute is a stammaitic creation. We will now consider the midrashim attributed to each amoraic position. According to R. Aha b. Yaakov, after Pesah R. Yehudah allows one to eat hametz owned by a non-Jew during Pesah—just as one can see the hametz of a non-Jew during Pesah, one can eat it **after Pesah**. As we saw above this makes perfect sense. All tannaim and amoraim allow one to see the hametz of a non-Jew during Pesah, and all agree that one can eat immediately after Pesah hametz owned by a non-Jew on Pesah. However, tannaim and amoraim never derive the permission to eat after Pesah hametz owned by a non-Jew on Pesah from the permission to see hametz owned by a non-Jew on Pesah. There was no need for such a derivation—the laws of eating hametz belonging to a non-Jew were abundantly clear: It was forbidden during Pesah and permitted afterwards. Nevertheless, the stam creates a principled explanation for R. Aha b. Yaakov, a midrash never found in tannaitic or amoraic literature. Just as one can see hametz owned by a non-Jew during Pesah, one can eat such hametz after Pesah.

This midrash follows the same reasoning employed in the situation described in the mishnah: Because a Jew transgresses by seeing hametz in his possession on Pesah, his hametz may not be eaten after Pesah. Both midrashim make sense, although only the latter, concerning hametz owned by a Jew, appears in non-stammaitic sources.

The stam then reasons that Rava, who disagrees with R. Aha b. Yaakov, must hold the opposite of the midrash. Just because one can see the hametz of a non-Jew during Pesah (a matter that all agree upon) does not indicate that one can eat such hametz after Pesah. As we saw above in our analysis of the creation of the statement attributed to Rava, this is an enormous innovation, one not found anywhere in earlier literature. The stam takes the midrash it created to explain R. Aha b. Yaakov—R. Yehudah derives the laws of eating hametz from the laws of seeing hametz—and mechanically attributes the opposite opinion to R. Aha b. Yaakov's disputant. If R. Aha b. Yaakov does not distinguish between seeing and eating, then Rava must necessarily distinguish between them

—one may see such hametz during Pesah, but not eat it, even after Pesah! As we shall see, the notion that R. Aha b. Yaakov and Rava dispute this midrash deeply impacts the stam's explanation of sugya 1, to which we now turn our attention.

## SUGYA 1, ANSWER 1

(1a) אמר רב אחא בר יעקב: לעולם רבי יהודה היא, ויליף שאור דאכילה משאור דראייה. מה שאור דראייה - שלך אי אתה רואה, אבל אתה רואה של אחרים ושל גבוה;

(1a) R. Aha b. Yaakov said: [The mishnah] follows R. Yehudah, who derives eating leaven from seeing leaven. Just as with seeing leaven— you may not see your own leaven, but you may see leaven belonging to non-Jews and to the Temple;

אף שאור דאכילה: שלך אי אתה אוכל, אבל אתה אוכל של אחרים ושל גבוה.

so too with eating leaven—you may not eat your own leaven, but you may eat leaven belonging to others or to the Temple.

(1b) ובדין הוא דאיבעי ליה למיתנא דאפילו באכילה נמי שרי, ואיידי דתנא דישראל אסור בהנאה - תנא נמי דנכרי מותר בהנאה.

(1b) And it should have taught that even eating [such hametz] is permitted, but since it taught that it is forbidden to derive benefit from [hametz] belonging to a Jew, it also taught that it is permitted to derive benefit from [hametz] belonging to a non-Jew.

(1c) ובדין הוא דאיבעי ליה למיתנא דאפילו בתוך זמנו מותר בהנאה, ואיידי דתנא דישראל לאחר זמנו תנא נמי דנכרי לאחר זמנו.

(1c) And it should have taught that it is permitted even during Pesah, but since it taught after Pesah concerning hametz owned by a Jew, it taught after Pesah concerning hametz owned by a non-Jew.

Again, the stam assumes that when R. Aha b. Yaakov states that the mishnah is in accordance with R. Yehudah, he relates to the entire mishnah. Thus R. Yehudah holds that it is permissible to derive benefit after Pesah from hametz owned by a non-Jew during Pesah, and it is prohibited, after Pesah, to eat hametz owned by a Jew during Pesah. The first section enlists the same midrash used to explain the other statement of R. Aha b. Yaakov that we saw above, "for he (R. Yehudah) derives eating leaven from seeing leaven." Just as one can see hametz owned by a non-Jew during Pesah, one can eat such hametz after Pesah. This, as we have seen, accords with all tannaitic halakhah.

Section 1b accurately reflects the literary development of the mishnah. The mishnah stated that it is permitted **to derive benefit** after Pesah from hametz owned by a non-Jew on Pesah so as to parallel the language in the second clause of the mishnah: "But that owned by a Jew [on Pesah], it is prohibited to derive benefit from it [after Pesah]." But were it not for such literary considerations, the mishnah could have taught that it is permitted to **eat** such hametz.

Section 1c finally introduces the strange notion that just as a Jew can see hametz owned by a non-Jew during Pesah, a Jew **can eat hametz owned by a non-Jew during Pesah!** This rather absurd notion is the result of midrashic equation of seeing and eating.[12] This midrash was originally created to defend a halakhah about which there was universal agreement—hametz owned by a non-Jew on Pesah is permitted after Pesah. But once this midrash linked seeing with eating, logic would dictate that any hametz one can "see" during Pesah one can eat even during Pesah. While this is a possible logical outcome of the midrash, it is obviously not a ruling that any sage would have issued.

## A Step-by-Step Development of Sugyot 1 and 2

In order to better understand the process that lead to the creation of this far-fetched stammaitic claim we will concisely retrace the steps of our analysis above. The stammaitic assertion that R. Yehudah would allow one

---

[12]   Rashi is the only medieval commentator who explicitly explains what the midrash clearly implies: One may eat hametz owned by a non-Jew on Pesah. Most commentators balk at the notion that a talmudic sage would allow a Jew to eat any hametz on Pesah. Therefore, they disagreed with Rashi, reasoning that it is physically impossible to eat hametz without first owning it. Once one picks up the hametz, it is no longer in the possession of the non-Jew. Therefore, there is really no way for a Jew to eat hametz while it is simultaneously owned by the non-Jew. Nevertheless, even this disagreement is basically an admission that if one could somehow eat hametz without first owning it, he would not have transgressed. In other words, the problem with eating hametz is ownership and not really the prohibition on consuming it.

to eat on Pesah hametz owned by a non-Jew is the result of a chain of literary and interpretive moves that might be summarized as follows:

1) First, the editor of the Mishnah combined two separate toseftan halakhot into one source that addresses both hametz owned by a Jew and that owned by a non-Jew. This conjoining of sources entailed the creation of a parallel structure between the two halves of the mishnah—the first clause, "permitted to **derive benefit** after Pesah from hametz owned by a non-Jew on Pesah," was formulated to mirror the second clause, "forbidden **to derive benefit** from hametz owned by a Jew on Pesah."

2) Subsequently, the amoraim argued over the attribution of the second clause of the mishnah, drawing on tannaitic opinions expressed in a relevant baraita. R. Aha b. Yaakov argued that this second clause of the mishnah accords only with R. Yehudah, and Rava argued that it accords even with R. Shimon. The amoraim did not need to address the first clause of the mishnah because it represented the unanimous opinion among tannaim, and thus all of the sources that comprise this sugya refer only to hametz owned by a Jew.

3) However, the stam assumed that each amora addressed both halves of the mishnah. If R. Yehudah (or R. Shimon for that matter) was the author of the second clause, then he must be the **sole** author of the first clause as well.

4) At the same time, the stam assumed that Rava attributes the mishnah **only** to R. Shimon. This leads to the strange notion that R. Yehudah would disagree with the first clause and hold that hametz owned by a non-Jew on Pesah is prohibited after Pesah.

5) This in turn leads to the creation of a midrash used by R. Aha b. Yaakov to justify why hametz owned by a non-Jew is permitted. The midrash equates seeing and eating the hametz of a non-Jew so as to permit eating such hametz after Pesah.

6) Once this midrash was created, its forceful logic overwhelmed all tannaitic halakhah—if the permission to see hametz is equated with the permission to eat such hametz, then a Jew could theoretically eat, on Pesah, hametz owned by a non-Jew. No doubt R. Yehudah would have been quite surprised to see that his stringency produced this leniency!

## Sugya 3

Returning to sugya 3, the only stammaitic addition to this sugya is found in section 3f where the stam claims that R. Aha b. Yaakov retracted his statement made in amoraic sugya 1, the sugya we have just analyzed.

| | |
|---|---|
| והא רב אחא בר יעקב הוא דאמר דרבי | But was it not R. Aha b. Yaakov who |
| יהודה יליף שאור דאכילה משאור | said that R. Yehudah derives eating |
| דראייה! אלא: הדר ביה רב אחא בר יעקב | leaven from seeing leaven! Therefore, |
| מההיא. | R. Aha b. Yaakov retracted his earlier statement. |

According to R. Aha b. Yaakov's statement in amoraic sugya 3, R. Yehudah would hold that hametz owned by the Temple on Pesah cannot be eaten after Pesah. Since it has no value, one who eats it during Pesah has not transgressed *me'ilah*. The problem is that earlier R. Aha b. Yaakov attributed the mishnah to R. Yehudah, and the mishnah allows one to eat after Pesah hametz owned by a non-Jew. If so, then hametz owned by the Temple should also be permitted after Pesah, for like hametz owned by a non-Jew, there is no prohibition of "seeing" on Pesah hametz owned by the Temple. The equation of hametz owned by a non-Jew with hametz owned by the Temple was even stated explicitly in the Tosefta analyzed above: "R. Shimon b. Gamliel and R. Yishmael b. R. Yohanan b. Berokah say: Even that belonging to the Temple is permitted after Pesah immediately." Thus R. Yehudah, proposed author of the mishnah, cannot say that hametz owned by the Temple on Pesah has no value after Pesah such that one who eats it has not transgressed *me'ilah*. On account of this difficulty, the stam suggests that R. Aha b. Yaakov retracted his earlier statement.

The stam's difficulty is based on the assumption that hametz owned by a non-Jew and hametz owned by the Temple have the same status. But as

David Weiss Halivni points out, in the Yerushalmi there are tannaitic opinions that distinguish between hametz owned by a non-Jew and hametz owned by the Temple. Thus, the laws of one case need not apply to the other.[13] For instance, the prohibition on seeing hametz on Pesah applies to Temple-owned hametz even though it does not apply to hametz owned by non-Jews:

| ירושלמי פסחים ב:ב (כט, א) | Yerushalmi Pesahim 2:2, 29a |
|---|---|
| *לא יראה לך* (שמות יג:ז) אית תניי תני לא *יראה לך* לך אין את רואה אבל רואה את לגבוה. | *Shall not be seen of yours* (Exodus 13:7): There are those who teach *Shall not be seen of yours*: "Of yours" you may not see, but you may see [hametz] belonging to the Temple. |
| אית תניי תני אפילו לגבוה. | There are those who teach: Even belonging to the Temple [you shall not see]. |

The first version of the baraita excludes hametz belonging to the Temple from the prohibition on seeing or possessing hametz, a halakhah that also appears in in tannaitic compositions.[14] The second version of the baraita prohibits a Jew from seeing or possessing hametz owned by the Temple.[15] Even though an individual Jew does not own such hametz, he still may not possess it, and therefore it would be forbidden after Pesah.

Thus R. Aha b. Yaakov could maintain that R. Yehudah is the author of the mishnah (and therefore agrees that hametz owned by a non-Jew is permitted after Pesah) and still say that R. Yehudah would hold that eating hametz owned by the Temple is not a transgression of *me'ilah,* because hametz owned by the Temple, like hametz owned by a Jew, is

---

[13] David Weiss Halivni, *Mekorot u-Mesorot: Tractates Eruvin and Pesahim* (New York: Jewish Theological Seminary of America, 1982), 352-353.

[14] Sifre Deuteronomy piska 131; Mekhilta de-R. Shimon b. Yohai 13:7.

[15] Friedman, *Tosefta Atikta*, 281-283, posits that there are other tannaitic opinions that hametz owned by the Temple is prohibited. He notes that Mekhilta de-R. Shimon b. Yohai 12:19 excludes hametz owned by non-Jews from the prohibition on seeing hametz but does not mention hametz owned by the Temple. He concludes by noting that "the rule that one may see hametz owned by the Temple is not found among the opinions of early tannaim, and it was added to a later baraita."

prohibited after Pesah.[16] The opinion in the baraita that holds that he did not trespass accords with R. Yehudah who maintains that hametz has no value after Pesah. The opinion in the baraita holding that he did trespass accords with R. Shimon, who maintains that hametz owned by the Temple has value after Pesah. This understanding of R. Aha b. Yaakov's statement leads to the conclusion that, despite the Talmud's claim that R. Aha b. Yaakov retracted his earlier statement, there is no reason for us to assume that he actually did.[17]

The stammaitic comment that R. Aha b. Yaakov retracted his earlier statement is a result of the fact that the stammaim are unaware of a source in which a tanna holds that it is prohibited for a Jew to possess hametz owned by the Temple. So, in order to account for R. Aha b. Yaakov's statement correlating the dispute, they manufacture a dispute on hametz belonging to a non-Jew, from which they could posit a similar dispute on hametz owned by the Temple. We should trace why and how this is accomplished.

First of all, the stam of course knows R. Aha b. Yaakov's statement correlating the dispute concerning one who eats hametz owned by the Temple with a dispute between R. Yehudah and R. Shimon. The stam does not have any source which explicitly prohibits after Pesah hametz that belonged to the Temple on Pesah, which means this dispute cannot correlate with the tannaitic dispute on hametz owned by a Jew (the original meaning of R. Aha b. Yaakov's statement). To create such a position, they imagine a new halakhic position, one not found anywhere in tannaitic or amoraic halakhah: Hametz owned by a non-Jew on Pesah is prohibited after Pesah. Continuing to assume that the status of hametz owned by the Temple on Pesah correlates with the status of hametz owned by a non-Jew, they now have a position which prohibits after Pesah hametz owned by the Temple. And since it clearly cannot be R. Shimon who prohibits, we are left to conclude that R. Yehudah prohibits after Pesah both hametz owned by a non-Jew and hametz owned by the

---

[16]   Halivni even draws a general methodological conclusion from this particular case. He notes that it is not unusual for a Babylonian amora (such as R. Aha b. Yaakov) to base his opinion on a tradition that was unknown to the Bavli, such as this source from Yerushalmi Pesahim. In other words, just because the Bavli quotes a particular version of a baraita, it does not mean that the amoraim who raise a difficulty or comment on it are reacting to the same version of the baraita.

[17]   See also Friedman, *Tosefta Atikta*, 164, n. 16.

Temple. Finally, this notion forces the stam to claim R. Aha b. Yaakov retracted his identification of the mishnah, which permits hametz owned by a non-Jew, with R. Yehudah.

## A Step-by-Step Development of Sugya 3

As we did above with sugyot 1 and 2, we will now concisely retrace the steps of our analysis above:

1) R. Aha b. Yaakov posits that the dispute over the status of Temple-owned hametz correlates with the dispute between R. Yehudah and R. Shimon concerning the status of hametz **owned by a Jew**.

2) The stam is unaware of any authority who prohibits hametz owned by the Temple after Pesah. He assumes that the same rules which apply to hametz owned by a non-Jew apply to Temple-owned hametz—both are permitted immediately after Pesah.

3) The stam creates a dispute between R. Yehudah and R. Shimon over hametz owned by a non-Jew; R. Yehudah prohibits and R. Shimon permits.

4) The creation of R. Yehudah's position which prohibits hametz owned by a non-Jew forces the stam to claim that R. Aha b. Yaakov retracted his attribution of the mishnah to R. Yehudah. This notion corresponds with the stam's explanation of Rava from sugya 2 that the mishnah accords solely with R. Shimon, and perhaps is even the source of this understanding.

Paradoxically, once the stam posits that R. Aba b. Yaakov retracted his earlier statement, there are now no amoraim who identify the mishnah with R. Yehudah, despite the fact that R. Yehudah's rule in the Tosefta was obviously the source for the mishnah's rule. What was obvious to the Yerushalmi, and what was probably obvious to the amoraim as well, is now not agreed upon by any amoraim in the Bavli. All ascribe the mishnah to R. Shimon, for R. Yehudah would prohibit after Pesah even hametz belonging to a non-Jew. But if the entire mishnah is R. Shimon, and R. Shimon holds that hametz belonging to a Jew is not prohibited by the Torah after Pesah, we are left with no amoraim who rule that hametz belonging to a Jew is prohibited by the Torah after Pesah. An anonymous mishnah, seeming to reflect the authoritative view of the mishnah's editors, has now been left on the cutting room floor of the stammaitic bet midrash.

## The Sugya's Impact on Halakhah

As we have seen, R. Shimon states in Sifre Deuteronomy that the biblical prohibition on eating hametz applies only during the festival of Pesah itself. When it comes to hametz after the sixth hour on the eve of Pesah, as well as hametz owned by a Jew after Pesah, the prohibition is merely rabbinic. As we saw in amoraic sugya 1, Rava rules according to R. Shimon with regard to **hametz after Pesah**. Clearly Rava's statement has nothing to do with hametz before Pesah, and indeed, the three amoraic sugyot out of which our sugya is constructed all deal directly or indirectly only with hametz after Pesah. Nowhere outside of the baraita does the sugya even refer to hametz after the sixth hour on the eve of Pesah.

However, since the editor of the sugya wove together baraitot dealing with hametz before and after Pesah, Rava's statement in which he rules according to R. Shimon concerning hametz after Pesah could be read as ruling according to R. Shimon even with regard to hametz before Pesah. While R. Shimon himself said only that hametz before Pesah is not prohibited according to biblical law and never said that it was permitted, there are also no sources in which he explicitly states that hametz is prohibited rabbinically after the sixth hour. This leads to the possibility that R. Shimon may have held that hametz is completely permitted until nightfall, a position which contradicts every other tannaitic and amoraic source. Moreover, since the halakhah follows Rava, this would indeed be the observed halakhic position.

Indeed, in line with the construction of this suga, there were medieval commentators who ruled that one could derive benefit from hametz after the sixth hour, which is also the time at which it must be destroyed.[18] In order to harmonize this ruling with all other sources which demand the destruction of hametz before the second half of the day, these

---

[18] See Tosafot Pesahim 28b ד"ה רבי שמעון אומר; R. Zerahiah Halevi, ha-Meor ha-Katan on the Rif 3a, ד"ה והא דאמר רב גידל; Ra'avad on Mishneh Torah Laws of Hametz and Matzah 1:8.

commentators suggested that R. Shimon would allow one to derive benefit from hametz while simultaneously destroying it. For instance, A Jew could use hametz in his oven as kindling to cook the food he will eat at the seder![19] R. Zerahiah Halevi, a 12th century Spanish authority, went even a step further, allowing one, at least *ex post facto*, to destroy hametz by eating it (!) on the second half of the day before Pesah.[20] While these rulings were certainly theoretical, they could only exist even in theory due to the editorial and compositional work of the stammaitic editors who created our sugya.

# Appendix:

# Let All Who Are Hungry Come and Eat—Except in Mehoza

The extended Babylonian sugya about hametz after Pesah concludes with a brief story that takes place at the house of R. Nahman, a third generation Babylonian sage. We shall consider this story because it provides a fascinating window into the practical challenges of strictly adhering to the laws of hametz on Pesah while living in a world controlled by non-Jews. It is also an excellent example of how the editing of a sugya can impact interpretation of earlier sources.

| בבלי פסחים ל ע"א | Bavli Pesahim 30a |
|---|---|
| ואזדא רבא לטעמיה, דאמר רבא: כי הוינן בי רב נחמן, כי הוו נפקי שבעה יומי דפסחא, אמר לן: פוקו וזבינו חמירא דבני חילא. | And Rava follows his own reasoning, for Rava said: When we were in the house of R. Nahman, when the seven days of Pesah were over, he would say to us: Go out and buy the leaven of the soldiers. |

The story is brought in the name of Rava, and in the context of the sugya it serves to support an earlier statement Rava has made. Rashi offers the following opinion on the connection between the story and Rava's earlier statement:

[19] See for instance Tosafot 28b s.v. רבי שמעון אמר; Ra'avad on the Rambam, Laws of Hametz and Matzah 1:5.
[20] Ha-Meor ha-Katan on the Rif, 3a. s.v. והא דאמר רב גידל.

## Rashi Pesahim 30a

**רש״י מסכת פסחים ל ע״א**

ואזדא רבא - דאמר הלכה כר' שמעון,
לטעמיה דאמר נמי בעלמא חמץ של
נכרי שעבר עליו הפסח מותר אף
באכילה הואיל וליכא למיקנס ביה מידי,
ואי ר' יהודה חמץ סתמא קאמר ואפילו
דנכרי.

"And Rava follows"—Rava, who says
the halakhah is an accordance with R.
Shimon, follows his own reasoning in
that he in general said that it is
permitted even to eat, after Pesah, the
hametz owned by a non-Jew on Pesah,
since there is no reason to penalize him.
For if he had held that the halakhah
followed R. Yehudah, [R. Yehudah]
said hametz in general [is prohibited
after Pesah] even that of a non-Jew.

בני חילא נכרים, אף על פי שאופיהו יום
זה שעבר, והוא פסח.

Soldiers—i.e. non-Jews, even though
they baked it the previous day, which
was Pesah [it is still permitted].

Rashi reads the story as illustrating that Rava ruled in accordance with R.
Shimon, who allows a Jew to eat the hametz of a non-Jew after Pesah. The
story proves that Rava holds like R. Shimon, for had Rava ruled in
accordance with R. Yehudah, hametz belonging to a non-Jew would have
been forbidden after Pesah. But as we demonstrated above, Rava himself
did not intend to imply that R. Yehudah would prohibit such hametz
after Pesah. Rava identified the mishnah with R. Shimon, but he did not
mean to suggest that R. Yehudah would forbid hametz of a non-Jew after
Pesah. This is a ruling ascribed to Rava **by the stam**. Rashi here is guided
by the stammaitic comment, "Rava follows his own reasoning," which
connects him all the way back to the stammaitic interpretation of Rava's
statement that appeared nearly an entire page earlier.

In contrast, R. Hananel explains Rava in light of a statement that Rava
made directly above: After Pesah, hametz in a mixture is permitted, even if
that hametz was owned by a Jew on Pesah. This ruling is consistent with
R. Shimon, who forbade hametz owned by a Jew only if the hametz was
unadulterated. R. Hananel writes:

## R. Hananel Pesahim 30a

**רבינו חננאל פסחים ל ע״א**

ואזדא רבא לטעמיה דאמר: כי
הוינא בי רב נחמן כי הוו נפקו יומי
דפסחא הוה אמר לן פוקו אייתו

Rava follows his own reasoning, that he
said: When we were in the house of R.
Nahman when Pesah was over he would

חמירא דבני חילא.

say to us, "Go buy the leaven of the soldiers."

מראין הדברים דחמירא דא דבני חילא ברשות ישראל הות, ואף על גב דכדידהו הות דמיא הוה שרי רב נחמן דהא על ידי תערובות היא.

We can see from here that this leaven belonging to the soldiers was in the possession of the Jews, and even though it was as if it was theirs, R. Nahman permitted the Jews to use it, for it was found in a mixture.

According to R. Hananel the hametz bought from the non-Jewish soldiers was in Jewish possession on Pesah, but since it was a mixture, it was permitted in accordance with R. Shimon's ruling. R. Hananel's interpretation that this hametz was in Jewish possession on Pesah is based on a similar story found earlier in the Bavli.

### Bavli Pesahim 5b

בבלי פסחים ה ע"ב

כי הא דאמר להו רבא לבני מחוזא: בעירו חמירא דבני חילא מבתייכו, כיון דאילו מיגנב ואילו מיתביד ברשותייכו קאי ובעיתו לשלומי כדילכון דמי, ואסור.

Like that which Rava said to the people of Mehoza: Destroy the leaven of the soldiers that is in your house, since if it is stolen or lost it will be considered to have been in your possession and you will need to compensate [them for it], therefore it is as if it is yours, and it is prohibited [to keep such leaven over Pesah].

In linking our story with this story earlier in the tractate, R. Hananel offers a more convincing reading of the reference to soldiers—these are not just any non-Jews. Our story refers specifically to soldiers who would store their hametz in Jewish homes. And, as we have seen, by linking our story with the issue of hametz owned by a Jew during Pesah but that has been mixed in with other permitted items after Pesah, R. Hananel offers a more compelling explanation of why this statement appears here in the Talmud immediately after Rava's statement about mixtures.

However, the major problem with R. Hananel's interpretation is that Rava's point would have been better illustrated by a story about the use of hametz that was obviously owned by a Jew during Pesah. Why illustrate the halakhah about mixtures with a story where the hametz does not seem to have been really owned by a Jew?

Separating the stammaitic introduction "Rava follows his own reasoning" from Rava's story of what happened at R. Nahman's house allows us to posit that the story was originally independent of either the context suggested by Rashi, or that suggested by R. Hananel. It was placed here at the end of the long sugya about hametz after Pesah because it is the only story in the Bavli concerning this subject. As is typical in the Bavli, stories of actual halakhic rulings are incorporated at the end of long theoretical discussions. After its placement here in the sugya, the stam added in the words "and Rava follows his own reasoning" to more closely tighten the independent sections of the sugya. Thus, only on the stammaitic level do we need to take into account the connection between the story and the previous statements of Rava. This frees us from interpreting the story in light of either of Rava's statements, the first identifying the mishnah with R. Shimon (Rashi) or the second, permitting hametz in a mixture after Pesah (R. Hananel).

We now turn our attention to analyzing the story itself. The story may be related to a halakhah found in the Tosefta:

**Tosefta Pesahim 2:4**    תוספתא פסחים ב:ד

The hametz of transgressors is permitted immediately after Pesah because they exchange their leaven.    חמיצן של עוברי עבירה מותר אחר הפסח מיד מפני שמחליפין את השאר.

Saul Lieberman provides the following explanation of this statement:

The simple interpretation of this baraita accords with that of most commentators, that the "transgressors," who wished to eat hametz after Pesah as soon as possible, were too frugal to buy leaven from non-Jews after Pesah, and would therefore prepare for themselves leaven before Pesah. At the end of Pesah they would exchange it with [the leaven] of non-Jews, for it would be easy to find someone to exchange leaven that had aged well with leaven that was only a day or two old. From here we can see that if they would leaven their dough with their own leaven that they had owned over Pesah, the bread would be prohibited, even though it was [a mixture most of which was] of a permitted substance.[21]

The assumed behavior of these Jews is fascinating both historically and sociologically. These Jews knew that they were not supposed to eat or make hametz on Pesah. Doing so would have been a blatant violation of Torah law, which they seem to have observed. They also knew that they could not eat—or perhaps other Jews would not eat—bread made with the leaven that they had possessed during Pesah. But these frugal Jews did not want to spend money buying new leaven. And so they switched the leaven they had made before Pesah with leaven that non-Jews had made a day or two before. Either they did not know that it was prohibited to possess leaven during Pesah, or they simply did not observe this halakhah. In any case, the Tosefta is reflective of what must have been a major problem in bread making in premodern times: how to make bread after Pesah without having to purchase expensive sourdough from non-Jews.

Lieberman goes on to cite our story from Pesahim 30a, along with R. Hananel's commentary. While Lieberman himself ultimately seems to prefer Rashi's interpretation, from a critical talmudic perspective it seems difficult not to connect our story to the story on 5a. As Lieberman demonstrates, the connection between the two stories also makes sense in light of a halakhic question found in Betzah 21a: "They asked of R. Huna: These village dwellers who were forced to take the flour from soldiers, can they bake it during the festival [during which one may bake, but only for the needs of a Jew]?" In order to appreciate the circumstances in which Jews took flour from soldiers to make hametz after Pesah, some historical context is necessary.

As Robert Brody has noted, these stories reflect a reality in which Jews in the Sasanian empire were forced to billet Persian soldiers, particularly in Mehoza, the place of Rava's residence, due to its proximity to Ctesiphon.[22] The story in Betzah illustrates that the soldiers would provide the flour for local residents to bake them bread. Thus there was potentially hametz owned by non-Jews in Jewish homes during Pesah.

---

[21] Saul Lieberman, *Tosefta Kifshuta: Moed Part IV* (New York: Jewish Theological Seminary of America, 1992), 489.

[22] Robert Brody, "Judaism in the Sasanian Empire," *Irano-Judaica II; Studies Relating to Jewish Contacts with Persian Culture throughout the Ages*, eds. Shaul Shaked and Amnon Netzer (Jerusalem: Ben-Zvi Institute, 1990), 59.

Rava on Pesahim 5a rules that a Jew must destroy such hametz before Pesah, not because it was really their hametz, but because if the hametz was stolen or lost, they would have responsibility to compensate the Persian soldiers for it. This was sufficient to make the Jew liable to destroy the hametz beforehand. From the story on Pesahim 30a, it seems likely that Jews did not in fact destroy such hametz, and we can surely understand why. After Pesah, this hametz was not considered to have been owned by Jews during Pesah, as Rava cites in the name of R. Nahman. And so, the hametz deposited in Jewish homes could be purchased by the Jew after Pesah and used immediately to bake bread, thereby solving the problem of how to leaven bread immediately after Pesah. The issue in this story is neither the status of Jewish hametz in a mixture after Pesah (R. Hananel) nor the status after Pesah of hametz owned by a non-Jew on Pesah (Rashi). Rather, the real issue is whether or not this hametz belonged to a Jew during Pesah or to the non-Jew. R. Nahman rules that it belonged to the non-Jew, and therefore it can be used immediately after Pesah.

Taken together, these stories offer an ingenious practical solution to a difficult halakhic question: how to make bread using good leaven immediately after Pesah without transgressing the pervasive prohibition of hametz after Pesah. If a Jew owns hametz outright on Pesah, it would be forbidden after Pesah because he has transgressed the biblical prohibition. But if it was only deposited in his house (Pesahim 5b), he may buy it after Pesah and use it immediately (Pesahim 30a). And if he exchanges leaven that he owned on Pesah with leaven owned by a non-Jew, the bread that he bakes after Pesah is permitted, because the leaven he used was not his own (Tosefta). Thus, while the "transgressors" in the Tosefta would exchange their old leaven with that of non-Jews, the Jews in Mahoza found a more halakhically acceptable solution—they would buy the leaven that they were forced to store in their own homes.

Interestingly, the fact that Persian soldiers would store their hametz with Jews helps us understand a comment on a line that later became a well-known part of the Pesah seder in the post-Talmudic period. The story appears in Bavli Taanit 20b-21a:

| | |
|---|---|
| **בבלי תענית כ ע״ב-כא ע״א** | **Bavli Taanit 20b-21a** |
| כי הוה כרך ריפתא הוה פתח לבביה ואמר: | When [R. Huna] would break bread, he would open the gates and exclaim, |

| | |
|---|---|
| כל מאן דצריך - ליתי וליכול. | "Anyone who needs, may come and eat." |
| אמר רבא: כולהו מצינא מקיימנא, לבר מהא דלא מצינא למיעבד משום דנפישי בני חילא דמחוזא. | Rava said: I can fulfill all these, except for this one, which I cannot do, because there are many soldiers in Mehoza. |

The Talmud relates the pious practice of R. Huna, who would share his food with anyone in need. Whenever he would eat a meal, he would open the gates and exclaim, "Anyone who needs, may come and eat." Rava responds that while in all other situations he would follow the meritorious practices of R. Huna, he could not offer his bread because of the many soldiers in Mahoza. Rashi explains that Rava feared that too many soldiers reside there and would come and eat all his food. But a more likely explanation, one that takes account of the stories we analyzed above, is that the soldiers would think he was giving away their bread, for they had deposited their flour with him. In the geonic period, R. Huna's words became part of the Ha-Lahma Anya opening of the Pesah seder, despite the fact that they initially had no connection to the festival. There is some irony that Rava could not say this line because of the presence of Persian soldiers, and yet the presence of these same soldiers allowed the Jews of Mehoza to find usable sour dough with which to bake bread after Pesah. Finally, we suggest that today when reciting this line, Jews can be grateful for our freedom not just from Egyptian overlords, but from Persian soldiers as well.

# CHAPTER FOUR

## A WOMAN IS ACQUIRED THROUGH MONEY: BETROTHAL IN JEWISH LAW

## KETUBOT 57B-58A; KIDDUSHIN 10A

## Introduction

In many societies throughout the world, the marital process is divided into two stages. The first stage is a promise between the two parties to get married, called betrothal (*kiddushin/erusin*)[1] or engagement. The second stage is when this promise comes to fruition, usually signified by the joining of the two parties into one household (*nisuin*).[2] The legal implications of the first stage vary among societies.[3] In the Torah there are strong legal consequences to betrothal. For instance, the sex with a betrothed girl is punished by stoning (Deuteronomy 22:23-24) whereas pre-marital sexual relations (Exodus 22:15-16; Deuteronomy 22:28-29) with a non-betrothed girl entail only a financial penalty. After betrothal,

---

[1]  The former word is rabbinic language whereas the latter is from the Torah. The rabbis use both words to mean betrothal.

[2]  For more on marriage in the rabbinic period see Adiel Schremer, *Zakhar u-Nekevah Bera'am* (Jerusalem: Merkaz Zalman Shazar, 2003); Michael Satlow, *Jewish Marriage in Antiquity* (Princeton: Princeton University Press, 2001); Mordechai Akiva Friedman, *Jewish Marriage in Palestine: A Cairo Geniza Study* (Tel Aviv: Jewish Theological Seminary of America, 1981).

[3]  See Philip Reynolds, *How Marriage Became One of the Sacraments* (Cambridge: Cambridge University Press, 2016), 157-180; Satlow, *Jewish Marriage*, 69-73.

sexual relations with another man is considered adultery.[4] Moreover, the separation from betrothal requires a formal divorce.[5] Indeed, these last two laws are standard throughout rabbinic literature: A betrothed woman requires a divorce to sever her relationship with her husband, and if she has relations with another man, she and he are both considered adulterers. Thus, according to both biblical and rabbinic law, a betrothed woman is already legally connected to her husband, despite the fact that they do not yet live together.

However, while a betrothed woman is certainly considered by the Torah to be legally bound to her husband, this does not necessarily mean that she is fully considered to be part of his household, which would have ramifications for several other realms of Jewish law. For instance, the Torah legislates that a man can annul the vows of a woman who is part of his household: A father can annul his daughter's vows, and a husband his wife's vows (Numbers 30). What about a betrothed girl?[6] Who, if anyone, annuls her vows? Another issue is inheritance: Should she die while betrothed, who inherits her estate—her father (or his family) or her husband? Is her husband financially obligated to provide for her while she is still betrothed? When can he begin to stake a financial claim upon her earnings? The discussion of these and other issues are part of the larger question of the status of a betrothed girl—is she part of her father's household or her husband's?

The question of whose household a betrothed woman belongs to arises most frequently and with greatest vigor in rabbinic literature with regard to the issue of eating terumah, agricultural produce set aside for the priests (kohanim). Is a woman betrothed to a kohen—while still living in her

---

[4]  The rabbis understand the Deuteronomy verses to refer to rape whereas the parallel in Exodus refers to seduction. However, this is not necessarily the simple meaning of the verses. See Tikva Frymer-Kensky, "Virginity in the Bible," in *Gender and Law in the Hebrew Bible and the Ancient Near East*, eds. Victor H. Matthews, Bernard S. Levinson, and Tikva Frymer-Kensky (Sheffield: Sheffield Academic Press, 1998), 91–92.

[5]  Although there may have been some tannaitic opposition to this requirement as well. See Tosefta Ketubot 4:9.

[6]  We use the terminology of betrothed girl to reflect the rabbinic practice of betrothal and marriage with girls soon after reaching sexual maturity. Schremer, above n. 2, estimates that in Eretz Yisrael girls were betrothed and married in their teenage years while in Babylonia the betrothal would often take place before reaching puberty.

father's home under his guardianship—allowed to eat terumah even before she actually enters her husband's household? As per the rabbinic understanding of Leviticus 22:10-13 and Numbers 18:11-13, only kohanim and the members of their household—wives, children, and slaves—may eat terumah.[7] The Torah contains no clear directive as to whether or not an Israelite (non-kohanic) woman betrothed but not yet married to a kohen can eat terumah. While this may seem to be a technical issue relevant only to kohanim and the rules governing their behavior, at the heart of this matter is the deeper question of whether we consider betrothal sufficient for a woman to be legally considered a member of her husband's household. Since a non-priest or one who is not a member of a priest's household who eats terumah is liable for "death at the hands of heaven,"[8] the ability to eat terumah is an effective way for the rabbis to clarify the status of the betrothed woman.

There is another reason why this specific aspect of the larger discussion concerning betrothal is particularly contentious in rabbinic discourse. With regard to financial matters there is no room for a distinction between law and practice—either her husband is responsible for her financially and benefits from her financially from the point of betrothal onward, or her father is responsible during this period. However, when it comes to the issue of terumah, there is room for bifurcation between theory and practice. We can imagine a system in which a betrothed woman could theoretically eat terumah while living in her father's home, for betrothal is strong enough to consider her to be effectively part of her husband's household. But in practice, she might not actually eat terumah until the point of marriage, for that is when she physically joins her husband in his home. We shall see that several rabbis indeed employ such a strategy.

Betrothal in rabbinic law seems to have generally been contracted by the husband giving money or an item of value to the woman (Mishnah Kiddushin 1:1; Bavli Kiddushin 12b). Allowing a betrothed girl to eat terumah, even theoretically, after this symbolic act has been performed is a statement that through the transfer of this money, the woman is

---

[7]   It is unclear whether these verses are referring specifically to terumah. Leviticus refers to either "holy things" (קודש) or "sacred gifts (תרומת הקדשים), a unique term. Numbers refers to either "holy things" or "gift offerings of their contributions (תרומת מתנם)."

[8]   Sifra, Dibura Dehova, parsha 9, perek 17; Bavli Sanhedrin 83a.

considered part of her husband's household.[9] Betrothal in rabbinic times did not occur simultaneous with marriage as it does in Jewish practice today (see for instance Mishnah Ketubot 5:2). According to this understanding, a woman would be considered part of her husband's household long before she actually moved from her father's home into his.

In contrast to the **symbolic** giving of money at betrothal, marriage was performed by a **physical act**, namely the woman moving into the husband's domain (see for instance Mishnah Ketubot 4:5). In rabbinic parlance, this is usually expressed as her "entering the huppah." While it is unclear what exactly the huppah was in rabbinic times, it was not a purely symbolic canopy as it is today. More likely it was a part of the husband's actual property—entering the huppah is thus synonymous with entering his domain. If a betrothed girl cannot eat terumah even theoretically until she enters her husband's home, then the acquisition formalized by kiddushin is not strong enough for her to be considered a member of his household. In other words, the intense rabbinic interest on this issue is not related just to the practical question of when a woman betrothed and then married to a kohen actually eats terumah. Rather, the significance is related to the strength of the bond created at betrothal. Allowing a woman to eat terumah at the point of betrothal is an unequivocal statement that betrothal places her legally in her husband's household.

Our exploration of this issue also has ramifications for the development of halakhic history as depicted in rabbinic literature. A mishnah in Ketubot and a parallel in the Tosefta mention a historical shift in the laws of when a betrothed girl eats terumah. According to this account, in earlier times a woman was allowed to eat terumah before marriage, but later rabbis decreed, for some reason unmentioned in tannaitic literature itself, that she must wait until marriage. Most scholars have accepted this presentation and posited that there was a change in the conception of betrothal in rabbinic law. Originally, betrothal considered strong enough to allow a betrothed girl to eat terumah, and in the late tannaitic period, betrothal was regarded as a weaker bond and, as a result, rabbis forbade her from eating terumah until entering her

---

[9]    On the exchange of money as a symbolic act of betrothal see Judith Hauptman, *Rereading the Rabbis: A Woman's Voice* (Boulder: Westview Press, 1998), 60-76. For a critique of this interpretation see Gail Labovitz, *Marriage and Metaphor: Constructions of Gender in Rabbinic Literature* (Lanham: Lexington Books, 2013), 29-62.

husband's home. In contrast, we will argue that this description of historical development was invented by later tannaitic editors in order to express their own halakhic viewpoint. Originally, this issue was debated by early tannaitic sages. Thus, instead of viewing these sources as accurate descriptions of halakhic history, we suggest that they were formulated in order to present a literary construction through which late tannaim chose sides in this heated debate.

In the last part of this chapter we will uncover the original meaning and setting of the amoraic explanation of the Mishnah and Tosefta dealing with the question of a betrothed woman eating terumah. Most tannaim rule that a woman betrothed to a kohen does not eat terumah until she enters the huppah; the amoraim attempt to explain this ruling. As frequently happens, the talmudic editors, the stammaim, took these statements slightly out of context, causing them to be significantly misunderstood. In addition, in the first appendix, we shall see how these editorial shifts caused a simple Greek word to be misunderstood by modern lexicographers. Finally, in the second appendix, we will consider how an internal contradiction in the Tosefta resulted in a later amoraic emendation of the earlier tannitic text.

## Mishnah Ketubot 5:2-3

The fifth chapter of tractate Ketubot deals with the legal rights and responsibilities of husbands and wives in marriage. The following mishnah is the primary source concerning when an Israelite woman betrothed or married to a kohen can begin eating terumah:

| משנה כתובות ה:ב- ג[10] | Mishnah Ketubot 5:2-3 |
|---|---|
| (1) נותנין לבתולה שנים עשר חדש משתבעה הבעל לפרנס את עצמה... | (1) A virgin is given twelve months from the [time her intended] husband claimed her, [in which] to prepare herself for marriage... |
| (2) הגיע זמן ולא נישאו, או שמתו בעליהן אוכלות משלו ואוכלות בתרומה. | (2) If the time has come and they were not married, or their husbands |

---

[10] The reading below is based on the Kaufmann manuscript of the Mishnah. For more on this important manuscript see Michael Krupp, "Manuscripts of the Mishnah," *The Literature of the Sages I*, ed. Shmuel Safrai (Philadelphia: Fortress Press, 1987), 252-262.

died,[11] they are entitled to receive maintenance from his estate and [if he is a priest] they may eat terumah.

(3) רבי טרפון אומר נותנין לה הכל תרומה.

(3) Rabbi Tarfon says: They give her [all of her food] in terumah.

רבי עקיבא אומר מחצה חולין ומחצה תרומה...

Rabbi Akiva says: One half unconsecrated food and one half terumah... [12]

(4) זו משנה ראשונה.

(4) This is the first mishnah.

בית דין של אחריהן אמרו: אין האשה אוכלת בתרומה עד שתכנס לחופה.

A later court ruled: A woman may not eat terumah until she has entered the huppah.

In section 1, the mishnah states that a betrothed virgin[13] receives twelve months to prepare herself for marriage, starting from the time the husband proposes marriage. In section 2, the mishnah penalizes the husband for not marrying her within this twelve-month period by obligating him to provide for her financial needs, including her food. Similarly, if he dies and has not yet married her, she is supported by his estate. In these situations, if he is a kohen, he (or his estate) may provide her with terumah. Allowing him to provide her with terumah is in fact a leniency on the husband, for terumah is cheaper than non-sacred produce; since only kohanim can eat terumah, there is less demand, which keeps prices down.

In section 3, Rabbi Akiva and Rabbi Tarfon debate how much terumah the husband may give his wife, once he is obligated to feed her. If she receives all of her food in terumah, she would face the problem that when she is a menstruant or otherwise impure, she would not be able to

---

[11] The words "או שמתו בעליהן" are not found in most talmudic manuscripts, but they are found in nearly all manuscripts of the Mishnah. See *Dikdukei Sofrim Hashalem: Ketubot II*, 18-19, n. 39. It seems most likely that this phrase refers to the husband's estate's obligation to provide her with food. If the husband dies, she is considered a widow and is provided for from his estate, as are all widows (Mishnah Ketubot 4:12; 11:1).

[12] We have skipped a portion of the mishnah concerning situations where the husband died before the time for marriage arrived and his betrothed awaits levirate marriage.

[13] The Hebrew word for virgin is also used to refer to a woman married for the first time, even if she is not technically a virgin.

eat it, for terumah cannot be eaten by one who is impure. If he were to provide her solely with terumah, she would need to sell it when impure and buy non-sacred food. Since this is difficult, and may cause her a financial loss, R. Akiva states that he is allowed to give her only half of her food-allowance in terumah; the rest must be provided in non-sacred produce.

At its end, the mishnah relates that the teaching in section 2 was the "first mishnah," meaning that it referred to an earlier historical stage. A later court decreed that a betrothed girl must wait until she enters the huppah, i.e. she is properly married, in order to be allowed to eat terumah. The mishnah offers no explanation as to why a later court decided to change the halakhah.

The tannaitic parallel to this mishnah is found in Tosefta Ketubot 5:1:

| תוספתא כתובות ה:א | Tosefta Ketubot 5:1 |
|---|---|
| (1a) ר' טרפון אומר: נותנין לה הכל תרומה. | (1a) R. Tarfon says: He can give her all her food in terumah. |
| (1b) במי דברים אמורים? מן האירוסין אבל מן הנשואין מודה ר' טרפון שנותנין לה מחצה חולין ומחצה תרומה. | (1b) To what does this refer? From betrothal. But after marriage, R. Tarfon agrees that he gives her half terumah and half non-sacred produce. |
| (1c) במי דברים אמורים? בבת כהן לכהן אבל בת ישראל לכהן הכל מודים שמעלין לה כל מזונותיה מן החולין. | (1c) To what does this refer? To a daughter of a priest betrothed to a priest. But daughter of an Israelite betrothed to a priest, everyone agrees that he gives all of her food as non-sacred produce. |
| (1d) ר' יהודה בן בתירה אומר: שתי ידות תרומה ואחת חולין. | (1d) R. Yehudah b. Batera says: He gives her two parts terumah and one-part non-sacred produce. |
| (1e) ר' יהודה אומר: מוכרת את התרומה ולוקחת בדמיה חולין. | (1e) R. Yehudah says: She sells her terumah and uses the proceeds to buy non-sacred produce. |
| (1f) רבן שמעון בן גמליאל אומר: כל מקום שהוזכרו שם תרומה נותן כפול חולין. | (1f) R. Shimon b. Gamliel says: In any case where terumah is mentioned, he gives her double the amount in non-sacred produce. |

(2) זו משנה ראשונה. רבותינו אמרו: אין האשה בת ישראל אוכלת בתרומה עד שתכנס לחופה והיבמה עד שתיבעל. אם מתה, בעלה יורשה.

(2) This is the first mishnah. Our rabbis said: An Israelite woman does not eat terumah until she enters the huppah. And a woman subject to levirate marriage [does not eat terumah] until she has relations. If she dies, her husband inherits her.

(3) אמר ר' מנחם בן נפח משם ר' ליעזר הקפר: מעשה בר' טרפון שקידש שלש מאות נשים להאכילן בתרומה שהיו שני בצרות.

(3) R. Menahem b. Nefah said in the name of R. [E]liezer Hakappar: It happened during years of famine that R. Tarfon betrothed 300 women in order to feed them terumah.

(4) וכבר שלח יוחנן בן בגבג אצל ר' יהודה בן בתירה לנציבין, אמר לו: שמעתי עליך שאתה אומר ארוסה בת ישראל המאורסת לכהן אוכלת בתרומה.
שלח לו ואמר: לו מוחזק הייתי בך שאתה בקי בחדרי תורה לדון קל וחומר אי אתה יודע!

(4) And Yohanan b. Bag Bag already sent to R. Yehudah b. Batera in Netzivin, saying: I heard that you have been saying that an Israelite woman betrothed to a priest can eat terumah.
He sent back saying: I assumed that you were an expert in the inner chambers of Torah but you don't even know how to make a *kal vahomer* argument!

ומה שפחה כנענית שאין ביאתה קונה אותה לאכול בתרומה כסף קונה אותה להאכילה בתרומה. בת ישראל שהביאה קונה אותה להאכילה בתרומה דין הוא שיהא כסף קונה אותה להאכילה בתרומה.

When it comes to a Canaanite slave, intercourse does not acquire her in order to allow her to be fed terumah, but money does acquire her to allow her to be fed terumah. Is it not therefore logical that for an Israelite woman, since intercourse does acquire her in order to allow her to be fed terumah, money should also acquire her in order to allow her to be fed terumah?

אבל מה אעשה שהרי אמרו חכמים אין ארוסה בת ישראל אוכלת בתרומה עד שתכנס לחופה. אם מתה, בעלה יורשה.

But what can I do for the sages have said that a betrothed Israelite woman does not eat terumah until she enters the huppah. If she dies, her husband inherits her.

Sections 1a and 1d-f are a parallel and an expanded form of section 3 of the mishnah concerning how much terumah a man may provide his betrothed wife. Sections 1b and 1c offer two important qualifications to these rulings. Section 1b relates to R. Tarfon's statement that she receives all her food in terumah, limiting his ruling to when she receives food as a betrothed woman. If he has already married her, he is allowed to give her only half of her maintenance in terumah. One potential explanation for the difference between a betrothed and a married woman is that a betrothed girl living in her father's house will have others to provide for her should she be impure and hence unable to eat the terumah given to her by her husband. But a married woman in her husband's home will not be able to rely on her father, and therefore she must be given half of her food in non-sacred produce. This way she will have food for the days in which she is not able to eat terumah.

Section 1c clarifies that all of the tannaim in sections 1a, d-f, who give permission to the husband to provide a woman a portion of her food in terumah while she is still betrothed, allow this only with regard to a daughter of a priest who is betrothed to a priest. In such a case, the woman goes from one situation in which she may eat terumah to another. If a priestly husband is providing his betrothed with food after the twelve-month period has elapsed, then he may provide her with at least part of the food in terumah. However, if her father is an Israelite, the husband must give her only non-sacred food. This section is crucial for our larger issue, for according to this section **all tannaim agree that a betrothed Israelite woman does not receive terumah**.

Section 2 is parallel to section 4 in the mishnah. Both recount a development in halakhah from an older position which allowed a betrothed Israelite woman to eat terumah, at least after the twelve-month waiting period had elapsed, to a more restrictive position prohibiting her from terumah until she enters the huppah. We should note that this section does not accord with section 1c, which stipulated that only a betrothed woman **of priestly descent** is allowed to eat terumah. It seems that these two clauses of the Tosefta are completely unaware of each other, both staking out the same essential ruling but in different ways. Section 1c uses a limitation (במי דברים אמורים) to achieve its goal of not allowing a betrothed Israelite woman to eat terumah. Section 2 achieves this same goal but presents it as a halakhic development: At one point in history, betrothed Israelite women could eat terumah, but a later court decreed against this. However, taken together, the two sections are inconsistent for, if according to section 1c an Israelite woman could not eat terumah until marriage, why would a later court decree the exact same halakhah? Indeed, Abaye, a fourth-generation Babylonian amora, emends this baraita so that these two lines accord more easily. (See Appendix II for a comparison.)

Section 3 relates that R. Tarfon, who was a priest, betrothed 300 women(!) in order to feed them terumah during a time of famine. In section 4, the Tosefta supports R. Tarfon's act by relating the precedent that R. Yehudah b. Batera permitted providing terumah for a betrothed Israelite. There is no explanation as to why this provokes R. Yohanan b. Bag Bag. R. Yehudah b. Batera defends his position by offering a *kal vahomer* midrashic argument, based on the fact that a handmaid eats terumah as soon as she is acquired by a priest. While he argues that his *kal vahomer* justifies allowing a betrothed woman to eat terumah, R. Yehudah b. Batera does not act in this manner because "the sages have said that a betrothed woman does not eat terumah until she enters the huppah." This story is key to understanding the historical development of this issue, so we will focus on it more closely below.

Before we do so, we should note the complex textual relationship between the Mishnah and Tosefta. We discussed the general relationship between the two tannaitic compositions in the previous chapter and noted that we share Shamma Friedman's assessment that the Mishnah is often (but not always) a redacted, later version of earlier material that appears in the Tosefta. For the most part, this seems to again be the case here, although the relationship is more complex. When it comes to the section concerning what percentage of terumah a man may give his wife, it seems that the Tosefta preserves the more original version, which was then abbreviated in the Mishnah into the two main positions. Sections 1b-c from the Tosefta, which limit these opinions, are found only in the Tosefta and may not have been known to the editors of the Mishnah. Section 2 in the Tosefta, which refers to a "first Mishnah," seems to have been a later addition, one based on section 4 of the mishnah. If this clause was added at a later period to the Tosefta, it would explain why it clashes with section 1c. In other words, originally both the Mishnah and the Tosefta claimed that a woman did not actually eat terumah until entering the huppah—the Mishnah by relegating the dispensation for a betrothed girl to eat terumah to an earlier ruling (*mishnah rishonah*), and the Tosefta by limiting the permission to give terumah to a betrothed woman to one of priestly descent. The Mishnah's clause was later added to the Tosefta, despite the superfluity.[14] As far as the stories in sections 3-4 of the toseftan halakhah, it is likely that they simply were not included in the Mishnah for the sake of brevity, especially since they do not add any new halakhic information.

## R. Yohanan b. Bag Bag and R. Yehudah b. Batera: The Conflict Between Theory and Practice

There are two specific questions we must ask about the vituperative interchange between these two sages. First of all, what provoked R. Yohanan b. Bag Bag to send a message to R. Yehudah b. Batera inquiring whether he really said that a betrothed woman eats terumah? We do not often hear of rabbis sending such messages to each other over mere differences of opinion. We must ask what occurred in this specific case to set off an accusatory letter and elicit such an angry response. The second question concerns the particulars of R. Yehudah b. Batera's *derashah*. If, as he himself admits, he cannot act upon his own words, why was it so important to him to offer midrashic justification for allowing a betrothed woman to eat terumah? It is understandable why a rabbi would "erect a fence around the Torah" and rule that the halakhah in practice is stricter than the Torah demands. But why would a rabbi go out of his way to note that the Torah is more lenient than the rabbinically ordained halakhah demands?

The key to answering the first question might be hinted at in the geographical location of these two sages. The Tosefta specifically states that R. Yohanan b. Bag Bag sends a message to R. Yehudah b. Batera in Netzivin (Nisibis), a city located in Asia Minor, on the southeastern edge of modern Turkey.[15] R. Yehudah b. Batera was known as a sage of some prominence who set up a center of rabbinic learning outside of the Land of Israel in Netzivin in the period immediately following the Bar Kokhba

---

[14]  There are, however, differences in language between the two clauses, making it possible that this clause entered the toseftan corpus before it was abbreviated in the mishnah.

[15]  For evidence that Netzivin is understood to be the home of R. Yehudah b. Batera, see Tosefta Yevamot 12:11; Yerushalmi Berakhot 3:4, 6c; Yerushalmi Sanhedrin 1:2, 19a; Bavli Pesahim 3a; Bavli Sanhedrin 32b.

revolt. This was a time when Jews, rabbis among them, would have found greater impetus to leave the Land of Israel. In a story from a reconstructed piece of Mekhilta Deuteronomy, several sages are even described as weeping as they leave the Land of Israel to learn Torah in Netzivin with R. Yehudah b. Batera.[16] The tension in this midrashic text is between the study of Torah, which is increasingly found in the Diaspora, and the inherent value of living in the Land of Israel.

This tension between the sages who remained in the Land of Israel and those who left in this moment of crisis provides a background for R. Yohanan b. Bag Bag's message to his colleague. R. Yohanan b. Bag Bag accuses R. Yehudah b. Batera of starting a new center of learning outside of the Land and contradicting the Torah and the practice of the Land of Israel, according to which a betrothed woman did not eat terumah until she entered the huppah. That this was the normative tradition throughout the tannaitic period is evidenced by the fact that **all tannaitic sources** (other than the Mishnah and Tosefta passages cited above) take as a given that only a married woman eats terumah.[17] The clearest example is Mishnah Yevamot 9:4-5: "A daughter of an Israelite betrothed to a priest does not eat terumah… A daughter of an Israelite married to a priest does eat terumah." Especially noteworthy is Sifra Emor, parashah 5, "From where do I know that if a priest **marries** a woman or buys slaves that they might eat terumah? Scripture states, 'a person who is a priest's property by

---

16   See Menahem Kahana, "Maalat Yeshivat Eretz Yisrael," *Tarbiz* 62, 4 (1993), 501-514.

17   See Mishnah Yevamot 9:4-5; Mishnah Eduyot 7:9; 8:2; Mishnah Niddah 5:4; Tosefta Yevamot 10:1-2; Tosefta Ketubot 4:3-4; Tosefta Eduyot 3:2. Mishnah Kiddushin 3:1 might be seen as implying that a woman betrothed to a priest can eat terumah, however the mishnah need not be read as saying so. The mishnah may instead be suggesting that when she enters the huppah with the man to whom she is now betrothed, she will be able to eat terumah. Cf. Shremer, *Zakhar u-Nekevah Bera'am*, 327. Indeed, the rule that the Torah prohibits a betrothed girl from eating terumah can be found even in amoraic literature. On Bavli Kiddushin 44b, there is a debate concerning a minor girl who was betrothed by her father and then was married in his absence and without his permission. Two amoraim use the issue of eating terumah to determine whether the marriage was valid despite the fact that the father did not express his consent. R. Asi says that she does not eat terumah lest her father return and it turns out that a non-priest eats terumah. R. Asi seems to think that even though she was undeniably betrothed to a priest, she would still be considered an outsider for the matter of terumah until marriage occurs.

purchase may eat of them (Leviticus 22:11).'" This is the same verse that is the basis of R. Yehudah b. Batera's *kal vahomer* proving the opposite, that a woman may eat terumah from the point of betrothal.[18] In the Sifra "property by purchase" is equated with marriage, whereas R. Yehudah ben Batera equates it with betrothal.

Furthermore, these traditions would have accorded with the simple understanding of Numbers 18:11-13, which twice states, "Any pure person *in your household* (בביתך) may eat of it." On the most basic level, "in your household" implies that for a woman to eat terumah she must be living with her husband, i.e. she must be married.[19] R. Yohanan b. Bag Bag is angry for he perceives that not only has R. Yehudah ben Batera set up a center of learning outside of the land, but he is rebelling against the practices observed in the Land and enshrined in the Torah itself.

Understanding the geographical tension between these two sages also serves to account for R. Yehudah b. Batera's heated response. R. Yehudah b. Batera anchors his halakhah in normative rabbinic midrashic thinking. He turns the accusation on its head. You, R. Yohanan b. Bag Bag, might be able to attack me for issuing an innovative halakhah, but I can anchor my halakhah in the standard patterns of interpreting the Torah. You, b. Bag Bag may be an expert in the "inner chambers of the Torah" and perhaps you are familiar with the traditions of halakhah. But, R. Yehudah b. Batera continues, you do not know how to argue a *kal vahomer* argument, a hallmark of rabbinic interpretive creativity. He then presents his *kal vahomer*, which leads to the conclusion that a betrothed Israelite woman should be allowed to eat terumah. But significantly, he concludes his words by reassuring R. Yohanan b. Bag Bag that despite his innovative interpretations from outside the land, he remains committed to the teachings of the sages.

Having provided the background to the emotional force of this exchange, we are left to interpret the specific content of the dispute. Why did R. Yehudah b. Batera contradict tradition and the simple meaning of the Torah in order to claim that the **Torah** would allow a betrothed

---

[18]  Mekhilta de-R. Yishmael Nezikin 1, concerning the Hebrew slave, similarly perceives that betrothal does not legally bind the woman to her husband. It states, *"And his wife goes out with him…with him—this excludes his betrothed who is not with him."*

[19]  This is stated explicitly in Yerushalmi Yevamot 9:6, 10c: "Any pure person in your house may eat it" and she is not in his house.

Israelite woman to eat terumah **before marriage?** The key to understanding his motivation is the comparison made in the *kal vahomer* itself. The crux of R. Yehudah b. Batera's argument is that acquisition through money is sufficient to consider a woman to be a part of her husband's household, just as it is sufficient to bring a slave into a master's household. The first mishnah of Kiddushin states that a woman is "acquired through money, a document, or intercourse." R. Yehudah b. Batera wishes to strengthen the nature of the acquisition through money, which is the way in which betrothal is described throughout rabbinic literature. He contends that acquisition through money alone, without the woman moving into her husband's house, is sufficient to allow her to be considered a member of his household and to eat terumah, the sine qua non of being a member of a priest's household. R. Yehudah b. Batera is not concerned with the fact that in practice he cannot enact his law. His *derashah* is meant to amplify the rabbinic theory that betrothal through money alone is strong enough to allow a woman to be considered part of her husband's household. Indeed, the importance of this theory in the eyes of the rabbis may be at least one answer to why that very mishnah in Kiddushin used the term "is acquired" as opposed to the root *k-d-sh*, the verb used elsewhere throughout the tractate. The Mishnah itself wished to strengthen the ties created by betrothal through money such that, after only having been betrothed, a woman could be considered a member of her husband's household.[20]

We can perhaps hear an echo of this argument in the beginning of Yerushalmi Kiddushin:

**Yerushalmi Kiddushin 1:1, 58b**

ירושלמי קידושין א:א (נח, ב)

כיני מתניתא או בכסף או בשטר או בביאה.

This is the correct interpretation of the mishnah: [She is betrothed] either with money, or with a document, or with intercourse.

---

[20] We do not deny that there are not other plausible reasons for why the Mishnah uses this word, a question that is already raised by the Babylonian amoraim. For instance, it is likely that the Mishnah wishes to preserve the literary continuity with the remainder of the chapter where the verb "acquire" is more appropriate. See David Weiss Halivni, "The Use of KNH in Connection with Marriage," *Harvard Theological Review* 57 (1964), 244-248.

ותני ר' חייה כן: לא סוף דבר
בשלשתן אלא אפילו באחד מהן.

And R. Hiyya also taught: It is not necessary for all three, for even one of them [is sufficient].

Here we find the Yerushalmi specifically negating what may have been an earlier understanding of the process of marriage: For a woman to be considered a full member of her husband's household, all three steps must occur. According to this rejected interpretation, the husband must first "acquire" her with money, then give her a document (assumedly the ketubah), and finally engage in sexual intercourse, which would take place upon her moving into his home. Taken together, these were clearly the three normal steps towards marriage. This is evident in one of the eleventh century ketubot examined in Mordechai Akiva Friedman's study of Cairo Geniza Ketbuot:

ואכניש יתה לביתיה וקידשה קידושין
גמורין בכסף ובשטר ובביאה.

He brought her into his house and took her in complete *kiddushin*, by money, by writ, and by intercourse.

The above ketubah was written when the bride was already betrothed. It declares that the groom has concluded the marriage process by giving his wife the ketubah and consummating the marriage.[21] The Yerushalmi adamantly negates this understanding of the mishnah: Any one of the three is sufficient to create a strong, status-changing betrothal, including and especially money alone.

We can thus understand R. Yehudah b. Batera's teaching as part of this trend to strengthen the force of betrothal performed through money alone. Even if R. Yehudah b. Batera admits that there are no practical ramifications to his words, it is important to him to emphasize that the Torah itself, through his midrash (the *kal vahomer*), is evidence of the fact that betrothal performed through money alone is sufficient for a woman to be considered part of her husband's household, even before she moves into his physical home.

---

[21]  See M.A. Friedman, *Jewish Marriage in Palestine*, 202-204.

## The Other Tannaim in the Mishnah and Tosefta

Sections 3 of the mishnah and section 1 of the toseftan halakhah are parallel sources which deal with how much terumah a priest is allowed to give to a woman whom he is responsible to feed. These sections can be read independent of the debate over when a woman begins to eat terumah. They are concerned with how much terumah her husband can give her whenever he might be obligated to feed her.[22] In Yerushalmi Ketubot 5:3, there even appears a baraita, parallel to this section of the mishnah and toseftan halakhah, which is completely independent of the debate over whether a betrothed woman can eat terumah. Perhaps section 3 appears at this point in our Mishnah because of the section (2) that immediately precedes it, "If the time has come and they were not married or their husbands died, they are entitled to receive maintenance from his estate, and [if he is a priest] they may eat terumah." Even if a betrothed woman does not eat terumah until entering the huppah, a daughter of a kohen marrying a kohen could certainly be given terumah. Section 3, concerning how much terumah the priest may give a woman, is therefore relevant here as soon as he begins to feed her. Ultimately, though, sections 2-3 do not provide us with much information about what these particular tannaim thought concerning the issue of when a woman begins to eat terumah.

According to the testimony of R. Menahem b. Kappah and R. Eliezer Hakappar in section 3 of the Tosefta, R. Tarfon, a contemporary of R. Akiva, betrothed three hundred women in order to feed them terumah. R. Tarfon seems to agree with—and even act upon—the position of R. Yehudah b. Batera: On principle, a woman betrothed to a priest can eat terumah; she is not considered a "foreigner" (see Leviticus 21:10) for whom terumah would be strictly forbidden even in the time of famine. However, the story is clearly not brought to demonstrate that **any woman** betrothed to a priest eats terumah. The significance of this testimony is that although general practice was not to give a betrothed woman terumah until she enters the huppah, exceptions could be made, for she is not truly considered a "foreigner." It is also extremely significant that this is the

---

[22] We are not including sections 1b-c of the Tosefta in the discussion here because, as we explained above, they may be secondary insertions into the Tosefta. Concerning 1c see the appendix below.

189

only story in rabbinic literature in which it is related that betrothed women actually ate terumah. R. Tarfon is the only sage whom we know to have actually acted upon R. Yehudah b. Batera's theoretical position. Presumably R. Yohanan b. Bag Bag would have been none too happy.

## Sifre Numbers: "Any Pure Person"—to Include a Betrothed Israelite

A midrash found in the tannaitic composition Sifre Numbers accords with R. Yehudah b. Batera's position that a betrothed woman may eat terumah:

| ספרי במדבר פיסקא קיז | Sifre Numbers piska 117 |
|---|---|
| *כל טהור בביתך יאכלנו* (במדבר יח:יג) *למה נאמר?* | *Any pure person in your home may eat of it* יאכלנו (Numbers 18:13): Why is this stated? |
| *והלא כבר נאמר כל טהור בביתך יאכל אותו ומה תלמוד לומר: כל טהור בביתך יאכלנו?* | For hasn't it already stated, *Any pure person in your home may eat of it* יאכל אותו (ibid 18:11)? Why then does it state, *Any pure person in your home may eat of it* יאכלנו? |
| *להביא את בת ישראל המאורסת לכהן שתהא אוכלת בתרומה.* | To include an Israelite woman betrothed to a priest that she should eat terumah. |
| *או אינו מדבר אלא בנשואה?* | Or perhaps it only speaks of a married woman? |
| *כשהוא אומר כל טהור בביתך יאכל אותו הרי נשואה אמורה.* | When it states, *Any pure person in your home may eat of it* יאכל אותו, it refers to a married woman. |
| *הא מה תלמוד לומר: כל טהור בביתך יאכלנו? להביא את בת ישראל המאורסת לכהן שתהא אוכלת בתרומה.* | Why then does it state, *Any pure person in your home may eat of it* יאכלנו? To include an Israelite woman betrothed to a priest that she should eat terumah. |

Sifre Numbers uses a different midrashic technique to support the same idea that was put forth in the Tosefta by R. Yehudah b. Batera: A woman can begin to eat terumah as soon as she is betrothed. The repetition of the term "may eat of it" is understood to teach something additional, namely that a betrothed woman may eat terumah. In other words, this midrash explicitly states what R. Yehudah b. Batera was hinting at above: A betrothed woman is considered to be part of her husband's household.

The continuation of this passage from the Sifre (not quoted above) relates the dispute between R. Yohanan b. Bag Bag and R. Yehudah b. Batera from the Tosefta. Considered as a whole, this midrash serves to bolster the notion that betrothal is strong enough for the woman to be considered part of her husband's household. Furthermore, when the author of the midrash rhetorically posits, "or perhaps it is only talking about a married woman," only to go on to dismiss this notion, he pointedly disagrees and perhaps may even be taking issue with R. Yohanan b. Bag Bag's insistence that the Torah allows only a married woman, who is physically in her husband's home, to eat terumah.

It is difficult to date this midrash, but it is clearly aware of the dispute between R. Yohanan b. Bag Bag and R. Yehuda b. Batera, suggesting that it comes later. The midrash sides with R. Yehudah b. Batera and musters additional support for the idea that the Torah consistently espouses a strong form of betrothal and allows a woman who is merely betrothed to a priest to eat terumah.

## "If the Time Came and They Were Not Married" (Mishnah, section 3)

We have not yet analyzed the third clause of the mishnah, "If the time came and they were not married [or their husbands died], they (the women) eat from their [husbands'] food and they may eat terumah [if the husband is a priest]." This clause complicates our exploration of the debate concerning when a woman betrothed to a priest may eat terumah. On the one hand, this clause does not state that she may eat terumah immediately at betrothal (the theoretical position of R. Yehudah b. Batera), but on the other hand it also does not state that she must wait until she enters the huppah (the position of R. Yohanan b. Bag Bag and the halakhah as practiced according to all other tannaitic sources and conceded to by R. Yehudah b. Batera).

This clause of the mishnah suggests that the arrival of the date upon which she was supposed to enter his household (marriage) creates a situation in which she is already considered to be in her husband's household.[23] The lapse of the twelve-month period means that the full responsibilities and rights of marriage kick in. As we know from other sources, a person is considered "in someone else's household" when the head of the household has a financial obligation to feed that person.[24] Therefore, from this point and onwards the betrothed woman is allowed to eat terumah, in accordance with Numbers 18:11-13, "Anyone pure in your household may eat of it." In other words, this clause fits the general practice agreed to by all parties: Practically, a woman begins to eat terumah once she is in her husband's household. Usually she becomes part of his household when she physically moves there. However, if he has delayed the marriage, he must treat her as if she is already in her household. Notably this clause has nothing to do with R. Yehudah b. Batera's midrash that she may eat terumah immediately upon betrothal, even before the twelve-month period has lapsed.

The idea of the husband's obligation to provide for his betrothed at the end of the twelve-month waiting period is mentioned in two other places in rabbinic literature. In Mishnah Nedarim it is ascribed to R. Eliezer:

| | |
|---|---|
| משנה נדרים י:ה | Mishnah Nedarim 10:5 |
| בוגרת ששהתה שנים עשר חדש ואלמנה שלשים יום: | A mature girl that has waited twelve months or a widow thirty days— |
| רבי אליעזר אומר: הואיל ובעלה חייב במזונותיה יפר. | Rabbi Eliezer says: Since her husband is obligated to provide her with food, he may break [her vows]. |
| וחכמים אומרים: אין הבעל מיפר עד שתכנס לרשותו. | The sages say: The husband does not break [her vows] until she enters his domain. |

---

[23] In talmudic times, marriage was simply the woman moving into her husband's household. While there clearly were marriage celebrations and feasts, the main rite of marriage is transfer of responsibility from her father's house to her husband's house. See Satlow, *Jewish Marriage in Antiquity*, 68-89. Therefore, it is not such a leap to think that tannaim would consider a woman whose husband has financial obligations towards her to be married, even though no celebration/ritual has actually occurred.

[24] Another example is the case where the father has transferred her to the husband's agents. According to Tosefta Ketubot 4:4, she does not eat until she actually enters her husband's home. Nevertheless, R. Asi in Bavli Ketubot 48b rules that she may eat terumah immediately upon transfer. It seems that whether a woman could eat terumah at these marginal moments was still debated.

R. Eliezer conflates the husband's obligation to feed his wife with his right to break her vows. As we mentioned in the introduction, the Torah teaches that a husband may break his wife's vows "in her husband's house" (Numbers 30:11). Rabbi Eliezer would extend the meaning of "in her husband's house" to any woman being supported financially by her husband's house. As we saw in our mishnah in Ketubot (5:2), after twelve months of delay, a husband is obligated for his betrothed wife's sustenance. Based on this mishnah, R. Eliezer concludes that the lapse of twelve months places her in her husband's household, and therefore the husband can break her vows without her father's consent.

In contrast, the other sages do not connect a husband's right to break his wife's vows with his obligation to feed her. These sages would interpret the biblical verse from Numbers literally—she must have already moved into her husband's house. So long as she is still living with her father, even if she is supported by her husband, she is not considered part of her husband's household.

A halakhah similar to that ascribed to R. Eliezer is found in Sifre Zuta Numbers 18:

**ספרי זוטא במדבר פרק יח**

בביתך (במדבר יח:יג), פרט לבת ישראל
עד שלא זכו במעשה ידיה.

מניין את מרבה משזכו במעשה ידיה
תלמוד לומר: *כל טהור בביתך יאכלנו*
(שם יח:יא).

**Sifre Zuta Numbers ch. 18**

*[Any pure person] in your home [may eat of it]* (Numbers 18:13). This excludes an Israelite woman before her husband has rights to her handiwork.

How do you know to include from the time that he has rights to her handiwork? Scripture states, *any pure person in your home may eat of it* (ibid. 18:11).

This midrash reflects the flip side of the mishnah in Ketubot. While the mishnah used the husband's responsibility to feed his wife as a barometer for when she eats terumah, Sifre Zuta uses his rights to her handiwork as the barometer. This midrash teaches that once he has a right to her handiwork, he may feed her terumah.[25] Presumably he has a right to her handiwork when he starts to provide for her, quid pro quo, even if she is

---

[25] This is a marker for marriage proper. See for instance Mishnah Ketubot 4:4.

still living in her father's home. This is not a synonym for entering the huppah or moving into his domain, for if it were, there would not be a need for the midrash to "include" the fact that she eats at this earlier point.[26] In sum, there are multiple tannaitic midrashim which provide the husband with various rights and responsibilities before the woman physically enters his home.

## The Halakhic Development—Section 4 of the Mishnah and Section 2 of the Tosefta

Both the Mishnah and Tosefta distinguish between an earlier ruling, a "*mishnah rishonah*," which allowed women to eat terumah before entering the huppah, and a "later court "or "rabbis" who ruled that she could not eat terumah until after she entered the huppah. Traditional and modern scholars alike have accepted this line as reflecting actual stages in halakhic history: Earlier sages allowed an Israelite woman betrothed to a priest to eat terumah, but later sages decreed against this halakhah, forbidding a woman from eating terumah until marriage proper.[27]

There are several problems with taking the historical account at face value. First and foremost, the very structure of the interchange between R. Yohanan b. Bag Bag and R. Yehudah b. Batera implies that there was no shift in halakhah from a "*mishnah rishonah*" according to which a betrothed woman could eat terumah to a more restrictive position. R. Yohanan b. Bag Bag's message to R. Yehudah b. Batera may even demonstrate the opposite trend in historical development. R. Yohanan b. Bag Bag is angered that R. Yehudah b. Batera is breaking longstanding

---

26  Cf. Menahem Kahana, *Sifre Bamidbar* (Jerusalem: Magnes Press, 2015), 898 and ibid n. 103.

27  Adiel Schremer, *Zakhar u-Nekevah Bera'am*, 326-333 accepts the presentation in the Mishnah as an accurate portrayal of historical development. See also Robert Brody, *Mishnah ve-Tosefta Ketubot* (Jerusalem: Magnes Press, 2015), 144, who suggests dating the change to the period between R. Tarfon and R. Yehudah b. Batera due to a lack of fastidiousness by non-priests in their treatment of terumah. In contrast, Shmeul Safrai, et. al, *Mishnat Eretz Yisrael: Tractate Ketubot* (Jerusalem: Mikhlelet Lifshits, 2013), 1:311-325 posits that this Mishnah reflected a halakhic division between customs in Judea, where a betrothed woman was treated as if she were already married, and the Galilee, where the separation between betrothal and marriage was more carefully preserved. The Mishnah's Galilean editors ruled according to their concept of betrothal.

custom that a betrothed woman cannot eat terumah until she enters the huppah. This seems to be the earlier, more normative, halakhic position, one that was challenged by R. Yehudah b. Batera's innovative midrash. Furthermore, R. Yehudah b. Batera, a mid-second century sage, already quotes this later court and defers to its authority. It seems exceedingly unlikely that "the later court" was already so well-established by the mid-second century, a period still relatively early in the development of tannaitic halakhah, such that even R. Yehudah ben Batera would not be able to rule against it.

Similarly, in the Tosefta we learned that R. Tarfon betrothed 300 women during the time of famine so that they could eat terumah. Because of the famine, R. Tarfon dispensed with the general prohibition on providing a betrothed woman terumah. This prohibition would have to be that of the later court. Had the earlier halakhah been in effect, R. Tarfon's halakhah would have been exceptional only because of the great number of women he betrothed. But clearly his actions are equally notable because they counter the normative halakhah. R. Tarfon also lived in the middle of the tannaitic period, rendering it unlikely that his actions should already reflect the decree of the "later court."

Strongest of all is the fact that all other tannaitic halakhot follow the later court's decree is suspicious. If there had indeed been a stage in halakhic history in which a woman could eat terumah at betrothal, we would have expected this practice to be reflected in tannaitic halakhah.[28] Typically, early halakhot and halakhic interpretations of biblical texts do not entirely disappear.[29] Rather, even if they are ultimately rejected, they remain at the margins of rabbinic literature, appearing when the direct subject of the halakhah is not addressed. But when the subject of when a woman begins to eat terumah is peripherally addressed, all tannaitic

---

[28] An excellent example of this is the progression with regard to the types of vessels that can be carried on Shabbat. According to Tosefta Shabbat 14:1, originally only three vessels could be carried. This stringency was originally lessened until nearly all vessels could be carried (Mishnah 17:3). However, other mishnayot still reflect the older halakhah, a fact acknowledged by the Bavli itself (Shabbat 123b-124a). It seems that mishnayot not directly related to the subject were not updated to match the latest halakhah.

[29] See for example Aharon Shemesh, *Onashim ve-Hataim min ha-Mikra le-Sifrut Hazal* (Jerusalem: Magnes Press, 2003), 14-18. This example is discussed in our excursus to chapter 8, "Warning a Pursuer."

sources are unanimous: she eats only upon entering the huppah, at marriage.

Finally, the Tosefta itself states in section 1c that an Israelite woman betrothed to a priest does not eat terumah. As we argued above, this clause of the Tosefta is unfamiliar with the description of historical development. In other words, the author of this clause was unfamiliar with the notion that a betrothed Israelite woman could eat terumah, and therefore the author limits any halakhah describing a husband giving terumah to his betrothed to cases of wives of priestly descent. If the *"mishnah rishonah"* was in actuality a normative halakhic position, it is hard to imagine why anyone would have deemed it necessary to add in this clause.

Rather than posit that this section reflects actual historical development in rabbinic halakhic decision making, a development that left no traces elsewhere, it seems more plausible to argue that the addition of this clause is a later editor's attempt to reject the notion that a woman actually begins to eat terumah after the twelve-month waiting period has elapsed.[30] As we saw above, the notion that after this period has passed the woman is considered to be a part of her husband's household is ascribed in Mishnah Nedarim to R. Eliezer and is also found in Sifre Zuta Numbers. Both R. Eliezer and the author of Sifre Zuta Numbers reasoned that since financial responsibilities (providing financially for the betrothed woman) or financial rights (the husband's rights to her handiwork) begin at this twelve-month point, so too do other rights granted by the Torah— the right for her to eat terumah and the right to break her vows.

Rabbi Eliezer and the author of Sifre Zuta Numbers are often "outlying figures" in tannaitic literature, representing marginal positions that are frequently opposed by the majority opinion.[31] Indeed, in Mishnah Nedarim we learn explicitly that the other sages disagree with R. Eliezer— according to the majority opinion, a husband does not annul his wife's

---

[30] J.N. Epstein also suggests that this is a later addition to the Mishnah albeit for different reasons, including the fact that the Naples printed edition of the Mishnah includes this line in Rashi script, indicating that it is a gloss. See *Mavo LeNusah HaMishnah* (Jerusalem: Magnes Press, 1964), 972-973.

[31] See Vered Noam, "Traces of Sectarian Halakhah in the Rabbinic World," *Rabbinic Perspectives: Rabbinic Literature and the Dead Sea Scrolls*, eds. Steven Fraade et. al (Leiden: Brill, 2006), 67-85;" Menahem Kahana, "The Halakhic Midrashim," *The Literature of the Sages. Second Part*, eds. Shmuel Safrai, et. al. (Philadelphia: Fortress Press, 2006), 92-92; Hillel Beitner, *Sifre Zuta Bamidbar le-Farashat Parah* (Jerusalem: Hebrew University Master's Thesis, 2011).

vows until she enters the huppah. Furthermore, in section 3 of Mishnah Ketubot 5:2-3, R. Akiva and R. Tarfon debate how much terumah a husband may provide for his wife. This debate follows section 2, which claims that the husband is allowed to give his wife terumah after the time for marriage has arrived. This structure gives the impression that the two tannaim agree that she may eat terumah before entering the huppah. Even though these two tannaim likely debate this question irrespective of when she may begin to eat terumah, the literary formation of the mishnah creates this impression.

According to this understanding, the final editor of this mishnah introduced the ruling of a "later court"—even though no such court existed—to counter R. Eliezer, Sifre Zuta, as well as a potential misinterpretation of R. Akiva and R. Tarfon. This section relegates the halakhah allowing the woman to eat terumah before she enters the huppah to an earlier point in halakhic history. According to the editor, while this may have once been a valid halakhah, it is no longer observed. We should note that the implication of this suggested reconstruction is that the final editor of the mishnah was adding onto an earlier mishnah consisting of sections 1-3. The ruling in section 2, as we saw, accorded with R. Eliezer and Sifre Zuta, while the final editor ruled according to the sages in Nedarim who disagreed with R. Eliezer.

The immediate question concerning this interpretation is that if section 4 of the mishnah was created in order to rule according to the sages from Mishnah Nedarim, why do Mishnah and Tosefta of Ketubot not simply state, "If the time has come and they were not married or their husbands died they are entitled to receive maintenance from the man's estate and [if he is a priest] they may eat terumah. **But the sages say a woman does not eat terumah until huppah**"? Why present two stages of halakhic history instead of a more straightforward dispute?

Presumably, the editors of Mishnah/Tosefta Ketubot needed to also avoid R. Yohanan b. Bag Bag's opinion. If Mishnah Ketubot had been phrased as a simple dispute, one side holding that she eats terumah after twelve months and the other that she does not until she enters the huppah, this latter position would have been synonymous with the opinion of R. Yohanan b. Bag Bag—**the Torah prohibits** a woman from eating terumah until she enters huppah under any circumstances. In order for the Mishnah to maintain a disagreement with R. Eliezer/Sifre Zuta and hold that in practice a woman does not eat terumah until huppah, while at the same time agreeing with R. Yehudah b. Batera that she theoretically may eat terumah at betrothal, the Mishnah and Tosefta stake a claim of historical development. This claim about historical development accords with R. Yehudah b. Batera by acknowledging the theoretical possibility of a woman eating terumah before huppah, a halakhah that was valid during the time of the "*mishnah rishonah.*" But this claim also echoes R. Yehudah b. Batera's admission that the sages have ruled that it is forbidden, contrary to R. Eliezer/Sifre Zuta's view. According to the mishnah, in practice a woman does not in fact begin to eat terumah (or have her husband break her vows) after the twelve-month period has elapsed, a halakhah ascribed to a decree made by the later court.

The following baraita in the Yerushalmi adds an additional layer to the historical development presented in the sources we have seen thus far regarding eating terumah during the betrothal period:

### Yerushalmi Ketubot 5:4, 29d

ירושלמי כתובות ה:ד (כט, ד)

| | |
|---|---|
| מתניתיתא לא כמשנה הראשונה ולא כמשנה האחרונה אלא כמשנה האמצעית. | Our mishnah is not like the first mishnah nor like the later mishnah but like the intermediary mishnah. |
| דתני: בראשונה היו אומרים ארוסה בת ישראל אוכלת בתרומה דהוון דרשין: *וכהן כי יקנה נפש קניין כספו* (ויקרא כב:יא) דלא כן מה בין קונה אשה ובין קונה שפחה. | As it is taught: At first they said that a betrothed Israelite woman eats terumah, for they expounded: *A person who is a priest's property by purchase* (Leviticus 22:11), for if not so, what would the difference be between a acquiring a wife and acquiring a slave! |
| חזרו לומר לאחר שנים עשר חדש לכשיתחייב במזונותיה. | Then they came back and said [that she eats terumah] after twelve months when he becomes liable to provide her sustenance. |
| בית דין של אחרון אמרו: לעולם אין האשה אוכלת בתרומה עד שתיכנס לחופה. | The last court said: A woman never eats terumah until she enters the huppah. |

This baraita completely historicizes all of the information found in the Mishnah, Tosefta, and Sifre Numbers concerning when a woman is allowed to eat terumah. The baraita goes even a step further than the tannaitic sources, which never stated that in practice a woman would receive terumah immediately upon betrothal. We now have a three-step historical process:

1) The originally practiced halakhic position was R. Yehudah b. Batera's: A woman would receive terumah immediately upon betrothal.

2) A second court decreed that a woman would not be able to eat terumah until the time in which her husband was obligated to provide for her had arrived, after twelve months.

3) The last court prohibited her from eating terumah until she enters her husband's home.

Some scholars have recognized that this baraita is a later construct, one that attempts to historicize and harmonize the varied information found in the Mishnah and Sifre Numbers.[32] But of course, if one is willing to accept that the baraita constructs historical development rather than reflects it, we should countenance the same possibility for the Mishnah and Tosefta themselves.[33]

## Amoraim and Stammaim

As we shall see below, the post-tannaitic sources which address this question all take the Mishnah and Tosefta at face value. The Torah, along with the earliest of rabbinic courts, allowed for a betrothed woman to eat terumah, but a later court ruled that she may only do so upon entering her husband's household. While the Mishnah and Tosefta are silent on the reason for the prohibition, much of the talmudic discussion attempts to account for the change. This question is never addressed in tannaitic literature for, as we saw through our reconstruction of the tannaitic material, there was no real need to answer this question. The Torah legislates that only members of the priest's household eat terumah; a betrothed woman, living in her father's home, is simply not a member of

---

32 See Schremer, *Zakhar u-Nekevah Bera'am*, 326-333.

33 The possibility that the Mishnah presents historical development as a means to achieve other editorial, legal, or pedagogical goals was also noted by Amram Tropper, *Ka-Homer be-Yad ha-Yotzer* (Jerusalem: Zalman Shazar, 2011), 27-45. For more on the concept of "*mishnah rishonah*" see J.N. Epstein, *Mevo'ot le-Sifrut ha-Tannaim* (Jerusalem: Magnes Press, 1957), 21-24.

his household. The practice not to give women terumah until huppah accorded easily with the Torah's laws and made abundant common sense—this particular right would be provided to the woman only after entering her husband's home. In the Tosefta, R. Yehudah b. Batera posited that a betrothed woman could theoretically eat terumah immediately upon betrothal. However, he never advocated for an actual change in practice.

There are two sugyot in the Bavli, one in Ketubot and one in Kiddushin, where amoraim discuss this tannaitic material. The small amount of material in the Yerushalmi on the subject has been addressed above or will be addressed in our discussion of the Bavli. We shall begin with the sugya in Ketubot, which we divide into two parts, considering each in turn. The first part may itself be divided into two major sections, numbered here:

## Bavli Ketubot 57b

 בבלי כתובות נז ע"ב

(1) **אמר עולא**: דבר תורה, ארוסה בת ישראל אוכלת בתרומה, שנאמר: *וכהן כי יקנה נפש קנין כספו* (ויקרא כב:יא), והאי נמי קנין כספו הוא.

(1) Ulla said: The daughter of an Israelite who is betrothed [to a priest] is, according to Torah law, permitted to eat terumah, for it said, *a person who is a priest's property by purchase* (Leviticus 22:11) and that [woman] also is his acquisition through money. What is the reason why they ruled that she is not permitted to eat [terumah]? Lest they mix her a cup [of terumah] in her father's home and she gives it her brother or sister to drink.

מה טעם אמרו אינה אוכלת?

שמא ימזגו לה כוס בבית אביה ותשקה לאחיה ולאחותה.

(1a) אי הכי, הגיע זמן ולא נישאו נמי!

(1a) If so, [the same should apply] if the time had come and they were not married?

התם דוכתא מייחד לה.

In that case, he would designate for her a special place.

(1b) אלא מעתה, לקיט כהן לישראל לא ליכול בתרומה, דלמא אתו למיכל בהדיה!

(1b) If so, a priest harvest worker [working] for an Israelite should not be allowed to eat terumah, since it is possible that [members of the

200

Israelite's household] would come to eat with him!

השתא מדידהו ספו ליה, מדידיה אכלי?

Now that they are feeding him from their own [food], would they really eat of his?

(2) רב שמואל בר יהודה אמר: משום סימפון.

(2) R. Shmuel b. Yehudah said: Because of *simpon*.

(2a) אי הכי, נכנסה לחופה ולא נבעלה נמי!

(2a) If so, [the same should be true] if she entered the huppah but had not yet had relations.

התם מיבדק בדיק לה והדר מעייל.

In that case, he could arrange for her to be first examined and only then take her in.

(2b) אלא מעתה, עבד כהן שלקחו מישראל, לא ליכול בתרומה משום סימפון!

(2b) If so, the slave of a priest, bought from an Israelite, should not be allowed to eat terumah on account of a *simpon*!

סימפון בעבדים ליכא.

There is no *simpon* for slaves.

---

| Tannaitic Source | Amoraic Source | Stammaitic Source |

The earliest stratum of this sugya is formed by the two amoraic statements the first by Ulla (section 1) and the second by R. Shmuel b. Yehudah (section 2). Both amoraim posit that according to the Torah's laws, a woman can begin to eat terumah at the time of betrothal, since she is acquired by her husband with money. They both explain why, in spite of this dispensation, the tannaitic sages ruled that a woman is not actually allowed to eat terumah until huppah. According to Ulla, it is because a woman still living in her father's home might share the terumah with her siblings. According to R. Shmuel b. Yehudah, it is because of *simpon*, a term understood by the amoraim as referring to a stipulation that could annul the betrothal, as we shall discuss more fully in the appendix below.

Most significantly, these amoraim do not directly explain the section of Mishnah Ketubot according to which a woman could eat terumah when the twelve-month period in which marriage was to have taken place has elapsed. Rather, they explain a system similar to that represented by R. Yehudah b. Batera in the Tosefta and reflected in Sifre Numbers, in which there is a dichotomy between biblical law and practice. Indeed, Ulla reiterates the exact point made by R. Yehudah b. Batera in his *kal vahomer*—betrothal performed through money "acquires" a woman and thereby allows her to eat terumah immediately, just as acquisition of a slave allows a slave to eat terumah. Again, we see sages using the issue of terumah to espouse their views on betrothal: Betrothal is strong enough to theoretically place a woman in her husband's household. R. Shmuel b. Yehudah would agree with this point. The only difference between the two amoraim is in their explanation as to why the sages did not allow her to eat terumah until she entered the huppah.

The stam, however, understands Ulla and R. Shmuel b. Yehudah to be explaining the difference between the Torah's rule—she eats at betrothal—and what was referred to in the mishnah as the "*mishnah rishonah*"—she may eat when the twelve-month period has elapsed. This creates significant interpretive difficulties for the stam. If the fear is that she will give terumah to her non-kohanic family (Ulla), why allow her to eat terumah while she still lives there, even after the twelve months have elapsed (1a)? And if the fear is that the marriage will be annulled due to a *simpon*—a term which the stam understands to refer to a physical defect, as we shall see below—then why should she be allowed to eat terumah even after entering the huppah but before having had relations with her husband? Couldn't the marriage be annulled between huppah and sexual relations? The stam offers extremely strained resolutions to these questions. In response to Ulla, the stam suggests that the groom designates a special place for her in spite of the fact that she is not yet in his home. In response to R. Shmuel b. Yehudah, the stam posits that the groom ensures there will not be an annulment because he sends his relatives to physically examine the bride. Clearly, we can sense that the amoraim themselves were not explaining this section of the mishnah. Rather, they were explaining why the sages prohibited women from eating terumah until they had entered the huppah.

The same stammaitic reinterpretation is found in the explanation of the second part of the mishnah, the later court's prohibition:

| בבלי כתובות נח ע"א | Bavli Ketubot 58a |
|---|---|
| זו משנה ראשונה כו'. | "This the first mishnah" |
| מאי טעמא? | What is the reason? |
| אמר עולא, ואיתימא רב שמואל בר יהודה: משום סימפון. | Ulla, or some say R. Shmuel b. Yehudah, say: Because of *simpon*. |

| | |
|---|---|
| בשלמא לעולא, קמייתא שמא ימזגו לה כוס בבית אביה, ובתרייתא משום סימפון. | This works well [if the statement was said by] Ulla. The first [decree] was lest they pour her a cup in her father's house and the later [decree] because of *simpon*. |
| אלא לרב שמואל בר יהודה, קמייתא משום סימפון, ובתרייתא משום סימפון, | But [if the statement was said by R. Shmuel b. Yehudah, the first was because of *simpon* and the latter [was also] because of *simpon*!? |
| מאי בינייהו? | What's the difference between them? |
| איכא בינייהו בדיקת חוץ, | The difference is an external examination: |
| מר סבר: בדיקת חוץ שמה בדיקה, ומר סבר: בדיקת חוץ לא שמה בדיקה. | One [the first decree] held that an external examination is an examination, and the other [the second decree] held that it is not. |

---

Tannaitic Source     Amoraic Source     Stammaitic Source

---

Remarkably, in this sugya the first opinion is attributed to either Ulla or R. Shmuel b. Yehudah, the authors of the two different opinions in the previously discussed sugya. Obviously, this is the exact same statement made by R. Shmuel b. Yehudah above, and simply placed later in the sugya and attributed, at least according to some opinions, to Ulla. This creates the possibility that Ulla could hold that there were three stages in the halakhah, like the baraita found in the Yerushalmi (see above). That is to say, once the stam understood the amoraim above as explaining why a woman could not eat terumah immediately (Torah law) but had to wait for the twelve-month period to elapse (*mishnah rishonah*), they then could take R. Shmuel b. Yehudah's opinion about the *simpon*, attribute it to Ulla, and use it to explain why according to a later court she had to wait until she entered the huppah.

The name of R. Shmuel b. Yehudah, however, was not entirely removed as an attribution of this statement, thereby creating the difficulty that both stages are explained using the same reasoning.[34] The resolution

---

[34] Perhaps the removal of this attribution was simply not possible, or at least unlikely, in the oral recitation of the sugya.

of this difficulty, which suggests the existence of examinations of different intensity, is extraordinarily strained, clearly a hallmark of the stam's strong desire to resolve all difficulties. According to this forced resolution, R. Shmuel b. Yehudah holds that originally the rabbis thought that a superficial external examination[35] was sufficient such that she should be allowed to eat when the time set for marriage had passed. This examination would ensure that the groom would not later push to abrogate the marriage. The later court thought that only a more intimate examination was sufficient to ensure that the marriage would not be annulled by *simpon,* and therefore they decreed that she must wait until huppah when he would be alone with her and could examine her himself.

Solid evidence that these amoraim were not interpreting the mishnah in Ketubot, but were rather explaining the difference between Torah law and the rabbinic stringency, can be found in Ravina's use of these same explanations on Kiddushin 10b in his explanation of the debate between R. Yohanan b. Bag Bag and R. Yehudah b. Batera:

### בבלי קידושין י ע"ב

רבינא אמר: מדאורייתא מיפשט
פשיטא ליה דאכלה, ומדרבנן הוא
דשלח ליה, והכי שלח ליה: שמעתי
עליך, שאתה אומר ארוסה בת ישראל
**אוכלת בתרומה, ולא חיישת לסימפון.**

שלח ליה: ואתה אי אתה אומר כן?
מוחזקני בך שאתה בקי בחדרי תורה,
לדרוש בקל וחומר אי אתה יודע!

ומה שפחה כנענית שאין ביאתה
מאכילתה בתרומה - כספה מאכילתה
בתרומה, ולא חיישינן לסימפון.

### Bavli Kiddushin 10b

Ravina said: It was obvious to him [R. Yohanan b. Bag Bag] that [she could eat] according to Torah law. He sent him a question concerning rabbinic law, and this is what he sent to him: I have heard about you, that you say that a betrothed Israelite woman can eat terumah **and that you are not concerned for *simpon.***

He [R. Yehudah b. Batera] responded: And you do not say this? I assumed that you were an expert in the inner workings of Torah but you do not even know a *kal vahomer* argument!

When it comes to a Canaanite slave, intercourse with her does not acquire her in order to allow her to eat terumah but money does acquire her to allow her to

---

[35] Rashi explains that the examination was conducted by the husband's relatives while she still lived in her father's home.

eat terumah **and we are not concerned about *simpon*.**

זו שביאתה מאכילתה בתרומה - אינו דין שכספה מאכילתה בתרומה, ולא **ניחוש לסימפון.**

This one for whom [acquisition] by intercourse with her does allow her to eat terumah should not [acquisition by] money also acquire her to eat terumah **and we should not be concerned about *simpon*.**

אבל מה אעשה, שהרי אמרו חכמים: ארוסה בת ישראל אינה אוכלת בתרומה עד שתכנס לחופה, משום **דעולא.**

But what can I do for the sages have said that a betrothed Israelite woman does not eat terumah until she enters the huppah **because of Ulla.**

According to Ravina's creative interpretation of the tannaitic debate, the tannaim, R. Yohanan b. Bag Bag and R. Yehudah b. Batera, argue about the same exact issue debated by the amoraim, Ulla and R. Shmuel b. Yehudah. Ravina has mapped the amoraic debate onto the early tannaitic one. The key difference between this source and the sugya in Ketubot is that there is no mention here of beginning to eat terumah after twelve months. Rather, according to Ravina's reconstruction, both tannaim hold that she could eat immediately after betrothal and debate only why the sages made her wait until marriage—exactly as do Ulla and R. Shmuel b. Yehudah according to our reconstrution.[36] Thus, Ravina has simply applied the opinions of Ulla and R. Shmuel b. Yehudah to the disputing tannaim. Indeed, it seems possible that Ravina was familiar with Ulla and R. Shmuel b. Yehudah's statements as explanations to this baraita and not as explanations to the mishnah in Ketubot.

We should also note that, by Ravina's time, the original meaning of R. Yohanan b. Bag Bag's opinion has completely changed. In the Tosefta, as we saw, R. Yohanan b. Bag Bag held that a woman may not eat terumah until she is married and enters her husband's household. There is no reason to assume that he does not believe that even the Torah would prohibit her from terumah before marriage. But according to Ravina, all tannaim—even R. Yohanan b. Bag Bag—agree that according to the Torah a betrothed girl can eat terumah. Since both tannaim agree that in practice she does not eat until huppah, the only disagreement which can

---

[36]   See Tosafot Kiddushin 11a, s.v. עד שתכנס לחופה.

remain between them is why the rabbis prohibited her from eating immediately upon betrothal. R. Yohanan b. Bag Bag believes it is prohibited because of *simpon* (R. Shmuel b. Yehudah) and R. Yehudah b. Batera forbids because of a fear she will feed the terumah to her family (Ulla). Ravina lived after Ulla and R. Shmuel b. Yehudah and clearly quotes their words, but whereas they both seem to have adopted R. Yehudah b. Batera's position (from the Torah she is allowed to eat terumah at betrothal but the sages prohibited it), Ravina has gone a step further and ascribed R. Yehudah b. Batera's position to R. Yohanan b. Bag Bag, the vocal champion of the opposite opinion! The following chart should help illustrate this process:

| Tosefta | Bavli Ketubot | Bavli Kiddushin |
|---|---|---|
| R. Yohanan b. Bag Bag: Torah prohibits terumah until marriage, presumably according to biblical law. | Ulla: Torah allows terumah before marriage, but rabbis prohibit lest she give to her family. | R. Yohanan b. Bag Bag: Torah allows terumah before marriage, but rabbis prohibit lest marriage is annulled. |
| R. Yehudah b. Batera: Torah allows terumah before marriage, but rabbis prohibit. | R. Shmuel b. Yehudah: Torah allows terumah before marriage, but rabbis prohibit lest marriage is annulled. | R. Yehudah b. Batera: Torah allows terumah before marriage, but rabbis prohibit lest she give to her family. |

Perhaps this transformation was a result of Mishnah Ketubot itself, which implies that according to all tannaim, a woman could theoretically eat terumah before entering the huppah. Heavily influenced by the mishnah, Ravina may have been unaware that anyone ever ruled according to the simple meaning of Numbers 18—the Torah prohibits a woman from eating terumah until she physically enters the husband's household.

# Appendix I
## What is a *Simpon*?

Scholars have demonstrated that the word *simpon* comes from Greek and means "codicil," a document that emends rather than replaces a previous agreement.[37] In our case, the *simpon* emends the kiddushin agreement and adds a condition to it, as can be seen from the following source in the Yerushalmi:

| ירושלמי קידושין ג:ב (סג, ד) | Yerushalmi Kiddushin 3:2, 63d |
|---|---|
| ר' אבהו בשם רבי יוחנן: סדר הסימפון כך הוא: אנא פלן בר פלן, מקדש ליך אנת פלניתא ברת פלן, על מנת ליתן ליך מיקמת פלן ומכנסיניך ליום פלן. ואין אתא יום פלן ולא כנסתיך, לא יהוי לי כלום. | R. Abahu [said] in the name of R. Yohanan: This is the order of the *simpon*: I, so and so, son of so and so, betroth you, so and so, daughter of so and so, on condition that I give you a certain thing and that I will bring you into marriage by a certain day. And if that day arrives and I have not yet married you, I will have nothing. |

The *simpon* agreement would annul the betrothal should the husband fail to provide his wife with a certain gift, perhaps an amount of money, and/or not marry her by a prescribed date. Such an agreement has many parallels in other contemporaneous cultures.[38] The word appears elsewhere in rabbinic literature, such as Mishnah Bava Metzia 1:8 and Tosefta Bava Metzia 1:13, where it has the same meaning. Indeed, the extended discussion concerning the *simpon* found in the continuation of this Yerushalmi passage seems to indicate that this was an institution of some practical importance in betrothal practice of their time.[39]

---

[37] See Shamma Friedman, *Mehkarei Lashon u-Minuah be-Sifrut ha-Talmudit* (Jerusalem: Academy of the Hebrew Language, 2014), 182-186; Daniel Sperber, *A Dictionary of Greek and Latin Legal Terms* (Ramat Gan: Bar Ilan University Press, 1985), 117.

[38] Asher Gulak, "Simpon be-Erusin lefi ha-Talmud ha-Yerushalmi," *Tarbiz 5* (1934), 126-133.

[39] Its usage may have continued even to a much later period. A fragment of a ketubah found in the Cairo Geniza reads, "דאתי לתלתא ירחין." M.A. Friedman, *Jewish Marriage in Palestine*, 1:196 suggests that this might be connected to the Yerushalmi's *simpon*.

However, other scholars claimed that in the talmudic passages that we have dealt with above (Bavli Ketubot 57b-58a, 58b and Kiddushin 10b-11a), the meaning of *simpon* is different and is derived from a different Greek word altogether. Some claimed it came from a word which means a bodily defect, while others explained that the word "*simpon*" actually came from the Greek word "*symptom*," as in the "symptom" of a disease; the "t" was accidentally dropped.[40] Yet it seems highly unlikely that the word "*simpon*" in Mishnah and Tosefta Bava Metzia and the same word "*simpon*" in Bavli Ketubot and Kiddushin are actually derived from two different Greek words.

If we analyze the two parallel Babylonian passages from Ketubot and Kiddushin, we can see that R. Shmuel b. Yehudah, who uses the word *simpon* in our sugya, understood it in the original way, to mean codicil. He explains that a woman eats terumah only once she enters the huppah because of *simpon*. This statement in and of itself can easily be explained in the same way as it appears in the Yerushalmi: A betrothed woman cannot eat terumah until she enters the huppah, lest the betrothal be annulled due to a stipulation on the agreement. After she enters the huppah (his domain), the betrothal could not be annulled through a *simpon,* so there would be no such concern. Similarly, Ravina's statement in Kiddushin, which is based upon R. Shmuel b. Yehudah's statement, is also reflective of the original meaning of the word: Ravina holds that, according to R. Yohanan b. Bag Bag, a woman could theoretically eat terumah immediately upon betrothal, but does not because we are concerned that the marriage might be annulled due to a *simpon*. There were several sages known as Ravina, but since Ravina argues here with R. Nahman b. Yitzhak, a late fourth century amora, we can date Ravina as being from a similar or slightly later period. In other words, towards the end of the Babylonian amoraic period, the word still seems to have been understood according to its original meaning.

The meaning of the word begins to change only in the stammaitic layer of the text. The stam understands that *simpon* refers to something that may cause the betrothal to be annulled. Perhaps the stam even understands that the term is connected to a condition placed on the kiddushin.[41] However, the stam is not familiar with the original legal

---

[40] See Sperber, ibid., who himself accepts this interpretation.
[41] This is Rashi's understanding in his commentary on Ketubot 57b.

context for such an annulment, the document described in the Yerushalmi. Not knowing what this *simpon* actually was, and not understanding the Greek word itself, the stam connects it with a law found elsewhere in the Mishnah concerning the annulment of betrothal, namely Mishnah Ketubot 7:7-8. According to these mishnayot, a man may make the betrothal conditional upon the woman not having physical defects. Thus, *simpon* becomes synonymous with physical defects—defects which can only be exposed by examining the woman, presumably by the husband at the time of their first sexual relations, which take place after she enters the huppah.

Scholars who have claimed that the word has a different derivation in the Bavli than it does in Eretz Yisraeli texts and that the "t" dropped out of the Greek word for "symptoms" were led astray by the different historical levels in the Bavli's sugya. The original derivation was known in Babylonia by a third generation amora (R. Shmuel b. Yehudah) and even by a member of the fifth or sixth generation (Ravina). The other interpretation, that the word means defects or diseases, was simply a misinterpretation by the stam.

# Appendix II
## Abaye's Emendation of the Tosefta

In our discussion of the baraita preserved in the Tosefta above, we noted that section 2 (which recounts a development in halakhah, from an older position which allowed a betrothed Israelite woman to eat terumah, to a more restrictive position prohibiting her from terumah until she enters the huppah) was inconsistent with section 1c (which stipulated that only a betrothed woman **of priestly descent** is allowed to eat terumah). That is, the early part of the baraita states that an Israelite woman betrothed to a priest receives only non-sacred produce, thereby precluding any situation whereby an Israelite woman would begin to eat terumah before entering the huppah. However, later in this same baraita, we hear that a later court decreed that an Israelite woman does not eat terumah until she enters the huppah. In the context of the Tosefta, this makes no sense, for earlier it was already stated that an Israelite woman does not eat terumah while still betrothed.

As we noted above, Abaye, a fourth century amora, emended this baraita so that the two sections would accord more easily. Below is a chart comparing the original toseftan baraita, Abaye's emendation as quoted in the Bavli, and the baraita as it appears in Bavli Ketubot:

| Tosefta Ketubot 5:1 | Abaye's statement, Bavli Ketubot 58a | Babylonian baraita, Bavli Ketubot 58a |
|---|---|---|
| ר' טרפון אומר: נותנין לה הכל תרומה. | | תניא נמי הכי, רבי טרפון אומר: נותנין לה הכל תרומה, ר"ע אומר: מחצה חולין ומחצה תרומה; |
| מן ?אמורים דברים במי האירוסין אבל מן הנשואין מודה ר' טרפון שנותנין לה מחצה חולין ומחצה תרומה במי דברים אמורים? בבת כהן לכהן אבל בת ישראל לכהן הכל מודים שמעלין לה כל מזונותיה מן החולין. | אמר אביי: מחלוקת - בבת כהן לכהן, אבל בבת ישראל לכהן - דברי הכל מחצה חולין ומחצה תרומה. | במה דברים אמורים - בבת כהן לכהן, אבל בת ישראל לכהן - דברי הכל מחצה חולין ומחצה תרומה. |
| R. Tarfon says: He can give her all her food in terumah. To what does this refer? From betrothal, but after marriage R. Tarfon agrees that he gives her half terumah and half non-sacred produce. To what does this refer? To a daughter of a priest betrothed to a priest. **But with regard to the daughter of an Israelite betrothed to a priest everyone agrees that he gives all of her food as non-sacred produce.** | Abaye said: There is a dispute concerning a daughter of a priest [betrothed] to a priest. **But with regard to a daughter of an Israelite betrothed to a priest everyone agrees [that he gives her] half non-sacred produce and half terumah.** | It was similarly taught in a baraita: R. Tarfon says: He gives her all her food in terumah. R. Akiva says: Half non-sacred produce, half terumah. To what does this refer? To a daughter of a priest betrothed to a priest. **But with regard to the daughter of an Israelite betrothed to a priest everyone agrees [that he gives her] half non-sacred produce and half terumah.** |

Abaye emends the original version as found in the Tosefta to read: "But with regard to a daughter of an Israelite betrothed to a priest everyone agrees [that he gives her] **half non-sacred produce and half terumah**." According to Abaye, an Israelite woman betrothed to a priest receives half of her food in terumah. This leaves room for the decree of the later court which prohibited an Israelite woman from eating terumah until marriage.

Abaye's rewording of the baraita impacted the transmission of the baraita itself and hence, when the Bavli quotes the baraita, it appears in its emended form and serves as a support for Abaye. For our purposes, this textual history demonstrates how difficult the baraita originally was. According to the authors of the section in the Tosefta which states that the betrothed daughter of an Israelite receives only non-sacred produce, there was never any need for a later court to decree that an Israelite woman did not eat terumah until entering the huppah. Such a halakhah never even existed.

# CHAPTER FIVE

## ALL MY SONS: ANCIENT NEAR EASTERN CUSTOM AND BIBLICAL INHERITANCE LAW

## KETUBOT 90B-91A

### Introduction: The *Benin Dikhrin* Clause

The last part of the fourth chapter of Mishnah Ketubot lists marriage contract conditions that are binding upon the husband even if he does not include them in the written marriage contract, the ketubah. This section is unique in the mishnaic landscape for several reasons. These legal stipulations were clearly part of the common marriage law of the Ancient Near East and are not rabbinic in origin or even "Jewish." This is evidenced not just by the fact that they are written in Aramaic, the lingua franca of the Near East and not the language typically used in the Mishnah, but also by the prevalence of these laws in Ancient Near Eastern law codes that originated over one thousand years prior to the Mishnah. Similar clauses, if not in wording then at least in content, appear in the Israelite marriage documents found in Elephantine, Egypt, in the fifth century B.C.E.[1] These clauses and their history have been discussed by Mordecai Akiva Friedman in his magisterial work, *Jewish Marriage in Palestine*.[2]

This chapter discusses the clause found in Mishnah Ketubot 4:10: "Male sons (בנין דכרין) that you will have through me, they will inherit your ketubah beyond the share with their brothers." The clause refers to a

---

[1] For more on the community and their documents see Yochanan Muffs, *Studies in the Aramaic Legal Papyri from Elephantine* (Leiden: Brill, 2002); Alejandro Botta, *The Aramaic and Egyptian Legal Traditions at Elephantine: An Egyptological Approach* (London: T & T Clark, 2009).

[2] Mordechai Akiva Friedman, *Jewish Marriage in Palestine: A Cairo Geniza Study* (Tel Aviv: Tel Aviv University, 1981).

case where a husband has more than one wife, either simultaneously, or one after the other. The stipulation guarantees that the sons of one wife will not inherit the ketubah of the other wife. The term ketubah in this clause and in other instances in rabbinic literature includes both the dowry given to the wife by her father and the marital payment contributed by the husband.[3] The clause becomes significant if the ketubah of one wife is greater than the ketubah of the other wife, or if one wife has more sons than the other. The intent of the clause is to incentivize the father-in-law to give a higher dowry to his daughter by increasing the likelihood that the property he gives will be inherited by his grandsons and thus remain within his biological family. For example, Jacob is married to two women—Rachel and Leah—who each enter the marriage with their own dowry. Rachel comes from a rich family and her dowry is significantly greater than Leah's. If Rachel dies before Jacob, he inherits her dowry and it becomes part of his estate. According to biblical law, when Jacob dies his estate will be divided equally among all of his children (with the firstborn taking a double share). This presents a problem because Leah's children, who have no biological connection to Rachel, will inherit part of Rachel's dowry. The *benin dikhrin* clause responds to this concern and ensures that only Rachel's sons will inherit her dowry.

This clause seems to have been the source of some angst in rabbinic circles and was not adopted wholeheartedly. We should note that according to rabbinic law, the *benin dikhrin* rights are limited to sons. Daughters do not inherit their mother's ketubah, at least not through the *benin dikhrin* clause. For instance, if a man is married to two women and they both predecease him, if he has only daughters, the inheritance would be divided equally among all of his daughters regardless of the disparity between their mother's ketubot, or a disparity in the number of daughters born to each mother. Only sons receive their mother's ketubah through the *benin dikhrin* clause. Clearly, this limitation is patterned after the general Jewish laws of inheritance, in which females have fewer rights than males.[4] Furthermore, were a girl to inherit her mother's ketubah from her father, and thereby deprive her brother (same father, different mother) of

---

[3]  See Friedman, ibid., 310-311.

[4]  As is stated in Bavli Ketubot 52b. On inheritance by daughters in tannaitic law see Jonathan Milgram, *From Mesopotamia to the Mishnah: Tannaitic Inheritance Law in Its Legal and Social Contexts* (Tübingen: Mohr Siebeck, 2016) 105-131.

some or even all of his inheritance from his father, the normal, biblical laws of inheritance would be all the more disrupted. Thus, the rabbis limited this clause to sons, and insisted that the phrase "male sons" be written explicitly in the ketubah itself. [5]

In contrast, pre-rabbinic ketubot found in the Judean desert do not contain the word *dikhrin*, Aramaic for male. In these marital documents, it is possible to understand "*benin*" as children, sons or daughters.[6] This seems to be largely true of these types of laws in Ancient Near Eastern law in general—the daughters of the mother inherit her dowry in the absence of sons.[7] After all, the logic of the clause, to ensure the passing of the dowry through bloodlines, should hold whether the offspring are male or female. Consider, for instance, the Laws of Hammurabi which do not specify whether it is males or females who inherit:

> If a man marries a wife and she bears him children, and later that woman goes to her fate, and after her death he marries another woman and she bears children, after which the father then goes to his fate, the children will not divide the estate according to the mothers; they shall take the dowries of their respective mothers and then equally divide the property of the paternal estate. *Laws of Hammurabi* 167

As we shall see, the application of this law to sons alone in rabbinic literature was only one of several limitations placed on the rule by the rabbis, many of which may be explained in light of the fear that *benin dikhrin* inheritance is a deviation from biblical law.

## *Benin Dikhrin* and the Fear of Overriding Biblical Inheritance Law

Even though it excludes girls from the right to inherit their mother's ketubah through their fathers, the *benin dikhrin* clause still disrupts the automatic nature of the Torah's laws of inheritance. The Torah requires a father to bequeath his firstborn son a double portion of inheritance

---

[5]   This limitation contrasts with the opinion of R. Zechariah b. Hakatzav in Tosefta Bava Batra 7:10, who rules that sons and daughters share equally in the inheritance of their mothers. See Friedman, ibid., 83; Milgram ibid., 115-118.

[6]   Friedman, ibid., 382.

[7]   See Milgram, ibid., 124-127.

(Deuteronomy 21:15-17). The anonymous voice of the mishnah demands a strict adherence to biblical inheritance law:

| משנה בבא בתרא ח:ה | Mishnah Bava Batra 8:5 |
|---|---|
| האומר איש פלוני בני בכור לא יטול פי שנים, איש פלוני בני לא יירש עם אחיו, לא אמר כלום, שהתנה על מה שכתוב בתורה. | A man who says, "So and so, my firstborn son, shall not receive a double portion" or "So and so, my son, shall not inherit with his brothers," has said nothing, for he has stipulated a condition contrary to what is written in the Torah. |

The firstborn son receives a double portion and the remaining sons divide the rest equally.[8] The rabbis do not allow individuals to make statements that undermine biblical law. In contrast, the *benin dikhrin* clause will almost always undermine these two principles. If the mother of the (father's) firstborn son has a lower ketubah than the mother of non-firstborn sons, he will end up receiving a lower portion. And the entire inheritance of the father will be distributed equally among the other sons only if the mother's ketubot were exactly equal. Therefore, both Talmuds connect the *benin dikhrin* clause with the opinion of R. Yohanan b. Berokah found in the same Mishnah.[9]

| משנה בבא בתרא ח:ה | Mishnah Bava Batra 8:5 |
|---|---|
| רבי יוחנן בן ברוקה אומר: אם אומר על מי שהוא ראוי ליורשו, דבריו קיימין. | R. Yohanan b. Berokah says: If he said this of one that was qualified to inherit from him, his words remain valid. |
| ועל מי שאין ראוי ליורשו, אין דבריו קיימין. | But if of one that was not qualified to inherit from him, his words do not remain valid. |

R. Yohanan b. Berokah allows the father to disrupt biblical inheritance and give preferential inheritance to any biblically-sanctioned inheritor.[10] And indeed, this is the intended effect of the *benin dikhrin* clause: to give

---

[8]  The mishnah continues with a description of a gift-giving process which allows the father to circumvent the Torah law. See Milgram, ibid. 43-52.

[9]  See Yerushalmi Bava Batra 8:5 (16b); Bavli Bava Batra 130a.

[10]  See Milgram, ibid. 85-89.

the sons of one wife preferential inheritance over the sons of another wife, all motivated by the father of the wife, who wishes to ensure that his property is transmitted to his own grandchildren.

This dislodging of biblical inheritance is mitigated in Mishnah Ketubot 10:2 (quoted below), according to which the sons receive their *benin dikhrin* ketubah only if there remains in their father's estate an extra dinar to be divided evenly, according to the rabbinic understanding of biblical inheritance. That is, the mother's dowry is removed from the estate and then divided evenly among her sons alone, but all the father's sons equally divide the extra dinar from their father's estate. Through this extra dinar, the laws of biblical inheritance are minimally fulfilled, and thereby not completely dislodged by the *benin dikhrin* inheritance.

There is no evidence of such a requirement in Ancient Near Eastern law or in pre-rabbinic marital documents. These laws and documents wish to ensure that a woman's dowry passes to her children (not just sons), and with such a goal in mind, it matters not whether any other estate remains to be divided equally. The angst concerning the relationship of *benin dikhrin* and biblical laws of inheritance is, as we surely would have expected, the result of the rabbinic desire to harmonize biblical law with normative practice. This angst is articulated in both Talmuds, but is expressed most clearly in the tenth chapter of the Yerushalmi, in a sugya related to a mishnah we discuss at length below:

| | |
|---|---|
| **Yerushalmi Ketubot 10:2, 33d** | ירושלמי כתובות י:ב (לג, ד) |
| Perhaps [*benin dikhrin* is valid] even if there is no extra dinar? | מעתה אפילו אין שם יתר דינר. |
| R. Avun said: When you can fulfill their (the sages') words and the words of the Torah, fulfill their words and the words of the Torah. | אמר ר' אבון: בשעה שאת יכול לקיים דבריהן ודברי תורה, את מקיים דבריהן ודברי תורה. |
| When you cannot fulfill their words and the words of the Torah, nullify their words and fulfill the words of the Torah. | בשעה שאת אין יכול לקיים דבריהן ולקיים דברי תורה, את מבטל דבריהן ומקיים דברי תורה. |

The solution is typical of the scholastic nature of rabbinic legalism, in which the rabbis seek to clearly define the parameters of biblical inheritance. Biblical law really is uprooted by the *benin dikhrin* clause, but the bare minimum necessary is still fulfilled in a symbolic manner. If, however, there is not enough in the estate for biblical inheritance to be fulfilled even minimally, biblical law is not allowed to be uprooted entirely.

## The Limits of *Ketubat Benin Dikhrin*

As we saw in the passage from the Laws of Hammurabi quoted above, the scenario used to illustrate the sons' preferential inheritance of their mother's dowry is the case where one wife dies before her husband and one after. In Near Eastern law, the order in which the women and their husband dies does not seem to matter—the right of the children to their mother's dowry is absolute. This accords with the goal of these clauses and laws in the first place—to offer absolute protection of the dowry. But Mishnah Ketubot 10:2-3 illustrates this law only in the case where both wives die while the husband is still alive:

| משנה כתובות י:ב-ג | Mishnah Ketubot 10:2-3 |
|---|---|
| מי שהיה נשוי שתי נשים ומתו ואחר כך מת הוא ויתומים מבקשים כתובת אמן ואין שם אלא שתי כתובות חולקין בשוה. | If a man was married to two wives and they died, and subsequently he died, and the orphans [of one of the wives] claim their mother's ketubah and there is only enough for the two ketubot, they [all the orphans] divide it equally. |
| היה שם מותר דינר אלו נוטלין כתובת אמן ואלו נוטלין כתובת אמן. | If there was a surplus of [at least] one dinar, these take their mother's ketubah and these take their mother's ketubah. |
| אם אמרו יתומים: אנחנו מעלים על נכסי אבינו יתר דינר כדי שיטלו כתובת אמן, אין שומעין להן אלא שמין את הנכסים בבית דין. | If the orphans [of one of the wives] says, "We are raising the estate of our father by a dinar [more than the total amount of the ketubot]," in order to take their mother's ketubah, they are not listened to; rather the estate is evaluated by the court. |

| | |
|---|---|
| היו שם נכסים בראוי אינן כבמוחזק. | If there was property that would soon belong to the estate, it is not [regarded] as [property held] in possession. |
| רבי שמעון אומר: אפילו יש שם נכסים שאין להם אחריות אינו כלום עד שיהיו שם נכסים שיש להן אחריות יותר על שתי הכתובות דינר. | R. Shimon says: Even if there was movable property, it is not regarded [as part of the estate] unless there was real estate worth one dinar more than [the total amount of] the two ketubot. |

According to the mishnah, in order for both sets of sons to inherit their mothers' *benin dikhrin* ketubah, the estate must be sufficient to cover both dowries and for there to remain an extra dinar to be divided equally, according to the biblical laws of inheritance as understood by the rabbis. The mishnah proceeds to add three details concerning this extra dinar. First, the sons are not allowed to artificially inflate the inheritance such that it would be sufficient to cover both dowries. Second, the evaluation of the estate includes only property currently in the estate's possession. Third, at least according to R. Shimon, the evaluation includes only real estate, not chattel.

The mishnah illustrates these halakhot in a case where both women die while the husband is still alive. It does not seem that the intent of the mishnah is to imply that the *benin dikhrin* clause is operable **only** when both women predecease the husband; it is likely that this example is chosen for the sake of simplicity. However, a limited reading of the mishnah could lead to the conclusion that the *benin dikhrin* inheritance may not take effect unless both wives predecease the husband.

The preceding mishnah in Ketubot considers the case where the husband predeceases his two wives:

### משנה כתובת י:א     Mishnah Ketubot 10:1

| | |
|---|---|
| מי שהיה נשוי שתי נשים ומת, הראשונה קודמת לשניה ויורשי הראשונה קודמים ליורשי שניה. | If a man was married to two wives and died, the first wife takes precedence over the second, and the heirs of the first wife take precedence over the heirs of the second. |

נשא את הראשונה ומתה, נשא שניה ומת הוא, שניה ויורשיה קודמים ליורשי הראשונה.

If he married a first wife and she died and then he married a second wife and he died, the second wife and her heirs take precedence over the heirs of the first wife.

If a man dies and leaves two wives, the first wife's ketubah takes precedence over that of the second wife because the debt to the first wife was incurred before the debt to the second wife. Therefore, if after the first wife collects her ketubah not enough money remains to pay the second wife, she will not receive her full ketubah. But if the first wife dies and then the man dies, then the second wife or her heirs collect first because they are collecting a normal ketubah and they are treated as creditors who come to collect a debt. In contrast, the first wife's inheritors are collecting an inheritance which they have received from their mother (as stipulated in the *benin dikhrin* clause), and the payment of debts always takes precedence over inheritance. Therefore, the second wife or her heirs receive their ketubah, and only if enough money remains will the first wife's heirs receive their ketubah.

The difference between the first wife's heirs and the second wife's heirs in the second part of the mishnah can be understood by considering what will happen when the second wife—the only one still alive when her husband dies—in turn dies some time after her husband's death. This second wife's children will inherit her ketubah/dowry directly from her when she dies, for the ketubah was owed to her from the moment her husband died, and her children are her primary inheritors. In other words, her husband never inherited her dowry from this wife, so her sons will not need to inherit their mother's dowry through their father.

The mishnah highlights the difference between biblical inheritance, directly from the mother, and rabbinic inheritance, the *benin dikhrin* ketubah, which is taken out of the inheritance of the father. In the first clause, both sets of sons are inheriting their mother's ketubah through their mother. Since the inheritance of both sets of sons is of biblical origin, the first debt must be paid first. But in the second situation, the claim of the first sons for their mother's ketubah/dowry is only of rabbinic origin through the *benin dikhrin* clause. Therefore, they lose their precedence over their brothers. In contrast, Ancient Near Eastern law and early marital documents make no such distinction—children inherit their mother's ketubah/dowry in all cases without exception. We might even assume that in non-rabbinic law, if there was not enough in the estate to cover both dowries, the first children would take precedence, for their marriage was first. But such a law is found nowhere in rabbinic literature—all rabbis distinguish between the biblical inheritance of the children of the second wife and the rabbinic inheritance of the children of the first. The attention paid to the theoretical origins of the law and not just its content and purpose is a hallmark of rabbinic thinking.

The tannaim, amoraim, and stammaim, however, do have a significant debate over whether the sons of the first wife in such a situation would receive their mother's dowry through the laws of *benin dikhrin* at all. The question could be framed in the following way: We know that according to the tannaim (Mishnah Ketubot 10:2), in order for there to be *benin dikhrin* ketubah inheritance, there must also be biblical inheritance, even if it is just a dinar. Can the sons of the second wife's inheritance of their mother's ketubah be considered biblical inheritance such that the first sons could subsequently inherit their mother's ketubah through the *benin dikhrin* clause? Or, because the second sons are inheriting from their mother and not their father, does the inheritance of the second sons' dowry not count as the required biblical inheritance? If the latter is true, this would mean that the second sons would inherit their mother's dowry and then the rest of the estate, **including the first wife's ketubah**, would be divided equally among **all** the children, in order for the biblical inheritance of the father's estate to occur. If the latter is not true, then then both sets of sons receive their mother's ketubah and the remainder is divided equally. To emphasize, the rabbis' insistence on the fulfilment of biblical inheritance could now undermine the entire intent of the *benin dikhrin* clause, because the dowry that originated with the father of the wife who predeceased her husband would be transferred to sons not related to him.

We shall now examine the tannaitic material on this question, and then note how it expands into an even broader dispute in the amoraic and stammaitic periods.

## Yerushalmi Baraita: Inheritors or Creditors?

Chronologically, the earliest material on this issue is found in a baraita in the Yerushalmi, one that has no parallel in the Tosefta but does in the Bavli.[11]

| ירושלמי כתובות י:א (לג, ד) | Yerushalmi Ketubot 10:1, 33d |
|---|---|
| ...ליורשי הראשונה. | ...take precedence over the heirs of the first wife. |
| אמר בן ננס: יורשי הראשונה אומרים ליורשי השנייה אם כבעל חוב אתם טלו את שלכם וצאו ואם לאו אנו ואתם נחלוק בשוה. | Ben Nanas said:[12] The inheritors of the first [wife] say to the inheritors of the second [wife]: "If you are creditors, collect what is yours and leave; and if not, we will divide [the inheritance] equally." |
| אמר לו רבי עקיבה: בני שנייה קפצה עליהן ירושת תורה, ונוטלין כתובת אמן וחוזרין וחולקין. | R. Akiva said to him: The inheritance according to Torah [law] jumped to the children of the second [wife]. They collect their mother's ketubah and then divide the remainder. |

The Yerushalmi begins with a brief reference to the final line of the mishnah, indicating that the proceeding baraita refers to a case where the first wife died while the husband was alive, and the second wife died after his death. It seems that even the wife who died after the husband's death has not yet collected her ketubah, which would have been the normal protocol in most situations. The children of the second wife are creditors—their father's estate owed the ketubah/dowry to their mother, and now the estate owes it to them. However, they are also inheritors of their father's estate. There is some potential conflict in terms of their role,

---

[11] David Weiss Halivni has convincingly demonstrated that the original version of this baraita is that found in the Yerushalmi, and that only through it, and not through the abbreviated parallel in the Bavli, can the original tannitic dispute be understood. The following interpretation of the baraita closely follows Halivni's interpretation. See Halivni, *Mekorot u-Mesorot: Seder Nashim* (Tel Aviv: Dvir, 1968), 235-238.

[12] This text is corrected based on Halivni's emendation. The Leiden manuscript mistakenly reads Ben Azzai. See ibid., 236.

for by taking their mother's ketubah/dowry and then expecting to divide the remaining estate equally, they are taking more than their share of the inheritance. Put another way, they simultaneously have the right to diminish the estate (as creditors of their mother's ketubah) and to divide it as inheritors. Sometimes it would be an advantage for them to act primarily as creditors, for instance if their mother's ketubah was greater than the amount of inheritance due to them. But it could also be advantageous for them to act as inheritors of their father's estate, for instance if the ketubah owed to their mother is less than the share owed to them in the inheritance. The dispute in the baraita is over whether they can be both—i.e. creditors vis a vis their mother's ketubah and at the same time inheritors of their father's estate and divide the remainder of the inheritance evenly.

Ben Nanas demands that the sons of the second wife must make a choice. They have the option to collect their mother's ketubah and then give the rest to the sons of the first wife as their *benin dikhrin* ketubah. Or they can act as inheritors and divide up the entire estate evenly, without either party receiving their mother's ketubah. But they cannot act as both inheritors and creditors. What this means is that if the sons of the second wife take their mother's ketubah, the sons of the first wife will receive their mother's ketubah. But if the second sons do not take their mother's ketubah, then the first sons will also not receive the ketubah of their mother—the entire estate will be divided among all sons equally as inheritance.

Ben Nanas ensures that there is some degree of fairness in the system, for in either case the two sons' rights are equal. Either both sets of sons receive their mothers' ketubot, or they all divide the inheritance equally. However, in reality the first wife's sons' rights are still more limited because the choice belongs to the sons of the second wife. They will always have the lower hand vis a vis the sons of the second mother—they will never get more than the lower of the two sums, their mother's ketubah or their share of the inheritance. In any case, it is difficult to ascertain Ben Nanas' stance with regard to the rights of the first sons to their mother's ketubah as *benin dikhrin* inheritors because their rights are entirely dependent on the choice made by the sons of the second wife. The lack of clarity on this thinking may have contributed to its modification in the Bavli, as we shall see below.

R. Akiva disagrees and holds that even if the sons of the second wife collect their mother's ketubah, they retain their rights as inheritors of their father's estate. The Torah inheritance "jumps" to them—meaning they have the luck to inherit both their mother's ketubah and their father's inheritance by biblical law. They may collect the ketubah debt and then still divide the rest of the inheritance equally with the sons of the first wife. The sons of the first wife will not receive their mother's ketubah because she died while her husband was still alive and he inherited her dowry. Since the second sons do not receive their mother's dowry through the *benin dikhrin* clause, for they received it as a biblical inheritance, the first sons also do not receive their mother's ketubah through *benin dikhrin*. *Benin dikhrin* inheritance, to Rabbi Akiva, would occur only when both sets of sons can inherit their mother's ketubah **through benin dikhrin**—if one set receives their mother's ketubah through biblical inheritance, then the entire *benin dikhrin* clause is inapplicable. Note, that R. Akiva's ruling limits the applicability of the *benin dikhrin* clause and shows a strong preference for the fulfillment of the normal order of biblical inheritance. The second sons inherit their mother's ketubah by biblical law, and then all of the sons divide the inheritance equally, again according to biblical law.

## Yerushalmi Amoraim: Is There an Extra Dinar?

In the Yerushalmi, two amoraim dispute the circumstances surrounding the tannaitic dispute, in light of the mishnah's requirement that there be an extra dinar in order to allow the enactment of the *benin dikhrin* ketubah:

| ירושלמי כתובות י:א (לג, ד) | Yerushalmi Ketubot 10:1, 33d |
|---|---|
| רבי מנא אמר: כשיש שם דינר יתר נחלקו, אבל אם אין שם דינר יתר אף רבי עקיבה יודה לבן ננס שאילו ואילו חולקין בשוה. | R. Mana said: The dispute is [in a situation] where there is an extra dinar, but if there is no extra dinar even R. Akiva would agree with Ben Nanas that these and those divide evenly. |
| אמר ליה רבי יוסי בי רבי בון הך דלא תניתא פליגא את עבד ליה פליגא. | R. Yose b. R. Bun said to him: That which was not taught as a dispute you are making into a dispute! |

אלא כשאין שם יתר דינר נחלקו אבל אם
יש שם יתר דינר אף בן ננס יודי לרבי
עקיבה בני השנייה קפצה עליהן ירושת
תורה ונוטלין כתובת אמן וחוזרין וחולקין

Rather, the dispute is [in a situation] where there is no extra dinar; but if there is an extra dinar, even Ben Nanas would agree with R. Akiva that inheritance according to Torah [law] jumped to the children of the second [wife]. They collect their mother's ketubah and then divide the remainder.

The chart below summarizes how these two amoraim frame the dispute between Ben Nanas and R. Akiva. As we shall see, half of each statement makes sense, namely their statements as to where the dispute exists, but the other half of each of their statements, where they determine the point of agreement, is in both cases exceedingly difficult.

|  | Extra Dinar | No Extra Dinar |
|---|---|---|
| R. Mana | Dispute:<br>Ben Nanas: Second sons have choice:<br>1) Take ketubah and then let first sons take theirs, and then divide extra<br>2) Divide the entire estate equally.<br><br>R. Akiva: Second sons take ketubah and the rest is divided equally | R. Akiva agrees with Ben Nanas: Both sets of sons divide the entire inheritance equally. |
| R. Yose | Ben Nanas agrees with R. Akiva: The second sons receive their mother's ketubah and then the rest is divided equally. | Dispute:<br>Ben Nanas: Second sons have choice:<br>1) Take ketubah and then let first sons take theirs, and then divide extra<br>2) Divide the entire estate equally.<br><br>R. Akiva: Second sons take ketubah and the rest is divided equally |

The first half of R. Mana's statement makes sense even if it does not precisely accord with the language of the baraita.[13] If there is an extra dinar, R. Mana says that Ben Nanas would give the sons of the second wife the choice to take the ketubah or divide the inheritance. Since there is an extra dinar beyond the value of the two ketubot to fulfill biblical inheritance, if the second wife's sons decide to take their mother's ketubah (collecting a debt) and then the sons of the first wife take their mother's ketubah as their *benin dikhrin* inheritance, there is still an extra dinar with which to fulfill biblical inheritance. If the second sons decide not to take their mother's ketubah, then all sons divide the entire estate as inheritance. In either case, biblical inheritance occurs. R. Akiva would say that the second sons collect their mother's ketubah as a debt and all of the sons divide the rest evenly as inheritance. R. Akiva, according to this view, holds that since one wife died after her husband's death, there is no *benin dikhrin* inheritance for any of their sons. It does not matter that there is an extra dinar beyond the value of the two ketubot.

The problem is with the second half of R. Mana's statement. According to R. Mana, if there is no extra dinar then all parties agree that the father's entire inheritance is divided equally. This is extremely problematic. Why would R. Akiva hold that in such a case the second sons lose their mother's ketubah? After all, this is a debt inherited directly from their mother. Under no circumstances should they lose the right to recover this debt. And why would Ben Nanas hold that the sons of the second wife do not at least have the option of collecting the ketubah debt? Again, since this is a debt, how can it be denied to the second sons?

Turning to R. Yose, we can again make sense of part of his statement, but not all of it. R. Yose opens with a difficulty against R. Mana—the latter posits a tannaitic dispute about a case not referred to in the baraita (where there is an extra dinar). The phrase "collect what is yours and leave" implies that the baraita refers to a case where there is no extra dinar that could be divided in inheritance after the division of the two ketubot. The second wife's sons collect their entire ketubah and leave because there will be nothing left to divide after the sons of the first wife collect their mother's ketubah. Therefore, R. Yose argues that it is specifically in the case where there is no extra dinar that the two tannaim dispute. According to Ben Nanas, even though there is no extra dinar, the sons of the second

---

13   As pointed out by Halivni, ibid., 237.

wife can still either take their mother's ketubah and let the first sons have the rest, or choose to divide the whole inheritance equally. R. Akiva would say that the first sons lose their mother's ketubah and the second sons can take their mother's ketubah and divide the rest of the inheritance with the first sons. This as we shall see, accords with an opinion in the Tosefta and with the opinion of R. Shimon in a baraita in the Bavli. Without an extra dinar, the sons of the first wife do not receive the *benin dikhrin* ketubah at all.

As was the case with R. Mana's statement, the second half of R. Yose's statement is exceedingly difficult. If there is an extra dinar, he posits that all **tannaim agree that the second sons receive their mother's ketubah and the rest is divided evenly**. Why, we would need to ask, would Ben Nanas hold that if there is an extra dinar the first sons lose their *benin dikhrin* ketubah? On the contrary, Ben Nanas should be all the more adamant that the first sons can receive their *benin dikhrin* ketubah in such a case, since there **is an extra dinar to be divided up as biblical inheritance!**

The classical commentators on the Yerushalmi—the P'nei Moshe, the Korban ha-Edah, and others—all agree that due to these difficulties, the Yerushalmi must be emended. Academic scholars are generally hesitant about emending texts in order to solve difficulties, but there are three justifications in this case:

1) The text of the Yerushalmi was preserved in its entirety in a single manuscript (Leiden) and the scribe of this manuscript himself testifies that the manuscript from which he copies is replete with errors.

2) The repetitive words in this section lend themselves to errors in copying. In such cases, once errors are made, they are at times incorrectly emended by subsequent copyists who may have inserted corrections into the wrong places.

3) The version preserved by Leiden and printed editions simply makes no sense. Any attempt to explain the sugya in its current form would be the result of a slavish devotion to justifying the reading of a text simply because it is the single text that survived.[14]

The classical commentators emend the text to read as follows:

---

[14] For more on the textual issues surrounding the Leiden manuscript see Yaakov Sussman, *Talmud Yerushalmi according to Ms. Or. 4720 (Scal. 3) of the Leiden University Library* (Jerusalem: Academy of the Hebrew Language, 2005), 17-35.

רבי מנא אמר: כשיש שם דינר יתר נחלקו, אבל אם אין שם דינר יתר אף בן ננס יודי לרבי עקיבה בני השנייה קפצה עליהן ירושת תורה ונוטלין כתובת אמן וחוזרין וחולקין.

R. Mana said: The dispute is [in a situation] where there is an extra dinar; but if there is no extra dinar, even Ben Nanas would agree with R. Akiva that inheritance according to Torah [law] jumped to the children of the second [wife]. They collect their mother's ketubah and then divide the remainder.

אמר ליה רבי יוסי בי רבי בון: הך דלא תנינתא פליגא את עבד ליה פליגא.

R. Yose b. R. Bun said to him: That which was not taught as a dispute you are making into a dispute!

אלא כשאין שם יתר דינר נחלקו אבל אם יש שם יתר דינר אף רבי עקיבה יודה לבן ננס שאילו ואילו חולקין בשוה.

Rather, the dispute is [in a situation] where there is no extra dinar; but, if there is an extra dinar, even R. Akiva would agree with Ben Nanas that these and those divide evenly.

This revision of the text, which flips the points of agreement, leads to a far more logical reading.

| | Extra Dinar | No Extra Dinar |
|---|---|---|
| R. Mana | Dispute:<br>Ben Nanas: Second sons have choice:<br>1) Take ketubah and then let first sons take theirs, and then divide extra<br>2) Divide the entire estate equally<br><br>R. Akiva: Second sons take ketubah and the rest is divided equally | Ben Nanas agrees with R. Akiva: The second sons receive their mother's ketubah and then the rest is divided equally. |

|  | **Extra Dinar** | **No Extra Dinar** |
|---|---|---|
| **R. Yose** | R. Akiva agrees with Ben Nanas: Both sets of sons divide the entire inheritance equally (unless the second sons wish to take their ketubah and let the first sons have theirs). | Dispute: Ben Nanas: Second sons have choice: 1) Take ketubah and then let first sons take theirs, and then divide extra 2) Divide the entire estate equally. R. Akiva: Second sons take ketubah and the rest is divided equally |

The cases of dispute remain the same as explained above. For R. Mana, in the case of the extra dinar, Ben Nanas allows the second sons to choose to act as inheritors or creditors. R. Akiva posits that it matters not that there is an extra dinar through which biblical inheritance could be fulfilled. R. Akiva simply holds that unless both women die while the husband is still alive, there is no *benin dikhrin* ketubah: The sons of the second wife collect their mother's ketubah as a debt and the rest is divided evenly. According to the emended version of the second half of R. Mana's statement, it is now Ben Nanas who concedes to R. Akiva when there is no extra dinar. Clearly, in such a situation, R. Akiva would retain his opposition to the application of the *benin dikhrin* clause. Ben Nanas' position would shift: Since there is no extra dinar as is required by the mishnah, the sons of the first wife do not receive their *benin dikhrin* ketubah, for this would uproot biblical inheritance. In this case, there is no choice but to give the sons of the second wife their mother's ketubah and to divide the rest evenly.

R. Yose criticizes R. Mana for positing a dispute in a case where there is no dispute. To R. Yose, there is no dispute when there is an extra dinar. In such a case, because there is biblical inheritance, even R. Akiva would agree that if the second sons decide to collect their *benin dikhrin* ketubah, the first sons may collect theirs; biblical inheritance will be carried out with the extra dinar. Alternatively, the second sons could decide to divide the entire estate evenly, and again biblical inheritance would be carried out.[15] The two tannaim dispute only if there is no extra dinar. In such a case, R. Akiva would say that since there is no extra dinar, there can be no *benin dikhrin* ketubah for the sons of the first wife. Ben Nanas would say that the first sons can still receive their mother's *benin dikhrin* ketubah if the sons of the second wife choose to take theirs. It is possible that Ben Nanas disagrees in principle with the mishnah that holds there must be an extra dinar beyond the value of both ketubot. Perhaps Ben Nanas is simply unconcerned that the biblical inheritance would be uprooted by the rabbinic *benin dikhrin* enactment. Alternatively, Ben Nanas may hold that this situation is different because the second sons are receiving some sort of "biblical inheritance"—they are inheriting the debt owed to their mother. This idea is given an abstract name in the Bavli—"the [second] ketubah can be considered the extra amount [needed for] the other ketubah [to be collected]." We shall discuss this idea in greater depth below.

If we boil these two opinions down, R. Yose really seems to hold that even R. Akiva would agree that there is a *benin dikhrin* ketubah if only one wife dies while the husband is still alive. R. Akiva simply limits this to a case where there is also an extra dinar such that there can be equally divided biblical inheritance. In essence, the tannaim do not have a principled disagreement over the applicability of the *benin dikhrin* ketubah in the case where only one wife dies first. The only issue is that biblical inheritance must still occur. This, as we shall see, is similar to Rabbah in the Bavli. In contrast, R. Mana would hold that R. Akiva objects to the *benin dikhrin* enactment unless both wives predecease the husband. Ben Nanas holds that the *benin dikhrin* clause is operative regardless of who dies first, so long as there is an extra dinar with which to fulfill biblical inheritance. This, as we shall see, is similar to R. Yosef in the Bavli. Read in this way, the opinions of these two amoraim are not merely

---

15 R. Yose only states that "all agree that they divide evenly." But since R. Akiva agrees with Ben Nanas, he must also agree that if the second sons wish to take their mother's ketubah, the first sons will also be able to do so. It seems that R. Yose has abbreviated R. Akiva's opinion. Clearly, the second sons always have a right to collect their debt. The thrust, therefore, of Ben Nanas' opinion is that if this is not advantageous to them, they can deny the first sons their right to their *benin dikhrin* ketubah and divide the whole estate equally. Thus, R. Yose quotes only the essential part of Ben Nanas' rule, not the obvious part. This same phenomenon occurs with R. Shimon's position in the Babylonian baraita discussed below.

an attempt to limit or frame the tannaitic dispute. They are in their essence the beginning of the abstraction of these opinions vis a vis the larger question of whether the *benin dikhrin* ketubah is applicable in all cases, even when one woman was still alive when her husband died.

## The Tosefta and the Bavli's Baraita

Continuing with our survey of tannaitic literature, the issue of whether the first sons receive their *benin dikhrin* ketubah if the husband predeceases one of the wives is discussed in the Tosefta and in a parallel baraita in the Bavli.

| בבלי כתובות צ ע"ב | תוספתא כתובות י:א |
|---|---|
| דתניא: נשא את הראשונה ומתה, נשא את השניה ומת הוא, **באין בניה של זו לאחר מיתה ונוטלין כתובת אמן.** | נשא את הראשונה ומתה נשא את השניה ומת הוא, |
| רבי שמעון אומר: אם יש מותר דינר - אלו נוטלין כתובת אמן ואלו נוטלין כתובת אמן. | והיה שם יתר דינר, אילו נוטלין כתובת אמן ואילו נוטלין כתובת אמן ושאר חולקין. |
| ואם לאו - חולקין בשוה. | ואם אין שם יתר דינר **שניה ויורשיה נוטלין כתובת אמן** והשאר חולקין בשוה. |

**Bavli Ketubot 90b**

If he married a first wife and she died and then he married a second wife and he died,

**the sons of this (second) come after her death and collect their mother's ketubah.**

R. Shimon says: If there is an extra dinar, these (the sons of the first wife) collect their mother's ketubah, and these (the sons of the second wife) collect their mother's ketubah, and if not, they divide [the estate] equally.

**Tosefta Ketubot 10:1**

If he married a first wife and she died and then he married a second wife and he died,

if there is an extra dinar, these (the sons of the first wife) collect their mother's ketubah, and these (the sons of the second wife) collect their mother's ketubah, and if not **the second wife or her sons collect their mother's ketubah,** and they divide the rest [of the estate] equally.

The Tosefta refers clearly to the same scenario found in the mishnah and discussed in the R. Akiva and Ben Nanas baraita. The major difference between the toseftan halakhah and its parallel in the Bavli is that the Tosefta contains only one opinion, which accords with R. Shimon in the Bavli. The Tosefta/R. Shimon simply plugs the normal laws governing *benin dikhrin* into this situation. If there is an extra dinar, then both sets of sons receive their mother's ketubah; biblical inheritance will be executed on this extra dinar. If not, the sons of the second wife receive their mother's ketubah[16] and the rest is divided equally. According to David Weiss Halivni, this is an interpretation of R. Akiva's rule from the baraita.[17] According to the Tosefta, R. Akiva did not offer principled objection to the application of *benin dikhrin* to this case; he only objected to it if it completely uprooted biblical inheritance. As long as there remains a dinar for all of the sons to divide equally, they each take their mother's ketubah and divide the rest evenly, just as they would if both mothers predeceased the husband. Furthermore, according to our emendation of the Yerushalmi (see above), the Tosefta/R. Shimon would agree with R. Yose's interpretation of R. Akiva's opinion. This also seems to be the simple reading of Mishnah Ketubot 10:1—the second sons have a priority in collecting their mother's ketubah, because it is a debt. But the first sons can still collect their mother's *benin dikhrin* ketubah if anything remains.

The baraita in the Bavli is clearly a parallel to the Tosefta, but it is also significantly different. Below, when discussing the Bavli, we will address the particulars of this baraita and how it differs from the Tosefta. Here we will just note the most significant change. Whereas the Tosefta contains only one opinion, the baraita contains both an anonymous opinion and the opinion of R. Shimon. According to a straightforward reading of this baraita, one that will ultimately be rejected in the Bavli, the authors of the first opinion hold that even if there is an extra dinar, the sons of the second wife receive their mother's ketubah and then the rest is divided evenly. There is only *benin dikhrin* when both women die while the

---

16 While R. Shimon does not explicitly state this, as we explained above, this has to be the meaning of his statement. Indeed, under no circumstances can the second sons be denied the right to their mother's ketubah since this is a debt. See Rashi s.v. חולקין בשוה.

17 Halivni, ibid., 237 attributes this opinion to R. Shimon based on the baraita in the Bavli.

husband is still alive. Halivni treats this clause a presenting an authentic tannaitic position, one absent in any text earlier than the Bavli. We will return to this issue below in our analysis of the Bavli. This opinion, according to Halivni, is a more expansive view of R. Akiva. R. Akiva objects in principle to the *benin dikhrin* clause unless both women died while their husband was still alive. We can also note that this reading of the first opinion in the Bavli is also a reflection of R. Mana's opinion, namely that even if there is an extra dinar, R. Akiva still holds that the second sons take their mother's ketubah and the rest is divided evenly. Thus, even if we might doubt whether this line is an authentic tannaitic creation, it does accurately represent an amoraic presentation of a tannaitic stance.

## Historical Development of the Bavli Sugya
## Bavli Ketubot 90b-91a

THREE STAMMAITIC DEDUCTIONS ON THE MISHNAH

| | |
|---|---|
| **נשא את הראשונה...** | **If he married the first woman...** |
| שמע מינה תלת: | Conclude from this three [laws]: |
| (1a) שמע מינה, אחת בחייו ואחת במותו - יש להן כתובת בנין דכרין, ולא חיישינן לאינצויי. | (1a) Conclude from it that if one [of the man's wives died] in his lifetime and one died following his death, then [the sons of the first wife] collect the *ketubat benin dikhrin* and we are not concerned that this would lead to quarreling. |
| | From where is it known? |
| ממאי? | From the fact that [the mishnah] |
| מדקתני: שניה ויורשיה קודמים ליורשי ראשונה מיקדם הוא דקדמי, הא איכא שקלי. | teaches: The second wife and her heirs precede the heirs of the first wife, [this implies] that they precede [the heirs of the first], but if there is [enough in the estate for all the claims against it], then the children of the first wife do take [their *ketubat benin dikhrin*]. |
| (1b) ושמע מינה, כתובה נעשית מותר לחברתה, | (1b) And conclude from it that one ketubah can be the surplus for the other. |
| ממאי? | From where is it known? |

מדלא קתני אם יש שם מותר דינר.

From the fact that [the mishnah] does not teach: If there is an extra dinar [in addition to the value of all the ketubot].

**(1c)** ושמע מינה, כתובת בנין דכרין לא טרפה ממשעבדי,

(1c) And conclude from it that a *ketubat benin dikhrin*, cannot be collected from encumbered property.

דאי סלקא דעתין טרפה ממשעבדי, ליתו בני ראשונה ולטרפינהו לבני שניה.

For if you should think that it can be collected from encumbered property, then let the sons of the first wife come and collect it from the sons of the second wife.

AMORAIC OBJECTION TO THE FIRST TWO DEDUCTIONS

**(2a)** מתקיף לה רב אשי: ממאי? דלמא לעולם אימא לך: אחת בחייו ואחת במותו - אין להן כתובת בנין דכרין,

(2a) Rav Ashi objected: From where do you know this? Perhaps I could actually say to you: If one [of the man's wives died] in his lifetime and one died following his death, no one is entitled to the ketubat *benin dikrhin*.

**(2b)** ומai קודמין? לנחלה קתני!

(2b) And what [does the mishnah mean when it says] "take precedence"? It teaches [the sons of the second wife collect the ketubat *benin dikhrin* before the remainder of] the inheritance [is divided among of the sons].

**(2c)** וכי תימא יורשי הראשונה למה לי? איידי דתנא שניה ויורשיה, תנא נמי ליורשי הראשונה.

(2c) And if you say, why do I [need the mishnah to mention] the heirs of the first wife? Since the mishnah mentions the second wife and her heirs, the mishnah also mentions [the parallel phrase]: The heirs of the first wife.

**(2d)** ודקאמרת: כתובה נעשית מותר לחברתה, דלמא לעולם אימא לך: אין כתובה נעשית מותר לחברתה, והכא הוא דאיכא מותר דינר.

(2d) And [regarding] that which you said—that one ketubah can be the surplus for the other—perhaps I could actually say to you that one ketubah cannot be the surplus for the other, and here [the mishnah refers to a case where] there is an extra dinar.

233

## INTRODUCTION OF A BARAITA

(3a) ואחת בחייו ואחת במותו תנאי היא,
דתניא: מתו אחת בחייו ואחת במותו, בן
ננס אומר: יכולין בני הראשונה לומר
לבני השניה: בני בעלת חוב אתם, טלו
כתובת אמכם וצאו. ר' עקיבא אומר: כבר
קפצה נחלה מלפני בני הראשונה ונפלה
לפני בני השניה.

(3a) The case where one wife died in his lifetime and one died following his death is [the subject of] a tannaitic dispute. As it is taught in a baraita: If they died, one in his lifetime and one following his death, Ben Nanas says: The sons of the first wife can say to the sons of the second wife: You are the children of a creditor, collect your mother's ketubah and leave. R. Akiva says: The inheritance already jumped away from the sons of the first wife and fell before sons of the second wife.

## STAMMAITIC EXPLANATION OF THE BARAITA

(3b) מאי לאו בהא קא מיפלגי? דמר
סבר: אחת בחייו ואחת במותו - יש להן
כתובת בנין דכרין, ומר סבר: אחת בחייו
ואחת במותו - אין להן כתובת בנין
דכרין.

(3b) Is it not that they disagree about this: One master (Ben Nanas) holds that [in a case] where one wife died in his lifetime and one died following his death, [the first wife's sons] collect the ketubat *benin dikhrin*. And one master (Rabbi Akiva) holds that [in a case] where one wife died in his lifetime and one died following his death, [the first wife's sons] do not to collect the ketubat *benin dikhrin*?

## AMORAIC DISPUTE OVER THE INTERPRETATION OF THE BARAITA

(4a) אמר רבה, אשכחתינהו לרבנן דבי
רב דיתבי וקאמרי: דכולי עלמא, אחת
בחייו ואחת במותו - יש להן כתובת בנין
דכרין, והכא בכתובה נעשית מותר
לחברתה והוא הדין לבעל חוב קמיפלגי:

(4a) Rabbah said: I found the rabbis of the school of Rav sitting and saying: Everyone agrees that [in a case] where one wife died in his lifetime and one died following his death, [the first wife's sons] collect the ketubat *benin dikhrin*. But here, there is a dispute if one ketubah can be the surplus for the other and similarly regarding a creditor.

234

מר סבר: כתובה נעשית מותר לחברתה
והוא הדין לבעל חוב, ומר סבר: אין
כתובה נעשית מותר לחברתה והוא הדין
לבעל חוב.

One master (Ben Nanas) holds that one ketubah can be the surplus for the other and similarly regarding a creditor. And one master (Rabbi Akiva) that one ketubah cannot be the surplus for the other and similarly regarding a creditor.

ואמינא להו אנא: בעל חוב - כולי עלמא
לא פליגי דהוי מותר, כי פליגי -
בכתובה.

And I said to them: [Regarding] a creditor, everyone agrees that it is permitted. They disagree in the [case of] the ketubah.

(4b) מתקיף לה רב יוסף: אי הכי, רבי
עקיבא אומר: כבר קפצה נחלה, אם יש
מותר דינר מיבעי ליה!

(4b) Rav Yosef objected: If that is so, [that the dispute is over whether the ketubah counts as a surplus] then why did [the baraita state] Rabbi Akiva says: The inheritance already jumped away? Rather, it should have stated: If there is an extra dinar!

אלא אמר רב יוסף: באחת בחייו ואחת
במותו קא מיפלגי.

Rather, Rav Yosef said: They disagree regarding [the case] where one wife died in his lifetime and one died following his death.

INTRODUCTION OF A BARAITA

(5a) והני תנאי כי הני תנאי:

(5a) And these tannaim are like those tannaim:

דתניא: נשא את הראשונה ומתה, נשא
את השניה ומת הוא, באין בניה של זו
לאחר מיתה ונוטלין כתובת אמן.

As it is taught in a baraita: If he married a first wife and she died and then he married a second wife and he died, the sons of this woman (the second wife) come after her death and collect their mother's ketubah.

רבי שמעון אומר: אם יש מותר דינר -
אלו נוטלין כתובת אמן ואלו נוטלין
כתובת אמן, ואם לאו - חולקין בשוה.

R. Shimon says: If there is an extra dinar, these (the sons of the first wife) collect their mother's ketubah, and these (the sons of the second wife) collect their mother's ketubah, and if not, they divide [the estate] equally.

STAMMAITIC EXPLANATION OF THE BARAITA

(5b) מאי לאו בהא קא מיפלגי, דמר
סבר: אחת בחייו ואחת במותו - יש להן
כתובת בנין דכרין, ומר סבר: אחת בחייו
ואחת במותו - אין להם כתובת בנין
דכרין!

(5b) Is it not that they disagree about this: One master (Rabbi Shimon) holds that in a case where one wife died in his lifetime and one died following his death, [the sons of the first wife] collect the ketubat *benin dikhrin*; and one master (the *tanna kamma*) holds that in a case where one wife died in his lifetime and one died following his death, [the sons of the first wife] cannot collect the ketubat *benin dikhrin*?

(5c) לא, דכולי עלמא אחת בחייו ואחת
במותו - יש להן כתובת בנין דכרין, והכא
בדינר מקרקעי קמיפלגי, מר סבר:
מקרקעי אין, מטלטלי לא, ומר סבר:
אפילו מטלטלי.

(5c) No, everyone agrees that [in a case] where one wife died in his lifetime and one died following his death, [the sons of the first wife] collect the *ketubat benin dikrhin*, but here they disagree if the [extra] dinar was in real estate: One master (the *tanna kamma*) holds that if [the extra dinar was in] real estate, then yes, [they can collect the *ketubat benin dikhrin*], but if [the extra dinar was in] movable property, then no, [they cannot collect]. And one master (R. Shimon) that [they can collect] even [if the extra dinar was in] movable property.

(5d) ומי מצית אמרת הכי?
והתנן, ר' שמעון אומר: אפילו יש שם
נכסים שאין להם אחריות - אינן כלום,
עד שיהא שם נכסים שיש להן אחריות
יתר על ב' כתובות דינר!

(5d) But how can you say that? Did not we learn in the Mishnah: R. Shimon says: Even if there was movable property, it is not regarded unless there was real estate worth one dinar more than [the total amount of] the two ketubot?

(5e) אלא, הכא בדינר משעבדי קמיפלגי,
מר סבר: מבני חורין אין, ממשעבדי לא,

(5e) Rather, here they disagree about a dinar of encumbered property: One

236

ומר סבר: אפילו ממשעבדי.

master (the *tanna kamma*) holds that if [the surplus was in the form of] free property [that is currently in the estate], then yes, [each can claim the ketubat *benin dikhrin*], but if [the surplus was in] encumbered property then no. And one master (R. Shimon) holds that [it is a surplus] even if it was encumbered property.

(5f) אי הכי, ר"ש אומר: אם יש שם מותר דינר, כיון שיש שם מותר דינר מיבעי ליה!

(5f) If that is so, [that the baraita refers to a case where there is encumbered property], [then why did the baraita state] "Rabbi Shimon says: If there is an extra dinar," it should have said: "Since there is an extra dinar"!

(5g) אלא בפחות מדינר קמיפלגי, מר סבר: דינר אין פחות מדינר לא, ומר סבר: אפילו פחות מדינר.

(5g) Rather, the dispute is regarding [a case] where there is less than a dinar: One master (the *tanna kamma*) holds that if [the surplus was worth] a dinar, then yes, [each can collect the ketubat *benin dikhrin*], but if it was less than a dinar then no. And one master (R. Shimon) holds even if it was less than a dinar.

(5h) והא ר' שמעון דינר קאמר! וכי תימא איפוך, תנא קמא דמתניתין נמי דינר קאמר!

(5h) But did not R. Shimon say: "If there is a dinar" [and not less]. And if you say: Reverse the [sons referenced in the interpretation of the baraita, that cannot be] because the *tanna kama* of the mishnah also said that a dinar [is necessary]!

(5i) אלא כי הנך תרי לישנאי קמאי ואיפוך.

(5i) Rather, [the dispute in the baraita must be explained] according to those first two interpretations, [that they disagree about movable property or encumbered property], and reverse [our understanding of the baraita: The *tanna kamma* holds the sons of the first wife may collect the ketubat *benin dikhrin* if there is an extra dinar of movable property or encumbered property, whereas R. Shimon holds that there must be an extra dinar of real estate that is not encumbered].

## AMORAIC HALAKHIC RULING

(6a) אמר מר זוטרא משמיה דרב פפא, הלכתא: אחת בחייו ואחת במותו - יש להן כתובת בנין דכרין, וכתובה נעשית מותר לחברתה.

(6a) Mar Zutra said in the name of R. Pappa: The halakhah in the case where one wife died in his lifetime and one died following his death is [that the sons of the first wife] collect the ketubat *benin dikhrin*, and one ketubah can be the surplus for the other.

## STAMMAITIC INTERPRETATION

(6b) בשלמא אי אשמעינן אחת בחייו ואחת במותו יש להן כתובת בנין דיכרין, ולא אשמעינן כתובה נעשית מותר לחברתה, הוה אמינא, אי איכא מותר דינר - אין, אי לא - לא, אלא לישמעינן כתובה נעשית מותר לחברתה, ואנא ידענא משום דאחת בחייו ואחת במותו יש להן כתובת בנין דכרין!

(6b) It makes sense, if he had taught only that [in a case] where one wife died in his lifetime and one died following his death, [the sons of the first wife] collect the ketubat *benin dikhrin*, and he would not have taught that one ketubah can be the surplus for the other, I would say that if there is an extra dinar, then yes, [the sons of the first wife can claim their ketubat *benin dikhrin*], but if not, then no. However, let him teach us only that one ketubah can be surplus for the other, and I would know that it is because if one wife died in his lifetime and one died following his death, [the sons of the first wife] collect the ketubat *benin dikhrin*!

(6c) אי אשמעינן הכי, הוה אמינא, כגון שנשא שלש נשים ומתו שתים בחייו ואחת במותו, והך דמיית לאחר מיתה יולדת נקבה היא, ולאו בת ירושה היא, אבל אחת בחייו ואחת במותו והא דלאחר מיתה יולדת זכר היא, אימא ליחוש לאינצויי, קא משמע לן.

(6c) If he would have taught only that, I would say [that this applies in a case] where a man married three women, and two of them died in his lifetime and one after his death, and that wife who died after his death had given birth to a daughter, and she is not eligible for inheritance. However, [in a case] where one wife died in his lifetime and one died after his death, where the one who died after his death had given birth to a son, one could say that there is a concern about quarreling. Therefore, [Mar Zutra] teaches us [both halakhot to clarify that this is not taken into account].

---

| Tannaitic Source | Amoraic Source | Stammaitic Source |

The Bavli's sugya can be broken into four sections whose order of appearance in the sugya does not reflect their historical development. Schematically the structure of the sugya is as follows:

Sections 1-2)    Two conflicting views, one anonymous and one attributed to R. Ashi, concerning how to understand the mishnah in light of the main issues in the sugya—does the law of the *benin dikhrin* ketubah apply when only one wife predeceases her husband? And, if it does, can the ketubah of the second wife be considered the "extra dinar" necessary for the first sons to collect their mother's ketubah?

| | |
|---|---|
| Sections 3-4) | A dispute between Rabbah and R. Yosef, two third-generation Babylonian amoraim, as to how to understand the Ben Nanas and R. Akiva baraita. |
| Section 5) | An analysis by the stam of the Babylonian version of the baraita from the Tosefta. |
| Section 6) | A halakhic ruling by Mar Zutra, another late Babylonian amora, accompanied by a few stammaitic remarks on his ruling. |

Even before we analyze each section, we can note the thread that runs throughout the entire sugya. In each section, there is a dispute about whether the first sons receive their *benin dikhrin* ketubah in the case under discussion, when only one wife predeceases the husband. What began in the tannaitic period as a dispute in which R. Akiva said that they never receive this ketubah and Ben Nanas said that they can receive this ketubah, but only if the second sons choose to take their mother's ketubah, is transformed by the end of the amoraic period into a undisputed halakhic ruling that they do receive the *benin dikhrin* ketubah, and that there is not even a necessity for an extra dinar in such a case because "one ketubah can be the surplus for the other."

We will now examine these sections, but not in the order of their appearance. Rather we will discuss them in the order of their historical development.

## Section 3: The Bavli Ben Nanas/R. Akiva Baraita

In this section Rabbah and R. Yosef, two mid-third century Babylonian amoraim, disagree over the interpretation of the Babylonian version of the Ben Nanas/R. Akiva baraita. As we noted earlier, this baraita has no parallel in the Tosefta, though it appears in the Yerushalmi. We will begin our discussion by examining the baraita itself, in comparison with the version found in the Yerushalmi.

The Babylonian version of the baraita differs in several critical ways from the version found in the Yerushalmi, and indeed these differences are one of the linchpins in understanding the history of the halakhot of the *benin dikhrin* ketubah.

**Bavli**

מתו אחת בחייו ואחת במותו,
בן ננס אומר: יכולין בני הראשונה לומר
לבני השנייה בני בעלת חוב אתם, טלו
כתובת אמכם וצאו.
ר' עקיבא אומר: כבר קפצה נחלה מלפני
בני הראשונה ונפלה לפני בני השניה.

**Yerushalmi**

אמר בן ננס יורשי הראשונה אומרים
ליורשי השנייה **אם** כבעל חוב אתם טלו את
שלכם וצאו **ואם לאו אנו ואתם נחלוק**
**בשוה.**

אמר לו רבי עקיבה בני שנייה קפצה **עליהן**
ירושת תורה ונוטלין כתובת אמן **וחוזרין**
**וחולקין.**

---

If they died, one in his lifetime and one following his death,

Ben Nanas says: The sons of the first wife can say to the sons of the second wife: You are the children of a creditor, collect your mother's ketubah and leave.

R. Akiva says: The inheritance already jumped away from the sons of the first wife and fell before sons of the second wife.

Ben Nanas said: The inheritors of the first [wife] say to the inheritors of the second [wife] **if** you are creditors, collect what is yours and leave, **and if not, we will divide [the inheritance] equally.**

R. Akiva said to him: The inheritance according to Torah [law] **jumped to** the children of the second [wife]. They collect their mother's ketubah **and then divide the remainder.**

---

Halivni cogently noted the difficulties in the Babylonian version of the Ben Nanas/R. Akiva baraita.[18] In the Bavli's version, Ben Nanas no longer provides two options to the sons of the second wife—take their mother's ketubah or share the inheritance equally. Rather, only the first section of his statement remains—the first sons say to the second sons, "take your mother's ketubah." The statement has become relatively cryptic—of course the sons of the second mother receive her ketubah; no one has ever doubted this. After all, the father owed their mother this money and they inherited their mother's debt as their biblical inheritance. Furthermore, why would the first sons say to the second sons something that is abundantly obvious and devoid of any legal significance? Ben Nanas could have just stated, "the second sons take their mother's ketubah," if this is what he wished to teach. Even more difficult, if his intent is to rule that the first sons also receive their mother's ketubah, as all amoraim understand, this stipulation is completely missing from the statement

---

18   See Halivni, ibid. 235-237.

itself. Why does he mention the ketubah of the second wife's sons when his intent is to refer to the ketubah of the first wife's sons?

The meaning of Ben Nanas' statement as preserved in the Bavli might be derived in either of the following ways. First, the phrase, "the sons of the first can say to the second" gives the impression that the sons of the first have some sort of right. This does indeed accord with the original form of Ben Nanas' statement as it appears in the Yerushalmi. Second, while we could try to uncover the meaning of Ben Nanas' statement from R. Akiva's, R. Akiva's statement is also cryptic. The force of his statement is lost because he no longer responds to Ben Nanas' claim that the second sons have the ability to choose. In the Bavli, R. Akiva no longer says "they go back and divide the remainder," leaving us with no real answer as to what R. Akiva believes should occur in this situation: Do the first sons receive their mother's ketubah, or are they left to split the remaining inheritance equally? Nevertheless, it does seem that R. Akiva is implying that the first sons have lost something—"the inheritance already jumped away." This line could be interpreted in accordance with the original meaning of R. Akiva as seen in the Yerushalmi, that the first sons do not receive their *benin dikhrin* ketubah. If this is the correct interpretation, we could construe a diametrical dispute between Ben Nanas and R. Akiva and conclude that Ben Nanas holds that the first sons do receive their mother's ketubah.

In any case, it is abundantly clear that the Babylonian version is an echo of the original found in the Yerushalmi. When exactly these changes occurred is not determinable. It is possible that they were the result of a Babylonian attempt to form "absolutes" out of the two opinions—i.e. one tanna (Ben Nanas) believes that the first sons receive their *benin dikhrin* ketubah, and one tanna (R. Akiva) believes that they do not. If this is so, then we should note that the Babylonian transmitters of the baraita chose to retain as much of the original language as possible. Rather than rewrite the entire dispute, they simply removed some of the words, despite some loss of coherence. There is also the possibility that a reverse process occurred—the baraita's transmission became garbled when it reached Babylonia, forcing the amoraim to offer a new interpretation, one that perceived the two positions as potentially opposite sides of a dispute over whether *benin dikhrin* applies in this case. While we tend to give less credence to such a history of texts, the possibility cannot entirely be ruled out.

# Section 4: Rabbah and Rav Yosef on the Baraita

However we understand the history of the Rabbi Akiva/Ben Nanas baraita, it is found in the Bavli only in this form. We now turn our attention to the topic of how the Babylonian amoraim interpreted it.

(4a) אמר רבה, אשכחתינהו לרבנן דבי רב דיתבי וקאמרי: דכולי עלמא, אחת בחייו ואחת במותו - יש להן כתובת בנין דכרין, והכא בכתובה נעשית מותר לחברתה והוא הדין לבעל חוב קמיפלגי:

(4a) Rabbah said: I found the rabbis of the school of Rav sitting and saying: Everyone agrees that [in a case] where one wife died in his lifetime and one died following his death, [the first wife's sons] collect the ketubat benin dikhrin. But here, there is a dispute if one ketubah can be the surplus for the other and similarly regarding a creditor.

מר סבר: כתובה נעשית מותר לחברתה והוא הדין לבעל חוב, ומר סבר: אין כתובה נעשית מותר לחברתה והוא הדין לבעל חוב.

One master (Ben Nanas) holds that one ketubah can be the surplus for the other and similarly regarding a creditor. And one master (R. Akiva) that one ketubah cannot be the surplus for the other and similarly regarding a creditor.

ואמינא להו אנא: בעל חוב - כולי עלמא לא פליגי דהוי מותר, כי פליגי - בכתובה.

And I said to them: [Regarding] a creditor, everyone agrees that it is permitted. They disagree in the [case of] the ketubah.

(4b) מתקיף לה רב יוסף: אי הכי, רבי עקיבא אומר: כבר קפצה נחלה, אם יש מותר דינר מיבעי ליה!

(4b) R. Yosef objected: If that is so, [that the dispute is over whether the ketubah counts as a surplus], then why did [the baraita state] "R. Akiva says: The inheritance already jumped away"? Rather, it should have stated: "If there is an extra dinar"!

אלא אמר רב יוסף: באחת בחייו ואחת במותו קא מיפלגי.

Rather, R. Yosef said: They disagree regarding [the case] where one wife died in his lifetime and one died following his death.

243

There are basically two competing interpretations of the Ben Nanas/R. Akiva baraita. According to R. Yosef, these tannaim have a principled dispute over whether the *benin dikhrin* ketubah is applicable in a case where one woman died after the husband. According to this interpretation, R. Akiva rejects the right of the sons of the first wife to the *benin dikhrin* **in all cases** in which the second mother was alive when the husband dies. This accords with R. Mana's interpretation of R. Akiva, as we have reconstructed it from the Yerushalmi. It also accords with the first opinion in the Babylonian version of the baraita in Tosefta Ketubot 10:1. The rationale behind this opinion seems to be that the *benin dikhrin* ketubah was originally instituted only in the situation where both wives die before the husband. In real terms, this position would be a significant limitation on the entire applicability of the *benin dikhrin* clause. Ben Nanas would hold the opposite: the *benin dikhrin* clause applies in all situations. The word "leave" implies that this would hold true even if there is no extra dinar, but R. Yosef does not make this point explicitly.

According to Rabbah, R. Akiva agrees that if there is an extra dinar, the first sons receive their mother's ketubah. R. Akiva and Ben Nanas disagree only if there is no extra dinar. Ben Nanas would hold that even without an extra dinar, the first sons still receive their mother's ketubah. This is because the second wife's ketubah counts as the extra dinar needed to fulfill biblical inheritance, and this would allow the sons of the first wife to receive their mother's ketubah. R. Akiva would hold that since there is not actually an extra dinar, the first sons do not receive their mother's ketubah. For the most part, this accords with R. Yose's opinion in the Yerushalmi, as well as R. Shimon in the Babylonian version of Tosefta Ketubot 10:1, and probably the author of the mishnah as well. However, there is one way in which Rabbah goes beyond the earlier framing of the dispute. According to Rabbah, if there is any other debt owed by the estate, the act of paying back the debt counts as biblical inheritance, such that the sons of the first wife may receive their *benin dikhrin* ketubah. He argues that all tannaim, even R. Akiva, agree with this principle. This is an even greater limitation of R. Akiva than was found in the Yerushalmi. The other rabbis, mentioned at the beginning of Rabbah's statement, disagree and hold that only Ben Nanas considers the external debt to count as the extra dinar.

We could summarize all of the opinions we have seen thus in the following way:

| | Extra Dinar | No Extra Dinar |
|---|---|---|
| Mishnah, Tosefta, R. Shimon in Babylonian baraita, R. Akiva according to R. Yose and Rabbah, Ben Nanas according to R. Yosef[19] | Everyone gets their mother's ketubah and the rest is divided evenly. | The second sons take their mother's ketubah and then the rest is split evenly. |
| The first opinion in the Babylonian baraita according to R. Yosef, R. Akiva according to R. Mana and R. Yosef | Even in this case the first sons do not receive their mother's ketubah. | |
| Ben Nanas according to R. Yose and Rabbah, the first opinion in the baraita according to the stam | | Even in this case the first sons do receive their mother's ketubah, because the second ketubah counts as the extra dinar. |

## Section 6: A Late Amoraic Halakhic Ruling

(6a) אמר מר זוטרא משמיה דרב פפא, הלכתא: אחת בחייו ואחת במותו - יש להן כתובת בנין דכרין, וכתובה נעשית מותר לחברתה.

(6a) Mar Zutra said in the name of R. Pappa: The halakhah in the case where one wife died in his lifetime and one died following his death is [that the sons of the first wife] collect the ketubat *benin dikhrin*, and one ketubah can be the surplus for the other.

Mar Zutra's halakhic ruling, which appears at the end of the sugya, the typical place for halakhic rulings in the Bavli, accords with Ben Nanas, as understood by Rabbah. As we shall see, it also accords with the stammaitic reading of the Babylonian baraita that immediately preceded it. As we

---

19   R. Mana may share this interpretation of Ben Nanas, but this is uncertain.

shall also see below, the stam throughout the sugya seems to be influenced by this position, and attempts to read it into tannaitic sources.

## Sections 1 and 2: The Mishnah and Its Derivations

שמע מינה תלת:

Conclude from this three [laws]:

(1a) שמע מינה, אחת בחייו ואחת במותו - יש להן כתובת בנין דכרין, ולא חיישינן לאינצויי.

(1a) Conclude from it that if one [of the man's wives died] in his lifetime and one died following his death, then [the sons of the first wife] collect the *ketubat benin dikhrin* ~~and we are not concerned~~ that this would lead to quarreling.

From where is it known?

ממאי?

מדקתני: שניה ויורשיה קודמים ליורשי ראשונה מיקדם הוא דקדמי, הא איכא שקלי.

From the fact that [the mishnah] teaches: The second wife and her heirs precede the heirs of the first wife, [this implies] that they precede [the heirs of the first], but if there is [enough in the estate for all the claims against it], then the children of the first wife do take [their *ketubat benin dikhrin*].

(1b) ושמע מינה, כתובה נעשית מותר לחברתה, ממאי?

(1b) And conclude from it that one ketubah can be the surplus for the other. From where is it known?

מדלא קתני אם יש שם מותר דינר.

From the fact that [the mishnah] does not teach: "If there is an extra dinar" [in addition to the value of all the ketubot.]

(1c) ושמע מינה, כתובת בנין דכרין לא טרפה ממשעבדי,

(1c) And conclude from it that a *ketubat benin dikhrin* cannot be collected from encumbered property.

דאי סלקא דעתין טרפה ממשעבדי, ליתו בני ראשונה ולטרפינהו לבני שניה.

For if you should think that it can be collected from encumbered property, then let the sons of the first wife come and collect it from the sons of the second wife.

The sugya opens by deriving three halakhot from the mishnah's ruling that "If he married the first one and she died, and then married a second wife and he died, the second wife and her inheritors take precedence over the inheritance of the first wife." The first halakhah is that "that if one [of the man's wives died] in his lifetime and one died following his death, then [the sons of the first wife] collect the *ketubat benin dikrin*." This has been the main topic of the entire sugya, and it does seem to accurately reflect the intention of the mishnah. The second derivation is a subset of the first. Once we know that the first sons have a principled right to their *benin dikhrin* inheritance, can we suspend the usual requirement that an extra dinar be divided equally as inheritance among all of the sons? The stam answers, in line with Rabbah (section 4a), that the ketubah of the second wife, which is paid as a debt to her sons, can count as this extra dinar. This too is an issue that reflects the amoraic discussion of this mishnah.

The third derivation, that the *benin dikhrin* inheritance cannot be taken from encumbered property, is less inherent to our sugya, and does not really belong here. It is related to an amoraic debate on Ketubot 45a and is mentioned also in a stammaitic dialogue on 42b. This issue appears again in this sugya only in the stammaitic discussion of Mar Zutra; it is not mentioned here by an amora. Furthermore, R. Ashi (section 2a) does not refer to this derivation from the mishnah in his response. Moreover, this conclusion is derived not from a precise reading of the mishnah, "from the fact that the mishnah teaches/does not teach," but rather from a general observation of the halakhic content of the mishnah. This third derivation is only here to fill in the requisite "learn from this three" format found throughout the Bavli. While the phrase "learn from this two" is found in the Bavli, it is never used in this way, to introduce derivations stemming from a tannaitic source.[20] When deriving more than one halakhah from an earlier source, the stam always learns three halakhot, never two and never more than three. But the sugya only discusses two related issues. To fill in the third, the stam added an issue related to *benin dikhrin* that is discussed elsewhere in Ketubot.

The stam's two primary halakhic derivations both accord with Rabbah from section 4. The first derivation is a point which, according to Rabbah, is not even a dispute between R. Akiva and Ben Nanas—all tannaim hold that the *benin dikhrin* clause in principle applies when one wife dies before the husband. The second derivation also accords with the framework

---

[20] For more on this see the introduction to this volume pp. 26-27.

which Rabbah provides for the baraita. While Rabbah does not explicitly rule as to whether the second ketubah can count as the extra dinar, by framing the tannaitic dispute as over this issue, he attributes this opinion to Ben Nanas. The stam goes one step further and locates this opinion in the mishnah itself, despite the lack of any real evidence.

R. Ashi then responds to the preceding anonymous passage. It may be surprising to find an amora commenting upon a stammaitic passage, since we generally assume that amoraic material predates the stam. But as Robert Brody has pointed out, there are stammaitic passages in the Bavli that should be dated to the amoraic period, and section 1 seems to be one such case.[21] The "learn from this three" section can even be divided into a Hebrew core and an Aramaic additional layer, as is typical of many amoraic statements. The Hebrew core lists the derivations themselves and the Aramaic core explains how they are anchored in the mishnah. R. Ashi rejects the derivations, thereby lending credence to the opposite opinion. Together, the anonymous portion and R. Ashi's response serve to introduce the issues of the sugya to the reader and relate them to the mishnah. The presentation of two interpretations, one anonymous and one attributed to R. Ashi, also creates a literary aesthetic with the next two sections of the sugya, each of which wavers between two explanations of a tannaitic source.

## Section 5: Stammaitic Acrobatics

As is sometimes the case, the editors of this sugya display a strong preference for one of the two positions debated throughout the sugya. This was evident in the opening "learn from this" section which we just analyzed. It is also evident in section 5, much of which is also stammaitic. The opening line of this section directly connects to the previous section, the dispute between Rabbah and R. Yosef, by correlating the tannaitic disputes at the heart of both.

(5a) והני תנאי כי הני תנאי:    (5a) And these tannaim are like those tannaim.

---

21    Robert Brody, "Stam ha-Talmud ve-Divrei ha-Amoraim," in *Ha-Mikra ve-Olamo: Sifrut Hazal u-Mishpat Ivri u-Mahshevet Yisrael,* ed. Baruch Schwartz, Abraham Melamed, and Aharon Shemesh (Jerusalem: Ha-Igud ha-Olami le-Mada'ei ha-Yahadut, 2008), 213-232.

דתניא: נשא את הראשונה ומתה,
נשא את השניה ומת הוא, באין בניה
של זו לאחר מיתה ונוטלין כתובת
אמן.

רבי שמעון אומר: אם יש מותר דינר
- אלו נוטלין כתובת אמן ואלו נוטלין
כתובת אמן, ואם לאו - חולקין בשוה.

(5b) מאי לאו בהא קא מיפלגי, דמר
סבר: אחת בחייו ואחת במותו - יש
להן כתובת בנין דכרין, ומר סבר:
אחת בחייו ואחת במותו - אין להם
כתובת בנין דכרין!

As it is taught in a baraita: If he married a first wife and she died and then he married a second wife and he died, the sons of this [second] wife come after her death and collect their mother's ketubah.

R. Shimon says: If there is an extra dinar, these (the sons of the first wife) collect their mother's ketubah, and these (the sons of the second wife) collect their mother's ketubah, and if not, they divide [the estate] equally.

(5b) Is it not that they disagree about this: One master (R. Shimon) holds that in a case where one wife died in his lifetime and one died following his death, [the sons of the first wife] collect the *ketubat benin dikhrin*; and one master (the *tanna kamma*) holds that in a case where one wife died in his lifetime and one died following his death, [the sons of the first wife] cannot collect the *ketubat benin dikhrin*.

To recall, in section 4, R. Yosef claims that Ben Nanas and R. Akiva dispute over whether the *benin dikhrin* ketubah is enacted when the husband predeceases one of his wives. The stam now uses the term "and these tannaim are like those tannaim" in order to transition into its interpretation of the Babylonian version of the Tosefta that we examined above. It is not entirely clear whether this phrase is amoraic, issued by R. Yosef, or stammatic. When this term is used elsewhere in the Bavli, it is usually clearly stammaitic; in only one other place (Bavli Sotah 20b) is it ascribed to an amora. The issue is not of great significance in this case, for even if the stam authored this entire section, it clearly offers one interpretation that is in the spirit of R. Yosef—the tannaim dispute the issue of whether the first sons receive their mother's ketubah.

This interpretation of the baraita seems particularly convincing, for if R. Shimon holds that the sons of the first wife do receive their *benin dikhrin* ketubah (as long as there is an extra dinar), then it seems most likely that the first tanna holds that they do not—even if there is an extra dinar, and all the more so if there is not. Furthermore, it seems most likely that the words "the sons of this woman" refer to the second wife, for their mother is the one that just died. Even if the first sons were to receive their mother's *benin dikhrin* ketubah, they would be receiving it only after their father's death. While obviously this is also after her death, the baraita would not need to say "they come after her death." This convincing interpretation of the baraita is artfully taken apart by the stam through the following highly stylized and pedagogical passage.

(5c) לא, דכולי עלמא אחת בחייו ואחת במותו - יש להן כתובת בנין דכרין, והכא בדינר מקרקעי קמיפלגי:

(5c) No, everyone agrees that [in a case] where one wife died in his lifetime and one died following his death, [the sons of the first wife] collect the *ketubat benin* dikrhin; but here they disagree if the [extra] dinar was in real estate:

מר סבר: מקרקעי אין, מטלטלי לא, ומר סבר: אפילו מטלטלי.

One master (the *tanna kamma*) holds that if [the extra dinar was in] real estate, then yes, [they can collect the *ketubat benin dikhrin*], but if [the extra dinar was in] movable property, then no, [they cannot collect]. And one master (R. Shimon) that [they can collect] even [if the extra dinar was in] movable property.

(5d) ומי מצית אמרת הכי?

(5d) But how can you say that?

והתנן, ר' שמעון אומר: אפילו יש שם נכסים שאין להם אחריות - אינן כלום, עד שיהא שם נכסים שיש להן אחריות יתר על ב' כתובות דינר!

Did not we learn in the Mishnah: "R. Shimon says: Even if there was movable property, it is not regarded unless there was real estate worth one dinar more than [the total amount of] the two ketubot"?

(5e) אלא, הכא בדינר משעבדי קמיפלגי, מר סבר: מבני חורין אין, ממשעבדי לא, ומר סבר: אפילו ממשעבדי.

(5e) Rather, here they disagree about a dinar of encumbered property: One master (the *tanna kamma*) holds that if [the surplus was in the form of] free property [that is currently in the

250

estate], then yes, [each can claim the *ketubat benin dikhrin*], but if [the surplus was in] encumbered property then no. And one master (R. Shimon) holds that [it is a surplus] even if it was encumbered property.

(5f) אי הכי, רבי שמעון אומר: אם יש שם מותר דינר, כיון שיש שם מותר דינר מיבעי ליה!

(5f) If that is so, [that the baraita refers to a case where there is encumbered property], [then why did the baraita state] "R. Shimon says: If there is an extra dinar," it should have said: "Since there is an extra dinar"!

(5g) אלא בפחות מדינר קמיפלגי, מר סבר: דינר אין פחות מדינר לא, ומר סבר: אפילו פחות מדינר.

(5g) Rather, the dispute is regarding [a case] where there is less than a dinar: One master (the *tanna kamma*) holds that if [the surplus was worth] a dinar, then yes, [each can collect the *ketubat benin dikhrin*], but if it was less than a dinar, then no. And one master (R. Shimon) holds even if it was less than a dinar.

(5h) והא ר' שמעון דינר קאמר! וכי תימא איפוך, תנא קמא דמתניתין נמי דינר קאמר!

(5h) But did not R. Shimon say: "If there is a dinar" [and not less]! And if you say: Reverse the [sons referenced in the interpretation of the baraita, that cannot be] because the *tanna kama* of the mishnah also said that a dinar [is necessary]!

(5i) אלא כי הנך תרי לישנאי קמאי ואיפוך.

(5i) Rather, [the dispute in the baraita must be explained] according to those first two interpretations, [that they disagree about movable property or encumbered property], and reverse [our understanding of the baraita: The *tanna kamma* holds the sons of the first wife may collect the *ketubat benin dikhrin* if there is an extra dinar of movable property or encumbered

property, whereas R. Shimon holds
that there must be an extra dinar of
real estate that is not encumbered].

The stam opens by rejecting the initial interpretation of the baraita,
instead suggesting that both sides of the baraita agree that the first sons
can potentially receive their *benin dikhrin* ketubah. The dispute is only
over the nature of the extra dinar necessary to fulfill biblical inheritance
and thus allow for the sons to collect their *benin dikhrin* ketubot. In
sections 5c-5g, the stam tries to invent an aspect of the nature of this extra
dinar over which the tannaim could dispute, and in each of the first three
cases, this attempt fails. Some of these suggestions seem startlingly easy to
reject and perhaps are only rhetorical or pedagogical. In other words, at
first glance it seems that the stam proposes interpretations of the baraita
that cannot possibly stand only to serve a pedagogical function: to
demonstrate interpretations that are not viable. However, there is a deeper
purpose to these suggestions. In the end of this entire section, what
seemed to be clearly rejected in sections 1 and 2, becomes authoritative in
section 5h-5i, when our understanding of the baraita is completely
reversed. This may be a demonstration of the stam's acumen in leading
the reader/listener down a path that seems to be errant, only to reveal at
the end that such a path does lead to ultimate resolution and truth.

This is clearest in sections 5c-5d, where it is proposed that the dispute
is over whether the extra dinar must be in real estate or whether it can be
movable property. The stam proposes that the first opinion holds that it
must be real estate, whereas R. Shimon holds that it may be movable
property. This is easily rejected based on the second mishnah of the
chapter, where R. Shimon explicitly says that the extra dinar to be shared
as equal inheritance must be land.

In sections 5e-5f, the stam proposes that the dispute is over whether
this dinar may even be encumbered property. The first opinion would
hold that even if this extra dinar is really owed to a third party, it still
counts as the extra dinar that would be divided equally as inheritance.
This notion is directly related to the opinion of Rabbah and the other
rabbis in his bet midrash (section 4), who held that inheriting a debt
counts as inheritance (see above). This connection is thus a sign of the
inspiration behind this section—to interpret the dispute in the baraita in

line with Rabbah. However, this interpretation is also rejected for it does not easily accord with R. Shimon's language.

Section 5g is most obviously a rhetorical framing of the dispute, without any chance of being accepted. The idea that R. Shimon would hold that the equally shared inheritance can be even less than a dinar directly contradicts his words. It is possible that the reason for a third interpretation is purely stylistic—the stam prefers tripartite structures.

This leads to sections 5h-5i, where the stam suggests reversing the understanding of the baraita. According to Rashi, the term "reverse" does not mean here that the tannaitic positions should be reversed, as it almost always does in the Bavli. Rather, we must "reverse" our understanding of which set of sons is referred to by the first opinion. According to this new interpretation of the baraita, the sons who come and claim the ketubah are the sons of the first wife not the sons of the second.[22]

We should emphasize the halakhic revolution that occurs here. According to this reading, the *tanna kamma* holds that **the sons of the first wife always receive their mother's ketubah**—the second sons' ketubah will count as the extra dinar to fulfill biblical inheritance. This, as we noted in the chart above, is in line with Rabbah's interpretation of the Ben Nanas and R. Akiva dispute, and most significantly, it accords with Mar Zutra's halakhic ruling. The stam here rereads the baraita so that the dominant, anonymous opinion accords with what it believes to be the halakhically accepted ruling. To emphasize, the original meaning of the baraita stated the opposite opinion—the **sons of the second wife receive their *benin dikhrin* ketubah and the sons of the first do not**. The stam, through some considerable pedagogic acrobatics, has proven that the simple meaning of the baraita is incorrect, and that the only correct reading is that which accords with the new halakhic ruling.

## The Tosefta and the Bavli's Baraita Revisited

The stam is able to suggest reversing the interpretation because of the ambiguity present in the Babylonian version of the baraita. In contrast, in

---

[22] The Tosafot raise many difficulties with Rashi's interpretation of the line and therefore provide an entirely different understanding of the term "reverse it." See Tosafot s.v. וכי תימא איפוך.

the Tosefta it is clear to whom the words "this one's sons come after her death" refer:

| בבלי כתובות צ ע"ב | תוספתא כתובות י:א |
|---|---|
| נשא את הראשונה ומתה, נשא את השניה ומת הוא, **באין בניה של זו לאחר מיתה ונוטלין כתובת אמן.** | נשא את הראשונה ומתה נשא את השניה ומת הוא |
| רבי שמעון אומר: אם יש מותר דינר - אלו נוטלין כתובת אמן ואלו נוטלין כתובת אמן, | והיה שם יתר דינר אילו נוטלין כתובת אמן ואילו נוטלין כתובת אמן ושאר חולקין |
| ואם לאו - חולקין בשוה; | ואם אין שם יתר דינר **שניה ויורשיה נוטלין כתובת אמן** והשאר חולקין בשוה. |

**Bavli Ketubot 90b**

If he married a first wife and she died and then he married a second wife and he died,

**the sons of [the second wife] come after her death and collect their mother's ketubah**

R. Shimon says: If there is an extra dinar, these (the sons of the first wife) collect their mother's ketubah, and these (the sons of the second wife) collect their mother's ketubah, and if not, they divide [the estate] equally.

**Tosefta Ketubot 10:1**

If he married a first wife and she died and then he married a second wife and he died,

if there is an extra dinar, these (sons of the first wife) collect their mother's ketubah, and these (the sons of the second wife) collect their mother's ketubah, and if not **the second wife or her sons collect their mother's ketubah**, and they divide the rest [of the estate] equally.

The Tosefta's line "the second wife or her sons collect their mother's ketubah" has been brought up into the first opinion of the baraita, with one small but significant modification. Instead of "the second wife" the

Bavli states more cryptically "of this wife."[23] Viewed through the lens of its transmissional history, "this one" clearly refers to the second wife, as the words did in their original position in the Tosefta. The stam (or perhaps R. Yosef) initially interprets the baraita this way as well. However, the fact that which wife is not specified allows the stam to reinterpret the phrase to refer to the sons of the first wife. The first opinion of the baraita now no longer rules in accordance with R. Akiva's original opinion, that the first sons never receive their *benin dikhrin* ketubah. Rather, **these sons always receive it!**

Having reversed the referent of the phrase "the sons of this one," the stam now can plug the interpretation of the baraita into the first two interpretations in the section (5c, 5e). Thus, the stam admits that even the first opinion requires that there be an "extra dinar" to be shared equally among all sons. However, the rules governing this extra dinar are exceedingly lenient—the extra dinar can even be movable property (5c). Most importantly, the extra dinar can even come from encumbered property (section 5e), which likely means that the ketubah of the second wife could count as the "extra dinar." In other words, the first sons will basically **always** receive their *benin dikhrin* ketubah, with the understanding that even a debt or a ketubah could count as the "extra dinar." R. Shimon is now understood to be the stricter opinion, ruling that there must be a real dinar. This is the same understanding of the debate proposed by Rabbah in section 2—the dispute is over whether the second ketubah can count as the extra dinar.

Finally, we should address the the baraita itself, specifically its authenticity. R. Shimon's opinion in this baraita is identical to the anonymous opinion in the Tosefta. The thornier question is with regard to the first section. As stated above, Halivni regards it as an authentic tannaitic opinion, a strict interpretation of R. Akiva—the first sons never receive their *benin dikhrin* ketubah (unless both wives predecease the husband). But there is strong evidence that this baraita is likely a post-tannaitic, perhaps even stammaitic, creation. First, this baraita is utterly absent from any tannaitic collection or in the Yerushalmi. If there were really a tannaitic dispute on this issue, we would have to wonder why

---

[23] MS Firkovitch 187 and Rabbenu Hananel both include readings which explicitly name the second wife, but these are likely explanatory glosses. See *Dikdukei Soferim Hashalem: Ketubot* ed. Moshe Hershler (Jerusalem: Institute for the Complete Israeli Talmud, 1977), 338-339.

Rabbah and probably R. Yosef did not know of it. Second, the fact that the ambiguous line in this baraita, "this one's sons come and collect her ketubah after her death," is explicit in the Tosefta, and appears in a different section of the halakhah, may indicate that the line was shifted and emended by a later editor. Indeed, its absence in R. Shimon's statement in the Bavli's version is glaring. As it stands, the baraita could be read as implying that the second sons do not receive their mother's ketubah. But this is impossible—since their father died before their mother, they have a biblical right to inherit her ketubah. This ambiguity forces Rashi, in essence, to restore the original reading, lest one think that "they divide equally" implies that even the second sons do not receive their mother's ketubah.

It seems likely that this baraita was emended in Babylonia to serve as a reflection of the earlier Ben Nanas/R. Akiva baraita. That is, the baraita was emended to prove that "these tannaim are like these tannaim." Furthermore, one cannot help but wonder if the baraita was intentionally formulated with such an ambiguity to allow for the creation of a position even more expansive than that of the Tosefta. While the Tosefta requires an extra dinar in order for the first sons to receive their *benin dikhrin* ketubah, in the end, after the stammaitic discourse, the first tanna of the baraita rules that even without a real extra dinar, the first sons collect their mother's ketubah. This is a reflection of Rabbah's reading of the Ben Nanas/R. Akiva baraita as well as Mar Zutra's halakhic ruling. Thus, a baraita that is originally cited as support for R. Yosef is transformed into potential support for his disputant, and as support for Mar Zutra's ruling which follows. The stam executes this maneuver by creatively reading the baraita, and perhaps by creatively and subtly emending it as well.

The following is the summary of the halakhic history of this issue as manifested in this sugya and related sources:

| Tannaitic period, Ben Nanas/R. Akiva | Tannaitic period, Tosefta | Early amoraic period | Late tannaitic period, stammaitic period |
|---|---|---|---|
| R. Akiva: The sons of the first wife do not receive their *benin dikhrin* ketubah. Ben Nanas: The sons of the first wife receive their *benin dikhrin* only if the sons of second wife claim their mother's ketubah. In reality, the sons of the first wife will receive their *benin dikhrin* ketubah only if it is smaller than their share of the inheritance. | The same rules that apply to normal cases of *benin dikhrin* apply here: If there is a real extra dinar, the first sons receive their *benin dikhrin* ketubah, but if there is no extra dinar, then the second sons take their mother's ketubah, and the rest is divided evenly. | Rabbah (Bavli) and R. Yose (Yerushalmi): All tannaim agree that if there is a real extra dinar, the first sons receive their *benin dikhrin* ketubah. Ben Nanas holds that even if there is no extra dinar, they receive the ketubah. R. Yosef and R. Mana: Ben Nanas rules that the first sons receive the *benin dikhrin* ketubah, and R. Akiva rules that they do not. | The final halakhic ruling accords with Ben Nanas, as understood by Rabbah: The first sons always receive their *benin dikhrin* ketubah, even without a real extra dinar. |

## Conclusion

The entire *raison d'être* of the *benin dikhrin* clause, and other such similar clauses in ancient Near Eastern inheritance law, was to ensure that the dowry a father provides for his daughter would not be transferred to offspring not part of his biological family. If his son-in-law had another wife, the father's own grandchildren, the offspring of his daughter, would receive their mother's marital payment (dowry plus money guaranteed to her by her husband) and not those of any other woman. The rabbis clearly understood the reason for this law, and the Mishnah already included it as a mandatory clause in its version of the marital contract, the ketubah.

However, the rabbis were keen to perceive that this clause would often overturn the biblical laws of inheritance, which require sons to divide the inheritance of their father equally. They reacted to this clash of ancient practice with biblical law in several ways. The primary one was to limit the applicability of the clause to male children, and thereby preserve the biblical preference for male inheritance. Another way of limiting it was to demand that *benin dikhrin* clauses would be effective only if biblical inheritance, shared equally by all of the brothers, could also be fulfilled. Finally, some tannaim limited the applicability to a case where both wives predeceased the husband. If one wife died first, and the other wife died after, the sons of the first wife would be denied their ability to collect their mother's ketubah. Inheritance would follow, in such a case, the normal biblical lines. All three of these shifts provided more of an opportunity for biblical inheritance to be carried out. The authors of these opinions exhibit fealty to the Torah's laws, beyond any fealty to Near Eastern legal tradition.

However, such fealty comes at a steep price, for the father's guarantee that his dowry would not be transferred to offspring not related to him would be severely limited. First of all, for the dowry to go to his grandchildren, his daughter would have to have male children. Second, the husband, if he takes a second wife, would have to leave a big enough estate to cover both ketubot plus an extra dinar. And finally, the father would have to hope (in a sort of grim fashion) that if his daughter predeceases her husband, her rival wife would as well. Some amoraim, including Mar Zutra, the only amora to offer a halakhic ruling on this case, as well as the stam, reverse the trend, and without being conscious of doing so, move the practice back closer to its Near Eastern roots. The requirement of an extra dinar has largely been fictionalized—even another debt will suffice. If one wife dies before her husband and one after, the first sons will still receive their mother's ketubah. Indeed, the only law that they do not undo is that which is ensconced in the language of the ketubah clause itself and is probably the most ancient and most difficult to reinterpret: the limiting of the clause to male children. It seems that even stammaitic acrobats occasionally fall to the ground.

# CHAPTER SIX

## RETURNING TO THE LAND OF ISRAEL, NOW AND AT THE ESCHATON

## KETUBOT 110B-111A

## Introduction

A large part of the rabbinic editorial process is reworking and adapting earlier material to fit new literary, legal, and social contexts. We find countless examples of late editors adapting and emending earlier texts and providing new meaning to existing sources by placing them in different contexts. The current chapter focuses on how the Babylonian editors employ these techniques when faced with a great theological and historical challenge: How can Babylonian Jews justify their decision to remain in exile in the face of a religious imperative to live in the Promised Land?

Babylonian encounters with Eretz Yisraeli sources extolling the virtues of life within the Land of Israel exemplify this struggle. One particularly poignant example is the final mishnah of Ketubot (13:11), which authorizes any party in a husband-wife or master-slave relationship to force the other party to move to the Land of Israel. The urgency of returning to the land from exile overrides the standard balance of these hierarchical relationships. The Bavli's sugyot linked to this mishnah present a broad array of halakhic and aggadic material praising the Land of Israel and exploring its relationship with Babylonia.[1] The Eretz Yisraeli sources overwhelmingly bestow lavish praise upon, and mystical significance to, living and dying in the Land of Israel. The rabbis of Babylonia confront the inherent tension present within these sources from

---

[1]  For an analysis of the entire passage see Jeffrey Rubenstein, "Hitmodedut Im Maalat Eretz Yisrael," *Merkaz Utefutzah*, ed. Isaiah Gafni (Jerusalem: Merkaz Zalman Shazar, 2004), 159-188.

their perspective in a variety of ways—at times accepting them wholly, at times tempering them, and at times going so far as to reject them altogether. As we shall see, the same Eretz Yisraeli sources and ideas which are used to attack those who remain in Babylonia and belittle the Babylonian communities as the diminutive "little sister" are used in the Bavli as a defense of their life in exile and a celebration of their centers of Torah learning.

## "A Person Should Always Live in the Land of Israel"

The final mishnah in Ketubot teaches that a wife can force her husband and a slave can force his master to move to the Land of Israel (or prevent a move away therefrom):

| משנה כתובות יג:יא | Mishnah Ketubot 13:11 |
|---|---|
| הכל מעלין לארץ ישראל, ואין הכל מוציאין. | Anyone may [forcibly] bring [the other] to the Land of Israel, but not everyone may remove [the other therefrom]. |
| הכל מעלין לירושלים, ואין הכל מוציאין. | Anyone may [forcibly] bring [the other] to Jerusalem, but not everyone may remove [the other therefrom]. |
| אחד נשים, ואחד עבדים.[2] | [This law applies] both to wives and slaves. |

Under normal circumstances, in the patriarchal society in which the rabbis lived, a woman would not be able to compel her husband to move, and the idea that a slave could compel his master to move sounds patently absurd in any slave-bearing society—when do slaves have any power to force their masters to do anything? This mishnah emphasizes the importance of the value of living in the Land of Israel by giving it the real teeth of economic consequence. The rabbis invoke a financial penalty in order to persuade the refusing party to consent. If a woman or slave demands to move to Eretz Yisrael, and the husband/master refuses, the refusing party will suffer economic consequences. In the case of the wife,

---

[2]  This is the dominant reading of the mishnah, found in good manuscripts and some geniza fragments. However, the Bavli (110b) was not familiar with " אחד עבדים" and therefore read it into the word "הכל." See *Dikdukei Soferim Hashalem*, Ketubot, v. 2, 530, n. 25.

the husband would be forced to divorce her and pay her ketubah. Normally speaking, wives do not have the ability to demand divorce; in this case they would. In the case of the slave, the master would be forced to set him free. This blatant disruption of the social hierarchy demonstrates in practical terms the value the rabbis placed on living in the Land of Israel.

The Bavli's sugya begins with a baraita which provides the ideological underpinnings for the extraordinary ruling found in Mishnah Ketubot 13:11:

| בבלי כתובות קי ע"ב | Bavli Ketubot 110b |
|---|---|
| תנו רבנן: לעולם ידור אדם בארץ ישראל אפילו בעיר שרובה עובדי כוכבים, ואל ידור בחוץ לארץ ואפילו בעיר שרובה ישראל, שכל הדר בארץ ישראל - דומה כמי שיש לו אלוה, וכל הדר בחוצה לארץ - דומה כמי שאין לו אלוה, שנאמר: *לתת לכם את ארץ כנען להיות לכם לאלהים* (ויקרא כה:לח). | Our Rabbis taught: A person should always live in the Land of Israel, even in a city with a non-Jewish majority, and should not live outside the Land, even in a city with a Jewish majority; for whoever lives in the Land of Israel it is as if he has a God, but whoever lives outside the Land it is as if has no God. As it says, *To give you the Land of Canaan, to be your God* (Leviticus 25:38). |
| וכל שאינו דר בארץ אין לו אלוה? אלא לומר לך: כל הדר בחוץ לארץ - כאילו עובד עבודת כוכבים. | And whoever does not live in the Land has no God? Rather [it is] to tell you, that whoever lives outside the Land it is as if he worships idols. |
| וכן בדוד הוא אומר: *כי גרשוני היום מהסתפח בנחלת ה' לאמר לך עבוד אלהים אחרים* (שמואל א כו:יט). | Similarly regarding David it says: *For they have driven me out today, so that I cannot have a share in the Lord's possession, but am told, "Go and worship other Gods"* (I Samuel 26:19). |
| וכי מי אמר לו לדוד לך עבוד אלהים אחרים? אלא לומר לך: כל הדר בחוץ לארץ כאילו עובד עבודת כוכבים. | Now, who said to David, "Go and worship other gods"? Rather [it is] to tell you that whoever lives outside the Land it as if he worships idols. |

| Tannaitic Source | Amoraic Source | Stammaitic Source |

261

The baraita declares that there is an existential preference for living in the Land, regardless of whether Jewish life there is even practical, at least in a communal sense.[3] One might have thought it preferable to live outside of Eretz Yisrael in a case where the majority of the local population is Jewish and a move to Eretz Yisrael would necessitate living among non-Jews. Instead, the baraita unequivocally rules that living in the Land of Israel is preferable and brings midrashic support for this ruling. The baraita makes the case for the lack of significance of Jewish community outside of the Land of Israel. Living outside the Land, even in a strongly Jewish community, is akin to living without God. The stam mildly attempts to soften the blow of this attack on diaspora Jewry by suggesting that those outside the Land of Israel are not entirely abandoned by God but are considered as if they worship idols.[4] Still, the baraita is quite clear—living outside the Land is an undesirable way for a Jew to live his life.

## R. Zera and R. Yehudah: Caught Between Babylonia and Eretz Yisrael

The Bavli continues with the story of R. Zera and R. Yehudah who, as we shall see, come to represent the two poles of thought regarding the preference of living in the Land of Israel at a time when the Jewish community in Babylonia is on the rise. R. Yehudah was the founder of the rabbinic school in Pumbedita and a dominant leader in the rabbinic movement of 3rd century Babylonia. R. Zera was his disciple.

| בבלי כתובות קי ע"ב-קיא ע"א | Bavli Ketubot 110b-111a |
|---|---|
| ר' זירא הוה קמשתמיט מיניה דרב יהודה, | R. Zera was avoiding R. Yehudah |
| דבעא למיסק לארץ ישראל, דאמר רב | because he wanted to go up to the |
| יהודה: כל העולה מבבל לארץ ישראל | Land of Israel, for R. Yehudah said: |
| *עובר בעשה, שנאמר: בבלה יובאו ושמה* | Whoever goes up from Babylonia to |

---

3     The parallel to this baraita in Tosefta Avodah Zarah 4:4-5 includes a section which forbids leaving the Land of Israel even in times of great economic hardship. The editors of the Bavli omit those passages because of the lack of relevance for those already living outside of Eretz Yisrael.

4     The same slight toning down of rhetoric can be found by comparing Tosefta Avodah Zarah 4:6, "Jews who live outside the Land are idol worshippers" with a teaching of R. Yishmael in Bavli Avodah Zarah 8a: "Jews who live outside of the Land are idol worshipers **in purity**." The Babylonian version again rebukes those living outside the Land but stops short of total condemnation.

*יהיו עד יום פקדי אותם נאם ה׳* (ירמיה כז:כב). the Land of Israel transgresses a positive mitzvah, for it is said: *They shall be brought to Babylon, and there shall remain, until I take note of them— declares the Lord of Hosts* (Jeremiah 27:22).

R. Yehudah utterly rejects the ideology reflected in the baraita and instead characterizes a move to the Land of Israel from Babylonia as a transgression of a biblical commandment. He quotes a verse from Jeremiah that refers to the Temple vessels which are to remain in Babylonia until the return of the exiles. R. Yehudah's teaching shifts the subject of the verse and applies it to the Jews who live in Babyonia—they are meant to remain in Babylonia, at least until God restores them to the Land. R. Zera, his disciple, is familiar with his master's opinion, but clearly disagrees with it. He strongly desires to move to the Land of Israel but so fears R. Yehudah's reaction that he hides from his master in anticipation of his move.

R. Yehudah's absolute rejection of the centrality of the Land of Israel is jarring. The value of living in the Land of Israel seems to be one of the central values of the Bible itself. His teaching undermines the entire historical and theological relationship between God and Israel, from God's promise to Abraham in Genesis to Moses' instructions in Deuteronomy. Although he provides a biblical prooftext, his reason for negating the ideological necessity of living in the Land of Israel is not explicitly revealed in his statement itself. While R. Yehudah's prooftext does lend itself to a messianic interpretation, an interpretation adopted by the stam which we will analyze below, we would like to suggest a different reading of his statement, one more in line with other statements made by R. Yehudah himself about the relationship between Israel and Babylonia. In other words, we suggest here employing a methodology we frequently use throughout our work: separating the amoraic material from its stammaitic interpretation.

In order to better understand R. Yehudah's teaching, we will examine three other statements attributed to him: two within this larger sugya in Ketubot 110b-112a about the merits of the Land of Israel and one in Kiddushin. Besides the statement we have already read above, Ketubot

111a records two other statements made by R. Yehudah which similarly elevate the status of Babylonia to that of the Land of Israel.

| בבלי כתובת קיא ע"א | Bavli Ketubot 111a |
|---|---|
| אמר רב יהודה אמר שמואל כשם שאסור לצאת מארץ ישראל לבבל כך אסור לצאת מבבל לשאר ארצות... | R. Yehudah said in the name of Shmuel: Just as it is forbidden to leave the Land of Israel for Babylonia, so it is forbidden to leave Babylonia for other lands... |
| אמר רב יהודה כל הדר בבבל כאילו דר בארץ ישראל שנאמר (זכריה ב, יא) הוי ציון המלטי יושבת בת בבל. | R. Yehudah said: Whoever lives in Bavel it is as if he lives in the Land of Israel, as it says: *Away, escape, O Zion, you who dwell in fair Babylonia* (Zechariah 2:11). |

The first statement takes for granted the prohibition on leaving the Land of Israel, a prohibition that would not have been relevant to R. Yehudah's assumed Babylonian audience, and applies it to leaving Babylonia. The baraita that opened the sugya posited that leaving the Land of Israel was abandoning God's presence, a sentiment that accords easily with normative biblical theology. Quite dramatically, R. Yehudah applies the same prohibition to leaving Babylonia, a land that is never referred to as "the place God will choose." According to R. Yehudah, living outside of Babylonia is its own Diaspora. The second statement goes even further, reading a verse as referring to those who dwell in Babylonia as "Zion," suggesting that Babylonia is the new Zion![5]

These two statements imply that rather than reading R. Yehudah's statement as a prohibition of moving to the Land of Israel until the messianic redemption, we should read him as emphasizing the imperative of remaining in Babylonia, "They shall be brought to Babylon, **and there shall remain.**" Messianism can explain why Jews must not move to the Land of Israel; it cannot explain why they must remain specifically in

---

5   On similar claims, see Isaiah Gafni, "How Babylonia Became 'Zion': Shifting Identities in Late Antiquity" in L. I. Levine and D. R. Schwartz (eds.), *Jewish Identities in Antiquity: Studies in Memory of Menahem Stern* (Tübingen: Mohr Siebek, 2009), 333-348. See also Daniel Boyarin, *A Traveling Homeland: The Babylonian Talmud as Diaspora* (Philadelphia: University of Pennsylvania Press, 2015), 33-53.

Babylonia and not move elsewhere. R. Yehudah is not emphasizing that Jews should not move to Eretz Yisrael; he is emphasizing that they must **remain in Babylonia**. But why should living in Babylonia be elevated to a value equivalent to living in the Land of Israel?

We will suggest two possible answers to this question. The first is hinted at in the discussion that follows R. Yehudah's prohibition on leaving Babylonia for any other land:

| בבלי כתובות קיא ע"א | **Bavli Ketubot 111a** |
|---|---|
| אמר רב יהודה אמר שמואל כשם שאסור לצאת מארץ ישראל לבבל כך אסור לצאת מבבל לשאר ארצות. | R. Yehudah said in the name of Shmuel: Just as it is forbidden to leave the Land of Israel for Babylonia, so it is forbidden to leave Babylonia for other lands. |
| רבה ורב יוסף דאמרי תרווייהו אפילו מפומבדיתא לבי כובי. | Both Rabbah and R. Yosef said: Even from Pumbedita to Be Kube. |
| ההוא דנפק מפומבדיתא לבי כובי, שמתיה רב יוסף. | A certain man went from Pumbedita to Be Kube. R. Yosef excommunicated him. |
| ההוא דנפק מפומבדיתא לאסתוניא, שכיב. | A certain man went from Pumbedita to Astunya[6] and died. Abaye said: If this |
| אמר אביי: אי בעי האי צורבא מרבנן הוה חיי. | student of the rabbis had desired, he could [still] be alive. |

Rabbah and R. Yosef, early fourth century Babylonian amoraim, prohibit a move within Babylonia, even to a neighboring area such as Be Kube, if it entails abandoning the city of Pumbedita, the location of R. Yehudah's academy.[7] The two stories which follow roundly condemn Jews who leave Pumbedita for other cities in Babylonia. These statements and the stories that accompany them imply that R. Yehudah considers the Torah of Babylonia to be superior to that of the Land of Israel, just as the Torah of Pumbedita was superior to that found in Be Kube or Astunya, cities that did not house Babylonian centers of learning. This difference may not have been one only of quantity—i.e. there are more Torah scholars in

---

[6] The spelling of this village varies greatly among the manuscript traditions.

[7] On the village of Be Kube see Aaron Oppenheimer, *Babylonia Judaica in the Talmudic Period* (Wiesbaden: L. Reichert, 1983), 83-86.

Babylonia than there are in Eretz Yisrael. It may also express a strong preference for the style of rabbinic learning characteristic of Babylonia. One of the major differences between Torah learning in Babylonia and the Land of Israel in the amoraic period was the Babylonian emphasis on dialectical acumen, as opposed to the Eretz Yisraeli emphasis on the meticulous collection and organization of traditions.[8] Babylonians believed that their form of Torah learning was superior for only they were able to engage in the intense type of analytical discourse that so typified the Babylonian style of study.[9] R. Yehudah's prohibition on leaving Babylonia is his way of stating that the highest form of Torah learning was found only in the Babylonian academies, and that a move to Israel or **any other place in the world** would entail abandoning a superior intellectual tradition.

An alternative, but not contradictory, explanation for R. Yehudah's preference of Babylonia over any other land is related to the issue of family lineage. Claims of purity of lineage play a crucial role in creating boundaries between communities. Rabbis express a hesitance—or even refusal—to marry their daughters to those whose lineage was compromised, whether it be to non-rabbis or even to Eretz Yisraeli rabbis. The Bavli even includes a meticulously delineated map of the communities in Babylonia which are of pure lineage. Isaiah Gafni, one of the most prominent scholars of the Babylonian talmudic Jewish community, reads the Babylonian mapping of their boundaries as a quasi-response, or perhaps equivalency, to the older Eretz Yisraeli mapping of their boundaries:

---

[8]  See Yerushalmi Horayot 3:5 (38c): "The collector of traditions (סודרן) takes precedence over the dialectician (פילפולן)." See also Bavli Berakhot 64a where the sages of Babylonia send a question to the sages of Eretz Yisrael asking which attribute is preferable in the head of the academy, a master of memorized traditions—"Sinai" or a master of dialectics—"an uprooter of mountains." They respond: "A Sinai takes precedence, as we have a tradition: All depend on the owner of wheat." See David Rosenthal, *"Mesorot Eretz-Yisraeliot ve-Darkan le-Bavel,"* *Katedra 92* (1999), 30-35 and Jeffrey Rubenstein, *The Culture of the Babylonian Talmud* (Baltimore: Johns Hopkins University Press, 2003), 48-51.

[9]  See Bava Metzia 38b: R. Sheshet praises those from Pumbedita who "bring an elephant through the eye of a needle;" Sanhedrin 17a: "R. Yehudah said in the name of Rav: We may appoint to the Sanhedrin only one who can purify a biblically impure *sheretz*." Both of these hyperbolic statements are meant to celebrate the dialectic prowess of the sage who through argumentation can deliver the impossible: pulling an elephant through a needle and purifying the impure.

Just as Eretz Israel requires a precise geographical demarcation for the purpose of ascertaining which portions of the land are bound by the various agricultural laws pertaining only to the Land of Israel, so the physical Land of Babylonia now required a similar demarcation, for only within its confines may we find those unadulterated Jews whom one may marry without hesitation.[10]

The fourth chapter of Bavli Kiddushin explores the issue of genealogy in relation to Mishnah Kiddushin 4:1, according to which there were ten classes of family lineage that moved from Babylonia to the Land of Israel in the time of Ezra.[11] This mishnah implies that in Babylonia, everyone knew their precise lineage. In the Bavli, R. Elazar attributes the division of the Babylonian Jewish community into precise lineages to Ezra himself: "Ezra did not go up from Babylonia before he rendered it like fine sifted flour" (Kiddushin 69b). R. Yehudah engages with this image and uses it to argue for the continued superiority of Babylonia over the Land of Israel:

| בבלי קידושין עא ע"א | Bavli Kiddushin 71a |
|---|---|
| אמר רב יהודה אמר שמואל: כל ארצות עיסה לארץ ישראל, וארץ ישראל עיסה לבבל. | R. Yehudah said in the name of Shmuel: All lands are dough to Israel, and Israel is dough to Babylonia. |

In R. Yehudah's metaphor, the Land of Israel is dough, a mixture of ingredients. The residents there do not preserve records of their lineage. He contrasts this with the "fine sifted flour of Babylonia" where pure lineage was best preserved.

---

[10]   Isaiah Gafni, "'Local Patriotism' in Sasanian Babylonia," *Irano-Judaica II; Studies Relating to Jewish Contacts with Persian Culture throughout the Ages*. Shaul Shaked and Amnon Netzer eds. (Jerusalem: Ben-Zvi Institute, 1990), 67. See also Yakir Paz, "'Meishan is Dead': On the Historical Contexts of the Bavli's Representations of the Jews in Southern Babylonia," *The Aggada of the Babylonian Talmud and its Cultural Worlds*, J. Rubenstein and G. Herman eds. (Providence: Brown University Press, 2018), 47-99.

[11]   For a literary analysis of the entire sugya about genealogy see Moulie Vidas, *Tradition and the Formation of the Talmud* (Princeton: Princeton University Press, 2014), 81-112.

Above we read a story of R. Yosef excommunicating a man who moved to Be Kube. In this sugya in Kiddushin, R. Yosef singles out the place as being of suspicious lineage:

| בבלי קידושין דף ע ע"ב | Bavli Kiddushin 70b |
|---|---|
| אמר רב יוסף: האי בי כובי דפומבדיתא כולם דעבדי. | R. Yosef said: Those of Be Kube of Pumbedita are all [descendants] of slaves. |

R. Yosef brands the inhabitants of Be Kube as slaves, effectively declaring them forbidden from marrying into rabbinic families. In the same sugya in Kiddushin, Ze'iri, a Bavli rabbi, rejects the offer of R. Yohanan, an Eretz Yisraeli rabbi, to marry his daughter:

| בבלי קידושין עא ע"ב | Bavli Kiddushin 71b |
|---|---|
| זעירי הוה קא מישתמיט מיניה דר' יוחנן, דהוה אמר ליה נסיב ברתי. | Ze'iri was avoiding R. Yohanan, for he [R. Yohanan] said to him: "Marry my daughter." |
| יומא חד הוו קאזלי באורחא, מטו לעורקמא דמיא, | One day they were walking along the way. They came to a puddle of water. |
| ארכביה לר' יוחנן אכתפיה וקא מעבר ליה. | [Ze'iri] put R. Yohanan on his shoulders and carried him across. |
| אמר ליה: אורייתן כשרה, בנתין לא כשרן? | He [R. Yohanan] said to him [Ze'iri]: Our teaching is fit, but our daughters are not fit? |

R. Yohanan, the head of the rabbinic academy in Tiberias, cries out against Ze'iri's hypocrisy. Ze'iri carries R. Yohanan across the river out of deference to R. Yohanan's Torah learning, and yet Ze'iri still refuses to marry R. Yohanan's daughter out of suspicion that her lineage is not pure. If Ze'iri is the same rabbi who avoided R. Yehudah and moved to the Land of Israel, then the irony is simply overwhelming.[12] R. Zera/Ze'iri avoids R. Yehudah in Babylonia because he wishes to move to Eretz Yisrael. But upon arrival in Eretz Yisrael, he must avoid his new master, R.

---

[12] There is a large amount of confusion surrounding the relationship between these two sages because of the similarity in their names and their biographies. See Hanokh Albeck, *Mavo LaTalmudim* (Tel Aviv: Dvir, 1969), 618-622.

Yohanan, out of fear that his lineage is not sufficiently pure to marry into his family.[13]

The proposal that R. Yehudah forbade leaving Babylonia because of its superior Torah learning and lineage is preferable to the stam's messianic interpretation for several reasons. First, it accords better with other statements made by R. Yehudah as to the superiority of Babylonia. If R. Yehudah's opposition was messianic, why the prohibition of moving from Babylonia to other countries? R. Yehudah and his students denigrate the lineage of Eretz Yisraeli Jews, and this alone would explain his preference for remaining in Babylonia. Second, an anti-messianic interpretation of R. Yehudah's teaching fails to explain why R. Zera, an individual acting alone, feared his rabbi would oppose his moving to Israel. R. Zera's personal decision to move to Eretz Yisrael is unlikely to be perceived as a messianic act, for there is no sign that he is emigrating as part of a larger, messianic movement. R. Yehudah and the other Babylonian sages maintain that the superior learning and lineage of Babylonia trump the existential superiority of the Land of Israel, certainly when it comes to practical behavior. Babylonian Jews may continue to emphasize the centrality of the Promised Land in their prayers, teachings, and theology, but in real life, they must remain in Babylonia, where one can marry into a family of pure lineage and study Torah on the highest level.

The same description of an amora wishing to move to the Land of Israel and therefore avoiding R. Yehudah appears at two other points in the Bavli: Shabbat 41a, again involving R. Zera, and Berakhot 24b, in reference to R. Abba. In each of these cases the amora decides to return to the bet midrash one final time before he leaves. There, he hears an obscure halakhah from R. Yehudah and declares: "Had I come only to hear this, it would have been enough." The amoraim in these sugyot are portrayed as fearing the loss of access to their master's teachings that will occur when

---

[13] On lineage and the academic hierarchy see Rubenstein, *The Culture of the Babylonian Talmud*, 80-101; Michael Satlow, *Jewish Marriage in Antiquity* (Princeton: Princeton University Press, 2001), 133-161. Richard Kalmin suggests that the emphasis on lineage among Babylonian rabbis corresponds to its significance in surrounding Persian culture. See Kalmin, *The Sage of Jewish Society in Late Antiquity*, 51-60. Cf. Yedidah Koren, "'Look Through Your Book and Make Me a Perfect Match:' Talking about Genealogy in Amoraic Palestine and Babylonia," *Journal for the Study of Judaism* 49 (2018), 1-32, who highlights the significance of lineage in Eretz Yisraeli sources.

they move to Eretz Yisrael. This is precisely the message that the editors of these sugyot wish to impart. Those hearing these stories will clearly receive the message that abandoning Babylonia causes a permanent loss of accessibility to high levels of Torah.

By choosing to move to the Land of Israel, R. Zera rejects his master's teaching and his methods. As with the stories of the amoraim who make one last trip to the bet midrash before abandoning their masters in Babylonia, the Bavli elsewhere recognizes R. Zera's loss in his "ascent" to the Land of Israel. Bava Metzia 85a recounts:

| בבלי בבא מציעא פה ע"א | Bavli Bava Metzia 85a |
|---|---|
| ר' זירא כי סליק לארעא דישראל יתיב מאה תעניתא דלשתכח גמרא בבלאה מיניה כי היכי דלא נטרדיה. | When R. Zera went up to the Land of Israel, he observed one hundred fasts to forget the Babylonian learning, in order that it not trouble him. |

R. Zera had to fast a hundred consecutive days in order to erase all vestiges of the style of Babylonian learning that had been so deeply ingrained in his mind by R. Yehudah. Babylonian Torah is so penetrating and pervasive that it requires a super-human effort to uproot it. The teachings of the sages of Eretz Yisrael will simply find no place in his head until he forgets his Babylonian Torah. This story admits that R. Zera did in the end abandon his master, but portrays him as still recognizing the superiority of his master's learning.

Other Babylonian stories also portray a certain amount of critique of R. Zera's move to the Land of Israel. The Yerushalmi (Shevi'it 4:7, 35c) recounts that R. Zera was so eager to enter the Land of Israel after leaving Babylonia that he swam across the Jordan river in his clothing. This story may simply highlight R. Zera's willingness for self-sacrifice in adhering to the value of living in the Land. It may also allude to the original entrance of the nation of Israel into the Land, which also entailed the crossing of a river. In contrast, the Bavli both dramatizes the episode and includes the voice of a heretic mocking R. Zera's hastiness:

| בבלי כתובות קיב ע"א | Bavli Ketubot 112a |
|---|---|
| רבי זירא כי הוה סליק לארץ ישראל, לא אשכח מברא למעבר, נקט במצרא וקעבר. | When R. Zera went up to the Land of Israel he could not find a ferry to cross. He held the rope [of the bridge] and crossed. |

אמר ליה ההוא מינא:[14] עמא פזיזא
דקדמיתו פומייכו לאודנייכו, אכתי
בפזיזותייכו קיימיתו!

A certain heretic said to him: An impetuous nation which placed its mouth before its ears, you remain in your impetuousness.

אמר ליה: דוכתא דמשה ואהרן לא זכו
לה, אנא מי יימר דזכינא לה!

R. Zera said to him: [I am traveling to the] place where Moses and Aaron did not merit [entering], who is to say that I will merit!

R. Zera has no patience to wait for the next ferry and takes the more difficult route to make it to the other side. Awaiting him immediately on his arrival is not a great rabbi, as he might have expected, but a heretic who mocks his impatience, referring to the Israelites' acceptance of the Torah at Sinai before even hearing its laws (Exodus 24:7).[15] R. Zera responds that the opportunity before him is of biblical proportions and that he is determined to do all in his power to ensure that he merits making his home in the Land of Israel. Ultimately, this story does confirm R. Zera's choice—he is going beyond where Israel's ancestors had the opportunity to go. But it does at least leave the echo of criticism in our ears—R. Zera, as the heretic points out, has no idea what he is getting into.

## And R. Zera? Defending the Rebellious Student

Returning to the amoraic story of R. Zera avoiding R. Yehudah, the sugya continues with an imagined amoraic debate between the two sages. The stam does not read R. Yehudah as mandating that Jews remain in Babylonia due to its superior Torah and lineage, as we read him in line with his other statements. Rather, the stam reads R. Yehudah as prohibiting moving to the Land of Israel due to an opposition to messianism. It is difficult to know why the stam would shift the meaning of this statement, and any interpretation of ours will be highly conjectural.

---

14  The Vilna edition reads צדוקי as a result of the emendation of the censor.
15  The storyteller imports the words of the heretic from Bavli Shabbat 88a. In its original context, his critique is part of a larger sugya about revelation at Sinai. There, the heretic mocks Rava who unknowingly injures himself because he is so deeply immersed in his study.

Still, we might suggest that this shift is related to a shift in the historical situation of the Jews in Babylonia. In the early talmudic period in Babylonia, Babylonia and the Land of Israel competed with each other for authority, and we can imagine why R. Yehudah would have to insist on the superiority of Babylonia over Eretz Yisrael. By the end of the talmudic period, the rabbinic movement in the Land of Israel had dramatically diminished.[16] R. Yehudah need not argue that Babylonia's Torah is superior—everyone knows it is. Jews who wished to leave Babylonia for the Land would not be doing so because they sought better Torah learning or better marriages. The only reason to leave Babylonia for the Land of Israel in the late fifth and early sixth centuries C.E. would have been the inherent historical value of the Land. But the historical/theological value of the Land of Israel is unlike the superiority of its Torah and lineage—the latter can change, the former cannot. Therefore, the stam rereads R. Yehudah's statement in a different light, using it to prove that, despite the Land's eternal, undeniable value, Jews still may not move there. R. Yehudah no longer opposes moving to the Land of Israel; he opposes moving their **now**.

The stam expresses this debate over messianism by placing it in a format used commonly by the stammaim throughout the Bavli. In this format each rabbi responds to the interpretation of the other rabbi's verse or uses another verse to account for a halakhic position that requires Scriptural proof. Since R. Yehudah used a verse to prove that moving to the Land of Israel was forbidden, R. Zera must open with his response:

| | |
|---|---|
| בבלי כתובות קיא ע״א | **Bavli Ketubot 111a** |
| ורבי זירא? | And R. Zera? |
| ההוא בכלי שרת כתיב. | That [verse] refers to the Temple vessels. |
| ורב יהודה? | And R. Yehudah? |
| כתיב קרא אחרינא: *השבעתי אתכם* | Another verse is written: *I adjure you, O* |

---

[16] Despite the continuity of the Eretz Yisraeli academies through the 11th century, the sages of the Land of Israel were clearly in an inferior position to their Babylonian colleagues. Robert Brody writes: "Palestinian rabbinic scholars were unable to contend as equals with their Babylonian counterparts, in those fields in which the Babylonians specialized during this period, namely Talmud and halakhah...there seem to be some indications, albeit indirect and undated, that the Palestinians themselves suffered from a sense of inferiority in these areas." See Brody, *The Geonim of Babylonia and the Shaping of Medieval Jewish Culture* (New Haven: Yale University Press, 1998), 117.

בנות ירושלים בצבאות או באילות השדה, וג' (שיר השירים ב:ז).

maidens of Jerusalem, by gazelles or by the hinds of the field, [Do not wake or rouse love until it please] (Song of Songs 2:7).

ורבי זירא?

And R. Zera?

ההוא שלא יעלו ישראל בחומה.

That [verse teaches] that Israel shall not go up in a unified manner.

ורב יהודה?

And R. Yehudah?

השבעתי אחרינא כתיב.

Another *I adjure you* is written.

ורבי זירא?

And R. Zera?

ההוא מיבעי ליה לכדרבי יוסי ברבי חנינא,

That [verse] is needed for [a midrash] like that of R. Yose b. R. Hanina,

דאמר: ג' שבועות הללו למה?

who said: These three oaths, why [do they exist]?

אחת, שלא יעלו ישראל בחומה

1. That Israel shall not go up in a unified manner

ואחת, שהשביע הקדוש ברוך הוא את ישראל שלא ימרדו באומות העולם;

2. The Holy One, blessed be He, adjured not to rebel against the nations of the world

ואחת, שהשביע הקדוש ברוך הוא את העובדי כוכבים שלא ישתעבדו בהן בישראל יותר מדאי.

3. And that the Holy One, blessed be He, adjured the idolaters not to oppress Israel too much.

ורב יהודה?

And R. Yehudah?

אם תעירו ואם תעוררו כתיב.

It is written, *Do not wake or rouse.*

ורבי זירא?

And R. Zera?

מיבעי ליה לכדרבי לוי,

That [verse] is needed for [a midrash] like that of R. Levi,

דאמר: שש שבועות הללו למה?

Who said: These six oaths, why do they exist?

תלתא - הני דאמרן,

1-3. These three as was said,

אינך -

and the others,

שלא יגלו את הקץ,

4. That they will not reveal the End of Days,

ושלא ירחקו את הקץ,[17]

5. That they will not delay the End of Days,

---

[17] Manuscript traditions differ between ירחקו (delay) and ידחקו (press for). The similarity between the *daled* and *resh* often make them difficult to discern in written texts. Rashi provides an explanation for both versions. See Rashi s.v. ושלא ירחקו.

273

ושלא יגלו הסוד לאומות העולם.

6. That they will not reveal the secret to the Nations of the World.

*בצבאות או באילות השדה* (שיר השירים ב:ז):

*By the gazelles, and by the hinds of the field* (Song of Songs 2:7):

אמר רבי אלעזר, אמר להם הקדוש ברוך הוא לישראל: אם אתם מקיימין את השבועה מוטב, ואם לאו - אני מתיר את בשרכם כצבאות וכאילות השדה.

R. Elazar said: The Holy One, blessed be He, said to Israel, "If you will keep the oath, it is well; but if not, I will permit your flesh like the gazelles and the hinds of the field."

In an attempt to dissuade R. Zera from moving to Eretz Yisrael, R. Yehudah had quoted a verse from Jeremiah: "*They shall be brought to Babylon, and there shall remain, until I take note of them.*" While originally the verse referred to the Temple's vessels, R. Yehudah applied the verse to the people, who also must remain in Babylonia. According to R. Zera's imagined response, R. Yehudah has taken the meaning of the verse out of context. Only the Temple's vessels must remain, not the exiled people.

Having R. Zera reject R. Yehudah's prooftext allows the stam to open up an entirely new avenue of discourse, where we can clearly sense that the issue has shifted to messianism. R. Yehudah responds to R. Zera (as he must) by citing another verse to prove that Israel may not return to Eretz Yisrael. The verse is from Song of Songs 2:7 and is read here (as it always is in rabbinic literature) allegorically: The people of Israel may not push for the messianic redemption until God is ready for its arrival. (We will analyze this midrash in depth below). Israel may not initiate the arousal of God's love until the time to do so has arrived.

On behalf of R. Zera, the stam responds that the prohibition alluded to in Song of Songs is limited to a move to the Land of Israel "in a unified manner," meaning en masse. In contrast, R. Zera acted only as an individual, and an individual moving to the Land of Israel is not necessarily a messianic act. R. Zera's response, differentiating between an individual and a group, again demonstrates the stam's reading of R. Yehudah against the background of messianism. R. Zera can move to Eretz Yisrael because he is not acting in a messianic manner. In contrast, in its original framework as an expression of Babylonia's superior Torah learning and lineage, R. Yehudah's ideology would not have distinguished between individuals and the masses.

Most importantly, the stam here radically tempers the original voice of R. Zera, the Babylonian representative of the imperative found in the Tosefta, "A person should always live in the Land of Israel." According to the stam, R. Zera accepts R. Yehudah's prohibition of mass immigration but regards himself as an exception to the rule. The Jewish community, **according to both rabbis**, must remain in Babylonia. Only individuals may go up to the Land of Israel, and even that is only according to one opinion. This reconstructed dialogue and reframing of the debate between these two amoraim thus serves as yet another excellent example of how the Bavli rewrites and reframes its sources, tilting them more in the direction of their own ideological positions.

## "For They Did Not Return En Masse": Rebuking the Babylonians

Having analyzed the history of the dispute between R. Zera and R. Yehudah, we now turn our attention to the midrash and terminology invoked by the stam in constructing the imagined discourse between them. The terminological key to this sugya is the phrase " שלא יעלו ישראל חומה"—which we have rendered, "That Israel should not go up [to Eretz Yisrael] in a unified manner."[18] Aside from this passage in the Bavli, this phrase appears only in Shir Hashirim Rabbah. This midrashic composition was redacted in the sixth-seventh centuries and is comprised mainly of exegeses on the verses of Song of Songs. These exegeses were culled by the editor from earlier Eretz Yisraeli sources, including the Yerushalmi, Bereshit Rabbah, Vayikra Rabbah, and Pesikta de-Rav Kahana. There are midrashim preserved in Shir Hashirim Rabbah which are not extant in parallel sources and whose original source has probably been lost. There is, however, no content in the midrash directly sourced from the Bavli.[19] In other words, when content found in Shir Hashirim Rabbah appears in the Bavli, it is likely that the redactors of the Bavli drew from content found in Shir Hashirim Rabbah, or from a common source, and modified it.

---

[18] In most manuscripts of Shir Hashirim Rabbah, the word appears simply as חומה, without any modifier. This matches the form of the phrase as it appears in Joel 2:7 describing the plague of locusts.

[19] See Tamar Kadari, "On the Redaction of Midrash Shir Hashirim Rabbah" (Ph.D. Dissertation: Hebrew University of Jerusalem, 2004), 1-10.

The phrase שלא יעלו חומה appears in Shir Hashirim Rabbah in a midrash on Song of Songs 2:7 (which will be discussed below) and 8:8-9. The verses in chapter 8 read:

| שיר השירים ח:ח-ט | Song of Songs 8:8-9 |
|---|---|
| אחות לנו קטנה, ושדים אין לה. מה נעשה לאחתנו ביום שידבר בה? | We have a little sister, whose breasts are not yet formed. What shall we do for our sister when she is spoken for? |
| אם חומה היא, נבנה עליה טירת כסף; ואם דלת היא, נצור עליה לוח ארז. | If she be a wall, we will build upon it a silver battlement; if she be a door, we will panel it in cedar. |

While the simple meaning of the Song of Songs describes the intense love between a man and woman, the rabbis (and Church Fathers) read the Song as a parable for the relationship between God and God's people.[20] The rabbis' allegorical reading of the verses identifies the sister through a midrashic play on the description of her physical appearance.

| שיר השירים רבה ח:ט | Song of Songs Rabbah 8:9 |
|---|---|
| (1) רבנן פתרין קרא בעולי גולה: *אחות לנו קטנה* - אלו עולי גולה. "קטנה" - שהיו דלים באכלוסין... | (1) The rabbis interpreted the verse as referring to the returning exiles: *We have a little sister*—these are the returning exiles. "Little"—for they were few in number... |
| (2) *מה נעשה לאחותינו*: מה נעשה ביום שגזר כורש ואמר: 'די עבר פרת עבר, די לא עבר לא יעבר' | (2) *What shall we do for our sister?*: What shall we do on the day when Cyrus decreed: "Whoever crosses the Euphrates shall cross, whoever does not cross shall not cross." |
| (3) *אם חומה הוא*: אלו ישראל עלו חומה מבבל - לא חרב בית המקדש בההיא פעם שנייה. | (3) *If she be a wall*: If Israel had gone up in a unified manner (*homah*) from Babylonia, the Temple would not have been destroyed a second time. |

---

[20] See Ephraim Urbach, "The Homiletical Interpretations of the Sages and the Expositions of Origen on Canticles and the Jewish-Christian Disputation," *Scripta Hierosolymitana*, 22 (1971) 247-275.

**(4)** ר' זעירא נפיק ליה לשוקא למזבן מקומה.[21]

(4) R. Zera went out to the market to buy something.

אמר ליה לדין דהוא תקיל: תקיל יאות.

He said to the one weighing: Weigh correctly.

ואמר ליה: לית את אזיל לקמן הכא בבלייא דין דחרבון אבהתיה בית מוקדשא.

He said to him: You should not have come here, Babylonian, whose fathers destroyed the Temple.

בההיא ענתה אמר ר' זעירא: לית אבהתי כאבהתהון דהדין?

At that moment R. Zera said: Are my fathers not like this one's fathers?

עאל לבית וועדא, ושמע קליה דר' אילא יתיב דריש: *אם חומה היא*: אילו עלו חומה מן הגולה לא חרב בית המקדש פעם שנייה.

He went into the academy and heard the voice of R. Ila who was sitting and expounding: *If she be a wall*—had they come up in a unified manner from exile, the Temple would not have been destroyed a second time.

אמר: יפה לימדני עם הארץ.

[R. Zera] said: The common man has taught me well.

The rabbis suggest that the "little sister" in the verse refers to the exiles returning to Eretz Yisrael from Babylonia (section 1). This "sister" is little not because of her age but because the group who returned from Babylonia was few in number. Section 1 partially aids in clarifying the meaning of the phrase עלו חומה in section 3. This phrase has biblical origins in Joel 2:7, where the connotations are clearly militaristic: "They rush like warriors; they scale a wall (יעלו חומה) like fighters." The rabbis invoke this phrase to argue that had the Israelites returned in large numbers, the Second Temple (as the Song of Song's "silver battlement" is allegorically interpreted) would never have been destroyed. However, the rich implications of this phrase, חומה, are understood better when we take into consideration the similarity between the Hebrew word for wall and the Greek homonym, *homa*. The Greek word *homa* when used in its adverbial form means "in a unified manner."[22] Thus, this line is

---

21  The word from the root קום means an object. See Sokoloff, 327.

22  We would like to thank Hanan Mazeh for his insight on the Greek wordplay at the core of this midrash and his help in analyzing the Shir Hashirim Rabbah passage.

intentionally playing on the similarity between the Hebrew word for wall in verse 9 and the Greek word. The *darshan* is adding that not only were the numbers few, but the manner of the return to Zion was not unified.[23]

The passage continues with a story of R. Zera which takes place after his move to the Land of Israel (section 4). R. Zera enters the marketplace and warns the local shopkeeper not to try to take advantage of him. By portraying R. Zera as asking the shopkeeper to weigh his purchase correctly, the storyteller captures this sage's immigrant mindset, and his fear that he will be defrauded by a local businessman. Perhaps the fear that his fellow Jew will cheat him reflects the lack of unity between the community of returnees and the residents of the land.

R. Zera's request to be treated fairly is met with an unexpected response. The shopkeeper immediately recognizes from his spoken Aramaic that his customer is Babylonian and, without explaining why, he blames the entire community of Babylonian Jews for the destruction of the Second Temple. This surprises R. Zera, who had imagined himself as a fellow Jew—"are my fathers not like his fathers?" When R. Zera enters the academy, he learns the reason for the resentment of the Babylonians. The rabbis residing in Eretz Yisrael harbor contempt towards the Babylonians because they chose to remain safe and secure in exile rather than taking on the burden of reestablishing the Land of Israel as the religious epicenter of Judaism. The denouement of the story occurs with the capitulation of R. Zera, who accepts the ancestral blame for the destruction of the Temple taught to him by an "*am ha'aretz*," a non-rabbi.[24] The use of the term *am ha'aretz*, literally translated as a "person of the Land," may imply that R. Zera, the learned Babylonian, has been upstaged by a commoner, whose merit is attributed not to his Torah learning but to the fact that his ancestors never left Israel.

This meaning of the term *homa* is confirmed by its appearance later in the same section of midrash:

---

[23] This is perhaps a harbinger of the Bavli's notion that the Second Temple was destroyed due to "baseless hatred." See Bavli Yoma 9b.

[24] Yerushalmi Berakhot 2:8 (5c) relates a different story of R. Zera's encounter with a shopkeeper following his move to the Land of Israel. In this humorous tale, R. Zera is duped by a butcher into believing that any purchase of meat is accompanied by a blow from the butcher. This, and other stories, are analyzed by Saul Lieberman in the aptly titled, "So It Was So It Will Be: The Jews of the Land of Israel and World Jewry in the Period of the Mishnah and Talmud," *Katedra* 17 (1981), 3-10.

## Shir Hashirim Rabbah 8:9

שיר השירים רבה ח:ט

ריש לקיש כד הוה חמי להון מצמתין בשוקא הוה אמר להון: בדרו גרמיכון!

Resh Lakish said: When I saw them gathered in the marketplace, I would say to them: Disperse yourselves!

אמר להם: בעליתכם לא נעשיתם חומה, וכאן באתם לעשות חומה!

He said to them: When you came up [to the Land of Israel] you did not make yourself a unified group (*homah*), but here you came to make a unified group (*homah*)!

Resh Lakish encounters a group of Babylonians in the marketplace in Eretz Yisrael. Upon seeing them gathering together, he becomes enraged and rebukes them for maintaining their homogenous character in the public market. Resh Lakish's reaction is multifaceted. There is clearly a xenophobic tone to this story, especially against immigrants who maintain their old identities in their new surroundings. On top of that, Resh Lakish invokes the tortuous history between Babylonians and Eretz Yisraeli Jews. Resh Lakish rhetorically argues that their unity as immigrants in the third century C.E. is too late—had their ancestors been able to muster the same unity hundreds of years earlier, Jewish history might have taken a much more positive turn.

A similar story involving Resh Lakish rebuking a Babylonian appears in Bavli Yoma 9b.[25] The editors of the Bavli, however, offer a response to Resh Lakish which nullifies his harsh critique:

## Bavli Yoma 9b

בבלי יומא ט ע"ב

ריש לקיש הוה קא סחי מיא בירדן. אזל רבה בר בר חנה יהב ליה ידא.

Resh Lakish was swimming in the Jordan. Rabbah b. b. Hannah came and extended his hand [in assistance].

אמר ליה: מאלהא, סנינא לכו, דכתיב *אם חומה היא נבנה עליה טירת כסף ואם דלת היא נצור עליה לוח ארז.*

He [Resh Lakish] to him: By God! I hate you (pl.), for it is written: *If she be a wall* (homah*), we will build upon it a silver battlement; if she be a door, we will panel it in cedar.*

---

25  For a full literary analysis of the sugya see Yonatan Feintuch, "Sanina Lechu: Sippur Pegishatam shel Resh Lakish ve-Rabbah b. b. Hannah al ha-Yarden," *JSIJ* *12* (2013), 1-23.

אם עשיתם עצמכם כחומה ועליתם בימי עזרא - נמשלתם בכסף שאין רקב שולט בו, עכשו שעליתם כדלתות - נמשלתם בארז שרקב שולט בו...

Had you made yourself like a wall (*homah*) and come up in the days of Ezra, you would be compared to silver, which cannot rot. Now that you have come up like doors, you are like cedar, which rots...

כי אתא לקמיה דרבי יוחנן אמר ליה: לאו היינו טעמא, אי נמי סליקו כולהו בימי עזרא לא הוה שריא שכינה במקדש שני, דכתיב *יפת אלהים ליפת וישכן באהלי שם* (בראשית ט, כז).

When he [Rabbah b. b. Hannah] came before R. Yohanan, he [R. Yohanan] said to him: That is not the reason, even if you had all come in the times of Ezra, the *Shekhinah* would not have dwelled in the Second Temple, as it says: *May God enlarge Yafet, and let him dwell in the tents of Shem* (Genesis 9:27).

אף על גב דיפת אלהים ליפת - אין השכינה שורה אלא באהלי שם.

Although God enlarges Yafet, the *Shekhinah* only dwells in the tents of Shem.

The dramatic encounter between the two sages takes place on the banks of the Jordan, the natural border of the Land of Israel and the very same river that R. Zera was so eager to cross.[26] Rabbah b. b. Hannah extends his hand in a gesture of kindness, in an effort to breach the physical barrier between the sages. Resh Lakish rebukes the rabbi who comes to his aid, regarding him as a representative of all Babylonians (as evidenced by his use of the plural), for the destruction of the Temple. Similar to the passage in Shir Hashirim Rabbah, Resh Lakish acts with great disdain towards all Babylonians, even when they are not gathered in a group. Based on the juxtaposition found in the original verse, "If she be a wall, we will build upon it a silver battlement; if she be a door, we will panel it in cedar," the midrash explains that the return was a failure due to the weakness of the returning exiles. The return to Zion from Babylonia was "like doors"— weak and penetrable. Had it been strong and impenetrable, like a wall, the Second Temple would never have been destroyed.

---

[26]  In fact, the Talmud raises questions about the chronological accuracy of the story and R. Pappa suggests that the story may actually describe an encounter between Resh Lakish and the Babylonian sage Ze'iri. On the relationship between R. Zera and Ze'iri see above, n. 12.

We should note in the Bavli the word "חומה" does not have any implication of "unified manner" as it did in the Eretz Yisraeli midrash and story, which makes sense, given that the Babylonian Jews would have been less familiar with Greek terminology. Furthermore, like the butcher who rebuked R. Zera in the Bavli, Resh Lakish is angry at the presence of even an individual Babylonian, and not at their gathering in the public marketplace. This Babylonian story may testify to the loss of the understanding of the pun between the Greek and Hebrew words, and to the secondary use of a midrashic motif that originally appeared in the Eretz Yisraeli sources.

The sugya concludes with words of consolation from R. Yohanan. R. Yohanan, well-known as Resh Lakish's teacher and contemporary, explains that even if all the Babylonian exiles had returned, the Temple would not have reached the status of God's dwelling. This comment, which we shall explain below, offers some solace to the Babylonian audience through the voice of the most authoritative Eretz Yisraeli amora, who explains that the Babylonians are not actually responsible for the failure of the Second Temple.

R. Yohanan's nullification of Resh Lakish's harsh rebuke does not appear in the above Eretz Yisraeli sources. Rather, the Babylonian editors have created this statement from other related sources to provide a conclusion more amenable to a Babylonian audience. The claim that the Second Temple did not contain God's divine presence appears in Bereshit Rabbah 36:8:

| בראשית רבה לו:ח | **Bereshit Rabbah 36:8** |
|---|---|
| יפת אלהים ליפת זה כורש שגזר שיבנה | *May God enlarge Yafet*—this is Cyrus |
| בית המקדש, אפעלפיכן *וישכן באהלי* | who decreed that the Temple be built, |
| *שם*, אין שכינה שורה אלא באהלי שם. | even so *let Him dwell in the tents of Shem*, the *Shekhinah* only dwells in the tents of Shem. |

The midrash connects the verse from Noah's blessings and curses to his sons in Genesis to Cyrus' decree allowing the Babylonian exiles to return to the Land of Israel and rebuild the Temple. God did not dwell in the Second Temple because the initiative for rebuilding it came from the

Persian king, a descendent of Yafet.[27] God will reside only in a Temple built by the children of Shem, as was the case with the First Temple built by Solomon. The midrash in Bereshit Rabbah has nothing to do with the lack of Babylonian participation in the building of the Second Temple. Rather, it is an explanation for the lack of God's presence in the rebuilt Temple. The Babylonian editors rework this midrash in order to achieve the desired amelioration of Resh Lakish's rebuke, ascribing it to R. Yohanan, Resh Lakish's teacher.[28] Again, we witness Babylonian editors emending the content of Eretz Yisraeli sources to temper their anti-Babylonian sentiment, rather than omitting these sources entirely.

These stories reveal a fascinating dynamic in the Eretz Yisrael/Babylonia relationship during the rabbinic period. The Eretz Yisraeli sources bitterly blame the Babylonians for their historic failure to return to the Land of Israel to aid in the rebuilding of the Temple. Eretz Yisraeli amoraim believe that had there been a mass return of the exiles, the Temple would never have been destroyed. They fault their Babylonian contemporaries for the sins of their fathers. Bavli Yoma responds to the rebuke by attributing a midrash to R. Yohanan which discredits the claim that the Babylonians are solely responsible for the failure of the Second Temple. Rather, it was beyond the control of both the Babylonian and the Eretz Yisraeli Jews that the Second Temple was fated never to rival the glory of the First.

## "That They May Not Return En Masse": From Rebuke to Oath

The Eretz Yisraeli sources cited above rebuke Babylonian Jewry for not returning en masse, *homa*, to the Land of Israel. And yet the Bavli uses this same word as a defense of the choice to remain in exile—even R. Zera professes that Israel may not return *homa* to the Land. The concept that Jews living in the Diaspora are prohibited from returning en masse to the Land also has its origins in Shir Hashirim Rabbah. We begin with the full citation of Song of Songs 2:7 referenced above:

---

27  The Medeans are the direct decedents of Yafet (Genesis 10:2). When Cyrus conquers the Medians around 550 BCE, he unifies the kingdoms (see Esther 1:3). Due to this link between the nations, rabbinic literature identifies the Persians as the decedents of Yafet.

28  Bavli Megillah 9b preserves a different midrash on Genesis 9:22 attributed to R. Yohanan.

<table>
<tr>
<td dir="rtl">

שיר השירים ב:ז

השבעתי אתכם בנות ירושלם בצבאות
או באילות השדה אם תעירו ואם
תעוררו את האהבה עד שתחפץ.

</td>
<td>

Song of Songs 2:7

I adjure you, O maidens of Jerusalem, by gazelles or by hinds of the field: Do not wake or rouse love until it please!

</td>
</tr>
</table>

The rabbis' allegorical interpretation of the verse explores the identity of the person taking the oath ("I adjure you") and the meaning of the oath ("do not wake or rouse love"). The midrash on this verse presents two alternatives for the number of the oaths referred to in the verse, one attributed to R. Yose b. R. Hanina and one to R. Helbo:

<table>
<tr>
<td dir="rtl">

שיר השירים רבה ב:ז

ר' יוסי בר' חנינא אמר: שתי שבועות יש כאן :אחת לישראל ואחת לאומות העולם.

1. נשבע לישראל שלא ימרדו על עול מלכיות,

2. ונשבע למלכיות שלא יקשו עול על ישראל, שאם מקשים עול על ישראל הם גורמים לקץ לבוא שלא בעונתו ...

ר' חלבו אמר: ארבע שבועות יש כאן:

1. השביע לישראל שלא ימרדו על המלכיות.

2. ושלא ידחקו על הקץ.

3. שלא יגלו מסטירין שלהם לאומות העולם.

4. ושלא יעלו חומה מן הגולה.

אם כן למה מלך המשיח בא לקבץ גליותיהן של ישראל?

</td>
<td>

Song of Songs Rabbah 2:7

R. Yose b. R. Hanina said: There are two oaths, one made by Israel and one by the nations:

1. He adjured Israel not rebel against the yoke of the kingdoms.

2. And he adjured the kingdoms not to intensify the yoke over Israel, for if they intensify the yoke over Israel, they will cause the End of Days to arrive before their time...

R. Helbo said: There are four oaths:

1. He adjured Israel not to rebel against the kingdoms.

2. That they will not press for the End of Days.

3. That they will not reveal their secret to the nations of the world.

4. That they will not go up in a unified manner (*homah*). [For] if so, why does the Messiah come to gather Israel's exiles?

</td>
</tr>
</table>

R. Yose b. R. Hanina's explanation of the verse is based on the doubling of the verb "awaken": "אם תעירו ואם תעוררו, do not wake or rouse love." He reads the verse as connoting a reciprocal oath: Israel is adjured not to revolt ("do not wake") and the nations are adjured not to awaken something within God ("do not rouse").[29] The subject of the oath is found in the continuation of the verse: "love until it please." The love referred to is God's love manifest in Israel's redemption at the End of Days. God implores both Israel and the nations to passively wait for the redemption to come at its appropriate time ("until it please"). The midrash calls for a repression of a revolt of Israel against the ruling authority. In return, God reassures Israel through the oath He administers to the nations of the world not to (overly?) oppress Israel. The core assumption of the midrash is that there is a specific predetermined time when God will bring about Israel's final redemption. When considered in its historical context, this type of midrash has been read by scholars as a corrective for the acute messianism which brought about the Bar Kokhba revolt. The monumental failure of the revolt, which jeopardized Judaism's very existence, motivated the rabbis to shift their messianism into the realm of faith and passivity; redemption is to be brought about by God alone.[30]

In the continuation of the midrash, R. Helbo doubles the number of oaths referred to in the verse. The suppression of messianic fervor also lies at the core of his explanation of the oaths, but he does not read the verse as referring to reciprocal oaths between Israel and the nations. Instead, he explains that all four oaths were made by Israel. This reading better fits with the actual wording of the biblical text, since "maidens of Jerusalem," interpreted as Israel, are the ones being adjured. Like R. Yose b. R. Hanina, R. Helbo expounds the double language of awakening which leads him to two oaths. The other two oaths are added because the same verse appears in chapter 3 verse 5—doubling the number of oaths for a total of four.[31] The first oath is verbatim the same oath described by R. Yose b. R. Hanina. The second oath, similar to the first, is that Israel will not press for an early arrival of the End of Days. In the continuation of the midrash (not quoted above) there is a list of four different leaders:

---

[29] The difficulty with this interpretation is that the subject of the verse is "the maidens of Israel." It is, therefore, unclear how R. Yose b. R. Hanina explains the verse as referring to the nations.

[30] See Gershom Scholem, *The Messianic Idea in Judaism and Other Essays on Jewish Spirituality* (New York: Schocken, 2006), 57.

[31] Song of Songs 8:4 uses extremely similar language, but 2:7 and 3:5 are identical verses.

Amram, Denai, Bar Kokhba, Shutelah b. Efrayim—who each "pressed for the End" by inappropriately rebelling against ruling authorities.[32]

The third oath adjures Israel not to reveal the secret date (מיסטיריון) of the End of Times. This word is derived from the Greek *mysterion*, meaning secret.[33] Revealing the secret, like the two oaths listed before it, is related to bringing about an early redemption. According to the rabbinic thought in these *derashot*, certain people are in possession of the date of redemption and they are charged with keeping it secret until it is divinely revealed to the entire world. The strict restrictions surrounding the calculation of the End of Days are a reflection of the prominence of eschatological calculations in the ancient Jewish world. During the Second Temple period and the first centuries C.E. a variety of Jewish groups, ranging from the members of the Qumran sect, to early Christians, to the authors of the various apocalypses, each believed in their own way that it was living at the End of Days. For various reasons, the rabbis living in the post Second Temple period seem to have strongly opposed these messianic beliefs.[34]

The final oath described by R. Helbo strikingly uses the exact same phrase found in chapter eight of Shir Hashirim Rabbah, שלא יעלו חומה, where it appeared as a critique of Babylonian Jewry for not having returned en masse to the Land of Israel when the Temple was rebuilt. The unusual phrase originated in the midrashic context in chapter eight, where it served as a word play on Song of Songs 8:9. R. Helbo, a Babylonian amora who moved to the Land of Israel, reads the lack of mass return in an entirely different way. Rather than a failure to bring about the redemption, i.e. the eternality of the Second Temple, it was a reflection of God's demand that Israel await deliverance through a divinely appointed

---

[32] The latter two cases are easily identified: (3) the Bar Kokhba rebellion of 132-135 CE and (4) the rabbinic interpretation of the incident described in I Chronicles 7:20-22 (see Mekhilta Beshalah and Bavli Sanhedrin 92b). There is, however, much debate over the proper identification of the first two generations.

[33] In the Bavli, the word is changed to the Hebrew סוד. The same term "*mistorin*" is found in Bereshit Rabbah (parashah 98) in a midrash describing Jacob's desire to reveal this secret date to his children on his deathbed: "*What is to befall you in the days to come* (Genesis 49:1)—it comes to teach that he wanted to show them the End Times (*mistorin*) and it was obscured from him.

[34] See for example Bavli Sanhedrin 97b. For more see Oded Irshai, "Dating the Eschaton: Jewish and Christian Apocalyptic Calculations in Late Antiquity," *Apocalyptic Time*, ed. Albert Baumgarten (Leiden: Brill, 2000), 113-153.

messiah. Importantly, his teaching inextricably imbues a mass return to the Land of Israel with deep eschatological significance. Returning to the Land of Isarel en masse is a messianic process, one that should not or cannot be initiated by human political activity.

## R. Yehudah, R. Zera, and the Oaths

Bavli Ketubot transforms the material from Shir Hashirim Rabbah into an unconditional defense of life in the Diaspora. First, R. Yehudah's rebuke of R. Zera, which is also based on Songs of Songs 2:7, prohibits even lone individuals to move to the Land of Israel. In Shir Hashirim Rabbah, there was at most a prohibition on moving to Eretz Yisrael en masse. As a result of R. Yehudah's midrash prohibiting emigration altogether, the Bavli ascribes the position which prohibits a mass move to R. Zera, the very amora who was pushing to move to Eretz Yisrael in the first place. Thus, a position that was expressed only by R. Helbo in Shir Hashirim Rabbah is in the Bavli attributed even to his disputant and is, in the end, unanimous, as is evident when we line up the midrashim in parallel columns.

| Bavli | Shir Hashirim Rabbah |
|---|---|
| [R. Yose b. R. Hanina] | [R. Yose b. R. Hanina] |
| אחת, שלא יעלו ישראל בחומה; ואחת, שהשביע הקדוש ברוך הוא את ישראל שלא ימרדו באומות העולם; ואחת, שהשביע הקדוש ברוך הוא את העובדי כוכבים שלא ישתעבדו בהן בישראל יותר מדאי. | נשבע לישראל שלא ימרדו על עול מלכיות, ונשבע למלכיות שלא יקשו עול על ישראל, שאם מקשים עול על ישראל הם גורמים לקץ לבוא שלא בעונתו. |
| 1. That Israel shall not go up in a unified manner | 1. He adjured Israel not to rebel against the yoke of the kingdoms. |
| 2. The Holy One, blessed be He, adjured Israel not to rebel against the Nations of the World | 2. And he adjured the kingdoms not to intensify the yoke over Israel, for if they intensify the yoke over Israel, they will cause the End of Days to arrive before their time. |
| 3. And the Holy One, blessed be He, adjured the idolaters that they will not oppress Israel too much… | |

ר' חלבו אמ': ארבע שבועות יש כאן:
השביע לישראל שלא ימרדו על
המלכיות,
ושלא ידחקו על הקץ,
שלא יגלו מסטירין שלהם לאומות
העולם,
ושלא יעלו חומה מן הגולה אם כן למה
מלך המשיח בא לקבץ גליותיהן של
ישראל.

לכדרבי לוי,
דאמר: שש שבועות הללו למה?
תלתא - הני דאמרן,
אינך - שלא יגלו את הקץ,
ושלא ירחקו את הקץ,
ושלא יגלו הסוד לאומות העולם.

...R. Levi who said: What are the six oaths [mentioned in the verse]?
1-3. Three, as were said;
And the others,
4. That they will not reveal the End of Days,
5. That they will not delay[35] the End of Days,
6. That they will not reveal the secret to the nations of the world.

R. Helbo said there are four oaths:
1. He adjured Israel not to rebel against the kingdoms
2. That they will not press for the End Times
3. That they will not reveal their secret to the nations of the world
4. That they will not go up in a unified manner.

While in Shir Hashirim Rabbah only R. Helbo portrays Israel as swearing not to go up in a unified manner, in the Bavli both R. Yose b. R. Hanina and R. Levi agree that this was one of the oaths. In the Bavli, the redactor seems to have taken the oath attributed to R. Levi and attributed it to his collocutor, R. Yose b. R. Hanina, such that he too prohibits emigrating en masse. However, as often happens in such situations, the redactor's agenda creates literary disruptions in the text. Here, the redactor's goal of portraying unanimous agreement as to a ban on mass immigration undermines the literary strength of the midrash. R. Yose b. R. Hanina's original midrash was based on the reciprocity of the oaths—"one made by Israel and one by the nations." This reciprocity is lost in the Bavli's version of the statement, where a third oath adjured only to Israel is added. Further proof that the first oath is a later addition is that the second oath opens with "God adjured Israel," even though the first oath was also an adjuration of Israel. Thus, the first oath was an addition to the

---

[35] See above n. 18.

source which originally contained two, as is found in Shir Hashirim Rabbah.

In the wake of the addition of an oath to R. Yose b. R. Hanina's statement, the editor must increase R. Helbo/R. Levi's oaths from four to six in order to maintain the doubling which, to recall, was based on the repetition of the same verse elsewhere in Shir Hashirim. The editor accomplishes this first by attributing R. Yose b. R. Hanina's original two oaths to R. Levi. In the context of the Bavli, this means that R. Levi agrees with all three of R. Yose b. R. Hanina's oaths. Together with R. Helbo/R. Levi's original two oaths, there are now a total of five. The additional oath, inserted here as the fourth oath, the first unique to R. Levi, "That they will not reveal the End of Days," is basically redundant with, "that they will not reveal the secret to the nations of the world" (the last of R. Levi's oaths). As we demonstrated above, the "secret" originally is none other than the date of the eschaton. Clearly the stam was just trying to get to the desired total of six. It accomplishes this at the cost of a high level of redundancy. We should also note that the stam is either hesitant or unable to create any new oaths—all six oaths found in the Bavli are essentially found in the four oaths in Shir Hashirim Rabbah. As often occurs, difficulties in texts are evidence of their textual development.

We should conclude by summarizing the shift that occurs from a broader perspective within this suyga. As we demonstrated above, the original amoraic dispute concerning the move to the Land of Israel was a question of the priority of Torah/lineage in Babylonia over the historical/theological centrality of the Land of Israel. The Bavli adapts a theme from Shir Hashirim Rabbah concerning the prohibition of a mass move to Israel, a prohibition against messianism, and attributes it to the Babylonian amoraim who would have argued over the appropriateness of an individual to move to the Land of Israel. In other words, the stam shifts the focus of R. Yehudah's prohibition from that of leaving Babylonia to an outright ban against moving to Eretz Yisrael. In turn, R. Zera's decision to ignore his teacher evolves from a defiant statement of connection to the Land into a supporting voice in the unified rabbinic chorus against messianism. Even R. Zera, who fervently wishes to move to the Land of Israel, admits that he may do so only as an individual. As a community, Babylonian Jews are like the Temple vessels—destined to remain in exile until God redeems them.

# The Enduring Legacy of Bavli Ketubot 111a: The Oaths and Zionism

The final redaction of the sugya in Ketubot introduced a rigid and uncompromising prohibition on moving to the Land of Israel en masse until God "will take note of them," i.e. until the messianic period. The verses in Song of Songs referring to God's adjuration of the daughters of Israel were interpreted as a series of prohibitions on returning to the Promised Land and hastening redemption. Aviezer Ravitzky has explored the impact of the oaths throughout Jewish history in his book *Messianism, Zionism and Jewish Religious Radicalism.*[36] We will now explore a few of the examples he cites in order to demonstrate how the sugya in Ketubot has played a significant role in rabbinic writings in medieval and modern Jewish history. In the twelfth century, Maimonides was the first to invoke the oaths in an effort to quell eschatological fervor among the Jews of Yemen. Maimonides wrote in his *Epistle to Yemen*:

> Solomon of blessed memory, inspired by the Holy Spirit, foresaw that the prolonged duration of the Exile would incite some of our people to seek to terminate it before the appointed time, and as a consequence they would perish or meet with disaster. Therefore, he admonished them and adjured them in metaphorical language to desist, as we read: *I adjure you, O maidens of Jerusalem, by gazelles or by the hinds of the field, do not wake or rouse love until it please.* Now, brethren and friends, abide by the oath, and stir not up love until it pleases. And may God, Who created the world with the attribute of mercy, grant us to behold the ingathering of the exiles to the portion of His inheritance.

Maimonides used the oaths from Ketubot in order to reject the messianic claims of a false prophet who was preaching a syncretistic religion which combined Judaism and Islam during a period of persecution of Yemen's Jews. Maimonides feared the prophet would bring about more political turmoil and disaster for the Jews, and attempted to reassure them with the

---

[36] Aviezer Ravitzky, *Messianism, Zionism, and Jewish Religious Radicalism* (Chicago: University of Chicago Press, 1996), 211-234.

belief that although the end of their suffering was near, they must still wait for deliverance from God.[37]

The oaths were also cited in the thirteenth century as part of a polemic against Jews from the French tosafist schools who began to move to and settle in the Land of Israel. Their decision to move was halakhically motivated by an intense desire to be able to fulfill those commandments that were conditional upon living in the Land of Israel.[38] The German Pietists harshly critiqued the move to the Land of Israel, citing the sugya from Ketubot and specifically R. Yehudah's teaching that one who moves to the Land transgresses a negative commandment. One particularly strident passage, penned by R. Eliezer b. Moshe of Wurzburg, creates a new midrash which alludes to the oaths of remaining in exile:

> *You shall set bounds for the people* (Exodus 19:12) around Jerusalem and around the Land of Israel. *Beware of going up to the mountain*—He adjured Israel not to force the End or to go up to the Land of Israel before the time and it says, *I adjure you… And when the ram's horn sounds they may ascend the mountain*, when will Israel leave the Exile and ascend to the Land of Israel? When the shofar [of redemption] sounds.

R. Eliezer of Wurzburg explains that the same restrictions on coming into contact with Mt. Sinai exist for entering the Land of Israel, and thus the Jews must wait for a clear sign of permission from God. He rejected the pious motivation of the French tosafist school, insisting that their move was in brazen defiance of God's adjuration of the Jews to remain in the Diaspora until He signals their return.[39]

In the modern period, the oaths played a particularly significant role in polemics concerning the religious validity of the establishment of the modern State of Israel. The Zionist call for action and a return to the Land of Israel was a direct attack on the rabbinic voice celebrating

---

[37] See Abraham S. Halkin, and David Hartman. *Epistles of Maimonides: Crisis and Leadership*. (Philadelphia: Jewish Publication Society, 1993), 163-172.

[38] See Ephraim Kanarfogel, "The Aliyah of 'Three Hundred Rabbis' in 1211: Tosafist Attitudes toward Settling in the Land of Israel," *The Jewish Quarterly Review* 76, 3 (1986), 191-215.

[39] Israel Ta-Shma, *Studies in Medieval Rabbinic Literature I: Germany,* (Jerusalem: The Bialik Institute, 2004), 254-260.

passivity which called for Jews to demonstrate their devotion to God by remaining in exile. In 1958, the Satmar Rebbe, Rabbi Joel Moshe Teitelabum, the prominent leader of the radical anti-Zionist movement, invoked the oaths as the cornerstone for his case against Zionism:

> ...In our generation one need not look far for the sin responsible for our calamity... The heretics have made all kinds of efforts to violate these oaths, to go up as a unified group and to seize sovereignty and freedom by themselves, before the appointed time, which is pressing the End time... it is no wonder that the Lord has lashed out in anger.

Teitelbaum identifies the Holocaust as the punishment for the heretical Zionists' violation of the oaths. He offers a theological explanation for the unexplainable and labels the Zionist movement as the source of the divine punishment. Even in the dark shadow of the Holocaust, Teitelbaum demands that Jews remain faithful to the oath of passivity in exile.[40]

On the other end of the spectrum, religious Zionist leaders were forced to contend with the oaths and argue that mass aliyah was halakhically valid, even for those who believe in the divinity of the oaths.[41] Rav Avraham Isaac Kook, for example, maintains the significance of the oaths but provides a new understanding of their meaning:

> ...it is for this reason that the Holy One, blessed be He, adjured the children of Israel not to press for the End, for He knew from the outset that when they recognized their bliss upon their return to the Land, they would not be able to control themselves to not [press for the End], and therefore He forbade it. So that they would not press for the End using means that are prohibited to the children of Israel.[42]

Rav Kook limits the restrictions of the oaths to the use of military force and taking action against the wishes of the nations of the world.

Rav Zvi Yehudah Kook, his son, takes a more dramatic step and argues that subsequent to the establishment of the State of Israel, the oaths are no longer binding:

---

[40]   See Ravitzky, ibid., 63-66.
[41]   Elie Holzer, "The Evolving Meaning of the Three Oaths: Within Religious Zionism," *Da'at* 47 (2001), 129-145.
[42]   *Sefer Arakhim* 1, 152

The Owner of the house, the Master of the Universe, He is pressing us. It is not the voice of a human being, rather the voice of the living God who has torn down the wall which divided us from our land, calling out to us, ascend![43]

Rav Kook harnesses the imagery of the wall, to claim that God Himself has torn down the barrier that had blocked the return to Zion and repealed the oaths once and for all.

## Conclusion

In May of 1980, Saul Lieberman addressed the relationship between Jews in Eretz Yisrael and the Diaspora during the talmudic period in a lecture delivered in memory of Moshe Haviv, who fell in battle in the Six Day War. The title of his lecture, "So It Was and So It Will Be," perfectly captures the timeless complexity of this relationship.[44] Indeed, Lieberman saw himself caught between the two worlds, as his own life was split between Israel and New York. In the lecture, Lieberman demonstrates how many of the familiar tropes of the poor, sandal-wearing Israeli who struggles to survive, and his rich, easy-living brother of the Disapora, are already evident in the stories of the Talmud. Those who made their home in Eretz Yisrael, in spite all the hardships, looked disparagingly on the Babylonians, who chose the comforts of the Diaspora over a commitment to the Promised Land. Their Babylonian counterparts, in turn, looked haughtily on the Jews in the Land of Israel, whose Torah learning and family connections they regarded as woefully inferior.

As Lieberman noted, the fundamental tensions underlying the conflicted relationship between Jews in the Diaspora and those in the Land of Israel in the talmudic era are the same tensions that govern this relationship today. Jews like R. Zeira, wherever they may find themselves, are drawn to the land of Israel, whereas others, like R. Yehudah, maintain that competing Jewish values prevent them from them from leaving their homes in the Diaspora. And in the Land of Israel, there will be always be those like Resh Lakish who have nothing but scorn for any Jews who elect

---

[43] Cited by Holzer, ibid, 144.
[44] See above n. 24.

to make their home anywhere else. In a sense, then, these Talmudic figures are archetypes for ourselves and our contemporaries, and in their struggles we can find a poignant reflection of our own.

# CHAPTER SEVEN

## FINDERS, KEEPERS, DECLARERS, DESPAIRERS: NAVIGATING THE LAWS OF RETURNING LOST OBJECTS

## BAVA METZIA 24A-24B

## Introduction

One of the aspects of the Bavli that makes it so fascinating to traditional students, modern academic scholars, and historians, is its tendency to both preserve and change the traditions that it has received. The Bavli preserves sources, voices from tannaitic and amoraic Eretz Yisrael or from earlier generations in Babylonia, that do not accord with later amoraic and stammaitic halakhah. The Bavli is thus unlike both earlier collections of halakhah and later codifiers. It is unlike the Mishnah, which is frequently a one-dimensional collection in which historical layers and voices from the past are hard—if not impossible—to recover or even detect. Neither is it at all like Maimonides' great code, the Mishneh Torah, which, patterned after the Mishnah itself, recasts its sources and usually cites only the accepted halakhic opinion with virtually no preservation of conflicting viewpoints. The Bavli is a compendium of the work of earlier generations, preserving its sources with a relatively large degree of accuracy, as can be seen by the thousands of parallels with earlier Eretz Yisraeli sources still found in the Tosefta, the halakhic midrashim, and the Yerushalmi.

However, the Bavli, and specifically the editors who gave it its final shape, also frequently insists on its own point of view. At times, the Babylonian editors did emend their received sources, as we have shown many times throughout our work. But more frequently, the Bavli achieves its desired result through contextualizing earlier sources such that they accord with the later halakhic views of the editors. These contextualizations are often forced, clashing quite obviously with what tannaim and earlier amoraim actually said and meant. And while these contextualizations do seem to have bothered medieval commentators, the Bavli itself seems to prefer them to the alternative: frequent contradictions between early and later halakhah.[1] These contextualizations allow the editors of the Bavli to preserve their fealty to earlier sages and at the same time guide the halakhah into new directions.

We have demonstrated this process many times throughout our work, but we believe that this chapter is the clearest demonstration of these tendencies and this process. It is the clearest case we have written about in which tannaitic halakhah rules in one way and stammaitic halakhah, influenced by some Babylonian amoraim, rules in another. Both sets of sources—the earlier and the later—are clear, and the strained contextualizations are obvious. As such, we hope this sugya about finding lost objects will help our readers find their way through the intricate and delicate process of preservation and innovation which is the hallmark of the incredible work of the stammaim, the ancient editors who produced the Bavli as we know it.

## The Biblical Commandment to Return a Lost Object

The biblical commandment regarding a lost object is found in Deuteronomy 22:1-3. The Torah requires the finder to initially care for an object he has found in order to be able to return it to its eventual claimant:

| דברים כב:א-ג | **Deuteronomy 22:1-3** |
|---|---|
| לא תראה את שור אחיך או את שיו נדחים, והתעלמת מהם; השב תשיבם לאחיך. | If you see your fellow's ox or sheep gone astray, do not ignore it; you must take it back to your fellow. |

---

[1]  The Bavli describes this preference on Menahot 55a: "R. Pappa said: Learn from this that we prefer to give a forced explanation to a tannaitic source as dealing with two different sets of circumstances rather than attribute it to two different authorities." The analysis of forced contextualization is a hallmark of David Weiss Halivni's methodology. See Jeffrey Rubenstein, "Translator's Introduction," *The Formation of the Babylonian Talmud*, by David Weiss Halivni (Oxford: Oxford University Press, 2013), xvii-xxx. For a comprehensive review of medieval and early modern commentators' engagement with this issue, see David Weiss Halivni, *Mekorot u-Mesorot: Nashim* (Tel Aviv: Dvir, 1968), 7-19.

ואם לא קרוב אחיך אליך ולא ידעתו,
ואספתו אל תוך ביתך והיה עמך עד דרש
אחיך אתו; והשבתו לו.

If your fellow does not live near you or you do not know who he is, you shall bring it home and it shall remain with you until your fellow claims it; then you shall give it back to him.

וכן תעשה לחמרו; וכן תעשה לשמלתו; וכן
תעשה לכל אבדת אחיך אשר תאבד ממנו
ומצאתה: לא תוכל להתעלם.

You shall do the same with his donkey; and you shall do the same with his garment; and so too shall you do with anything that your fellow loses and you find: Do not ignore it.

The Torah directly addresses a person who might be tempted to ignore a lost animal or object due to the inconvenience or expense of taking care of it for an indefinite period of time. If, for instance, he found a wandering animal, the Torah mandates that he bring the animal to his home and care for it until the owner claims it. To the finder, this could cause a significant loss of both time and money. The Torah therefore addresses the person tempted to intentionally overlook the lost animal. Speaking directly to such a person the Torah demands, "Do not ignore it." Noticeably, the Torah is not here concerned about theft, i.e. people gathering lost objects and claiming them as their own, but only about neglect of responsibility.

## Value and Identifying Marks

The Torah's law somewhat idealistically assumes that the owner will eventually be reunited with his lost item. More realistically, the tannaim create the institution of public declaration of lost objects in order to reunite owners with their missing property. The tannaim put limitations on the Torah's law and delineate exactly when the finder of a lost object is obligated to publicly declare what he has found in order to find the owner. There are three main principles which are at the core of the tannaitic discussion of a lost object:

1) What constitutes an identifying mark such that the owner could prove his claim;
2) The monetary value of the object;
3) The loss of hope of recovery by the owner.

Sifre Deuteronomy piska 224 (=Mishnah Bava Metzia 2:5) derives two of these requirements from the example of the garment found in the verse from Deuteronomy cited above:

| ספרי דברים פיסקא רכד | Sifre Deuteronomy piska 224 |
|---|---|
| אַף השמלה היתה בכלל כל אלו; ולמה יצאת? | The garment was included in the general rule; why then was it specified? |
| להקיש אליה: מה שמלה מיוחדת שיש לה סמנים ויש לה תובעים, כך כל שיש לו סמנים ויש לו תובעים. | In order to draw an analogy: Just as a garment is characterized by having identifying marks and having claimants, so too anything which has identifying marks and has claimants [must be declared]. |
| אין לי אלא אלו בלבד שאר אבדה מנין? תלמוד לומר: *לכל אבדת אחיך*. | I know only these particular objects, what about all other lost objects? Scripture states: *Anything your fellow loses.* |

The Sifre uses a garment as illustrative of the general rules of the obligation to declare a lost object. First, there is no mandate to care for a lost object unless it has a mark by which its owner could identify it as his own. If there is no such mark, there would be no way for the owner to substantiate his claim, thereby rendering the entire process futile. Mishnah Bava Metzia 2:1 provides examples of items which lack identifying marks, such as randomly scattered coins and pieces of meat. One who finds such objects may keep them for herself. Second, the finder is not required to care for the object if it is not valuable enough such that its owner would look for it. It must have "claimants"—that is, it must be of sufficient value for someone to want to claim it.

## Loss of Hope of Recovery

Another criterion used by the tannaim to determine when the finder is obligated to declare a found object is the assumption that, in certain situations, the owner would lose hope of recovery. The term for such loss of hope is יאוש, usually translated as "despair." If the owner can be assumed to have given up hope of being able to recover the object he has lost, the finder does not have to declare it.[2] The idea is that by giving up hope, the original owner actually renounces his ownership. Therefore, there is no longer an owner to return it to, and the finder is free to lay claim to the object. The Tosefta explains that location in which the object was found can serve to indicate that the owner has abandoned hope of recovery:

| תוספתא בבא מציעא ב:ב | Tosefta Bava Metzia 2:2 |
|---|---|
| וכן היה ר' שמעון בן לעזר אום' המציל | And so did R. Shimon b. [E]lazar say: |
| מפי הארי ומפי הזאב ומשניתו של ים | If one saves [an object] from the mouth |
| ומשניתו של נהר. | of a lion, the mouth of a wolf, the |
| | depths of the sea, the depths of the |
| | river; |
| המוציא באסרטיא ובפלטיא גדולה הרי | if one finds [an object] on the main |
| אילו שלו מפני שהבעלים מתיאשין מהן. | road, in the square—they are his, |
| | because the owners have abandoned |
| | hope of recovery. |

According to R. Shimon b. Elazar, an owner would give up hope of recovering any object lost in a place from which it would be physically difficult to recover it, such as in the proximity of wild animals or near the sea. The second clause refers to the broader, more likely scenario of objects lost in a public space. Although such objects are not physically challenging to recover, the owner would assume that recovery is unlikely—perhaps because the object was moved, because he cannot remember exactly where he lost it, or because someone else took it for himself. It is essential to note that there is no indication that R. Shimon ben Elazar distinguished between objects with an identifying mark and those without; in either case he assumes that the owner would abandon hope of recovery and, thus, the finder may keep the object. That is, according to R. Shimon b. Elazar, the finder may keep the object despite the fact that its owner may be able to identify it were the finder to declare it. Furthermore, there is no indication that the majority disagrees with his opinion. Both of these points will be important for our analysis of the Talmuds.

---

[2] While there is no tannaitic midrash which provides an explicit source for the principal of abandonment, there is an amoraic midrash found in Yerushalmi Bava Metzia 2:1 (53a) which identifies Deuteronomy 22:3 as the biblical source.

## Large Bundles Found in the Public Domain

Tosefta Bava Metzia 2:5 qualifies the previous halakhah by adding that the finder must also take into account the bulk of the object, which would impact how easily it may be recovered:

| תוספתא בבא מציעא ב:ה | Tosefta Bava Metzia 2:5 |
|---|---|
| מצא כריכות ברשות היחיד חייב להכריז. | If one finds a small sheaf in a private domain, he must declare it. |
| ברשות הרבים אין חייב להכריז. | In the public domain he does not have to declare it. |
| האלומות בין ברשות היחיד ובין ברשות הרבים חייב להכריז. | Larger bundles, whether in a private or public space, he must declare. |

From the first clause we can see that small bundles are recoverable, but only when found in the private domain. When found in the public domain, the owner would presume that they would be kicked around, trampled, and irrevocably lost. Like an object rescued "from the mouth of a lion," a small item lost in the public domain is assumed to be permanently irrecoverable. However, when one finds large bundles, he must declare them even if they were found in the public domain. This is due to the weight and size of the bundles. An owner would not lose hope of recovering such a mass of material, for large items are harder to truly lose.

We can extrapolate from this specific case to other cases: One who finds any large lost object would have to declare it, even if found in the public domain.[3] Different rules apply to smaller objects. If the object is identifiable and is found in the private domain, the owner would still hope to recover it under the assumption that with fewer people there, the item would be found and declared. But if he lost it in the public domain, we can assume that the owner would abandon hope of recovery, even if the item is of some value, and therefore the finder need not declare it.

---

[3]   See Shamma Friedman, "Metziot Birshut ha-Rabim," *Diney Yisrael 6* (1975), 175.

# Yerushalmi Bava Metzia: What is an Identifying Mark?

There are two relevant passages in the Yerushalmi which examine the subject of lost objects found in the public domain. The first, found in Bava Metzia 2:2 (8b), focuses on R. Yehudah's statement in the mishnah which requires that an object with a unique mark be declared: "Anything which has in it something unusual must be declared. How is this so? If he found a fig cake with a potsherd in it or a loaf with coins in it[—he must declare them]." The anonymous voice of the Yerushalmi questions the nature of the unique mark and asks whether an object with such a mark would have to be declared, even if it were found in the public domain:

| | |
|---|---|
| **ירושלמי בבא מציעא ב:ב (ח, ב)** | **Yerushalmi Bava Metzia 2:2 (8b)** |
| (1a) תני: במשוקע בו. | (1a) It was taught: [The identifying mark] must be pressed inside [the object]. |
| (1b) הכא את מר במשוקע בו וכא את מר בנתון בו דרך הינוח. | (1b) Here you say it must be pressed inside, but there you say [even] if it was placed on top [it is sufficient]! |
| (1c) הן דתימר במשוקע בו ברשות הרבים והן דתימר בנתון בו דרך הינוח ברשות היחיד. | (1c) When it says "it must be pressed inside," it refers [even] to [an object] in the public domain, and when it says "[even] it is was placed on top," it refers to [an object] in the private domain. |
| (1d) ואפילו ברשות הרבים בנתון בו דרך הינוח אני אומר דרך נפילה נפלה עליו... | (1d) And even in the public domain, if it is placed on top, I [could] say that it had [accidentally] fallen on it [and need not be declared]!... |
| (2) אמוריה דרבי יוחנן אשכח עזיל כריך במקטורא. אתא לגבי רבי יוחנן. אמר ליה: הן אשכחתיניה? בסימטא בפלטיא? | (2) R. Yohanan's speaker[4] found a spool of yarn wrapped in a coat. He came before R. Yohanan. He [R. Yohanan] said to him: "Where did you find it: On the footpath or in |

---

4  In rabbinic academies, the lecturer would teach in a low voice and the "speaker" would convey the material to the audience in a loud voice. In modern terms, we would think of the speaker as a human microphone.

the open space?"

דו בעי מיפתרינה כהדא דרבי שמעון בן
אלעזר דמתניתן.

He [R. Yohanan] wanted to interpret according to R. Shimon b. Elazar of the baraita.

Section 1a cites a baraita, which clarifies R. Yehudah's teaching and requires that the identifying mark be pressed into the object for it to be considered a valid indication of ownership. Such a mark is considered superior to one found external to the object because it is clear that it was intentionally placed there to signify ownership. Furthermore, the owner would not abandon hope of recovery because he would assume that a mark pressed into the object would remain in place. The anonymous voice then objects (section 1b) that the baraita contradicts a ruling found in the Tosefta which does not require the sign to be pressed into the object. Tosefta Bava Metzia 2:4 teaches:

תוספתא בבא מציעא ב:ד

כתוב בחרש ונתון על פי חבית בנייר
ונתון על פי עגול חייב להכריז.

**Tosefta Bava Metzia 2:4**

If [his name] was written on a potsherd and placed on the barrel, or [his name was written] on paper and placed on the [fig] cake it (the barrel or fig cake) must be declared.

The Tosefta relates directly to the examples given by R. Yehudah in the mishnah. According to the Tosefta, an identifying mark placed on the object is sufficient—it does not need to be pressed into the object. The anonymous voice in the Yerushalmi resolves the contradiction by differentiating between the locations in which the object was found (section 1c). In order for an object found in the public domain to require declaration, the mark must be pressed into the object. The owner has clearly marked his goods and he will assume the mark remains on them. A mark which is found external to the goods, however, may not remain in place. The owner will assume the mark fell off and abandon hope of recovery. On the other hand, if one finds an object in the private domain with an identifying mark placed upon it, he must declare it. In such a place the owner will hold out hope that the mark will remain on the object and will not become lost.

The sugya continues with a case in which a spool of yarn was found wrapped in a coat. The finder asks R. Yohanan whether he must declare the object. R. Yohanan responds by asking where the objects were found. If they were in a private space, the owner may have left them there on purpose or may be able to cite their location as an identifying mark. But if they were found in public, he may keep them because, relying on R. Shimon b. Elazar's ruling from the Tosefta (BM 2:2), one need not return objects found in the public domain. Notably, R. Yohanan's teaching does not engage with the ruling of the anonymous voice of the Yerushalmi which demands that certain objects with identifying marks must be declared even if they are found in the public domain. R. Yohanan seems to imply that R. Shimon b. Elazar's ruling is valid without any qualifications. This may be because R. Yohanan's ruling predated the qualification of the anonymous Yerushalmi.

In sum, the sugya clarifies two important points about objects found in the public domain. First, the anonymous voice of the Yerushalmi, based on the baraita, clarifies that an identifying mark pressed into an object is a valid signifier of ownership in the public domain, and thus an object with such a mark must be returned. Second, R. Yohanan's ruling indicates that amoraim explicitly rely on R. Shimon b. Elazar to allow the finder to keep an object found in the public domain, even if it has an identifying mark.

## Yerushalmi Shekalim: Identifying Marks as Symbols of Kashrut

The second sugya in the Yerushalmi is located in Shekalim. The seventh chapter of this tractate deals with items found in various locations in and around the Temple precincts. The sugya relates to mishnah 3, which covers the subject of meat which had been found in the Temple courtyard. The Yerushalmi uses this mishnah as an opportunity to discuss whether one can assume that found meat is kosher and therefore may be eaten. After bringing sources and stories that deal only with the issue of whether one can eat found meat, the Yerushalmi transitions to stories which discuss both the status of the meat as kosher and the status of the meat as a lost object—may it be kept by the finder?

## Yerushalmi Shekalim 7:3, 50c

### ירושלמי שקלים ז:ג (נ, ג)

(1) גדי צלי אישתכח באיסרטא דגופתא
והתירוהו משם שני דברים: משם מציאה
ומשם רוב מהלכי דרכים.

(1) A roasted kid was found on the road of Guftha and they allowed it for two reasons: (i) due to a found object; and (ii) due to the majority of the travelers.

משם מציאה דתני: המציל מיד הארי מיד
הגייס משונת הים ומשונת הנהר
ומאיסרטיא גדולה ומפלטיא גדולה הרי
אילו שלו מפני שהבעלים מתייאשין מהן.

"Due to a found object" as it is taught: If one saves [objects] from a lion, from the legions, from a shoal in the sea, from a shoal in the river, from the main road, from the square—they belong to him, because the owner has abandoned them.

משם רוב מהלכי דרכים משם שחיטת הגוי.
ואישתכח מן דבית רבי.

"Due to the majority of the travelers" [because they were Jews, there is no concern that] the slaughter was performed by a non-Jew. And it was discovered that it belonged to the house of Rabbi [Yehudah Hanasi].

(2) עיגול דגובנא אישתכח בפונדקא דלוי
והתירוהו משם שני דברים: משם מציאה
ומשם רוב מהלכי דרכים.

(2) A wheel of cheese was found in Levi's inn and they allowed it for two reasons: (i) due to a found object; and (ii) due to the majority of the travelers.

משם מציאה דתני: המציל מיד הגייס מיד
הארי משונת הים משונת הנהר מאיסטרטיה
גדולה ומפלטיא גדולה הרי אילו שלו מפני
שהבעלים מתייאשין מהן.

"Due to a found object" as it is taught: If one saves [objects] from a lion, from the legions, from a shoal in the sea, from a shoal the river, from the main road, from the square—they belong to him, because the owner has abandoned them.

משום רוב מהלכי דרכים משום גבינת גוי
ואישתכח מן דר' אלעזר בי ר' יוסי.

"Due to the majority of the travelers" [because they were Jews there is no concern for] cheese made by a non-Jew. And it was discovered that it belonged to R. Elazar b. R. Yose.

(3a) א"ר מנא קומי ר' יוסי: ואנן חמיין
רבנן מכרזין.

(3a) R. Mana said before R. Yose: Do we not see the sages declaring [lost objects]?

303

(3b) אמר ליה את אין הווייתה משכח לא
נסבת?

(3b) He said to him: If you found [a lost object,] would you not take it?

ר' יונה אבוך לא אמ' כן. אלא אמ' הלואי
כד נשכח נשכח מן פרוסדוס⁵ ולגיו.

Your father R. Yonah did not say this. Rather he said when I find [a lost object,] let me find it within the curved path [which leads into the city].

(3c) אפילו כן אשכח ולא נסב.

(3c) Even so he found [a lost object] and did not take it.

In the first two stories, the sages allow the finder to keep the object based on the opinion of R. Shimon b. Elazar in the Tosefta passage cited above. Since the object was found in a public space (the road of Guftha or Levi's inn), the owner is considered to have abandoned hope of recovery. Additionally, there is no concern for the kashrut of the object because the majority of the those traveling there were Jewish. It is essential to note that here the makeup of the population is relevant only to the kashrut of the object, and not to the issue whether it must be returned. Below we will see a different opinion in the Bavli.

Section 3 is more complicated. R. Mana questions the lenient rulings found in these stories, for he has witnessed sages declare lost objects with identifying marks found in the public domain. R. Yose responds (section 3b) that he is sure that if R. Mana were to find a lost object in the public domain, he too, like the rulings in the stories, would keep it. Furthermore, R. Mana's own father, R. Yonah, wished to extend the leniency of R. Shimon b. Elazar even further. R. Yonah declared that he hoped to find a lost object on the path which led from the main road into the city.[6] The force of this statement is that even this path is considered like the public domain, and therefore objects found there may be kept by the finder. A later anonymous voice, perhaps troubled by this extension of the leniency, adds (section 3c) that R. Yonah did find a lost object on the path but he did not take it. However, he also did not declare it lost because he was not required to do so. The final comment suggests that, on the one hand, the anonymous voice of the Yerushalmi is unsure of the extension of R.

---

[5] This word was changed in the citation to reflect the proper reading suggested by Saul Lieberman, *Ha-Yerushalmi Kifshuto* (New York: Jewish Theological Seminary,1994), 347.

[6] See Lieberman, ibid. Yerushalmi Eruvin 8:8 (25c) questions if the curved path leading into the city is considered the public domain.

Shimon b. Elazar's leniency, but, on the other hand, he does not rule that the finder of an object on such a path is responsible to locate the owner.

Both passages in the Yerushalmi demonstrate that Eretz Yisraeli amoraim rule according to the opinion of R. Shimon b. Elazar: Any object found in a public space—even if it has an identifying mark—may be kept because the owner has lost hope of recovery. The anonymous voice of Yerushalmi Bava Metzia, based on the mishnah and a baraita, provides one exception to the general rule: An object with a mark pressed into it must be declared even in the public domain because the owner would not abandon hope of recovery. Additionally, the anonymous voice at the end of Shekalim expresses concern over R. Yonah's desire to expand the leniency. The later voices in the Yerushalmi accept R. Shimon b. Elazar's ruling but provide certain limits or reservations pertaining to its application.

## Bavli Bava Metzia 24a-24b
## Part 1: Testing the Limits of R. Shimon b. Elazar

We will begin with a brief overview of part 1 of the Bavli sugya, and then move on to part 2, before returning to consider part 1 in greater depth. The sugya in the Bavli begins by quoting R. Shimon b. Elazar's ruling in the Tosefta, which it proceeds to analyze and interrogate at length:

OPENING TANNAITIC SOURCE

(1) And so did R. Shimon b. Elazar say: If one saves [an object] from a lion, a bear, a leopard, a panther,[7] the the depths of the sea, the depths of the river; If one finds [an object] on the main road, in the square, or in any place where there are crowds present,[8] they are his, because the owners have abandoned hope of recovery.

(1) וכן היה ר' שמעון בן אלעזר אומר:
המציל מן הארי ומן הדוב ומן הנמר ומן
הברדלס ומן זוטו של ים ומשלוליתו של
נהר;
המוצא בסרטיא ופלטיא גדולה ובכל
מקום שהרבים מצויין שם הרי אלו שלו
מפני שהבעלים מתיאשין מהן.

---

[7] The other animals are included in the baraita here because they are commonly grouped together in other tannaitic texts. See for example Mishnah Bava Kama 1:4.

[8] The clause "any place where there are crowds" is added into the Toseftan baraita in order to explain the Greek cognates סרטיא ופלטיא, which would not have necessarily been understood by the Babylonian audience.

## STAMMAITIC QUESTIONING TO DETERMINE HALAKHAH

(2a) אֵיבַּעְיָא לְהוּ: כִּי קָאָמַר רַבִּי שִׁמְעוֹן בֶּן אֶלְעָזָר בְּרוֹב גּוֹיִם אֲבָל בְּרוֹב יִשְׂרָאֵל לֹא? אוֹ דִּלְמָא אֲפִילוּ בְּרוֹב יִשְׂרָאֵל נָמֵי אָמַר?

(2a) They asked: Did R. Shimon b. Elazar say [that the object may be kept] only where the majority of the people are non-Jews,[9] but not where the majority are Jews; or perhaps he also said it [may be kept] where the majority are Jews?

(2b) אִם תִּמְצָא לוֹמַר אֲפִילוּ בְּרוֹב יִשְׂרָאֵל נָמֵי אָמַר, פְּלִיגִי רַבָּנָן עֲלֵיהּ אוֹ לֹא פְּלִיגִי?

(2b) And if you say he said this even where the majority are Jews, do the Rabbis disagree with him or not?

(2c) וְאִם תִּמְצָא לוֹמַר פְּלִיגִי - בְּרוֹב יִשְׂרָאֵל וַדַּאי פְּלִיגִי - בְּרוֹב גּוֹיִים פְּלִיגִי אוֹ לֹא פְּלִיגִי?

(2c) And if you say that they disagree—they certainly disagree where the majority are Jews—do they also disagree where the majority are non-Jews, or do they not disagree?

(2d) וְאִם תִּמְצָא לוֹמַר פְּלִיגִי, אֲפִילוּ בְּרוֹב גּוֹיִם הֲלָכָה כְּמוֹתוֹ, אוֹ אֵין הֲלָכָה כְּמוֹתוֹ?

(2d) And if you say that they disagree even where the majority are non-Jews, does the law follow him or does the law not follow him?

(2e) אִם תִּמְצָא לוֹמַר הֲלָכָה כְּמוֹתוֹ דַּוְקָא בְּרוֹב גּוֹיִם אוֹ אֲפִילוּ בְּרוֹב יִשְׂרָאֵל?

(2e) And if you say the law follows him [R. Shimon b. Elazar], does this apply only when the majority are non-Jews, or does it [apply] even when the majority are Jews?

## FIRST PROOF BASED ON A BARAITA

(3a) תָּא שְׁמַע: הַמּוֹצֵא מָעוֹת בְּבָתֵּי כְנֵסִיּוֹת וּבְבָתֵּי מִדְרָשׁוֹת וּבְכָל מָקוֹם שֶׁהָרַבִּים מְצוּיִין שָׁם הֲרֵי אֵלּוּ שֶׁלּוֹ מִפְּנֵי שֶׁהַבְּעָלִים מִתְיָאֲשִׁין מֵהֶן.

(3a) Come and hear: If one finds money in synagogues or in study houses, or in any other place where crowds are present, it belongs to him [the finder], because the owner has abandoned it.

---

[9] The Vilna printed edition, which is based on an earlier print edition that underwent Christian censorship, uses "Canaanites" instead of the term *goyim*. See Amnon Raz-Krakotzkin, *The Censor, the Editor, and the Text: The Catholic Church and the Shaping of the Jewish Canon in the Sixteenth Century* (Philadelphia: University of Pennsylvania Press, 2007), 127-128.

(3b) מאן שמעת ליה דאזיל בתר רובא? ר' שמעון בן אלעזר. שמעת מינה אפילו ברוב ישראל נמי.

(3b) Who did you hear say that we follow the majority? R. Shimon b. Elazar. Therefore, conclude that [he allows one to keep it] even with a majority of Jews.

(3c) הכא במאי עסקינן? במפוזרין.

(3c) What are we dealing with? With [a case where the money was] scattered.

(3d) אי במפוזרין, מאי איריא מקום שהרבים מצויין שם? אפילו אין הרבים מצויין שם.

(3d) But if [the money was] scattered, why specify places where crowds are present? [It would apply] even if crowds were not present!

(3e) אלא לעולם בצרורין, והכא במאי עסקינן? בבתי כנסיות של גוים.

(3e) Rather, [the baraita refers to money found] in bundles, and what are we dealing with? With synagogues of non-Jews.

(3f) בתי מדרשות מאי איכא למימר?

(3f) But what can you say about study houses?

(3g) בתי מדרשות דידן דיתבי בהו גוים.

(3g) [The baraita refers to] our study houses in which non-Jews sit.

(3h) השתא דאתית להכי, בתי כנסיות נמי דידן דיתבי בהו גוים.

(3h) Now that you have arrived at this conclusion, "synagogues" [can] also [refer to] our synagogues in which non-Jews sit.

(4a) תא שמע: מצא בה אבידה אם רוב ישראל חייב להכריז אם רוב גוים אינו חייב להכריז.

(4a) Come and hear: If one finds there a lost object, if the majority are Jews it has to be declared, but if the majority are non-Jews it does not have to be declared.

(4b) מאן שמעת ליה דאמר אזלינן בתר רובא? ר' שמעון בן אלעזר. שמעת מינה כי קאמר ר' שמעון בן אלעזר ברוב גוים אבל ברוב ישראל לא.

(4b) Who did you hear say that we follow the majority? R. Shimon b. Elazar. Therefore, conclude that when R. Shimon b. Elazar spoke, he was referring to a majority of non-Jews, but when there is a majority of Jews he cannot [keep what he finds]!

(4c) [No.] Whose opinion is this? It is the rabbis.

הא מני? רבנן היא. (4c)

(4d) Solve from this that the rabbis accept R. Shimon b. Elazar's view in the case of a majority of Jews [that the object may be kept]!

(4d)תפשוט מינה דמודו ליה רבנן לרבי שמעון בן אלעזר ברוב גוים!

(4e) Rather, it is indeed R. Shimon b. Elazar, and his ruling [that the object may be kept] applies even to a case of a majority of Jews, but here we are dealing [with a case where the object was] concealed.

(4e) אלא לעולם ר' שמעון בן אלעזר היא ואפילו ברוב ישראל נמי, והכא במאי עסקין? בטמון.

(4f) But if it was concealed, what is he doing with it? Have we not learned: If one finds a vessel in a trash, if covered up he may not touch it; but if uncovered he must take it and declare it."

(4f) אי בטמון מאי עבידתיה גביה? והתנן: מצא כלי באשפה מכוסה לא יגע בו מגולה נוטל ומכריז.

(4g) As R. Pappa explained: [The reference is] to a trash heap which is not regularly cleared away, and which [the owner] unexpectedly decided to clear away.[10]

(4g) כדאמר רב פפא: באשפה שאינה עשויה לפנות ונמלך עליה לפנותה.

(4h) Here too, [the reference is] to a trash heap which is not regularly cleared away, and which [the owner] unexpectedly decided to clear away.

(4h) הכא נמי באשפה שאינה עשויה לפנות ונמלך עליה לפנותה.

(4i) And if you wish, say this is indeed the view of the rabbis. Does [the mishnah] teach, "They belong to the finder?" It [merely] teaches, "He does not have to declare them." He leaves them, and a Jew will come and bring an identifying mark and take them.

(4i) ואיבעית אימא: לעולם רבנן. מי קתני הן שלו, אינו חייב להכריז קתני. ויניח ויתי ישראל ויהיב ביה סימנא ושקיל.

---

[10] Based on the sugya on 25a, R. Pappa's teaching included only the first half of the statement. See David Weiss Halivni, *Mekorot u-Mesorot: Bava Metzia* (Jerusalem: Magnes Press, 2003), 72 n. 5.

THIRD PROOF BASED ON AN AMORAIC STATEMENT

(5a) תא שמע דאמר רב אסי: מצא חבית יין בעיר שרובה גוים מותרת, משום מציאה ואסורה בהנאה. בא ישראל ונתן בה סימן מותרת בשתיה למוצאה.

(5a) Come and hear: R. Assi said: If one finds a barrel of wine in a city with a majority of non-Jews, it is permitted because of [the law of] a found object and he is forbidden to derive benefit from it. If a Jew comes and presents an identifying mark, the finder is permitted to drink it.

STAMMAITIC EXPLANATION

(5b) כמאן? כר' שמעון בן אלעזר.

(5b) Whom does this follow? R. Shimon b. Elazar.

שמע מינה כי קאמר ר' שמעון בן אלעזר ברוב גוים, אבל ברוב ישראל לא!

Conclude from it that R. Shimon b. Elazar says [that it may be kept] only where the majority are non-Jews, but not where there the majority are Jews!

(5c) לעולם אימא לך ר' שמעון בן אלעזר אפילו ברוב ישראל נמי קאמר, ורב אסי סבר לה כוותיה בחדא ופליג עליה בחדא.

(5c) [No.] I could nevertheless say to you that R. Shimon b. Elazar says [that it may be kept] even when the majority are Jews, but R. Assi agrees with him in one case [a non-Jewish majority] and disagrees from him in the other case [a Jewish majority].

(5d) וכי מאחר דאסירא בהנאה, מותרת משום מציאה למאי הלכתא?

(5d) But since it is forbidden to derive any benefit, what purpose does the law permitting him to keep it as a found object serve?

(5e) אמר רב אשי: לקנקנה.

(5e) R. Ashi said: [It refers] to the vessel.

---

| Tannaitic Source | Amoraic Source | Stammaitic Source |

After quoting R. Shimon b. Elazar's baraita from the Tosefta, the sugya continues with a multi-layered halakhic inquiry (sections 2a-2f) exploring this teaching. The stam asks two main questions:

1) Does R. Shimon b. Elazar maintain that an object found in the public domain may be kept even if the majority of the local population is Jewish?
2) Does the law follow R. Shimon b. Elazar?

The demographics of the local population are relevant because tannaitic halakhah establishes that Jews do not need to return lost objects owned by non-Jews. The rabbis base this halakhah on Deuteronomy 22:3, which stipulates that one must return the lost object of "your fellow (אחיך)." Tannaitic midrash interprets this to exclude the lost object of a non-Jew.[11] The stam then brings three sources in an attempt to answer these questions. The baraita (section 3a) seems to indicate that a lost object may be kept even if the majority of people in the location are Jews, while the mishnah (section 4a) and the amoraic statement (section 5a) seem to indicate that the object may be kept only if there is a non-Jewish majority. Throughout the sugya, the proofs offered as a way of answering these questions are rendered inconclusive by the use of extremely forced contextualiztions. This section has all the signs of a late stammaitic creation: The stam introduces the passage with a complicated question, weaves his discourse out of a collection of tannaitic and amoraic sources, and avoids prematurely answering these questions by rejecting the validity of the proofs through forced contextualizations.

## Part 2: Babylonian Case Law

(1) ההוא גברא דאשכח ארבעה זוזי דציירי בסדינא ושדו בנהר בירן. אתא לקמיה דרב יהודה, אמר ליה: זיל אכריז.

(1) A certain man once found four zuz tied up in a cloth and thrown into the Biran canal. He came before R. Yehudah who said to him, "Go and declare it."

---

[11] See Mekhilta Deuteronomy 23:3. See Menahem Kahana, "Dapim min ha-Mekhilta le-Devarim Parashot Ha'azinu ve-Vezot ha-Berakhah," *Tarbiz* 57 (1988), 182-185, 196. Later sources offer some reservations about the ruling. Yershalmi Bava Metzia 2:5 (8c) recounts a story where Shimon b. Shetah returns a lost object to a non-Jew as an act of piety, and Bavli Bava Kama 113b adds in the name of R. Pinhas b. Yair that if taking the lost object will lead to the profanation of God's name, it is forbidden. See Adiel Schremer, "Brotherhood, Solidarity, and the Rabbinic Construction of the Commandment to Return Lost Property," *Journal of Law, Religion and State* 3 (2014), 51-61.

והא זוטו של ים הוא?

But is this not [like retrieving an object from] the depths of the sea?

שאני נהר בירן כיון דמתקיל לא מיאש.

The Biran canal is different. Since it has a restricted flow, the owner does not abandon hope of recovering it.

והא רובא גוים נינהו?

But is it not a majority of non-Jews?

שמע מינה אין הלכה כר' שמעון בן אלעזר אפילו ברוב גוים!

Conclude from it that the law is not in accordance with R. Shimon b. Elazar even with a majority of non-Jews!

שאני נהר בירן דישראל סכרו ליה וישראל כרו ליה. כיון דישראל סכרו ליה אימור מישראל נפל וכיון דישראל כרו ליה לא מיאש.

The Biran canal is different since Jews dam it up and Jews dredge it. Because Jews dam it up, it may be assumed that [the coins] fell from a Jew, and because Jews dredge it, [the owner] did not abandon hope of recovering them.

(2) רב יהודה הוה שקיל ואזיל בתריה דמר שמואל בשוקא דבי דיסא.

(2) R. Yehudah once followed Mar Shmuel into the quarter of pounded wheat vendors.

אמר ליה: מצא כאן ארנקי מהו?

He asked him: What if one found a wallet here?

אמר ליה: הרי אלו שלו.

[Mar Shmuel] answered: It would belong to the finder.

בא ישראל ונתן בה סימן מהו?

What if a Jew came and brought an identifying mark?

אמר ליה חייב להחזיר.

[Mar Shmuel] answered: He would have to return it.

תרתי?

Both?

אמר ליה: לפנים משורת הדין.

[Mar Shmuel] answered: [This is] beyond the letter of the law.

כי הא דאבוה דשמואל, אשכח הנך חמרי במדברא ואהדרינהו למרייהו לבתר תריסר ירחי שתא; לפנים משורת הדין.

Like the case of the father of Shmuel who found some donkeys in a desert, and he returned them to their owner after a year of twelve months; [he went] beyond the letter of the law.

311

(3) רבא הוה שקיל ואזיל בתריה דר' נחמן בשוקא דגלדאי ואמרי לה בשוקא דרבנן.

(3) Rava once followed R. Nahman into the quarter of the leather workers (some say: into the quarter of scholars).

אמר ליה: מצא כאן ארנקי מהו?

He asked him: What if one found a wallet here?

אמר ליה: הרי אלו שלו.

He [R. Nahman] said to him: It would belong to the finder.

בא ישראל ונתן בה סימן מהו?

What if a Jew came and brought an identifying mark?

אמר ליה הרי אלו שלו.

He [R. Nahman] said to him: It would belong to the finder.

והלא עומד וצווח!
נעשה כצווח על ביתו שנפל ועל ספינתו שטבעה בים.

But is he not standing and shouting! It is as if he is shouting about his house collapsing or about his ship sinking in the sea.

(4) ההוא דיו דשקיל בשרא בשוקא ושדיה בצנייתא דבי בר מריון.

(4) A certain bird took [a piece of] meat from the market and dropped it among the *tzninita* palms of Bar Marion.

אתא לקמיה דאביי.
אמר ליה: זיל שקול לנפשך.

[Bar Marion] came before Abaye. Abaye said to him: Go and take it for yourself.

והא רובא דישראל נינהו?
שמעת מינה הלכה כר' שמעון בן אלעזר אפילו ברוב ישראל!

But is it not a Jewish majority? Conclude from it that the law follows R. Shimon b. Elazar even when the majority are Jews!

שאני דיו דכזוטו של ים דמי.

[Finding something dropped by] a bird is different, for it is like the depths of the sea.

והא אמר רב: בשר שנתעלם מן העין אסור?
בעומד ורואהו.

But did Rav not say: Meat which has disappeared from sight is forbidden? [In this case, Bar Marion] stood and watched it [the whole time].

(5) ר' חנינא מצא גדי שחוט בין טבריא לציפורי והתירוהו לו.

(5) R. Hanina once found a slaughtered goat between Tiberias and Sepphoris, and they permitted him [to take] it.

R. Ammi said: They permitted him [to take it due] to a found object in accordance with R. Shimon b. Elazar, and [they considered] its slaughter [to be ritually valid] in accordance with R. Hanania b. R. Yose Hagalili.

אמר רבי אמי: התירוהו לו משום מציאה כר' שמעון בן אלעזר, משום שחיטה כרבי חנניא בנו של רבי יוסי הגלילי.

For it has been taught: If one lost his goats or chickens and subsequently found them slaughtered—R. Yehudah forbids them, and R. Hanania b. R. Yose Hagalili, permits them. Rabbi [Yehudah Hanasi] said: The words of R. Yehudah seem correct in a case where they were found on a trash heap, while the words of R. Hanania b. R. Yose Hagalili seem correct when they were found in a house.

דתניא: הרי שאבדו לו גדייו ותרנגוליו והלך ומצאן שחוטין, ר' יהודה אוסר ורבי חנניא בנו של רבי יוסי הגלילי מתיר. אמר רבי: נראין דברי רבי יהודה כשמצאן באשפה ודברי רבי חנניא בנו של רבי יוסי הגלילי כשמצאן בבית.

Since they were permitted in regard to ritual slaughter, the majority must have been Jews!

מדהתירוהו לו משום שחיטה, רובא ישראל נינהו!

Conclude from it that the law is according to R. Shimon b. Elazar even when there are a majority of Jews.

שמעת מינה הלכה כר' שמעון בן אלעזר אפילו ברוב ישראל.

Rava said: [That was a case where] there the majority was non-Jews but the majority of the butchers [were] Jewish.

אמר רבא: רוב גוים ורוב טבחי ישראל.

(6) R. Ammi once found some slaughtered pigeons between Tiberias and Sepphoris.

(6) רבי אמי אשכח פרגיות שחוטות בין טבריא לציפורי.

When he appeared before R. Assi (some say: before R. Yohanan; and some say: in the house of study) they said to him: "Go and take them for yourself."

אתא לקמיה דר' אסי, ואמרי לה לקמיה דר' יוחנן ואמרי לה בי מדרשא, ואמרו ליה: זיל שקול לנפשך.

(7) R. Yitzhak Napaha once found some balls of thread spun at the spinners.

(7) רבי יצחק נפחא אשכח קיבורא דאזלי ביה אזלויי.

אתא לקמיה דר' יוחנן ואמרי לה בבי
מדרשא, ואמרו ליה: זיל שקול לנפשך.

When he appeared before R. Yohanan
(some say in the house of study) they
told him: "Go and take them for
yourself."

| Tannaitic Source | Amoraic Source | Stammaitic Source |

The second part of the sugya consists of a series of seven legal cases in
which various amoraim render decisions with regard to lost objects found
in the public domain. The cycle of stories begins with the stringent
position of R. Yehudah (case 1), who requires the declaration of a lost
object with an identifying mark even when found in a public place where
the majority are non-Jews. The cycle continues with two cases (2, 3) in
which an amora rules that a lost object found in the public domain need
not be declared and returned to its owner, but adds that one should go
beyond the letter of the law and declare the object in any case. The sugya
concludes with four cases in which an amora allows a lost object to be
kept by the finder, a halakhah consistent with the tannaitic and Eretz
Yisraeli sources we have seen up until the point—lost objects found in the
public domain may always be kept by the finder.

We will begin our analysis by examining a few of the amoraic cases
found in part 2 in light of a relevant sugya from earlier in chapter 2 of
Bava Metzia which played a crucial role in shaping the stammaitic
approach to lost objects found in the public domain. We will then return
to part 1 in order to demonstrate how the stam's halakhic opinion, which
stands in contrast to the Eretz Yisraeli halakhah, contributes to the forced
explanations which characterize the first part of the sugya.

## Rav Yehudah (Part 2, Section 1): All Objects with Identifying Marks Must Be Declared

R. Yehudah's ruling in part 2 of the sugya (that the person who found the
money in the Biran canal must declare it because it has an identifying
mark) is the earliest case in which a sage rules against R. Shimon b. Elazar.
As we have detailed above, all tannaim and Eretz Yisraeli amoraim rule
that any object found in the public domain, or in a place such as the sea
where recovery is unlikely, may be kept by the finder under the

314

assumption that the owner would lose all hope of recovery. In contrast, R. Yehudah rules that since the money can be identified due to the cloth in which it is wrapped, it must be declared, despite the fact that it was found in the Biran canal, a place from which recovery is unlikely.

This unprecedented halakhah, diametrically opposed to R. Shimon b. Elazar, is debated by Babylonian amoraim one generation later on Bava Metzia 22b. We will cite the source without its stammaitic interpolations (see below):

| בבלי בבא מציעא כב ע"ב | Bavli Bava Metzia 22b |
|---|---|
| אלו מציאות שלו... כריכות ברשות הרבים... | These are the found objects that he may keep... sheaves in the public domain... |
| אמר רבה: ואפילו בדבר שיש בו סימן. | Rabbah said: Even an item which has an identifying mark. |
| רבא אמר: לא שנו אלא בדבר שאין בו סימן, אבל בדבר שיש בו סימן - חייב להכריז. | Rava said: [The mishnah refers] only to an item which has no identifying mark, but an item which has an identifying mark must be declared. |

Based on the mention of the public domain in Mishnah Bava Metzia 2:2, Rabbah and Rava debate whether one can keep an object with an identifying mark found in the public domain. Rabbah, relying completely upon R. Shimon b. Elazar, allows the finder to keep the object. Rava, who lived a generation after Rabbah, argues that the mishnah allows one to keep objects found in the public domain only if they have no identifying mark. If there was an identifying mark on the item, the finder must declare it, even if found in the public domain. The sugya concludes (23a) with the Babylonian amora R. Zevid ruling in accordance with Rava. From this point on, the Bavli accepts that an identifying mark is the most significant factor in cases of lost objects. If there is such a mark the finder must assume that the owner has not lost hope of recovery and, therefore, he must declare it.

## "But is He Not Standing and Shouting!"

In part 2, case 3, R. Nahman rules in accordance with Eretz Yisraeli halakhah. The wallet found in the public domain may be kept even

though it has an identifying mark. Rava objects to R. Nahman's ruling—
how could the wallet be kept even if the Jewish owner stands and shouts
that he wants his wallet back? The fact that the owner has come to claim
the object with the identifying mark must indicate that he has not
despaired of recovery, and therefore it may not be considered ownerless.

Rava's argument reflects a change in focus in the law concerning lost
objects. Taking their cue from the Torah, the tannaim focus their energy
on prohibiting one who finds a lost object from ignoring it. Their concern
is to legislate exactly in what cases a finder must declare the object and in
what cases he need not. Their emphasis, in short, is on delineating and, at
times, alleviating the burden placed on the finder. R. Yehudah and Rava,
both Babylonian amoraim, drastically shift the focus towards concern for
the loss of the owner. With the owner's rights in mind, they maintain that
as long as there is a clear identifying mark, the object must be returned
even if found in the public domain.

Neither the earlier law nor the later law is perfect. The tannaim, the
Eretz Yisraeli amoraim, and some Babylonian amoraim who were
concerned with delineating the obligations of the finder created the legal
presumption that the owner would lose hope of recovery of an object lost
in the public domain and, in such a case, the finder could keep it. This
halakhah might at times create a situation in which a finder could
rightfully keep the object, even if he knew to whom it belonged. The
decision to return such an object is an act of piety that goes beyond the
letter of the law. In contrast, Rava (and R. Yehudah before him) was
concerned with maximizing the potential for an owner to recover his own
lost object. Therefore, he rules that as long as ownership can be
established through an identifying mark, the object must always be
returned. Such a ruling would occasionally create a situation in which
someone would find an object in the public domain, be forced to declare
it, but have little chance of finding the owner, for the owner had already
lost hope of recovery and would no longer be searching for what he had
lost.

## Local Population and Lost Objects

As we have seen, R. Yehudah's requirement to declare lost objects with
any identifying mark, even if found in the public domain, is a departure
from earlier halakhah. We shall now show how Rava, who ruled like R.

Yehudah, attempts to reconcile this ruling with an earlier Eretz Yisraeli source (part 2, section 5). This source is parallel to one of the sections from Yerushalmi Shekalim which we analyzed above. In order to highlight Rava's contextualization of this source, we will present the amoraic statements in the Bavli (with the stammaitic interpolation removed) alongside their parallels in the Yerushalmi:

| Yerushalmi | Bavli |
|---|---|
| גדי צלי אישתכח באיסרטא דגופתא והתירוהו משם שני דברים: משם מציאה ומשם רוב מהלכי דרכים. | ר' חנינא מצא גדי שחוט בין טבריא לציפורי והתירוהו לו. |
| משם מציאה דתני: המציל מיד הארי מיד הגייס משונת הים ומשונת הנהר ומאיסרטיא גדולה ומפלטיא גדולה הרי אילו שלו מפני שהבעלים מתייאשין מהן. | אמר רבי אמי: התירוהו לו משום מציאה כר' שמעון בן אלעזר, |
| משם רוב מהלכי דרכים משם שחיטת הגוי. | משום שחיטה כרבי חנניא בנו של רבי יוסי הגלילי. |
|  | **אמר רבא: רוב גוים ורוב טבחי ישראל.** |
| A roasted kid was found on the road of Guftha and they allowed it for two reasons: (i) due to a found object; and (ii) due to the majority of the travelers. | R. Hanina once found a slaughtered goat between Tiberias and Tzipori, and they permitted him [to take] it. |
| "Due to a found object" as it is taught: If one saves [objects] from a lion, from the legions, from the depths of the sea, from the depths of the river, from the main road, from the square—they belong to him, because the owner has abandoned them. | R. Ammi said: They permitted him [to take it due] to a found object in accordance with R. Shimon b. Elazar, |
| "Due to the majority of the travelers" [because they were Jews there is no concern that] the slaughter was performed by a non-Jew. | and [they considered] its slaughter [to be ritually valid] in accordance with R. Hanania b. R. Yose Hagalili. |
|  | **Rava said: [That was a case where] there the majority was non-Jews but the majority of the butchers [were] Jewish.** |

The Yerushalmi is concerned with the makeup of the population only because of its impact on the kashrut of the animal. If the majority was Jewish, one can assume that the animal was ritually slaughtered in a proper fashion. But the population demographic does not affect the status of the meat as a lost object. Since it was found in the public domain, it need not be declared, regardless of the fact that the majority was Jewish.

The case of the lost goat is problematic for Rava, who holds that found objects in the public domain must be declared if they have any identifying mark. Since R. Ammi said that this rule is in accordance with R. Shimon b. Elazar, we have to assume that the goat was identifiable, but was found in a place that does not require declaration. Were it not identifiable, then this ruling would be in accordance with everyone—objects without identifying marks never need to be declared. R. Ammi's permission to keep the meat thus clashes with Rava's perception that objects with identifying marks found in the public domain must be declared. To resolve this contradiction, Rava refers to a rule found in Mishnah Makhshirin 2:8: If one finds a lost object in a place where the majority are non-Jews, they need not declare it because, according to tannaitic halakhah, there is no obligation to return lost objects to non-Jews. However, the consequence of solving this problem creates an even greater problem for Rava: If the majority were non-Jews, how could the meat be assumed to be kosher? To answer this, Rava further qualifies the case and explains that despite the non-Jewish population, the majority of the butchers were Jews. As we have seen—and as we will continue to see below—such forced contextualizations are usually a sign that sources are being read against their original meaning.

## Non-Jews in the Synagogues and Study Houses of Jews

The strained stammaitic explanations that characterize this sugya are mostly a result of the stam's use of Rava's Babylonian halakhah to contextualize and reinterpret the Eretz Yisraeli halakhah. The stam agrees with Rava: Lost objects with an identifying mark must be declared, even if they are found in the public domain, as long as it is in a place where the majority are Jews.

To recall, R. Shimon b. Elazar ruled that objects found in the public domain may be kept, because the sheer volume of people passing through would cause the owner to assume that recovery is impossible. For R.

Shimon b. Elazar, the makeup of the population is irrelevant. In contrast, according to Rava, the makeup is critical. The finder may keep it only if the majority of people in the public domain are non-Jews. In such a case, the finder may assume that either a non-Jew dropped the object and there would be no requirement to return it, or that the owner would lose hope of recovery thinking that a non-Jew, who does not necessarily observe the laws of returning lost objects, had found it and kept it for himself. In either case, the owner would abandon all hope of recovery.[12] However, if the majority is Jewish, the finder must assume that it was dropped by a Jew, to whom he must return it.

In part 1 of the sugya, the stam is faced with the challenge of reconciling Rava's halakhah with earlier sources. The stam rereads these earlier sources in order to rule that lost objects found in the public domain must be returned as long as the majority is Jewish. We will briefly examine each of these sources independently. We should note at the outset that we will not explain every line in this sugya and its source history. We are focusing only on one issue: the Babylonian transformation of the halakhah of declaring lost objects in the public domain.

The baraita (3a) teaches that lost objects found in synagogues and study houses, or other places with large groups of people, may be kept. According to the simple meaning of the baraita, these lost objects may be kept by the finder due to the fact that there are large numbers of people in such places, and thus we can assume that the owner would have abandoned hope of recovery. The stam, however, rightly suggests that the detail of the synagogue and study house implies that the tannaim rule that even in a case of a Jewish majority, the object may be kept, a halakhah which would contradict Rava. The stam resolves this contradiction by offering the difficult resolution that the baraita refers to a synagogue or a study house where the majority of people are non-Jews (3e-3h).

The next source reread by the stam is Mishnah Makhshirin (4a), which teaches two principles: 1) lost objects need not be returned to non-Jews; 2) lost objects are assumed to have belonged to a member of the majority of the population. The mishnah does not teach anything about the location in which the object was found or the owner's loss of hope of recovery—the mishnah says only that the finder need not return the object because he can assume that it fell from a non-Jew. In other words,

---

12  See Tosafot s.v. כי קמאר ר"ש.

the mishnah rules that if the majority were non-Jews, one does not need to declare the object. It does not say that if the majority are Jews, one always needs to declare the object, no matter where it is found. In such a case it would depend upon whether the object was found in the private or public domain. But it is exactly this inference the stam tries to prove: If the majority of the population is Jewish, one always needs to declare the object. Needless to say, this logic is faulty.

The third and final earlier source reread by the stam is an amoraic statement by R. Assi (5a). In its original context, R. Assi rules that if the majority of the population are non-Jews, one is permitted to keep found wine, but prohibited to drink it because it is considered forbidden, non-Jewish wine. The finder may keep the vessel but must dump out the wine (5e). But if a Jew provides an identifying mark, then the wine may be drunk. Although R. Assi does not state so explicitly, if the majority of the population is Jewish, then the finder would be able to keep the wine and drink it. R. Assi needs to discuss the makeup of the population because it is relevant to the status of the wine (like the goat and cheese in the Yerushalmi), and not because it is relevant to its status as a lost object. However, the stam perceives the fact that R. Assi explicitly mentions the case of the non-Jewish majority as relevant to both issues—the ability of the finder to keep the object, and the prohibition of drinking the wine. In other words, the stam reads R. Assi as allowing the finder to keep the object only if the majority of the population are non-Jews. To the stam, if the majority of the population were Jewish, the wine could be drunk, but would have to be returned to the Jewish owner.[13]

In part 2 of the sugya, the stam also provides forced contextualizations in order to rule leniently. The stam must contend with R. Yehudah's stringency, which requires the declaration of all lost objects with an identifying mark regardless of their location, even if the population was non-Jewish. In order to soften R. Yehudah's position, the stam provides the difficult explanation that the Biran canal is considered to be a location with a Jewish majority (part 2, section 1b-1f).

---

[13] Although R. Ashi seems to be responding to the stam, he may simply be explaining R. Assi. What can a Jew do with a barrel of wine assumed to have fallen from a non-Jew—it is forbidden to derive any benefit from it! The answer is that he can use the jug. The fact that the wine was found in the public domain is irrelevant.

The sugya concludes with the rulings of two Eretz Yisraeli amoraim (part 2, sections 6 and 7) who allow the finder to keep a lost object found in the public domain, and do not seem to take the makeup of the population into account at all. While this makes sense in terms of the historical development of the halakhah—Eretz Yisraeli amoraim do not take into account the makeup of the population and allow the finder to keep lost objects found in the public domain—it is difficult in light of the stammaitic implementation of Rava's stringency. In case six, R. Assi allows R. Ammi to keep slaughtered pigeons found between two cities. Based on all of the stammaitic explanations which precede the case, the reader would have to assume that R. Ammi had found the pigeons in a location with a non-Jewish majority. But if this were the case, how could R. Ammi eat the pigeons? Surely one cannot assume that they were ritually slaughtered. This blatant contradiction did not escape the attention of the medieval commentators. Rashba, the thirteenth-century Spanish talmudist, resolves the difficulty by applying Rava's explanation of the previous case—that the majority was non-Jewish, but the majority of the butchers were Jewish—to R. Ammi. He begins by quoting the Ra'avad, a twelfth-century French commentator:[14]

אבל הראב"ד ז"ל כתב דממעשה דפרגיות דר' אמי איכא למשמע דהלכה כר' שמעון אפילו ברוב ישראל מדהתירו לו משום שחיטה שמע מינה ברוב ישראל,

But the Ra'avad of blessed memory wrote that from the incident of R. Ammi's pigeons we may learn that the law follows R. Shimon [b. Elazar], even in a case with a Jewish majority, for, since they allow him to [keep] the slaughtered [pigeons], we can learn there was a Jewish majority,

וליכא למימר ברוב נכרים ורוב טבחי ישראל, שאין טבחים לעופות שכל איש שוחט לעצמו ואוכל.

and we cannot say there was a non-Jewish majority with a majority of Jewish slaughterers, because there are no slaughterers for fowl, for every person slaughters for themselves and eats them.

ואינו מחוור בעיני דאם כן הוה להו למידק מינה הכין בגמרא ולימא שמע מינה הלכה כרשב"א אפילו ברוב

But the [Ra'avad's explanation] is not clear to me, for if so, the Talmud should have inferred as much and concluded

14 Rashba Bava Metzia 24b s.v. אמר רבא.

ישראל כדדייקי בעובדא דגדי שחוט, "the halakhah follows R. Shimon b. Elazar even with a Jewish majority," as they inferred in the case of the slaughtered goat. Rather it seems to me that here too we must say that there is a non-Jewish majority with a majority of Jewish trappers, and it is the way of trappers to slaughter [the birds] so that they do not run away from them.

אלא נראה לי דהתם נמי איכא למימר ברוב נכרים ורוב ציידי ישראל דדרכן של ציידים לשחוט כדי שלא יברחו ממנו.

The Ra'avad reads the final two cases as a rejection of the forced explanations of Rava and the stam. According to his reading, the sugya concludes with the stories of the Eretz Yisraeli amoraim in order to reaffirm the original halakhah which allows the finder to keep objects found in the public domain, no matter the composition of the population. Rashba rejects this reading because he, like the stam, accepts Rava's halakhah. He is forced to explain the lenient ruling of R. Assi using Rava's earlier contextualization in order to ensure that the sugya is halakhically consistent throughout.

## Identifying Marks in the Public Domain Revisited

We will conclude by noting that the stammaitic acceptance of R. Yehudah and Rava's halakhah—objects with identifying marks found in the public domain must be declared—forces the stam to reinterpret the debate between Rabbah and Rava found on Bavli Bava Metzia 22b which we discussed above. We now present that source again, this time including the stammaitic interpolations:

| בבלי בבא מציעא כב ע"ב | **Bavli Bava Metzia 22b** |
|---|---|
| אלו מציאות שלו ... כריכות ברשות הרבים | These are the found objects that he may keep... sheaves in the public domain... |
| (1a) אמר רבה: ואפילו בדבר שיש בו סימן. | (1a) Rabbah said: Even an item which has an identifying mark. |
| (1b) אלמא קסבר רבה: סימן העשוי לידרס לא הוי סימן. | (1b) Therefore, Rabbah is of the opinion that an identifying mark which is prone to be trampled is not considered an identifying mark. |

(2a) רבא אמר: לא שנו אלא בדבר
שאין בו סימן, אבל בדבר שיש בו
סימן - חייב להכריז.

(2a) Rava said: [The mishnah refers] only to an item which has no identifying mark, but an item which has an identifying mark must be declared.

(2b) אלמא קסבר רבא: סימן העשוי
לידרס הוי סימן.

(2b) Therefore, Rava is of the opinion that an identifying mark which is prone to be trampled is considered an identifying mark.

---

| Tannaitic Source | Amoraic Source | Stammaitic Source |

To recall, the mishnah allows one to keep sheaves found in the public domain. Rabbah extrapolates and holds that all objects found in the public domain may be kept, even if they have an identifying mark. Rava disagrees because he holds like R. Yehudah—objects with an identifying mark must always be declared. But the stam cannot tolerate Rava and Rabbah disagreeing on this fundamental issue because of the belief that everyone holds that objects with identifying marks found in the public domain must be declared. Therefore, the stam reframes the amoraic debate by limiting the dispute between Rava and Rabbah so that it is no longer a general disagreement about lost objects with identifying marks found in the public domain, but pertains only to the specific case of the bound sheaves mentioned in the mishnah. According to the stam (1b), Rabbah rules that since the mark on the sheaves will fall off, it does not count as an identifying mark. Since the owner will not rely on the mark remaining on his sheaves, he will despair of recovery, and thus the finder may keep them. Rava (2b), on the other hand, rules that although the sign may fall off, it still can serve as an identifying mark; thus, the owner will not despair, and the sheaves must be declared. Most significantly, with regard to other objects with a mark that would not fall off when trampled, **all amoraim agree that it must be declared even if found in the public domain.**

The addition of the contextualization to the amoraic debate clearly demonstrates the stammaitic drive for consistency. Once the Bablyonian amoraim accept the ruling that lost objects with identifying marks found in the public domain must be declared, the stam demands a comprehensive rereading of all early sources which rule precisely the opposite.[15] This leads to the strained interpretations that epitomize this sugya including: a new meaning given to the tannaitic phrase "it need not be declared," and the outlandish suggestion of a study houses frequented by a majority of non-Jews. Earlier, we saw that some identifying marks were pressed onto the objects so that the mark would not fall off. We might say, then, that the stam takes the opinion of Rava—that all objects with identifying marks found in the public space must be declared—and presses it into Rabbah, whose original opinion may still be found in this source, but requires a fair amount of searching.

---

[15] For more on the attitude towards lost objects in the Bavli, see Shai Secunda, "Gaze and Counter-Gaze: Textuality and Contextuality in the Anecdote of Rav Assi and the Roman (b. Baba Mesi'a 28b)" in *The Aggada of the Bavli and its Cultural World*, eds. Geoffrey Herman and Jefferey Rubenstein (Providence: Brown Judaic Studies, 2018), 149-171.

# Chapter Eight

## Warning a Pursuer

## Sanhedrin 72b

## Introduction

Rabbinic law makes it extremely difficult, if not impossible, to convict and execute a criminal. Two tannaim, R. Tarfon and R. Akiva, famously declare, "Had we been members of the Sanhedrin, no person would ever have been put to death" (Mishnah Makkot 1:10). The rabbinic restrictions on convicting a criminal of a capital crime are best articulated in a midrash found in Mekhilta de-R. Yishmael Kaspa parashah 20:

**Mekhilta de-R. Yishmael Kaspa 20**

They saw him pursuing his fellow to kill him with a sword in his hand. They said to him: "Know that he is a member of the covenant, and the Torah has said: *Whoever sheds the blood of man, by man shall his blood be shed* (Genesis 9:6)," and he said to them, "I know, it is because of it [that I am doing it]." And the witnesses turned their eyes away and after some time found the slain convulsing, and the sword dripping blood from the hands of the murderer. I might have thought he would be guilty? Scripture states: *An innocent or righteous person, do not kill* (Ex 23:7).

מכילתא דר' ישמעאל כספא פ' כ
ראוהו רודף אחר חבירו להרגו והסייף בידו. אמרו לו: "הוי יודע שהוא בן ברית, והתורה אמרה: *שופך דם האדם באדם דמו ישפך* (בראשית ט:ו)," ואמר להם, "יודע אני, על מנת כן." והעלימו עדים את עיניהם, ולאחר זמן מצאוהו הרוג מפרפר והסייף מנטף דם מיד ההורג, שומע אני יהא חייב, תלמוד לומר: *ונקי וצדיק אל תהרוג* (שמות כג:ז).

325

This midrash describes an exaggerated scenario where every step of the procedure necessary to convict a murderer has been scrupulously followed—except for the actual witnessing of the crime. The two witnesses have issued a proper warning and the perpetrator has acknowledged the warning. The knife is dripping with blood from the hand of the suspect and the victim lies convulsing on the floor. But without the actual witnessing of the act of murder, the criminal may not be convicted. The rabbis anchor their ruling with an innovative reading of the verse, "An innocent or righteous person, do not kill." Why, the rabbis ask, would the Torah deem it necessary to state that an innocent person should not be killed? As a response to the overly obvious and therefore unnecessary verse, the rabbis turn the biblical text on its head, such that even a person who is clearly guilty—who is not clean and literally has blood on his hand—is considered innocent until the actual crime has been witnessed. To put it in modern terms, even "unreasonable doubt" is sufficient for the rabbis to prevent execution.

This chapter will focus on the procedure by which criminals are warned, an aspect of the judicial process that renders conviction virtually impossible. We will begin by exploring the warning procedure as a means of determining criminal intent. We will then transition to a brief discussion of tannaitic sources concerning self-defense and the issue of preemptively killing a pursuer. While all rabbinic sources assume that a person has the right to defend themselves and a responsibility to protect others, there are different perspectives as to the justification for preemptive killing. These two distinct topics—determining the intent of a would-be criminal and preemptively killing one person to protect another—are later woven together into a single sugya in the Babylonian Talmud. The Bavli radically reworks earlier tannaitic and amoraic sources in order to explore an issue which does not appear at all in tannaitic or amoraic literature: whether a bystander who witnesses one person pursuing another in order to cause harm must warn the perpetrator before killing him to protect the victim. The Bavli raises the possibility that despite the immediate threat to the life of the victim, the bystander must still unequivocally determine criminal intent before taking action and thereby adhere to the rabbinic judicial process required for the prosecution of capital crimes.

# Warning the Offender: Establishing Intent

The requirement to warn a criminal, found in the midrash with which we began this chapter, and which constitutes a key element of the procedure that make conviction nearly impossible in rabbinic law, is most clearly articulated in chapter eleven of Tosefta Sanhedrin:

| תוספתא סנהדרין יא:א | Tosefta Sanhedrin 11:1 |
|---|---|
| (1) ושאר חייבי מיתות בית דין אין מחייבין אותן אלא על פי עדים, והתראה, ועד שיודיעוהו שחייב מיתה בבית דין. ר' יוסי בר' יהודה אומר עד שיודיעוהו באיזו מיתה הוא מת. | (1) All other criminals [suspected of] a capital crime cannot be convicted without two witnesses, a warning, and until they inform him that he is liable for capital punishment. R. Yose b. R. Yehudah said: [He cannot be convicted] until they inform him of the manner in which he will be executed. |
| (2) בין שהיתרו בו כל עדיו בין שהיתרו בו מקצת עדיו חייב. ור' יוסי פוטר עד שיתרו בו כל עדיו שנאמר: *על פי שנים עדים* (דברים יז:ו) - עד שיהו שני עדים מתרין כאחד. | (2) He is liable whether some or all of his witnesses warned him. R. Yose exempts until all of his witnesses warn him, as it is written: *Only by the word of two or three witnesses* (Deuteronomy 17:6)— until two witnesses warn him together. |
| ומודה ר' יוסי שאם היתרה בו הראשון והלך לו השיני והלך לו שהוא חייב. | R. Yose agrees that he is liable if the first [witness] warns him and departs, and the second [witness] warns him and departs. |

The Tosefta stipulates three conditions necessary for convicting a criminal of a capital crime:

1) the crime must be witnessed by two valid witnesses;
2) the criminal must be forewarned that what he is about to do is a crime; and
3) the criminal must be informed that the punishment for his crime is death.

The first of these requirements, two witnesses, appears explicitly in Numbers 35:30 and Deuteronomy 17:6 and 19:15. In contrast, the requirement that the criminal be aware of the severity and repercussions of his actions are not mentioned anywhere in the Torah.

The second and third requirements, to forewarn the perpetrator and inform him of the consequences of his actions, seem to emerge from both the Torah's differentiation between the consequences for intentional and unintentional sin as well as the extreme rabbinic reluctance to even theoretically mandate execution in a case where it is not required by the Torah. The notion that there are different consequences for intentional and unintentional sin is prevalent in the Torah. For instance, according to Numbers 35 an intentional murderer must be executed, whereas the accidental killer may escape to the city of refuge. Leviticus 4 prescribes various offerings for accidental sinners, including, presumably, an individual who transgresses the Sabbath laws. In contrast, Exodus 31:14-15 prescribes the death penalty for Sabbath transgressions. However, the Torah contains no formal mechanism whereby the witnesses are to ascertain the intentionality of the transgressor before committing the transgression. At most, Numbers 35 provides some *ex post facto* criteria by which to roughly determine whether the court should presume that a murder was intentional. For instance, if the murderer acted with violent aggression or ambushed the victim, we can assume that the murder was intentional. But this is a strong *ex post facto* assumption, and not an *a priori* affirmation that the murder (or other sin) was committed intentionally. To execute a criminal who committed a capital crime without full intent would constitute, in the rabbinic mind, bloodshed. To prevent any possibility of the court executing a criminal who does not deserve the death penalty, the rabbis create a two-part examination that the witnesses must administer prior to the transgression to determine that it is being performed with the highest level of awareness of what exactly is being done and the consequences of the action. Only with this information in mind can the court be certain that the sin was done intentionally.

Thus, the warning procedure functions as an extreme means to establish *mens rea* (criminal intent). This is stated explicitly by R. Yose b.

R. Yehudah, in a baraita cited in the Bavli: "An associate (*haver*)[1] does not need warning because warning is only given to differentiate between unwitting and intentional actions." If the potential criminal is someone who is expected to know the law (a *haver*), then he does not need a prior warning in order to be punished for his crime. For instance, a *haver* would not need to be informed what constitutes a Shabbat violation. In contrast, an unlearned person may not know, say, that writing is forbidden on Shabbat, and therefore in order for him to be subsequently punished, he must be warned before he transgresses. If he goes ahead despite the warning and writes on Shabbat, it would be clear that he had intentionally transgressed.

In section 2 of the Tosefta, the rabbis require the warning to be delivered by at least one witness in order to convict (see also Mishnah Sanhedrin 5:1). R. Yose is even more stringent and will not convict without a warning from both witnesses, a requirement he derives from Deuteronomy 17:6: "A person shall be put to death only by the word of two or three witnesses…" According to his reading, the "word" of the witnesses does not refer to the testimony they deliver at court, but rather to the warning which must be issued to the perpetrator by both witnesses before the commission of the crime.

The continuation of the Tosefta describes how the warning procedure is to occur, demonstrating just how exacting the tannaim were in establishing that the criminal was fully aware of the nature of his crime before he commits it.

### תוספתא סנהדרין יא:ב-ד / Tosefta Sanhedrin 11:2-4

מתרין בו ושותק, מתרין בו ומרכין בראשו, אף על פי שאמר "יודע אני" פטור, עד שיאמר "יודע אני ועל מנת כן אני עושה."

If they warn him and he is silent, or he nods his head, even if he said: "I know," he is exempt until he says, "I know and it is because of it that I am doing it!"

כיצד? ראוהו שמחלל את השבת, ואומרין לו: "הוי יודע שהיא שבת ואמר: *מחלליה מות יומת* (שמות לא:יד)" אף

How so? If they saw him profaning Shabbat and they said to him, "Know that it is Shabbat and it is said *He who*

---

[1]    The term was originally used as a designation for an individual who is meticulous in his observance of laws of purity and tithing. In later rabbinic literature the term becomes almost synonymous with the rabbis.

עַל פִּי שֶׁאָמַר, "יוֹדֵעַ אֲנִי" פָּטוּר, עַד
שֶׁיֹּאמַר "יוֹדֵעַ אֲנִי וְעַל מְנָת כֵּן אֲנִי
עוֹשֶׂה."

כֵּיצַד? רָאוּהוּ שֶׁהוֹרֵג אֶת הַנֶּפֶשׁ, וְאָמְרִין
לוֹ: "הֱוֵי יוֹדֵעַ שֶׁהוּא בֶּן בְּרִית וְנֶאֱמַר
*שׁוֹפֵךְ דַּם הָאָדָם בָּאָדָם דָּמוֹ יִשָּׁפֵךְ*
(בְּרֵאשִׁית ט:ו)," אַף עַל פִּי שֶׁאָמַר "יוֹדֵעַ
אֲנִי" פָּטוּר, עַד שֶׁיֹּאמַר "יוֹדֵעַ אֲנִי וְעַל
מְנָת כֵּן אֲנִי עוֹשֶׂה."

*profanes it shall be put to death* (Exodus 31:14)" even if he said: "I know," he is exempt until he says, "I know and it is because of it that I am doing it!"

How so? If they saw him [going] to kill someone and they said to him, "Know that he is a member of the covenant and it is said: *Whoever sheds the blood of man, by man shall his blood be shed* (Genesis 9:6)" even if he said: "I know," he is exempt until he says, "I know and it is because of it that I am doing it!"

The Tosefta provides two examples of warning. In the first, the witnesses verify that the potential transgressor knows that today is Shabbat and therefore his actions are punishable by death. In the second, the individual is warned that the person he is about to kill is Jewish. Killing a non-Jew would not result in capital punishment (see Tosefta Avodah Zarah 8:5), and so in order to ensure that the perpetrator is aware of the consequences, they must be certain he knows that the potential victim is a Jew.[2] In all cases, the witnesses must cite the specific verse in the Torah which states that the act is a capital crime. Likewise, the criminal must explicitly state that he is performing the prohibited act with full intent and that he is aware of the repercussions. Any digression from this procedure, even in a case of murder, renders execution forbidden. We should also note that these two particular warnings might be appropriate even for a *haver*, one aware that profaning Shabbat and murdering are both capital offenses. Even a *haver* might not know the day of the week, and even a *haver* might not know that the victim is a Jew. Thus, the Tosefta may be

---

[2] For more on this issue see Christine Hayes, "Were the Noahide Commandments formulated at Yavne?: Tosefta Avoda Zara 8:4-9 in Cultural and Historical Context" in *Jews and Christians in the First and Second Centuries; the Interbellum 70-132 CE*, eds. Joshua Schwartz and Peter J. Tomson (Leiden: Brill, 2018), 225-264; Steven Fraade, "Navigating the Anomalous: Non-Jews at the Intersection of Early Rabbinic Law and Narrative," in *Legal Fictions; Studies of Law and Narrative in the Discursive Worlds of Ancient Jewish Sectarians and Sages* (Leiden: Brill, 2011), 345-363.

alluding to the notion, in contrast to the opinion of R. Yose b. R. Yehudah, that even a Jew fully aware of the law must be warned before he commits the crime.

## The Pursuer: Saved at the Cost of His Life

Bystanders observing an attack on another person's life can of course perform another role besides testifying against the criminal *ex post facto*: They can intervene to prevent the crime from happening in the first place. Several rabbinic texts justify or demand that a bystander save the life of the victim. Here we should note that legal texts do not generally need to accord people the right to act in self-defense or to defend other innocent citizens.[3] But legal systems do need to codify the conditions under which preemptive killing is justified and when such an act is considered a transgression.

The primary rabbinic texts on the subject of self-defense are found in the eighth chapter of tractate Sanhedrin. Following chapter seven, which lists the capital crimes punished by stoning, chapter eight continues with a detailed description of the unique case of the rebellious son (Deuteronomy 21:18-22), who is also punished by stoning. The laws concerning the rebellious son have posed a challenge to rabbinic commentators for two main reasons. First, the death sentence is meted out to a child who has not reached the age of legal culpability; and second the child has not committed any crime that would otherwise be punishable by stoning.[4] It is beyond the scope of the current chapter to engage in the important moral questions surrounding this case. Our focus, rather, is on understanding the case of the rebellious son as an act of preemptive killing to prevent him from committing a violent crime in the future.

We shall analyze the final three mishnayot in the chapter because of their relevance to our discussion:

---

[3]    The exceptions to this rule are usually cases where the victim is of a far lower status than the perpetrator, such as a slave being struck by his master.

[4]    On the preemptive punishment of the rebellious son see Halbertal, *Mahapekhot Parshaniyot be-Hithavutan*, (Jerusalem, 1997): 42-68 and Ethan Tucker http://mechonhadar.s3.amazonaws.com/mh_torah_source_sheets/CJLVRebelliou sSon.pdf

<table>
<tr>
<td>משנה סנהדרין ח</td>
<td>

**Mishnah Sanhedrin 8**
</td>
</tr>
</table>

(ה) בן סורר ומורה נדון על שם סופו:
ימות זכאי ואל ימות חייב.

שמיתתן של רשעים הנאה להן והנאה
לעולם, ולצדיקים רע להן ורע לעולם...

(5) A "wayward and rebellious son" is judged on account of his end: Let him die innocent and let him not die guilty.

For the death of the wicked is a benefit for them and a benefit for the world; [and the death] of the righteous is bad for them and bad for the world...

(ו) הבא במחתרת נדון על שם סופו...

(6) [The thief] who tunnels his way [into someone's home] is judged on account of his end...

(ז) ואלו הן שמצילין אותן בנפשן:
הרודף אחר חבירו להרגו, אחר הזכור,
ואחר הנערה המאורסה.

אבל הרודף אחר הבהמה, והמחלל את
השבת, והעובד עבודה זרה, אין מצילין
אותן בנפשן.

(7) These are the ones to be saved at the cost of their lives: One who pursues his fellow to kill him, [or] after a male [to rape him], or after a betrothed girl [to rape her].

But one who pursues an animal [to commit bestiality], and one who [intends] to desecrate the Sabbath, and one who [intends] to worship idols, these may not be saved at the cost of their lives.

Mishnah five grapples with the moral and legal problems of the rebellious son by positing that "he is judged based on his end." The earlier sections of this chapter in the Mishnah seem to intimate that the rebellious son's current gluttony and thievery indicate that he will commit even worse crimes in the future, namely murder. His preemptory execution is beneficial for the criminal, for he will die innocent and not guilty of a greater crime, and it is also obviously a benefit for society as well.

In mishnah 6, the rabbis apply the same concept to the tunneling thief (Exodus 22:1-2), that is, the thief who burrows his way stealthily into his victim's home—he too is "judged based on his end." In truth, there is no great need to justify the homeowner's killing of the tunneling thief—it is an act of self-defense. The homeowner cannot be sure if the thief intends to rob him or kill him and therefore, due to the potential danger to his life, the Torah allows him to protect himself. But remarkably, self-defense is not sufficient for the rabbis to justify killing a potential murderer. The rabbis are reluctant to rely solely on self-defense as validation of the homeowner's lack of culpability for having killed another human being. They read the tunneling thief in light of the rebellious son to provide additional justification for killing the thief. They contend that killing the thief before he commits murder would be beneficial to the thief as well, for he will die without having committed the heinous sin of bloodshed.

The difference between the rebellious son and the tunneling thief is that while the former is executed by the court, the latter is killed by his potential victim. Mishnah 7 continues by enumerating other types of individuals who are intent on harming a victim in committing a capital crime, all of whom are described as pursuers. This mishnah defines a pursuer who can be killed as one who fulfills two criteria: 1) he presents an imminent danger to another human being; and 2) his intended action is a capital crime: murder or rape punishable by death. Mishnah 7 describes this principle as "he is saved at the cost of his life," meaning that the pursuer is preemptively killed to save him from committing a severe transgression of Torah law.[5] These are the same criteria that existed for the rebellious son and the tunneling thief—they both pose a danger to others and are likely to commit a crime punishable by death. Here the mishnah moves beyond the self-defense of the homeowner himself and allows a third party to save the victim from physical harm and the pursuer from sin.

The Sifra, the tannaitic midrash on the book of Leviticus, anchors the mishnah's law in a verse from the Torah:

**Sifra Kedoshim Parashah 2 Ch. 4**  ספרא קדושים פרשה ב פרק ד

From where [do we know] that one  ומנין לרודף אחר חבירו להורגו, ואחר

who pursues his fellow to kill him,  הזכור, ואחר נערה המאורסה חייב אתה

---

5   The ambiguous language of "his life" leads to disagreement among medieval commentators regarding the precise meaning of the mishnah. Rashi maintains that the subject is the pursuer. He is saved from transgression at the cost of his own life. This reading is supported by the use of the phrase in Tosefta Sanhedrin 11:9. Maimonides and Yad Ramah, however, both interpret the mishnah to refer to the pursued who is saved at the cost of the life of the pursuer.

| | |
|---|---|
| להצילו בנפשו? תלמוד לומר: *לא* <br> *תעמוד על דם רעך* (ויקרא יט:טז). | [or] after a male [to rape him], or after a betrothed girl [to rape her] that you must save him at the cost of his life? Scripture states: *You shall not stand by the blood of your fellow* (Leviticus 19:16). |

The midrash supports the law in the mishnah with a creative reading of Leviticus 19:16, which forbids standing idly by when another person is in life-threatening danger. The plain meaning of the text identifies the "fellow" as the victim. The midrash, however, suggests that the "fellow" may also refer to the pursuer. One may not stand idly by when another is about to commit a heinous crime which transgresses Torah law. The bystander has a responsibility to kill the pursuer to save him from transgression and to spare his victim from harm.

## The Pursuer: An Evil Person is Put to Death

Whereas the Mishnah justified the killing of a pursuer by a third party in order to save the pursuer himself from sinning, another tannaitic source offers a more common-sense justification for killing a pursuer. According to Sifre Zuta Numbers 35:12, the pursuer may be killed because doing so serves to save the life of the victim.[6] However, the midrash uses virtually the same language as the Mishnah to make this argument.

| | |
|---|---|
| ספרי זוטא במדבר לה:יב | **Sifre Zuta Numbers 35:12** |
| (1) הרי מי שהיה רודף אחר חבירו להורגו, | (1) A man was pursuing his fellow to kill him, |
| אמרו לו: "בן ברית הוא הוי יודיע שכתוב בתורה *שופך דם האדם באדם דמו ישפך* " (בראשית ט ו). אמר להן "אף על פי כן" הורג הוא. | They said to him: "He is a member of the covenant, and know that it is written in the Torah, *Whoever sheds the blood of man, by man shall his* |

---

6  Sifre Zuta Numbers, the tannaitic midrash on Numbers associated with the school of Rabbi Akiva, did not survive in its entirety. In the 19th century, it was reconstructed from citations in medieval texts and Cairo geniza fragments. Our passage is found in a geniza fragment published in 1894 by Solomon Schechter, and thus is assumed to be a tannaitic midrash and not a later medieval composition.

blood be shed" (Genesis 9:6). If he said to them "even so," he is a murderer.

(2) אמר: *רשע למות* (במדבר לה:לא) קדם הורגהו, הצל נפשו של זה בנפשו של זה...

(2) It says, *An evil [person] is to be put to death* (Numbers 35:31). Kill him first, save the life of this one [the pursued] at the cost of the life of that one [the pursuer]!...[7]

(3) יכול יהרגו אותו משהרג ,.... תלמוד לומר: *ולא ימות הרוצח*, עד מתי? *עד עומדו לפני העדה למשפט* (במדבר לה:יב).

(3) Perhaps they should kill him after he has murdered...? Scripture states *and the murderer shall not die*. Until when? *Until he has stood trial before the assembly* (Numbers 35:12).

Section 1 is basically the scenario set forth in the Tosefta: Witnesses see a person about to commit a murder and set out to warn him beforehand. These sections presuppose the halakhah of the Tosefta which stipulates that without a proper warning, post-crime conviction is impossible. Only if the criminal says "even so" can he be considered an intentional murderer, liable for the death penalty. Section 2 shifts the focus from the issue of warning the pursuer to what is obviously a preferred solution to dealing with a pursuer—kill him before he commits the crime. The Sifre creates a midrash on Numbers 35:31, reading it out of context as if to say that there is a point at which an evil person can be killed without a trial, namely immediately before he commits a crime. The Sifre justifies this dispensation by alluding to a line from the Mishnah: "These are the ones who are saved at the cost of their lives." In the Mishnah, this line meant that the pursuer was saved at the cost of his own life. But here in the Sifre it clearly refers to two distinct people, and thus must be rendered, "save the victim at the cost of the life of the pursuer." After having clarified that a bystander should kill a pursuer before he commits a crime, section 3 emphasizes that once the crime has been committed, justice must wait for trial. In such a case, "the murderer shall not die." Killing a murderer after the crime is vengeance, not justice.

The inclusion of the warning procedure in the midrash might lend the impression that the bystander may not preemptively kill the pursuer

---

[7]   The midrash continues by applying the same exegesis to a comparable case of a man who pursues a married woman to rape her.

unless he first issues a warning. According to this line of thought, even defense of the innocent would require a prior warning. However, despite the fact that such a position does appear in the Bavli, it seems highly unlikely that it was the intention of the author to create such an impractical position—must witnesses first warn a pursuer before saving the life of the pursued? Doesn't saving a life precede almost all considerations in Jewish law? Rather, this midrash is an amalgam of three issues stemming from two different texts, the Mishnah and the Tosefta. The first text is concerned with preemptive warning in order to allow conviction (Tosefta), the second with preemptive killing to protect the innocent victim (Mishnah), and the third with prohibiting extrajudicial vengeance. The warning in section 1 is not relevant to the preemptive killing in section 2 but to the judicial killing alluded to section 3.

## Bavli Sanhedrin 72b: Warning a Pursuer

In a single midrash, Sifre Zuta addresses two distinct issues that presumably reflect two different scenarios:

1) Witnesses must issue a warning before the crime is committed to determine the intent of the criminal. (We must assume in this case they cannot, for whatever reason, stop the crime from occurring).

2) Under certain circumstances, the bystanders should strive to stop the crime before it occurs.

The Bavli is the only rabbinic source that fully combines these two scenarios suggesting that a bystander must warn a pursuer before saving the life of the potential victim. Even in this text, such a position is not directly attributed to any amora. However, the editors of the Bavli create discourse which gives the impression that some rabbis do indeed hold such a strange position: Pursuers may never be killed without a prior warning. As we shall see, an original amoraic discussion concerning treating a minor as a pursuer led to the creation of a general position that all pursuers require a warning. We will begin with a brief explanation of the sugya following Rashi's commentary, and then demonstrate how the earlier sources are reframed by the editors of the Bavli to explore the issue of warning a pursuer.

AMORAIC STATEMENT

**(1a)** אמר רב הונא: קטן הרודף ניתן להצילו בנפשו.

(1a) R. Huna said: A minor who pursues can be saved at the cost of his life.

STAMMAITIC INFERENCE

**(1b)** קסבר רודף אינו צריך התראה לא שנא גדול ולא שנא קטן.

(1b) He holds that a pursuer, whether an adult or a minor, need not be warned.

AMORAIC CHALLENGE

**(1c)** איתיביה רב חסדא לרב הונא: יצא ראשו אין נוגעין בו לפי שאין דוחין נפש מפני נפש.

(1c) R. Hisda challenged R. Huna: But if the head has come out, one may not touch him, for one may not set aside one person's life for that of another.

ואמאי? רודף הוא!

But why? Is he not a pursuer!

RESOLUTION

**(1d)** שאני התם, דמשמיא קא רדפי לה.

(1d) There it is different, for she [the mother] is pursued by heaven.

ATTEMPTED SUPPORT OF R. HUNA

**(2a)** נימא מסייעא ליה: רודף שהיה רודף אחר חבירו להורגו, אומרין[8] לו: ראה שישראל הוא ובן ברית הוא והתורה אמרה שופך דם האדם באדם דמו ישפך (בראשית ט:ו). אמרה תורה הצל דמו של זה בדמו של זה!

(2a) Shall we say that the following supports him? If a man was pursuing his fellow to kill him, they [the witnesses] say to him, "See, he is an Jew, and a member of the covenant, and the Torah has said: *Whoever sheds the blood of man, by man shall his blood be shed* (Genesis 9:6)." The Torah has said, save the blood of this one [the pursued] with the blood of that one [the pursuer]!

REJECTION OF SUPPORT

**(2b)** ההיא רבי יוסי ברבי יהודה היא. דתניא: רבי יוסי בר' יהודה אומר: חבר אין צריך התראה לפי שלא ניתנה התראה אלא להבחין בין שוגג למזיד.

(2b) That accords with R. Yose b. R. Yehudah. For it has been taught: R. Yose b. R. Yehudah said: A *haver* does not need warning because warning is

---

8    The plural form is based on the MSS Munich, Karlsruhe, and Yad HaRav Herzog.

given only to differentiate between accidental and intentional actions.

### ATTEMPTED REFUTATION OF R. HUNA

(3a) תא שמע **רודף שהיה רודף אחר** חבירו להורגו, אומרין לו: ראה שישראל הוא ובן ברית הוא והתורה אמרה שופך דם האדם באדם דמו ישפך (בראשית ט, ו). אם אמר יודע אני שהוא כן, פטור; על מנת כן אני עושה, חייב.

(3a) Come and hear: If a man was pursuing his fellow to kill him, they [the witnesses] say to him, "See, he is an Israelite, and a member of the covenant, and the Torah has said: *Whoever sheds the blood of man, by man shall his blood be shed* (Genesis 9:6)." If he said, "I know," he is exempt. If he said, "I know and it is because of it that I am doing it!"—he is liable.

### RESOLUTION

(3b) לא צריכא, דקאי בתרי עיברי דנהרא, דלא מצי אצוליה. מאי איכא? דבעי איתויי לבי דינא, בי דינא בעי התראה.

(3b) No, this [baraita] is needed [in a case] where they are standing on two opposite sides of the river, so that he cannot save him. What is [to be done]? He must bring him before a court and a court requires a warning.

(3c) איבעית אימא: אמר לך רב הונא אנא דאמרי כתנא דמחתרת דאמר מחתרתו זו היא התראתו.

(3c) An alternative answer if you wish: R. Huna would tell you: My ruling agrees with the tanna of the tunneling thief, who holds that his tunnel is his warning.

---

| Tannaitic Source | Amoraic Source | Stammaitic Source |
|---|---|---|

The sugya begins with R. Huna, who teaches that bystanders may kill a minor pursuing a victim. The innovation in his ruling is that the minor may be preemptively killed as a pursuer, even though legally he cannot be considered to have the intent to kill. The danger to the victim overrides the fact that the minor cannot legally be described as having intent.

The stam then extrapolates a general principle from R. Huna's teaching (1b). Bystanders who can stop a person about to commit a murder need not warn him before preventing the crime. The stam derives this principle from the fact that R. Huna allows for killing a minor for whom warning is not relevant since minors cannot stand trial for their crimes. From the fact that minors about to commit a crime can be killed, the stam extrapolates that all pursuers can be killed without warning before they commit the crime. Warning is necessary only for post-crime conviction; it is not necessary for preemptive killing. While this is an intuitive position, and does reflect tannaitic halakhah, it is the first time any text has recognized the possibility that pursuers would need to be warned. And most importantly, a "קסבר" statement always implies that other sages disagree. Thus, immediately the reader is alerted to the startling notion that some other authority who disagrees with R. Huna would require bystanders to warn pursuers before they are prevented from committing the crime.

The sugya continues with R. Hisda's objection to R. Huna (1c) from Mishnah Ohalot 7:6. The mishnah discusses whether it is permissible to abort a fetus in order to save the life of the mother. While still in the womb, the fetus's life does not take precedence over the mother's. However, once most of the infant has emerged, nothing may be done to harm the infant because it is forbidden to take one life (the infant) in order to save the life of another (the mother). R. Hisda presents the case of a fetus as a paradigm for the minor pursuer, and thus as a direct difficulty on R. Huna. Read in light of section 1b, R. Hisda would argue that the infant cannot be harmed because it cannot be warned. By implication, all other pursuers, must be warned before they can be killed. The Bavli immediately rejects this interpretation by explaining that the case of the infant differs from that of a normal pursuer because "Heaven" is directing the infant's pursuit of its mother. The infant cannot be considered a pursuer because he lacks gross motor skills. He is not preemptively killed because he is not even in control of his motions. This is unlike a minor pursuer who, while legally lacking the capacity for intent, is in control of his faculties and thus can be killed. The issue is not the capacity to receive a preemptive warning—no pursuer needs to be warned. Rather, the issue is control over the body—one can be preemptively killed only if his mind is controlling his body.

Section 2a cites a baraita in support of R. Huna, to whom is attributed the position that pursuers need not be warned. At first glance, the baraita seems to contradict R. Huna, for it does appear to require warning a pursuer. According to Rashi and other medieval commentators, the fact that the baraita does not include a statement of acknowledgment by the pursuer that he is knowingly about to commit a crime forbidden by the Torah indicates that he need not be warned before the bystander kills him. In other words, without acknowledgment by the pursuer of the warning, the warning is considered not to have been issued. Therefore, this baraita, which is read as if it does not require a pursuer to acknowledge the warning, is brought as support for an implication drawn from R. Huna. The stam rejects this use of the baraita by explaining that it follows the opinion of R. Yose b. R. Yehudah, who does not require warning in every capital case. If it is clear that the offender knows that he is transgressing, as we must assume in the case of a *haver*, there is no need to warn him. Rashi explains that the baraita follows R. Yose b. R. Yehudah because it refers to a case of a non-*haver*. The warning is delivered to ensure that the assailant has criminal intent, but the non-*haver* does not have to accept the warning because R. Yose b. R. Yehudah does not require any criminal to acknowledge a warning. Following the logic of the sugya, if the baraita which does not require a warning accords with R. Yose b. R. Yehudah then we must assume that the sages who disagree with him would require a warning in all cases, even when the intent to sin is clear. If R. Yose b. R. Yehudah does not require warning a pursuer, then the other sages do.

In section 3a, a baraita is brought as a challenge against R. Huna. The baraita states that a pursuer must be warned before he is preemptively killed in protection of the victim. This baraita seems to be the clearest instance in which a tannaitic or amoraic text actually demands that pursuers be warned. The stam concludes by providing two explanations (3b and 3c) for why this baraita does not actually contradict R. Huna. These sections will be explored in detail below.

In summary, the stam has crafted this sugya by weaving together the two issues we discussed above: the warning necessary for post-murder conviction and the preemptive killing of a pursuer. We will now show how the stam rereads its tannaitic sources and reframes the amoraic debate to create the heretofore unknown position that despite the urgency of saving an innocent victim's life, pursuers may not be killed without a prior warning.

# Killing a Minor Pursuer: The Amoraic Sugya as Found in the Yerushalmi

The Yerushalmi preserves an amoraic dispute over the interpretation of the mishnah in Ohalot which demonstrates that the stam in the Bavli has reframed the original amoraic dispute. This short sugya appears three times in the Yerushalmi, including in chapter 8 of Sanhedrin (23c), the direct parallel to the Bavli's sugya. However, due to textual issues we will cite the version found on Shabbat 14:4, 14d (=Avodah Zarah 2:2, 40d).[9]

| | |
|---|---|
| **ירושלמי שבת יד:ד (יד, ד)** | **Yerushalmi Shabbat 14:4, 14d** |
| רב חסדא בעי: מהו להציל נפשו של גדול בנפשו של קטן? | Rav Hisda asked: Can one save an adult [by taking] the life of a minor [who is pursuing him]? |
| התיב רבי ירמיה: ולא מתניתא היא?! יצא רובו אין נוגעין בו שאין דוחין נפש מפני נפש (אהלות ז:ו). | R. Yirmiyah responded: Is it not a mishnah?! "But if the greater part has come out, one may not touch it, for one may not set aside one person's life for that of another" (Mishnah Ohalot 7:6). |
| רבי יוסה בי רבי בון בשם רב חסדא: שנייא היא תמן, שאין את יודע מי הורג את מי. | R. Yose b. R. Bun in the name of R. Hisda: There it is different, for you do not know who is killing whom. |

R. Hisda asks the question answered by R. Huna in the Bavli passage cited above: Can a bystander kill a minor pursuing an adult? R. Yirmiyah infers from Mishnah Ohalot that the prohibition of killing an infant to save the life of the mother implies that there is a similar prohibition in regard to all minors. Just as the infant is unaware of his actions and cannot be killed in order to save the mother, so too minors in general cannot be killed in order to save the lives of others.

R. Yose b. R. Bun rejects R. Yirmiyah's answer on the grounds that the two cases are different. The mishnah from Ohalot describes a situation of two individuals, each of whose lives is threatened by the existence of the

---

[9] See Leib Moskovits, "Sugyot Makbilot u-Mesorot Nusah," *Tarbiz 60,4* (1991), 529.

other; it is not clear who the aggressor is in such a situation. In contrast, R. Hisda's question imagines a situation in which an adult is actively being pursued by a minor. R. Yose b. R. Bun's distinction implies, although he does not say so explicitly, that as long as the aggressor can clearly be identified, he can be categorized as a pursuer even if he is a minor. The danger to the life of the pursued (the adult) is sufficient justification to kill the pursuer (the minor) even if the pursuer may not fully understand the ramifications of his actions. Intent is not strictly necessary to justify the preemptive killing of a pursuer. All that is necessary is establishing the facts of who is trying to kill whom. Notably, the Yerushalmi makes no mention of the warning procedure. The issue in the Yerushalmi is simple: Can a minor pursuer be killed?

Removing section 1b from the Bavli makes the two sugyot nearly identical:

| Yerushalmi | Bavli |
|---|---|
| רב חסדא בעי: מהו להציל נפשו של גדול בנפשו של קטן? | אמר רב הונא: קטן הרודף ניתן להצילו בנפשו. |
| התיב רבי ירמיה: ולא מתניתא היא?! יצא רובו אין נוגעין בו שאין דוחין נפש מפני נפש. | איתיביה רב חסדא לרב הונא: יצא ראשו אין נוגעין בו לפי שאין דוחין נפש מפני נפש. ואמאי? רודף הוא! |
| רבי יוסה בי רבי בון בשם רב חסדא: שנייא היא תמן, שאין את יודע מי הורג את מי. | שאני התם, דמשמיא קא רדפי לה. |
| | |
| R. Hisda asked: Can one save an adult [by taking] the life of a minor [who is pursuing him]? | R. Huna said: A minor who pursues can be saved at the cost of his life. |
| R. Yirmiyah responded: Is it not a mishnah?! "But if the greater part has come out, one may not touch it, for one may not set aside one person's life for that of another." | R. Hisda challenged R. Huna: "But if the head has come out, one may not touch him, for one may not set aside one person's life for that of another." But why? Is he not a pursuer! |
| R. Yose b. R. Bun in the name of R. Hisda: There it is different, for you do not know who is killing whom. | There it is different, for she [the mother] is pursued by heaven. |

In both Talmuds, the amoraim debate if criminally significant intent is necessary to justify killing the pursuer. One side suggests that the mishnah in Ohalot proves that children may not be killed as pursuers because they do not have intent. The other position ignores the issue of intent and is solely concerned with identifying the victim. As long the bystanders know who the victim is, they are permitted to kill the pursuer. The issue of warning is not raised at all in the Yerushalmi, or in what we have identified as the proto-Babylonian sugya, because warning is necessary only for post-criminal conviction, not for preemptive killing.

## The Stammaitic Reinterpretation of the Tannaitic Sources

By adding in section 1b, the stam reframes the debate such that is not over the narrow topic of preemptively killing a pursuing minor, but over the broad topic of whether pursuers ever need to be warned. The stam in the Bavli now pursues this broad topic with vigor. The remainder of the Babylonian sugya consists of tannaitic sources which the stam refashions into support or rejection of each side in this imagined debate. As we saw above, the tannaitic sources did not address the necessity to warn a pursuer in order to allow for preemptive killing to save the life of a victim. Common sense dictates that criminal pursuers may be stopped when lives are immediately at stake. What tannaitic sources do insist upon is that criminals may not be convicted by a court without having been warned before committing the crime. The Babylonian editor reworked these sources so that they reflect one side or the other in the debate over warning a pursuer.

Section 2a of the Babylonian sugya is a baraita brought as a support for R. Huna's position, that pursuers do not require warnings. This baraita may be compared to its tannaitic antecedent in Sifre Zuta:

| Sifre Zuta Numbers | Bavli |
|---|---|
| מי שהיה רודף אחר חבירו להורגו, אמרו לו: בן ברית הוא, הוי יודע שכתוב בתורה *שופך דם האדם באדם דמו ישפך*. אמר להן אף על פי כן, הורג הוא. אמר: *רשע למות*, קדם הורגהו הצל נפשו של זה בנפשו של זה. | רודף שהיה רודף אחר חבירו להורגו, אומרין לו: ראה שישראל הוא, ובן ברית הוא, והתורה אמרה *שפך דם האדם באדם דמו ישפך*, אמרה תורה: הצל דמו של זה בדמו של זה. |

343

## Sifre Zuta Numbers

A man was pursuing his fellow to kill him. They said to him: "He is a member of the covenant, and know that it is written in the Torah, *Whoever sheds the blood of man, by man shall his blood be shed*" (Genesis 9:6). **If he said to them "even so," he is a murderer.**

It says *an evil [person] is to be put to death* (Num 35:31) kill him first, save the life of this one [the pursued] at the cost of the life of that one [the pursuer]!

## Bavli

If a man was pursuing his fellow to kill him, they [the witnesses] say to him, "See, he is a Jew, and a member of the covenant, and the Torah has said, *Whoever sheds the blood of man, by man shall his blood be shed*" (Genesis 9:6).

The Torah has said, save the blood of this one [the pursued] with the blood of that one [the pursuer]!

At the outset, we should note that there are no tannaitic sources that state explicitly that a pursuer need not be warned, because this position is exceedingly obvious. As we stated above, in tannaitic literature warning is relevant only for post-crime conviction. Babylonian editors, however, looking for tannaitic sources relevant to the possibility that a pursuer would need to be warned, would clearly find this baraita from Sifre Zuta germane to the discussion. In Sifre Zuta this baraita is an amalgam of two distinct topics: 1) warning a potential criminal in order to achieve post-murder conviction; 2) the mandate to kill a pursuer. However, while Sifre Zuta can easily be read as maintaining the distinction between these two issues, the Bavli needs to combine them such that we have a source that supports R. Huna—preemptive warning is not necessary to stop a pursuer. To accomplish this, the Bavli omits one line from the original baraita, "If he said to them 'even so,' he is a murderer." By omitting the phrase, "If he said to them 'even so'" the baraita, which once contained a warning, now can be read (albeit with great difficulty) as if it does not.[10] Second, the Bavli must omit the phrase "he is a murderer." In Sifre Zuta, this line emphasizes that once the pursuer affirms his awareness that he is

---

[10] Rashi explains that without the pursuer's acknowledgement ("even so") that he understands the ramifications of his actions, it is as if no warning has been issued. Y.Z. Dinnur *Hiddushei ha-Ritzad Nezikin*, 3:304 offers another equally implausible interpretation that in the phrase "they say to him:" "him" is not the pursuer, but yet another bystander. The witnesses cannot protect the innocent pursued person, so they yell out to other bystanders urging them to save the life of the pursued who is a "member of the covenant."

about to kill a Jew, a crime punishable by death, "he is a murderer" and may be convicted **after the crime** by a court. The Bavli omits this line because it is not interested in the issue of post-crime conviction, it is only interested in pre-crime warning. Thus, by omitting both parts of this one line, the redactor has emended a source to allow it to be understood as stating that a pursuer may be preemptively killed without a warning, something so obvious that the tannaim never felt the need to say it.

After reworking a tannaitic source to support R. Huna, the redactor seeks to balance the imagined amoraic debate by citing a tannaitic source supporting the position attributed to R. Hisda (a pursuer must be warned). This strange position is, of course, not located in any tannaitic source and therefore the editor is again forced to emend an earlier text, namely the passage from Tosefta Sanhderin that describes the details of the warning procedure:

| Tosefta | Bavli |
|---|---|
| **ראוהו שהרג את הנפש** אמרו לו הוי יודע שהוא בן ברית ונאמר *שופך דם האדם באדם דמו ישפך* אף על פי שאמר יודע אני פטור עד שיאמר יודע אני ועל מנת כן אני עושה. | **רודף שהיה רודף אחר חבירו להורגו**, אמר לו: ראה שישראל הוא, ובן ברית הוא, והתורה אמרה: *שפך דם האדם באדם דמו ישפך*. אם הוא אמר: יודע אני שהוא כן - פטור, על מנת כן אני עושה - חייב. |
| **If they saw him [about to] murder someone**, they say to him, "Know that he is a member of the covenant, and it is said: *Whoever sheds the blood of man, by man shall his blood be shed* (Genesis 9:6)," even if he said "I know," he is exempt until he says, "I know and it is because of it that I am doing it!" | **If a man was pursuing his fellow to kill him**, they [the witnesses] say to him, "See, he is an Israelite, and a member of the covenant, and the Torah has said, *Whoever sheds the blood of man, by man shall his blood be shed* (Genesis 9:6)," if he said "I know," he is exempt. If he says, "I know and it is because of it that I am doing it!" he is liable. |

As we saw above, the passage from the Tosefta is not concerned with stopping a pursuer before he commits a crime, but rather with convicting a criminal in court. Without a properly issued warning, a murderer may not be executed lest he did not know that his victim is a Jew and that the Torah prescribes the death penalty for killing a Jew. Similar to the case of transgressing Shabbat, the halakhah teaches that warning and acknowledgement are necessary for conviction. The Babylonian redactor changes the language of the introduction to the baraita into the language used in the Mishnah in the context of killing a pursuer before he commits a crime. The redactor has now created a tannaitic source which explicitly requires warning a pursuer.

The modified baraita serves to challenge the position ascribed to R. Huna: Bystanders may preemptively kill a pursuer without warning. The very position which seemed intuitive and incontrovertible is now attacked by an emended tannaitic source. The stam provides two possible defenses of R. Huna. The first (3b), that the baraita refers to a case in which the witnesses are not able to save the victim, returns to the original tannaitic halakhah: The warning is necessary only for post-crime conviction. To convict, the witnesses must warn; but had they been able to save the life of the victim, no warning would have been necessary.

The second defense of R. Huna is again a slightly modified quote of an earlier tannaitic source, this time from Mekhilta de-R. Shimon b. Yohai 22:2.[11] We will begin by explaining this midrash in its original form:

**Mekhilta de-R. Shimon b. Yohai 22:2**     מכילתא דרשב"י כב:ב

Perhaps he needs witnesses? Scripture states: *While tunneling* (Exodus 22:2). It is a tunnel; it is the testimony [against him].

יכול יהא צריך עדים, תלמוד לומר: *במחתרת* (שמות כב:ב), היא מחתרת היא עדותו.

Why then is *is found*, stated?...     אם כן למה נאמר נאמר *ימצא*...

The midrash follows the standard יכול...ת"ל formula, which presents a possible reading of a verse which is subsequently rejected. The midrash begins with the supposition that the tunneling thief could not be preemptively killed unless witnesses were present to ascertain his lethal intentions. This wrong supposition is not the result of an actual counterposition that a pursued person (in this case a homeowner) cannot kill an intruder without first warning him. In other words, this is not an "it could be" reading that reflects a real halakhic position, as sometimes appears in halakhic midrashim. Rather, this "straw" position is a midrashic response to the appearance of the word ימצא in the verse, "if the

---

[11] This same baraita is quoted in the previous sugya found in the Bavli, immediately before R. Huna's statement.

thief is found (יִמָּצֵא) while tunneling." Rabbis here and elsewhere read this word as indicative of the need for witnesses.[12] In other cases, eyewitness testimony is required for criminal conviction, and read in this situation, the word would indicate that here too witnesses are needed for establishing *mens rea*. To reject this supposition, the midrash notes the particulars of the situation: The thief's entrance by tunneling obviates the need for witnesses. The fact that the thief tunneled into the house allows him to be categorized as an assailant and not a houseguest. The midrash then goes on to explain that the word "is found" here refers to a different issue altogether.

The baraita in section 3c of the Bavli, "his tunnel is his warning," is basically the same as the Mekhilta de-R. Shimon b. Yohai source, with one word changed: "testimony" becomes "warning." The change fits the baraita to the current context while maintaining its original argument. Just as the tunneling thief, whom the tannaim classify as a pursuer, does not require standard judicial procedures, so too any pursuer's actions justify preemptive killing. More importantly, though, the entire structure of the midrash has been removed. Instead of the incorrect supposition that a tunnelling thief cannot be killed unless there are witnesses (a position based on the usual midrashic reading of the word יִמָּצֵא), the position "his tunnel is his warning" is simply stated as a legal fact. This presentation gives the impression that it is one side in a tannaitic debate. In other words, while the midrash utterly dismissed the possibility that the tunnelling thief requires witnesses, the Babylonian version presents a simple opinion ("his tunnel is his warning"), an opinion that can be disputed. Finally, the stam explicitly attributes to R. Huna the implication that this baraita is one side of a tannaitic dispute: "R. Huna will tell you: My ruling agrees with the tanna of the tunneling thief, who holds that his tunnel is his warning." R. Huna here acknowledges that while at least one tanna agrees with him that pursuers do not require warning, others, like R. Hisda, would hold that they do.

## Conclusion

The rabbis created a legal system that was extraordinarily stringent when it comes to the rules of testimony and the determination of criminal intent.

---

[12] See Sifre Deuteronomy piska 148.

Such a system leads to the virtual impossibility of ever carrying out an execution, a result reflective of the rabbinic belief in the sanctity of all human life. Already in the Mishnah, we find evidence of the need to justify the killing of a pursuer beyond the common-sense reason of protecting the victim; thus, we are told that the pursuer must be killed because he is being saved from committing a terrible sin! In other words, taking the life of the pursuer is justified because it is for the pursuer's own benefit. Nevertheless, there is not a shred of doubt in tannaitic texts that a pursuer may be preemptively killed without warning. In pre-stammaitic texts, the issue of warning is relevant only for post-criminal conviction. Only in the Bavli do we encounter the notion that all pursuers must be warned before the life of the victim can be protected.

This development, of course, raises the obvious question: Why would the editors of the Bavli create such an impractical position? The answer may lie in the mishnah in Ohalot, cited by R. Yirmiyah in the Yerushalmi. To recall, in the Yerushalmi, R. Hisda asked whether a minor pursuer could be killed to save the life of the adult being pursued, and R. Yirmiyah answered in the negative: Just as an infant may not be killed to save the life of the mother, so too no minor pursuer can be killed. The reason can only be that like an infant, a minor does not have criminal intent. The Bavli sugya begins with the assumptions explored in the Yerushalmi and takes them to their next logical steps. If a minor pursuer cannot be killed because he does not have intent, then the reason an adult pursuer is killed is precisely because of his intent. But intent cannot simply be assumed; it must be ascertained through the warning procedure. Therefore, all pursuers must (potentially) be warned before they are preemptively killed in order to verify intent.

We should emphasize that the extension made by the Bavli moves from a real assessment of the minor's lack of intent to legal formalism: The intent of an adult can and must be determined only through legal warning. In other words, obviously an infant has no intent to kill, and obviously a person chasing another with a dangerous weapon does. But from a legal perspective, intent cannot be determined without the acknowledgment of the perpetrator and, therefore, a pursuer's intent must be clarified. Furthermore, through its adherence to legal formalism, the Bavli undermines the entire *raison d'etre* of the warning. Whereas originally the necessity of warning would serve to make execution exceedingly difficult and thus spare human lives, the necessity to warn

**before** a murder is committed would not in essence save any life, for in this case either the pursuer or pursued will die. The development of this issue from the tannaitic to the late talmudic sources is an excellent example of how the stammaim extend a principle to its logical extreme, even if by doing so the principle becomes entirely dissociated and distorted from its original function.

# EXECUTION: REVEALING THE RABBIS

## SCHOLARSHIP ON THE DEATH PENALTY IN RABBINIC LITERATURE

The rabbinic texts about execution raise questions about the role these laws played in the rabbinic world. Most modern scholars agree that the tannaim did not have the political power to execute criminals. The very few cases in rabbinic literature in which a sage testifies to an execution were not carried out according to rabbinically prescribed halakhah. For instance, in Mishnah Sanhedrin 7:2 and Tosefta Sanhedrin 9:11, R. Elazar b. R. Tzadok testifies that as a child riding on his father's shoulders, he saw a daughter of a priest burned alive for the sin of adultery. Similarly, Bavli Sanhedrin 52b records a story of Rav Hama b. Tuvia burning alive an adulteress daughter of a priest. This contradicts rabbinic halakhah according to which execution by burning is carried out by other means. In Mishnah Sanhedrin 6:4, R. Eliezer relates that Shimon b. Shetah hanged eighty women in Ashkelon (for sorcery according to Yerushalmi Sanhedrin 6:9, 23c). This too is against rabbinic halakhah which does not call for the hanging of women, nor allow multiple executions in one day. Bavli Sanhedrin 46a records a man executed for riding a horse on Shabbat, despite the fact that this is not considered to be an executable crime.[13] In short, the extreme philosophical reluctance to execute even certain criminals, the paucity of texts that refer to actual executions, and the historical position of the rabbis as subject to Roman authority, makes it almost certain that rabbis never carried out an execution.[14]

Nevertheless, despite the fact that these laws have no immediate practical ramification, the rabbis devote considerable attention to prescribing the details of how a court executes a criminal. Mishnah Sanhedrin contains a comprehensive description of the trial procedure, several chapters devoted to the performance of executions, and precise lists as to which criminals are executed in which manner. There is even

---

[13] In a passage excised from older printed editions, Bavli Sanhedrin 43a also describes Jesus's execution. This seems likely to be more of an echo of awareness of Christian stories than an actual preserved rabbinic tradition.

[14] On the historical reality of Jewish execution see Beth Berkowitz, *Execution and Invention: Death Penalty Discourse in Early Rabbinic and Christian Culture* (Oxford: Oxford University Press, 2006), 12-17.

material on the primary and secondary burial of the criminal and how he is to be mourned. The Tosefta, the halakhic midrashim, and the Talmuds greatly supplement this material. These detailed descriptions, which cannot all be explained as interpretations of biblical law or narrative, force scholars to delve into the paradox of why rabbis lacking the power to execute would discuss the death penalty at such great length.

We must also consider the question of the rabbis' famed leniency. Even a cursory glance at a description of the trial of capital crimes reveals that rabbinic law makes it extremely difficult, if not impossible, to actually convict and execute a criminal. This culminates in the famous statement of R. Tarfon and R. Akiva, "Had we been members of the Sanhedrin, no person would ever have been put to death" (Mishnah Makkot 1:10). Why did these rabbis not heed R. Shimon b. Gamliel's warning found in that same mishnah, "They would have multiplied murderers in Israel?"

Finally, the four methods of execution found in rabbinic literature—stoning, burning, decapitation, and strangulation—have, at most, a nominal affinity with those in the Bible. In rabbinic law, stoning is not carried out by simply throwing stones at the criminal until he dies; rather the convict is pushed off a two-story scaffolding (Mishnah Sanhedrin 6:4). Criminals are burned not by being cast into a fire or surrounded by a burning pyre; rather they are forced to drink hot molten lead (ibid 7:2). Decapitation and strangulation are never even mentioned in the Bible. Whereas, in the Bible and Second Temple literature, stoning seems to be the default methods of execution, in rabbinic literature strangulation is the default method (Mekhilta de-Rabi Ishmael Nezikin 5; Sifra Kedoshim Parashah 10 ch. 9). Scholars must account for why these methods of execution differ so radically from simpler interpretations of the biblical texts, interpretations that were shared by nearly all other Jewish writers in the Second Temple period: Jubilees, Philo, Josephus, Dead Sea Scrolls, Apocryphal literature, the New Testament, and others. Why do the rabbis envision execution so differently from all other Jewish writers of the period?

Various scholars have revisited these questions in recent years. Their respective approaches, which we explore below, differ from those of their predecessors in ways that bear exploring. Understanding this shift in scholarship on the death penalty is significant, as it is an excellent example of how scholarship in general has changed over the past generation. How current talmudic scholars and historians approach a subject that has historical significance contributes to an overall understanding of how critical talmudic study has shaped our views on the nature of rabbinic literature.

First, today scholars are far less likely to rely on external, non-rabbinic parallels as the sole or primary background for the analysis of rabbinic methods of execution. While scholars have not entirely abandoned the search for parallels to rabbinic literature in Greco-Roman sources, in contemporary non-rabbinic Jewish compositions, and elsewhere, it has become clear that noting the existence of an external parallel is not sufficient to account for the presence of any aspect of rabbinic law.[15] After all, even if a parallel for a certain rabbinic phenomenon can be identified in some other culture or legal system, we must still ask why the rabbis would have adopted such an element into their legal system. Furthermore, isolated parallels do not contribute to an understanding of how rabbinic law and thinking operate as a whole.

Second, rabbinic literature has justifiably been abandoned as a source of knowledge for the trial and crucifixion of Jesus or for other events from the Second Temple period. There is general consensus that Mishnah Sanhedrin and later rabbinic literature has little relevance for a historical reconstruction of the Second Temple period.

Finally, although some modern Jewish thinkers and legalists continue to marshal rabbinic dicta in the perpetual argument over the ethics of execution, scholars who specialize in rabbinics do not overtly engage in such polemics.

Our survey below focuses on five recent approaches to answering the question of what light the rabbinic discussions of execution can shed on the rabbis, their beliefs, their hermeneutics, and their texts in general. We have entitled the approaches: (i) Execution as Ethics, (ii) Execution as the Study of God and Humanity, (iii) Execution as Jurisprudence, (iv) Execution as Exegesis, and (v) Execution as Discourse.

---

[15] On the challenge of comparative research see Shai Secunda, *The Iranian Talmud: Reading the Bavli in Its Sassanian Context* (Philadelphia: University of Pennsylvania Press, 2014), 111-126.

## I. Execution as Ethics

Scholarship from the nineteenth century onwards focused on the claim that the rabbis were concerned either with the suffering of the convicted criminal or with preserving the intactness of his body. Moshe Halbertal's work on this issue, which appears as a chapter in his book, *Interpretive Revolutions in the Making* (Hebrew, 1997), nonetheless marks a watershed for several reasons.[16] Halbertal's study of the death penalty is embedded in a larger work which claims that ethical considerations drive rabbinic interpretation of the Torah's legal passages. That is, rabbis approach the Torah with predetermined ethical considerations and attempt to shape the Torah's legislation to match their own ethics (138). Rabbinic midrash is often revolutionary in that it overturns older and more literal interpretations in favor of interpretations which derive from ethical concerns. In short, ethics fuels exegesis.

When it comes to the death penalty, the central value that the rabbis wished to propagate was the sanctity of the body. Halbertal claims that the rabbis shifted the purpose of execution from the destruction of the body to the termination of the soul, the inner life source (146-149). While the death penalty in the Bible is directed at the utter destruction of the body either through stoning or burning,[17] the central rabbinic precept can be summarized as "the burning of the spirit (*neshamah*) while the body (*guf*) remains" (Sifra Shmini 1; Bavli Sanhedrin 52a).

Halbertal demonstrates his thesis regarding three of the four methods of execution. We shall begin with burning (Halbertal 146-149). Burning, a punishment in the Torah for only two crimes—intercourse with a mother and daughter (Leviticus 20:14) and a priest's daughter's fornication (Leviticus 21:9), consists of burning the body whole. The rabbis were aware of this manner of carrying out the execution of a criminal, yet in their own legislation the penalty is described as pouring hot lead down the criminal's throat (Mishnah Sanhedrin 7:2; Sifra Shmini 1; Bavli Sanhedrin 52a). Here Halbertal reveals what, in his opinion, is the ultimate motivating principle in the rabbinic shaping of executions. It

---

[16] Moshe Halbertal, *Interpretive Revolutions in the Making: Values as Interpretive Considerations in Midrashei Halakhah* (Jerusalem: Hebrew University Magnes Press, 1997).

[17] Or both in the case of Akhan. See Joshua 7:24.

is not, as some scholars have understood, a desire to demonstrate kindness to the criminal, but rather an ethics of preserving the body.

A similar and equally striking shift occurs with stoning (149-154). Stoning in the Torah involves the entire community throwing stones at the condemned until his body is utterly destroyed. In contrast, the rabbis describe a ritual in which the condemned is pushed off a two-story scaffold. Only if the fall fails to kill him do the witnesses, followed by the rest of Israel, place single stones upon him until he dies (Mishnah Sanhedrin 6:4). Tellingly, the scaffold must be no lower and no higher than two stories. The Babylonian Talmud (Sanhedrin 45a) asks why it must be this precise height, and answers with an ethical consideration. A lower height would be cruel because it might maim but not kill him, and the Torah states: "Love your neighbor as yourself (Leviticus 19:18)— choose for him a good death." A higher height, on the other hand, would be too disfiguring. Halbertal proceeds to analyze other elements of this method of execution, demonstrating that each element is meant to preserve the body of the criminal as much as possible while still technically carrying out the biblical punishment of stoning.

The very existence of execution by strangling serves, according to Halbertal (154-159), to advance his overall thesis that ethical considerations guide the formation of rabbinic laws and exegesis. In the Torah, stoning seems to be the default death penalty. In contrast, according to the dominant opinion in rabbinic literature, when the Torah does not prescribe a method of execution, the execution is to be performed by strangling, which, as mentioned, is not even found in the Torah. When defending this idea, the tannaim raise considerations that are, according to Halbertal, ethical in nature (Sifra Kedoshim 9; Halbertal 155). Again, the details of strangulation support this point. The rope used to strangle the criminal (Mishnah Sanhedrin 7:3) or pry open his mouth so that the lead can be poured down his throat in the execution of burning (Mishnah Sanhedrin 7:2) consists of "a hard rope put into a soft one." The only reason for such a seemingly extraneous detail is the overall goal of preserving the body of the criminal even while his life force, his *neshamah*, is being taken away (Halbertal 156).

With regard to post-mortem hanging (which is, according to rabbinic law, not a method of execution but something done to the body after the criminal has been executed), Halbertal again demonstrates how details in the rabbinic prescription reveal the rabbis' goal of preserving the body and their disgust at its disfiguration (159-162). While Deuteronomy 21:23 mandates that the body be taken down before nightfall, the rabbis insist that "when they hang him, one ties and one unties [immediately] in order to fulfill the commandment of hanging" (Tosefta Sanhedrin 9:6). The hanging is a commandment which must be performed because it is stipulated in the Torah, but it is to be done as speedily as possible in order to avoid disfiguring the body (159-162).

We must note that the one method of execution which Halbertal and other scholars have difficulty explaining is decapitation (Halbertal 158, n. 24). Mishnah Sanhedrin 7:2 admits how disfiguring this method of execution would be, and Tosefta Sanhedrin 9:11, in reference to one form of decapitation, cites the same text quoted with regard to the height of the scaffold: "R. Yehudah says: *Love your neighbor as yourself* (Leviticus 19:18)—choose for him a good death." Here "a good death" according to R. Yehudah is not the one that is the least disfiguring, but one that does not treat the Jewish criminal as do the Romans. Neither do the other rabbis who disagree with him as to how decapitation is to be carried out seem to strive to prevent physical disfigurement; after all, they too condone decapitation.

Nevertheless, deeper analysis may reveal that an attempt to cause less disfigurement to the body may have played some role in shaping this method of execution as well. A passage in Sifre Deuteronomy piska 94 (see also Mekhilta de-R. Shimon b. Yohai to Exodus 21:12]), commenting on Deuteronomy 13:16, demonstrates that some rabbis preferred certain methods of death by sword over others because they perceived them as less disfiguring. The passage reads, "'*By the sword* (lit. by the mouth of a sword):' By the side of the sword that it should not disfigure them." If an execution must be performed by shedding blood, then the sword is the least disfiguring of options (Halbertal 158, n. 24; Lorberbaum 223-224). Whether this is indeed true is irrelevant. What is relevant is the rabbis' cognizance of the ethical principles which guide their interpretive choices. Nevertheless, it is hard to comprehend how decapitation could ever be considered anything but disfiguring. Had the rabbis wished to create a method of execution that would have shed blood without overly disfiguring the criminal, they could have legislated cutting his or her wrists. Indeed, the rabbis were aware of this means of execution and rejected it (Mekhilta de-R. Yishmael Nezikin parashah 4). It seems quite clear that in this particular case, rabbinic interpretations were shaped by other considerations besides the preservation of the body.

Despite this difficulty, Halbertal's central argument is convincing. Ethics clearly plays a strong role in rabbinic exegesis. However, Halbertal is perhaps a bit quick to dismiss the technical elements of rabbinic midrash. There are many midrashic passages whose exegetical choices and legal conclusions do seem to be "forced"—that is to say, they do not accord well with what seems to be the original intent and simple meaning of the passage. Nevertheless, it is possible that when we examine them closer, exegetical considerations, mainly harmonizing biblical passages, do indeed drive these interpretations. This is a point that is amply demonstrated by Aharon Shemesh, whose work we will discuss below. The difference between the approaches of Halbertal and Shemesh highlights a tension that is critical for understanding modern interpretation of rabbinic literature as a whole: Should the scholar start by attempting to detect the exegetical layer and then admit that points that cannot be explained by exegesis are the result of other considerations? Or does the scholar begin by cataloguing these other considerations, and when they cannot be detected, admit that there is a purely exegetical motivation at play?

Finally, Halbertal never entirely explicates why the rabbis make such ethical choices. Why do the rabbis consider it ethical to preserve the body of the criminal and unethical to utterly destroy his body so that he might serve as a more powerful deterrent for the larger community? This question is addressed by Yair Lorberbaum, whose work we turn to now.

## II. Execution as Study of God and Humanity

The central thesis of Yair Lorberbaum's book, *In God's Image* (Hebrew, 2004),[18] is that to the rabbis the concept of *imago dei*, in Hebrew *tzelem elohim*, denotes that human beings are **physical** representations of God and that there is tangible divine presence within every human being. As "images" of the Divine, human beings function as icons in a manner

---

[18] The book was translated into English, *In God's Image: Myth, Theology and Law in Classical Judaism* (New York: Cambridge University Press, 2015). References here are to the Hebrew edition, *Tzelem Elohim: Halakhah ve-Aggadah* (Tel Aviv: Schocken Publishing House, 2004).

similar to the way idols function in the pagan world: They draw God's presence into themselves, blurring the borders between representation and form. The infusion of God's presence into the human body dictates that human beings are embodied with significant theurgic powers, meaning that acts upon the human body have direct impact on the Divine. This concept impacts primarily upon two areas of halakhah: the death penalty and procreation. Since humans are representations of God, execution is equivalent in some ways to deicide—it diminishes the divine image. Conversely, procreation is mandated because it increases God's physical manifestation in the world by creating more vehicles which embody God's presence.

Using this theoretical framework, Lorberbaum examines the four methods of execution in rabbinic literature. His overall analysis does not differ greatly from that of Halbertal (as Lorberbaum himself notes, 175-176), for he too states that the rabbis radically reshaped the methods of execution so as to limit the physical destruction of the body. Where he differs from Halbertal is in his understanding of why the rabbis shaped the death penalty in this way. For Lorberbaum, the concept of *tzelem elohim* is the underlying force that shapes nearly every aspect of the treatment of the death penalty in rabbinic literature. At its extreme, execution becomes akin to murder, which is itself akin to deicide. Hence the noted rabbinic reticence to execute is not a result of the rabbis' fear of executing an innocent criminal, but a result of their wish to avoid an act that they viewed as destructive of the Divine itself (234).

Lorberbaum's work is most convincing in his lengthy discussion of post-execution hanging (249-277). As he notes, several texts relevant to this subject explicitly mention or at least overtly allude to the concept of *tzelem elohim*. Deuteronomy 21:22-23 reads, "Now when a man has sin (resulting in) a sentence of death, and is put to death, and you hang him up on a tree, you are not to leave his corpse overnight on the tree, rather you shall certainly bury him on that day, for an insult to God is a hanging person (*kilelat elohim talui*)—that you should not render unclean the land which the Lord your God is giving you as an inheritance." For Lorberbaum, the most important implication that the rabbis drew from this verse was that since God is iconically present in the human body even after death, the hanging body is a curse to God and must be taken down immediately (Tosefta Sanhedrin 9:6). Other rabbinic texts concerning post-mortem hanging become a *locus classicus* for the rabbinic expression of *tzelem elohim* (286-292). In these texts, R. Meir provides a parable in which the hanging body of the criminal is seen by passersby as the identical twin of God (Tosefta Sanhedrin 9:7), and when the body is hanged God feels pain in his own arms and head (Mishnah Sanhedrin 6:4). Indeed, had God known that hanging the criminal would cause suffering to God as well, God would not have ordained it (292).

Ultimately, according to Lorberbaum, the idea of *tzelem elohim* and the iconic presence of God in human beings is what led to the severe rabbinic restrictions on the possibility of implementing execution and to the words of R. Tarfon and R. Akiva we have quoted from Mishnah Makkot 1:10. The rabbis—or at least a dominant strain among the rabbis—did not fear the execution of an innocent human being, as is commonly thought; they opposed the execution of even known criminals (348). Execution is ultimately murder, even if it is authorized by the court. R. Akiva states, "All who spill blood diminish the divine image (*demut*), as it says, *The one who spills the blood of a human being, by a human being his blood shall be spilled, [for in the image of God He made man]* (Genesis 9:6)" (Tosefta Yevamot 8:4). In this interpretation, the verse no longer **demands** execution for the murderer, but rather means that all bloodshed results in a diminishing of the divine image; capital punishment is no exception (353). The entire rabbinic legal corpus concerning capital crimes is shaped by this mytho-theurgic ethos: Execution diminishes the divine presence and is therefore to be legislated out of existence. Of course, the rabbis, confined by the rules of the Torah, could not entirely legislate the death penalty out of existence. They addressed the problem, as is typical, by making the threshold for execution virtually impossible to reach (370).

In the end, Lorberbaum proposes that execution (and procreation) were discussed at such great length by the rabbis, not because of their practical importance, but because it was the opportunity for the rabbis to elaborate upon one of their central theosophical and anthropological tenets: the claim that human beings are iconic representations of an embodied God. Rabbis of the mishnaic and talmudic periods did not write philosophical treatises or comprehensive theologies. Rather, they encoded their beliefs through halakhah and aggadah. There is, perhaps, no better example of such a phenomenon than the halakhot and aggadot concerning the death penalty.

## III. Execution as Jurisprudence

In the first chapter of her book *Punishment and Freedom* (2008), Devora Steinmetz offers various critiques of Halbertal and Lorberbaum's understanding of the overarching goals of the rabbinic laws concerning the death penalty.[19] She is particularly critical of their claim that strangulation was instituted as a method of execution so as to preserve as much as possible the intactness of the body of the criminal (5-11). Instead, Steinmetz suggests that we pay more attention to the notion that in strangulation the human court mimics "death by the hands of heaven." Strangulation takes the air, the life spirit, out of a person, mimicking the way in which people die natural deaths (12-13).

Steinmetz then explores the implications of a legal system in which a court-imposed execution mimics the way that people naturally die (15). The answer lies, for Steinmetz, in the overall structure of the rabbinic penal code. In rabbinic law, as we have seen, a criminal cannot be executed unless he is first warned of the punishment for his impending crime (*hatra'ah*), and he must indicate that he is fully aware of the consequences of the crime he is about to perform (16). The criminal specifically must state, "I know and I do it on that condition." By accepting that he is about to commit a crime that will condemn him to death, the criminal gives himself over to death before he even comes to court. With the very act of committing the crime, he he has relinquished his right to life. The rabbis derive this notion from the phrase in Deuteronomy 17:6, "יומת המת," which could be translated as "the [already dead one] shall die." The court then merely implements the punishment that in a sense has been incurred. As Steinmetz concludes, "Execution, then, is not the court's killing a person; it is the court acting as a human agent in the relinquishing of life that the person has acceded to in choosing to violate God's command" (17). Thus, to Steinmetz, creation of strangulation as the default death penalty is a reflection of the rabbis' overall theory of jurisprudence. It is their way of articulating the role accorded to a human court in enacting God's laws.

---

[19] Devora Steinmetz, *Punishment and Freedom: The Rabbinic Construction of Criminal Law* (Philadelphia: University of Pennsylvania Press, 2008).

## IV.Execution as Exegesis

Aharon Shemesh's book, *Punishments and Sins* (Hebrew, 2003), serves as a foil for the work of the scholars surveyed above.[20] For Halbertal, Lorberbaum, and Steinmetz, the death penalty discussions expose broader concerns, be they ethics, anthropology/theosophy, or jurisprudence. In contrast, according to Shemesh, at the heart of the rabbinic discussions concerning the death penalty lies the rabbinic endeavor to interpret the Torah, to solve exegetical difficulties, and to create a unified, coherent structure out of the Torah's disorganized penal system. Shemesh agrees with the other modern scholars that the rabbis had no political authority to implement their penal code and hence all discussions are theoretical, but he disagrees as to the impulse underlying them.

As with Halbertal, Lorberbaum, and Steinmetz, Shemesh too is fascinated by the implementation of strangulation as the default method of execution by the rabbis. He, of course, recognizes that strangulation is not to be found in the Torah, but he nonetheless believes that this method of punishment has biblical roots (29-33). He contends that strangulation as a death penalty was born as an attempt to solve the seeming contradiction between Deuteronomy 22:22, where the adulterer and adulteress are punished by death but no method of execution is specified, and Deuteronomy 22:23-24, which specifies stoning for adultery with a **betrothed** girl. If all adultery is punished by stoning, why does the Torah single out adultery with a betrothed girl? In addition, the rabbis needed to interpret Leviticus 20:10, "If a man commits adultery with a married woman, committing adultery with another man's wife, the adulterer and the adulteress shall be put to death (*mot yumat*)." To what type of adultery does Leviticus refer? Most rabbis solved these problems by answering that Deuteronomy distinguishes adultery with a married woman from adultery with a betrothed girl because the punishment for the two differs: Adultery with a married woman is punished by strangulation, and adultery with a betrothed girl by stoning. In other words, the notion that adultery with a married woman is not punished by stoning, as is adultery with a betrothed woman, is a product of rabbinic exegesis.

---

[20]  Aharon Shemesh, *Onashim ve-Hata'im: Min ha-Mikra le-Sifruit Hazal* (Jerusalem: The Hebrew University Magnes Press, 2003).

Shemesh's reasoning still does not explain why adultery with a married woman is not punished by one of the other methods of execution already prescribed in the Torah. In other words, we now know why adultery with a married woman cannot be punished by stoning, but we still do not know why the rabbis chose strangulation and not, for instance, burning. Here Shemesh offers an extraordinarily sharp reading of rabbinic texts. He notes (29) that there are actually three different opinions as to the punishment for adultery with a married woman: stoning (R. Eliezer, Sifre Deuteronomy piska 221), decapitation (an anonymous midrash in the Mekhilta de-R. Yishmael Nezikin 4), and strangulation (the normative opinion found in Mishnah Sanhedrin 9:1 and in most other texts). For R. Eliezer, stoning is the default method of execution, applied to every case in which the Torah does not specify how the criminal is to be executed (20-24). As is characteristic of the portrayal of this sage, R. Eliezer follows an older halakhic system, one with traces in Jubilees, Philo, Josephus, and the New Testament, all of which assume that adulterers are punished by stoning (Shemesh 14-18; Halbertal 156-158). Interestingly, it seems that R. Eliezer was more interested in preserving the earlier halakhah than solving the seeming superfluity of the Deuteronomic verses. Here we sense a tension between the needs of exegesis and the requirement of maintaining tradition. The rabbis who held that the adulterer is punished by the sword (decapitation) were also operating exegetically (147-148), based on Ezekiel 16:38-40, "I will inflict upon you the punishment of women who commit adultery and murder... I will deliver you into their hands... then they shall assemble a mob against you to pelt you with stones and **pierce you with swords**." These rabbis solved the exegetical problem by differentiating between adultery with a betrothed girl (stoning) and adultery with a married woman (decapitation). However, this position is found only at the margins of rabbinic literature, and is no where located in the halakhic compositions (Mishnah, Tosefta, and the two Talmuds).

The puzzling opinion is the choice of strangulation. Here Shemesh is almost forced to admit that ethical (Halbertal) or theosophical/anthropological (Lorberbaum) considerations cause the rabbis to invent a new method of execution, a method that because of exegetical considerations eventually becomes the default method of execution. The following is a brief outline of how this process unfolded, according to Shemesh:

1) The rabbis sensed an exegetical need to distinguish between adultery with a married woman (Leviticus 20:10 and Deuteronomy 22:22) and adultery with a betrothed girl (Deuteronomy 22:23-24).
2) They chose strangulation as the method of execution for adultery with the married woman because it is the least disfiguring.
3) Once the punishment of adultery with a married woman was established as strangulation, the phrase *mot yumat*, found in Leviticus 20:10, was understood to **always** mean strangulation. Such an interpretation was then applied to the other instances in which the Torah uses the same language, and strangulation became the default method of execution.

Shemesh does not disagree completely with Halbertal or Lorberbaum, he just limits the use of ethics/theology to one step in the overall development of these laws (step 2). The other steps were governed by exegetical considerations. If for Halbertal ethics guided exegesis, for Shemesh exegesis is guided by ethics.

Another example of Shemesh's claim that exegesis drives these discussions is his analysis of the ranking of the four death penalties. In Mishnah Sanhedrin 7:1, R. Shimon and the sages debate the severity of the four methods of execution, ranking them from most to least severe. Shemesh (37-38) notes that the tannaim support their arguments by asking why certain crimes (the fornicating daughter of a priest who is burned [Leviticus 21:9] or the blasphemer who is stoned [Leviticus 24:16]) are punished with certain methods of execution (Mishnah Sanhedrin 9:3). Neither R. Shimon nor his disputants claim that a certain penalty is more severe because it is more painful or more disfiguring. Shemesh concludes (55) that much of the discussion ranking the four death penalties arises from the fact that the rabbis are trying to forge one detailed coherent legal system out of biblical laws that are often imprecise and even contradictory.

Shemesh further demonstrates that the rabbis did not actually rule that strangulation was the default execution for every criminal whose execution was not specified in the Torah (11-13). According to the rabbis, when the Torah states *damav bo/damehem bahem* ("his blood is upon him"/"their blood is upon them"), the criminal is to be executed by stoning even though the Torah did not state so explicitly (see, for instance, Sifra Kedoshim 11). Similarly, Mishnah Sanhedrin 9:4 prescribes stoning for two crimes (sorcery and bestiality) for which the Torah neither prescribes stoning nor uses the aforementioned phrases. The fact that the rabbis did not limit stoning just to those for whom it is specifically prescribed in the Torah proves that biblical exegesis and not "leniency" was the motivating factor in their determining who receives what death penalty. This is a direct challenge to the views of Halbertal and Lorberbaum surveyed above.

Shemesh's work does not completely overturn that of Halbertal, Lorberbaum, and others. Shemesh admits that non-exegetical considerations do play a role in determining rabbinic halakhah; they account, for instance, for why the rabbis institute strangling as the fourth method of execution, as opposed to a more disfiguring form of execution. Exegesis cannot explain many aspects of these passages—such as why the rabbis modified stoning and burning, and the minor but significant detail of the coarse rope placed inside the soft rope used in strangling and burning. However, Shemesh does demonstrate that when analyzing these passages, one must **first** analyze them in terms of their potential exegeses, which is after all probably the most significant rabbinic intellectual endeavor. Only **after** properly attributing these passages to potential exegetical impulses and necessities should other factors be taken into consideration.

## V. Execution as Discourse

In *Execution and Invention: Death Penalty Discourse in Early Rabbinic and Christian Cultures* (2006), Beth Berkowitz argues that rabbinic discourse concerning the trial and execution of a criminal was itself an exercise of rabbinic power.[21] Step by step, she examines the capital trial as portrayed in tractate Sanhedrin and uncovers a nuanced discourse among the rabbis concerning their own imagined power in a world dominated by Roman authorities. As a marginal group within the larger Jewish society, itself utterly colonized by the Romans, the rabbis seized upon the trial of capital crimes and execution as an opportunity to exercise their own power, even if that power was only discursive. Berkowitz realizes how counterintuitive her claim sounds—how can a realm of law which was completely

---

[21] Beth Berkowitz, *Execution and Invention: Death Penalty Discourse in Early Rabbinic and Christian Culture* (Oxford: Oxford University Press, 2006).

imagined, even fantastical, and therefore utterly removed from actual implementation, be the very realm through which a group exercises its political power? This is indeed the central question she explores (19): "How might the experience of being punished be channeled to create a new regime that, paradoxically, has the power to punish?"

Berkowitz attempts to show how rabbinic authority is portrayed as "self-restrained, reluctant to exercise violence" but at the same time its legitimacy is based on "its capacity to exercise violence" (77). For example, by granting speech to the condemned criminal the rabbis empower him, allowing him an opportunity for self-exculpation; yet, at the same time, they preserve their ultimate authority by instituting that the judge examines him to see if there is "substance in his words" (Mishnah Sanhedrin 6:1; Berkowitz 79-80). Moreover, the rabbis instruct the convicted criminal to confess, thereby enabling him to earn a place in the world to come, and yet at the same time they dictate the words of his confession, not allowing him to question the justness of the verdict (Mishnah Sanhedrin 6:2; Berkowitz 83-85). Similarly, when the rabbis provide an opportunity for those in the crowd to argue for the criminal's innocence, in the end, when no one speaks up for him, the crowd becomes complicit in his execution, thereby bolstering rabbinic justice and authority (83).

The rabbis' confrontation with their own authority is evident in their reluctance to cast themselves as actual executers (142-150). Descriptions of rabbis performing executions are quite rare in rabbinic literature. In the few cases in which we do hear of an execution, the executer is either unjustified in executing or has executed in a wrongful manner and is therefore either accused (Tosefta Sanhedrin 6:6) or marginalized (Mishnah Sanhedrin 6:4; 7:2). In contrast, when Shimon b. Shetah refrains from executing an obviously guilty murderer, he is vindicated (Tosefta Sanhedrin 8:3). The rabbis shed tears when confronted with a criminal who blames them for wrongly convicting him (Tosefta Sanhedrin 8:5). Overall, we are presented with rabbis who distance themselves from the power of execution, preferring to situate the authority over life and death with the abstract body of law they have created instead of with themselves as judges.

Berkowitz's argument that the rabbis used execution to negotiate their place in the Roman world is most convincing in her discussion of decapitation, where the texts explicitly compare Jewish and Roman practice. By decapitating in the way "that the kingdom does" (Mishnah Sanhedrin 7:3), rabbis appropriate Roman power for themselves (162), employing mimicry, a well-attested survival strategy of the colonized.[22] At the same time, some rabbis express discomfort with this approach, as if to argue, "You cannot be a Rabbi and look like a Roman" (163). Berkowitz eloquently summarizes the dilemma: "If rabbinic power is to look nothing like Roman power, then it is not power. If rabbinic power is to look too much like Roman power, then it is not rabbinic (165)."

Methodologically, Berkowitz's work is significant because it analyzes tannaitic literature in its broader cultural context. In the past few decades, scholars have increasingly come to understand and appreciate that the rabbis were a powerless, marginal group within Jewish society. Earlier generations of scholars typically analyzed rabbinic literature—and especially the execution texts—with the assumption that the rabbis had some degree of political power, or that, at the very least, the content of their discussions was influenced by the laws of other social groups who did have political power. Berkowitz avoids both of these approaches, positing that just because a group is removed from the center of political authority does not mean that its writings are devoid of political aspirations and implications. She, like the other scholars which we have discussed here, have largely abandoned history altogether, examining the internal world of rabbinic literature independent of outside forces.

## Conclusion

The last few decades have witnessed a remarkable flourishing of scholarship on the death penalty and execution in rabbinic literature, a development which mirrors some general trends in the study of rabbinic literature. Scholars have largely abandoned the search for external historical connections and explanations and taken up a closer examination of the inner workings of the rabbinic bet midrash. Of course, the rabbis were a part of history and could no more hide themselves from it and its influences than can any other group living in a political world. But any historical study of the rabbis must first take into account the rabbis' own

---

[22] See Ishay Rosen-Zvi, "Rabbis and Romanization: A Review Essay," *Jewish Cultural Encounters in the Ancient Mediterranean and Near Eastern World*, edited by Mladen Popović, et. al (Leiden: Brill, 2016), 218-245.

*sitz im leben.* Only when life inside the bet midrash has been properly explored and revealed can the place of the rabbis in broader political and intellectual history be approached. In our specific case, this means first asking questions such as: What were the rabbis trying to achieve in their creation of the vast edifice of rabbinic literature? What did these discussions mean to them and to the limited audience who may have heard their words? The fact that there are several different and overlapping answers to this question makes the study of the death penalty discussions so fascinating. They allow us to peer into the bet midrash and ask what is really going on inside, and what is truly at stake.

# CHAPTER NINE

ARE YOU GOING TO THE AVODAH ZARAH FAIR? MYRTLE,
ROSE, HANDMAIDENS AND SLAVES

AVODAH ZARAH 6A-B; 12B-13A

## Introduction

While the Torah—and especially the book of Deuteronomy—is adamant
that the Israelites are to utterly destroy all idols, altars, and places of
worship belonging to the seven Canaanite nations,[1] Mishnah Avodah
Zarah focuses on how to interact with the non-Jews (pagans) that occupy
the Land of Israel after the destruction of the Second Temple.[2] The
Mishnah proscribes certain forms of interaction, but tacitly permits all
others. It prohibits the use of certain objects but does not mandate their
widespread destruction; on the contrary, even its prohibitions are
relatively limited. Many scholars have noted the radical change in focus
from the biblical text to the rabbinic texts, attributing it to either socio-
economic factors, the historical circumstance of living under Roman rule,

---

[1]  See for example Deuteronomy 7:1-10; 12:2-3
[2]  On the tannaitic approach to interaction with non-Jews see Moshe Halbertal,
    "Co-Existing with the Enemy: Jews and Pagans in the Mishnah," *Tolerance and
    Intolerance in Early Judaism and Christianity* (Cambridge: Cambridge University
    Press, 1998), 159-172; Amit Gvaryahu, "A New Reading of Three Dialogues in
    Mishnah Avodah Zara," *Jewish Studies Quarterly* 19 (2012), 207-229.

or a shift in ideology.[3] While some have questioned whether all rabbis shared such an approach to the world of idolatry, there is little doubt that the Mishnah's overall program is to prevent certain problematic interactions between Jews and non-Jews while tolerating others.[4]

The following chapter can be divided into two parts. In the first half, we will address the economic participation of Jews in pagan festivals and in their fairs, a topic discussed in the first chapter of Avodah Zarah. We will trace a development in the understanding of this prohibition. The earlier explanation focuses on the Jew—his participation is akin to idol worship—while the later understanding focuses on the pagan—Jewish participation will abet pagan idol worship. Methodologically, we will note how tannaitic and early amoraic sources can be explained differently—and often more cogently—when we separate them from later amoraic and stammaitic explanations.

In the second half of the chapter, while we continue to discuss other texts that refer to Jewish participation in pagan fairs and festivals, we take a broader view of the tendency of later rabbis to relax earlier prohibitions. Indeed, this drive towards leniency is one of the most outstanding features of the rabbinic approach to living and participating in the pagan world and permeates rabbinic literature at all levels, from the Mishnah to the

---

[3]  According to Halbertal, ibid., because the rabbis did not have the political ability to rid their environment of idols and idolaters, they adapted strategies as to how operate in a pagan world. Ephraim E. Urbach emphasizes both socio-economic factors and a lack of concern for pagan influence on Judaism as the source of the change. See Urbach, "The Rabbinical Laws of Idolatry in the Second and Third Centuries in the Light of Archaeological and Historical Facts," *Israel Exploration Journal* 9 (1959), 229-245. Christine Hayes critiqued Urbach for overreading historical, social, and economic conditions as the source of rabbinic thought. In its place, Hayes suggests that first the reader pay careful attention to literary, textual, and analytic factors which often account for changes that occurred to rabbinic texts in the course of the their development. See *Between the Babylonian and Palestinian Talmuds* (Oxford: Oxford University Press, 1997). For a more recent appraisal of this issue see Yair Furstenburg, "The Rabbinic View of Idolatry and the Roman Political Conception of Divinity," *Journal of Religion* 90, 3 (2010), 335-366.

[4]  On the tannaitic interpretations of the biblical laws prohibiting idolatry see Ishay Rosen-Zvi, "Rereading 'Herem': Destruction of Idolatry in Tannaitic Literature" in *The Gift of the Land and the Fate of the Canaanites in Jewish Thought* eds. Katell Berthelot, Joseph E. David, and Marc Hirshman (New York: Oxford University Press, 2014), 50-65.

redaction of the Bavli. Critical talmudic studies can enrich our understanding of these leniencies both by comparing them with sources outside rabbinic literature, particularly Christian patristic texts, and by comparing later texts within the rabbinic corpus with their earlier parallels. Most importantly, such analysis will help us categorize three types of leniencies: 1) those which reflect the way rabbis actually acted (or at least portray themselves as having acted); 2) those which are the result of rabbinic discourse internal to the bet midrash; 3) those which were created only by later editors weaving together imagined talmudic dialectics.

## Part 1: Idolatrous Fairs and Festivals

The first mishnah of Tractate Avodah Zarah begins:

| משנה עבודה זרה א:א-ב | **Mishnah Avodah Zarah 1:1-2** |
|---|---|
| לפני אידיהן של גוים שלשה ימים אסור מלשאת ומלתת עימהן, מלהשאילן ומלהשאיל עימהן, מלהלוותן ומללוות מהן, מלפורען ומלפרע מהן. | For three days preceding the festivals of non-Jews, it is forbidden to do business with them, to lend to them or to borrow from them, to loan them money or to borrow money from them, to pay back a debt to them or to recover a debt from them. |
| רבי יהודה אומר: נפרעין מהן מפני שהוא מצר. | R. Yehudah says: One can recover a debt from them since it causes him distress. |
| אמרו לו: אף על פי שהוא מצר עכשיו שמח הוא לאחר זמן. | [The Sages] said to him: Even though he might be distressed now, later he will be joyful. |
| ר' ישמעאל אומר שלשה לפניהן ושלשה לאחריהן אסור. | R. Yishmael says: [The above] is forbidden for three days before them and for three days after them. |
| וחכמים אומרים לפני אידיהן אסור. לאחר אידיהן מותר. | But the Sages say: Before the festivals it is forbidden, after the festivals it is permitted. |

The mishnah's prohibition is clear, but its underlying justification is not. Why are economic exchanges with non-Jews prohibited for three days before their festivals, or for that matter, why are they prohibited even on their festivals? Both Talmuds devote considerable attention to this question, and it has attracted the eyes of modern scholars as well due to the light it sheds on the socioeconomics of the Jews during the first centuries C.E. in Roman Palestine. To uncover the original meaning of this prohibition, we must start by examining tannaitic sources and other contemporaneous texts composed outside of the rabbinic milieu. As we shall see, early Christian texts are particularly useful in shedding light on this prohibition as well.

At the outset, we must emphasize that the mishnah presents a blanket prohibition on any economic interaction between Jews and non-Jews around the time of their festival. The prohibition includes, but is not limited to, providing a non-Jew with goods that he may use in sacrificial service or other idolatrous acts. The rabbinic approach can be contrasted with the Damascus Covenant,[5] a text attributed to the Dead Sea sect, which prohibits selling particular items to non-Jews:

| ברית דמשק יב:ח-ט | **Damascus Covenant 12:8-9** |
|---|---|
| אל ימכר איש בהמה ועוף טהורים לגוים בעבור אשר לא יזבחום. | No one should sell pure animals or birds to non-Jews lest they sacrifice them. |
| ומגורנו ומגתו אל ימכר להם בכל מאדו. | And he should not sell them anything from his granary or his press, at any price. |
| ואת עבדו ואת אמתו אל ימכור להם אשר באו עמו בברית אברהם. | Neither should he sell his servant or maidservant to them, for they entered the covenant of Abraham with them. |

The Dead Sea sect prohibited selling items used in idolatrous ceremonies: pure (sacrificable) animals, birds, grain, and wine. There was also a prohibition on selling slaves who would be forced to become idolaters after they had already been Judaized. This rule applies throughout the year, without any connection to the festivals of idolaters. In contrast, the

---

5   The Damascus Covenant is a sectarian work found in the Cairo Geniza and in fragments of the Dead Sea Scrolls. There is nearly universal agreement today among scholars that the rules found in the scroll were composed by Jews living in Qumran between the 3rd and 1st centuries B.C.E.

mishnah proscribes any economic exchange whatsoever, but only before (or according to R. Yishmael even after) the festival. As we shall see, some interpretations of the mishnah would read it as if it states a similar rule to the Damascus Document, but this does not seem to be the mishnah's original intention.

The mishnah's all-encompassing prohibition on any economic engagement means that the concern is not simply abetting idol worship. Rather, the festival (איד) and, as we shall see, the fair (יריד), were both points in the pagan calendar in which economic activity and idolatrous worship were so thoroughly intertwined that a Jew who traded in the markets of such an event would be tacitly participating in its idolatrous aspects as well.[6] There simply was no way to distinguish between economic and ritual spheres, for in Greco-Roman culture, such a distinction did not exist. Fairs and markets were dedicated to specific gods, and worshippers who went to visit shrines served as customers for local merchants.[7] A Jew who engaged in any sort of business or exchange with a non-Jew on either of these occasions was, *ipso facto*, flirting with idolatrous worship. In other words, the problem was not that the Jew was enabling the non-Jew to worship by providing him with particular goods necessary for the cult. The problem was that the Jew herself was coming too close to idolatrous practice.

The rabbis articulate this notion in a toseftan passage concerning idolatrous fairs:

[6]  Emmanuel Friedheim, "A New Look at the Historical Background of Mishna Aboda Zara 1:1," *Zion* 71 (2006), 291-294, believes that the festival and the fair are basically identical—the former occurs on the latter. See also Rashi 11b s.v. עיר. However, this is not borne out in the rabbinic texts themselves which relate to each institution on its own. See Ze'ev Safrai, *The Economy of Roman Palestine* (London: Routledge, 1994), 135-147, and Hayim Lapin, *Economy, Geography, and Provincial History in Later Roman Palestine* (Tübingen: Mohr Siebeck, 2001), 141-145.
[7]  See Friedheim, ibid. 296-297 and Ramsay MacMullen, "Market-Days in the Roman Empire," *Phoenix* 24, 4 (1970), 333-341.

## Tosefta Avodah Zarah 1:15[8]

Jews who go to the fair—it is permitted to engage in business with them. But upon their return it is forbidden for they have engaged in idolatry.[9]

תוספתא עבודה זרה א:טו
ישראל הולכין לירוד מותר לשאת ולתת עמהן, ובחזירה אסור מפני שנהגו בעבדה זרה.

And the non-Jews—it is permitted [to engage in business with them] both when going and returning.

והגוים בין בהליכה בין בחזרה מותר.

Non-Jews participating in an idolatrous parade (*tarput*)—it is prohibited to engage in business with them.

גוים ההולכים בתרפות אסור לשאת ולתת עמהם.

But on their return it is permitted, for this is like a case of an idol abandoned by its worshippers.

ובחזירה מותר מפני שהוא כעבודה זרה שהניחוה עובדיה.

And [with regard to] a Jew it is forbidden [to engage in business with him] whether he is going or returning.

וישראל בין בהליכה בין בחזירה אוסר.

A Jew may not travel in the caravan of the idolatrous parade (*tarput*), even to go out, even before dawn, even after dusk, even if he is afraid of non-Jews, robbers, or an evil spirit, as it is said: *Do not follow other gods* (Deuteronomy 6:14).

לא יטייל אדם ישראל עם שיירה בתרפות אפילו לצאת, אפילו מקדים, אפילו מחשיך, אפילו מתיירא מפני גוים, מפני ליסטים, מפני רוח רעה שנאמר: *לא תלכון אחרי אלהים אחרים* (דברים ו:יד).

The Tosefta distinguishes between the fair and the parade of worshippers on their way to the pagan temple parade, referred to by the deragotory

---

[8]    This text follows the Vienna manuscript. The Erfurt manuscript contains obvious scribal errors.

[9]    The Yerushalmi's version of the baraita reads "because he has benefitted on account of idol worship."

word, *tarput*, a Semitic word meaning disgrace or obscenity.[10] Travelling to the fair is not yet participation in anything close to idolatry, and therefore one may engage in business with a Jew or non-Jew on the way to the fair. But, once at the fair, the Jew is participating in a social institution that is associated with idolatry, and thus, on his return, one cannot buy any of his products. In contrast, those participating in the idolatrous parade are already engaged in idol worship—the parade is part of the worship process, and thus the laws are stricter. What is clear from this source is that the participating in the fair is considered participation in idolatry.

Another halakhah from the Tosefta treats items acquired at the fair with the same stringency that the Mishnah treats items thought to have been used in idolatry (Mishnah Avodah Zarah 3:3; 4:9). Tosefta Avodah Zarah 3:19 states:

| Tosefta Avodah Zarah 3:19 | תוספתא עבודה זרה ג:יט |
|---|---|
| One who engages in business at a pagan fair—[if he acquires] an animal, it must be rendered useless; clothing or vessels, they should be left to rot; coins or metal vessels, the equivalent in benefit must be thrown into the Dead Sea. | הנושא והנותן ביריד של גוים: בהמה תיעקר, כסות וכלים ירקבו, מעות וכלי מתכות יוליך הנאה לים המלח. |

Despite the fact that the fair is not a place dedicated solely to idol worship, the items acquired at the fair are treated as if they were profits gained from idolatry and therefore they (or the equivalent value) must be destroyed.[11] Thus, while the fair is not a pagan temple, a Jew who engages in business at the fair is treated as if he engaged in idol worship, or at least "the dust of idol worship," a term that appears in the first chapter of Tosefta Avodah Zarah in reference to economic interaction on the festival:

---

10  R. Yohanan in the Yerushalmi connects the term to the Greek word *thorubos*, lit. uproar or tumult, which scholars connect to the parade surrounding the transfer of the statue of Dionysus from one temple to another. See J.N. Epstein, *Mavo le-Nusah ha-Mishnah* (Jerusalem: Magnes Press, 1948), 119-120.

11  See Sifre Deuteronomy piska 96.

| תוספתא עבודה זרה י:יג | Tosefta Avodah Zarah 1:13 |
|---|---|
| אבק עבודה זרה: לא ישא אדן ויתן עם הגוי ביום אידו מפני אבק עבודה זרה. | The dust of idol worship: One should not engage in business with a non-Jew on the day of his festival because this is the "dust" of idol worship. |

Clearly, economic interchanges are not really idol worship. When it came to defining what "really" constitutes idol worship, punishable in theory by stoning, the rabbis were quite limiting in their definition (see Mishnah Sanhedrin 7:6). But participating in the festival or fair is close enough to the "real" prohibition that it too is proscribed.

Another text found in the same chapter of the Tosefta prohibits a Jew from even being seen in the proximity of the fair—again, because others (Jews and non-Jews alike) would think he is attending the fair:

| תוספתא עבודה זרה א:ה | Tosefta Avodah Zarah 1:5 |
|---|---|
| יריד שבאותו הכרך אין הולכין לאותו הכרך ולא לעיירות הסמוכות לו מפני שהוא כנראה הולך ליריד דברי ר' מאיר. | A fair in a particular city—one should not go to that city or to the towns close to it because it would look like he is going to the fair. [These are] the words of R. Meir. |
| וחכמים אומרים: אין אסור אלא הכרך בלבד. | But the Sages say: Only that city is prohibited. |

Other texts in the Tosefta go even further in proscribing any type of significant social interchange between Jews and non-Jews on their festivals:

| תוספתא עבודה זרה א:ב-ג | Tosefta Avodah Zarah 1:2-3 |
|---|---|
| לא ישא אדם ויתן עם הגוי ביום אידו. | A person should not engage in business with a non-Jew on the day of his festival. |
| ולא יקל עמו את ראשו. | Nor should he be light-headed with him. |
| ולא ישאל בשלומן במקום שמתחשב. | Nor should he ask concerning his welfare, in a place where this is considered significant. |

| | |
|---|---|
| מצאו לפי דרכו שואל בשלומו בכובד ראש. | If he has a chance encounter with him, he can ask concerning his welfare with solemnity. |
| שואלין בשלום הגוים באידיהן מפני דרכי שלום. | One may ask concerning the welfare of non-Jews on their festivals due to the ways of peace. |

The Tosefta prohibits even greeting a non-Jew on his festival, if such a greeting is the type that would be considered of significance, presumably due to the high social standing of the Jew. The final line does indeed permit Jews to greet non-Jews on the festival. But the stark contrast between this line and everything which precedes it leads us to suggest the possibility that it was drawn from Mishnah Gittin 5:9, "And [Jews] may greet them [non-Jews] because of the ways of peace." The editor may have added in the word "on their festivals" in order to rule that the concerns for the ways of peace in Mishnah Gittin override the concerns for the "dust of idol worship" in Tosefta Avodah Zarah. In any case, even if this line is an original part of the Tosefta passage, it still implies that in principle, a Jew should not even inquire into the welfare of non-Jews on their festivals. Simply put: On these days of the year, a Jew should have nothing to do with the neighboring culture.

We have emphasized this point at length because many of the scholars who have addressed the issue of the prohibition on economic activity on or before the festival have framed the issue in light of the Bavli, which provides two main reasons for the prohibition:

1) The non-Jew will thank his god for the economic (or other) benefit he gained from the Jew;
2) The Jew is enabling the non-Jew to worship idols.

The second reason does not accord with the simple reading of the mishnah which prohibits all economic activity—even that which would not enable the non-Jew to worship his god. The first reason also has no grounding in the Mishnah and is not mentioned in any pre-Babylonian text. Most significantly, both of these interpretations in the Bavli focus on the non-Jew: If the Jew participates in the fairs or festivals of the non-Jew, he will somehow enable or encourage the non-Jew to worship idols. In contrast, the tannaitic texts focus mostly on the Jew. Participation in the fairs and festivals is something a Jew should not do; it is the "dust of idol worship."

## Tertullian and the Mishnah

The writings of Christian thinkers contemporary with the rabbis can often provide a fuller appreciation of the religious milieu in which both groups were active, and aid in understanding the background of rabbinic law, thought, and practice. After all, both groups were battling against the paganism still rampant throughout the Roman Empire. In the case of economic interactions between Jews and pagans, the writing of the early Church Father Tertullian (155-240 C.E., Carthage) is particularly instructive.

In her book-length comparison and discussion of Tertullian and Mishnah Avodah Zarah, Stephanie Binder highlights convincing parallels between these two texts. Even if Tertullian was not familiar with the Mishnah itself (and clearly the rabbis were not familiar with Tertullian), these parallels suggest a common struggle with the surrounding pagan society.[12] In chapter thirteen of Tertullian's work, *On Idolatry*, the Church Father writes:

> There are certain days on which presents are given, nullifying for some a reason to pay homage, for others a debt of wages. "Should not I then," you say, "receive what is my due or pay to another what is due to him?" If people have sanctified this custom for themselves, out of superstition, why do you, who are beyond every one of their vanities, take part in festive offerings to idols, as if also for you there existed a rule concerning this day, i.e. that you should not pay or receive what you owe to a person or what a person owes to you except on the day of observance? You should set the rule by which you wish to be dealt with. For why should you conceal yourself, thus contaminating your conscience because of the other man's ignorance? If it is not unknown that you are a Christian, you are put on and act contrary to the other's knowledge as if you were not a Christian—certainly people will even pretend not to know you are a Christian—you have been tested and

---

[12] Stephanie Binder, *Tertullian, on Idolatry and Mishnah 'Avodah Zarah: Questioning the Parting of the Ways between Christians and Jews in Late Antiquity* (Leiden: Brill, 2012).

condemned. In any case, either in the latter or in the former way, you are guilty of shame in the Lord.[13]

Tertullian describes certain pagan festivals whose celebration entails the giving of gifts and repayment of debts.[14] He criticizes those Christians who participate in the economic aspects of the festival. Such Christians claim that they are simply accepting what belongs to them or paying back what is owed. They are not, so they claim, participating in the festival, but merely engaging in economic activity. Tertullian denigrates such behavior as a "custom they have sanctified out of superstition." In his eyes, a Christian who either pays back a debt to a pagan or receives a debt from him on one of those specific days is "taking part in festive offerings to idols." Participation of any sort in a pagan festival is a denial of Christian identity. One who conceals his identity before doing so is obviously "guilty of shame in the Lord." But one whose Christian identity is known also brings shame to the Lord by not attesting to his own beliefs.

Tertullian's words echo our interpretation of the blanket prohibition found in the Mishnah: A Jew who participates in the economic activity that occurs at the festivals and pagan fairs is acknowledging the validity of idol worship. The fear is not precisely that the Jew will be directly worshiping idols. After all, as we have said, Mishnah Sanhedrin does not regard these transactions as idolatrous practices. The bigger issue is that the Jew will be seen by others as conferring legitimacy on idolatrous practice, which is considered the "dust of idol worship."

Tertullian's exhortations are transformed into law in later Christian legislation which explicitly prohibits a Christian from participating in pagan festivals and fairs. The following is from the *Constitutiones Apostolicae* 2.62.4, a late fourth-century Christian work:[15]

---

[13] Translation by J.H. Waszink and J C.M. van Winden, *De Idololatria*, (Leiden: Brill, 1987) 47-49.

[14] The modern editors of Tertullian's work identify the festival as Saturnalia, see Waszink and van Winden, ibid., 227. This is one of the three holidays mentioned in Mishnah Avodah Zarah 1:3.

[15] Cited by Yehudah Cohn, "The Graeco-Roman Trade Fair and the Rabbis," *Journal of the American Oriental Society*, 131,2 (2011), 192. The translation above partially relies upon Andrew Dalby, "Fairs and Markets," *Encyclopedia of Ancient Greece*, ed. Nigel Wilson (New York: Routledge, 2006), 291.

> Let us not, by collectively participating in the festivals that they celebrate in honor of the demons, share also in their impiety. Both their fairs and the ceremonies connected with them are to be avoided. For a believing person must not go near a fair, except in order to buy a slave (and thus save his soul) or to buy one of the necessities of life.

Christians were simply to avoid participating in pagan festivals and fairs altogether because it abets idol worship. Any participation in festivals and fairs and their attendant ceremonies constitutes sharing in their impiety. By participating, the Christian herself is engaged in a transgression. The purchase of slaves and items absolutely necessary for sustenance is permitted—we shall see that the rabbis permitted this as well—but these are exceptions. Any other type of economic interaction must be avoided.

## "Because it Makes Him Rejoice"

The tannaitic sources we have considered thus far have interpreted the prohibition on engaging in business before or during the festival as focused on the Jew. Any sort of Jewish participation in a pagan festival is prohibited because it is flirting with Jewish recognition of idolatry. The prohibition at its core was not related to the impact it would have on the non-Jew. However, tannaitic texts raise the possibility that if the Jewish participation has a negative impact on the non-Jew, the prohibition may not apply. In other words, any Jewish participation in a pagan festival that aids the non-Jew's celebration is forbidden, but Jewish participation that impairs the non-Jew's celebration may be permitted, according to some opinions.

Perhaps the best example of such an opinion is R. Yehudah's statement in the mishnah that a Jew may recover a debt from a non-Jew on his festival, because repaying debts causes distress. One might deduce from this statement that R. Yehudah regards the prohibition on participating in pagan festivals as a way of preventing Jews from acting in any way that would cause the non-Jew to rejoice on or before his festival. If the Jew causes distress to the non-Jew, he will not contribute to the general levity of the festival, and thus the act is permitted. Nevertheless, it seems more likely that R. Yehudah would hold that economic engagement with non-Jews before and on their festival is prohibited for the reason we outlined above—the Jew is sharing in their impiety—but that the prohibition is waived if Jewish participation causes the non-Jew distress. Furthermore, R. Yehudah's statement may be better understood as a case where the law (collecting debts is permitted) preceded its justification (because this causes distress) and not the other way around. That is, it was not the underlying purpose of the prohibition (to refrain from causing the non-Jew to rejoice) which led to the law (collecting debts is permitted). Proof that R. Yehudah's statement is an *ad hoc* justification for a relaxation of the prohibition can be found in the Tosefta, where R. Yehoshua b. Korhah offers a different reason why a Jew may, at least under certain circumstances, recover a debt:

**Tosefta Avodah Zarah 1:1**

תוספתא עבודה זרה א:א
ר' יהושע בן קרחה אומר: כל מלוה שבשטר אין נפרעין הימנו. ושאינה בשטר נפרעין הימנו מפני שהוא כמציל מידם.

R. Yehoshua b. Korhah says: One may not collect from them a loan written in a document. But one may collect a loan not written in a document because this is like saving something from them.

R. Yehoshua b. Korhah allows one to recover a debt that was not secured by a document because such debts are difficult to recover. Any chance to recover an unsecured debt is considered an opportunity to "save one's property." Thus, there are at least two reasons why the general prohibition is relaxed in the case of debt collection: 1) it is "saving something from them;" 2) the non-Jew will not be happy about paying back the debt. R. Yehudah in the mishnah is not revealing the underlying cause of the entire prohibition, he is merely attempting to bolster a particular leniency.

Whereas R. Yehudah in the mishnah permits an action because it causes the non-Jew distress, the Tosefta prohibits an action because it causes the non-Jew to rejoice:

**Tosefta Avodah Zarah 1:3**

תוספתא עבודה זרה א:ג
ואף על פי שגמר את כליו לפני אידו לא יוליכם לו ביום אידו מפני ששמח ביתו.

And even though he completed [working with] his vessels before his festival, he may not bring them to him on his festival because this will cause his household to rejoice.

This halakhah refers to a case where a Jewish craftsman or repairman is working on a project commissioned by a non-Jew. The Tosefta seems to refer to a situation where the Jew has already been paid, completed the work, and merely needs to deliver the object to the non-Jew. According to Mishnah Bava Metzia 6:4 and Tosefta Bava Metzia 7:18, the status of such a craftsman is that of unpaid guardian. His work is completed and the financial arrangement with the non-Jew is basically over. Technically, it is the client who is responsible for retrieving the object. We might have thought that it is permitted to return the object because the business arrangement was in any case completed—the Jewish craftsman would be giving the non-Jew what is already rightfully his. However, the halakhah prohibits a Jewish craftsman from going to the non-Jew's home right before the festival to return his wares. This source does not imply that the entire reason for the prohibition was to prevent Jews from giving cause to non-Jews to rejoice on their festivals; it means only that specific actions that might seem to be permitted are prohibited because they cause the non-Jew to rejoice.

The Yerushalmi pushes the notion of not causing the non-Jew to rejoice even further. R. Yishmael, in the first mishnah cited above, rules that the prohibitions continue for three days following the festival. The Yerushalmi questions the rationale behind R. Yishmael's stringency:

**Yerushalmi Avodah Zarah 1:1, 39b**

**ירושלמי עבודה זרה א:א (לט, ב)**

Havraya say: The reason for R. Yishmael is the festival feast.[16]

חברייא אמרי: טעמא דרבי ישמעאל משום בריה דמועדא.

R. Ba said: Since he knows that it is forbidden for you to engage in business with him, he will reduce the rejoicing on his festival.

אמר רבי בא: כיון שהוא יודע שאסור לך לישא וליתן עמו הוא ממעט בשמחת אידו.

The "havraya"[17] ascribe R. Yishmael's reasoning to the continuation of the feast for three days after the festival. R. Ba suggests that on the festival the non-Jew will know that for the subsequent three days the Jews will not

---

[16] On the translation of this phrase see Christine Hayes, *Between the Babylonian and Palestinian Talmuds*, 216 n. 44.

[17] This term seems to refer to a group of scholars or students. See Michael Sokoloff, *A Dictionary of Jewish Palestinian Aramaic* (Ramat Gan: Bar Ilan University Press, 1992), 185.

engage in business with him, and this will cause a reduction in his celebration. We should note that this justification for the prohibition has now reached or perhaps exceeded its conceptual limits. R. Yehudah allowed for a specific interaction with a non-Jew—collecting debts—that would cause him distress. The Tosefta explained that while returning certain items would seem not to fall under the rubric of "business," it is still prohibited because it increases the joy of the festival. But in the Yerushalmi, R. Ba purports that even the abstention from economic interaction will cause the non-Jew distress. Obviously, this is a strained piece of reasoning—would the non-Jew even notice that Jews were not engaging in business with him?[18] The strained nature of this explanation for R. Yishmael's prohibition is further evidence that the fear of causing the non-Jew to rejoice was not the original reason for the prohibition in the first mishnah of Avodah Zarah. It was prohibited to engage in business with non-Jews not because the avoidance of such interaction would cause them to be distressed. It was prohibited because Jews should not participate in idolatrous fairs and festivals.

In sum, early texts occasionally dispense with aspects of the blanket prohibition against economic interaction if it can be mitigated by the notion that engaging in business will distress the non-Jew. It is only R. Ba, a third generation amora, who attempts to explain the prohibition as being based on a desire to cause the non-Jew distress, and this interpretation leads to a certain level of forced reasoning.

## Understanding Mishnah Avodah Zarah 1:1: Yerushalmi and Rava

We now turn our attention to the sugyot in the Bavli and the Yerushalmi that most directly explain the prohibition on engaging in business interactions with non-Jews on their festivals. As we shall see, these later sources shift the focus from the problem of the Jew participating in idolatrous festivals and fairs to what effect such participation has on the non-Jew.

---

[18] For a similar difficulty, see Tosafot Bavli Avodah Zarah 2a s.v. לפני אידיהן.

| | |
|---|---|
| **ירושלמי עבודה זרה א:ב (לט, ב)** | **Yerushalmi Avodah Zarah 1:2, 39b** |
| (1) ניחא מלהשאיל, מלשאול מהן? מפני שהוא כמשיאו שם. | (1) It makes sense that lending to them should be prohibited. But why [is it prohibited] to borrow? For this gives him a good name. |
| (2) ניחא מלהלוותן, מלהלוות מהן? מפני שהוא כמשיאו שם. | (2) It makes sense that lending them money should be prohibited. But why [is it prohibited] to borrow money? For this gives him a good name. |
| (3) ניחא מלפורען, מליפרע מהן? שלא יאמר עבודה זרה שלו סייעה. | (3) It makes sense that repaying a loan should be prohibited. But why [is it prohibited] to collect repayment? So that he should not say his idol aided him. |

The Yerushalmi's line of questioning demonstrates the conceptual shift in focus from the Jew to the non-Jew. It is "easy" for the Yerushalmi to understand why one may not lend objects or money or pay back a debt to a non-Jew during this period. Such an action would provide tangible monetary gain to the non-Jew immediately before his festival, and thereby could in some ways be construed as abetting his celebration. This understanding is already echoed in the Tosefta passage we examined above, which highlights the impact that Jewish acts will have on the non-Jew on or before his festival—will they cause him distress or make him rejoice? That *ad hoc* justification for one particular aspect of the prohibition is applied in the Yerushalmi to all aspects of the mishnah. However, the Yerushalmi is well aware that this is not a satisfactory explanation of the entire mishnah. If the concern is augmenting the non-Jew's joy on his festival, why not borrow from him (money or objects) or receive a debt in return? Such actions, so it would at first be assumed, do not cause the non-Jew to rejoice. The Yerushalmi responds by broadening the scope of what it means to provide benefit to another person. Borrowing money or objects from a non-Jew has the effect of bestowing upon them a good name.

The notion that lending bolsters a person's reputation is consistent with a halakhah found elsewhere in the Tosefta.

| תוספתא כתובות ז:ד | Tosefta Ketubot 7:4 |
|---|---|
| הדירה שלא להשאיל נפה, וכברה, רחיים, ותנור, יוציא ויתן כתובה מפני שמשיאה שם רע בשכינותיה. | If [a husband] made [his wife] take a vow that she should not lend out a sieve, sifter, mill, or oven, he must divorce her and pay her ketubah, for this gives her a bad name among her neighbors. |
| וכן היא, שנדרה שלא להשאיל נפה, וכברה, רחיים, ותנור, תצא שלא בכתובה מפני שמשיאתו שם רע בשכונתו. | Similarly, if she took a vow not to lend out a sieve, sifter, mill, or oven, she may be divorced without her ketubah, for this gives him a bad name among his neighbors. |

Refusing to lend household objects to neighbors gives a "bad name" to a woman and to her husband. The converse is clear: Lending benefits a person's reputation. Thus, a Jew should not borrow from a non-Jew on the festival because this gives them a good name, and a Jew should not provide material or even social gain to a non-Jew during his festivities.

The Yerushalmi provides a different justification for the final prohibition, that of receiving a debt from the non-Jew. Paying back a debt does not seem to bolster one's reputation, as does lending objects or money. So, the Yerushalmi must come up with another reason: The non-Jew will say that his god helped him to repay his debt. We should note that this reasoning applies, of course, only on (or before) the festival. Jews are allowed to recover debts from non-Jews at other times of the year. But if the non-Jew repays his debt on the festival, he will think that the gods helped him pay back the debt, because the festival is considered a lucky day in which the gods aid people in paying back their debts.

The Yerushalmi's justification is reminiscent of Tertullian's explanation quoted above. However, we can again notice a subtle shift from the tannaitic focus on the Jew to the Yerushalmi's interpretation. For Tertullian, when a Christian receives a debt on the festival, he is tacitly acknowledging people's superstitions about that day. It is **the Christian** who transgresses by participating in the festival. In contrast, the Yerushalmi identifies the pagan's reaction as the reason for the prohibition: Because it was repaid on (or before) the festival, **the non-Jew** will believe that his god has helped him repay his debt. If a Jew accepts repayment for the debt, he will be abetting pagan worship.

The Bavli contains a sugya that exhibits clear parallels with the Yerushalmi. It too finds the first element in each dyad to be easily understandable and the second problematic. However, as we shall see, the differences between the Talmuds attest to a further development in the interpretation of the mishnah.

| בבלי עבודה זרה ו ע"ב | Bavli Avodah Zarah 6b |
|---|---|
| (1a) **להשאילן ולשאול מהן.** בשלמא להשאילן - דקא מרווח להו, אבל לשאול מהן - מעוטי קא ממעט להו! | (1a) **To lend or borrow from them.** It makes sense [to forbid] lending them articles, for this causes them to profit; but borrowing from them diminishes them! |
| (1b) אמר אביי: גזרה לשאול מהן אטו להשאילן. | (1b) Abaye said: Borrowing from them is prohibited as a decree lest one lend to them. |
| (1c) רבא אמר: כולה משום דמודה[19] הוא. | (1c) Rava said: It is all on account of their offering thanks. |
| (2a) **להלוותם וללוות מהן.** בשלמא להלוותם - משום דקא מרווח להו, אלא ללוות מהן - אמאי? | (2a) **To lend them money or borrow money from them.** It makes sense [to forbid] lending them money, for this causes them to profit; but borrowing from them, why not? |
| (2b) אמר אביי: גזרה ללוות מהן אטו להלוותם. | (2b) Abaye said: Borrowing money from them is prohibited as a decree lest one lend to them. |
| (2c) רבא אמר: כולה משום דמודה הוא. | (2c) Rava said: It is all on account of their offering thanks. |
| (3a) **לפורען ולפרוע מהן.** בשלמא לפורען - משום דקא מרווח להו, אלא לפרוע מהן - מעוטי ממעט להו! | (3a) **To repay a debt, or recover a debt from them.** It makes sense [to forbid] repaying them a debt, for this |

---

[19] The printed edition reads "דאזיל ומודה" but manuscripts leave out the first word.

causes them to profit; but recovering a debt diminishes them!

(3b) אמר אביי: גזירה לפרוע מהן, אטו לפורען.

(3b) Abaye said: Recovering a debt from them is prohibited as a decree lest one repay them a debt.

(3c) רבא אמר: כולה משום דמודה הוא.

(3c) Rava said: It is all on account of their offering thanks.

(4a) וצריכי, דאי תנא לשאת ולתת עמהן, משום דקא מרווח להו ואזיל ומודה, אבל לשאול מהן דמעוטי קא ממעט להו - שפיר דמי.

(4a) And all [the cases listed in the mishnah] are necessary. For if it had taught only engaging in business with them, [I might have thought it is forbidden] because it causes them to profit and they will go and thank [their god] for it; but to borrow from them, which diminishes them, would be permitted.

(4b) ואי תנא לשאול מהן, משום דחשיבא ליה מילתא ואזיל ומודה, אבל ללוות מהן - צערא בעלמא אית ליה, אמר: תוב לא הדרי זוזי.

(4b) And if it had taught only borrowing articles from them, [I might have thought it is forbidden] because this is considered important, so he would go and thank [his god]; but to borrow money would be distressful to him, as he might say, "My money may not be returned."

(4c) ואי תנא ללוות מהן, משום דקאמר: בעל כרחיה מיפרענא, והשתא מיהא אזיל ומודה, אבל ליפרע מהן דתו לא הדרי זוזי - אימא צערא אית ליה ולא אזיל ומודה, צריכא.

(4c) And if it had taught only borrowing money, [I might have thought it is forbidden] because he might say, "I can force him to pay me back" and he would go and thank his god; but to collect a debt from them [in which case] the money will never return [to him], I might have said that is distressful to him so he would not go and thank [his god]—[therefore all the cases] are needed.

Tannaitic Source | Amoraic Source | Stammaitic Source

Abaye's statement is similar to the Yerushalmi, which finds the first half of each dyad easily understandable but is forced to offer a strained explanation for the second half. While the Yerushalmi did not state so explicitly, it is likely that the underlying explanation for the prohibition is the same for the first half of each dyad as is explained in the Bavli: Lending the non-Jew objects or money or repaying a debt causes him to profit, and a Jew should not give profit to a non-Jew so close to his festival. The major difference between Abaye and the Yerushalmi is that Abaye basically admits that the activities listed in the second half of each dyad should be permitted. They are prohibited only due to rabbinic decree. The rabbis decreed against them lest one engage in the more problematic activity: providing material gain to the non-Jew.

Rava disagrees with Abaye with regard to all three activities, and provides the same explanation for every aspect of the mishnah. To Rava, all such activities, even cases where the non-Jew gives something to the Jew, will ultimately lead the non-Jew to thank his god on the festival.

While it is possible that the amoraim were commenting on all three facets of the mishnah's prohibition, Rava's words seem far more appropriate in reference to the third clause—the prohibition of accepting repayment of a debt. One who pays back a debt will certainly feel a sense of relief, as was noted already by the sages in their response to R. Yehudah in the mishnah ("even though he might be distressed now, later he will be joyful"). In the wake of such joy, Rava fears that the non-Jew will thank his god. Furthermore, this context is best related to the Yerushalmi's understanding of why it is prohibited to receive a debt. According to the Yerushalmi, there is a fear that the non-Jew will say that his god helped him pay back the debt. It would be quite natural to take this one step further: The non-Jew will now go and thank his god for having been able to pay back the debt. In contrast, Rava's reasoning does not work particularly well in reference to the non-Jew lending goods or money to the Jew. Would a non-Jew really thank his god for having the opportunity to lend his kitchen utensils to a Jew? While there might be a small gain in social standing, it seems hardly grounds to offer thanks to one's god.

Again, we should emphasize how the understanding of the mishnah has subtly shifted from problematic Jewish behavior to the causation of problematic pagan behavior. Originally, the prohibition was to prevent Jews from participating in pagan festivals and fairs. Such behavior was deemed "the dust of idolatry"—not quite idolatry, but close enough. The

Yerushalmi notes that a Jew who receives a debt from a non-Jew is in general bolstering the reputation of the idolatrous practice, giving the impression that these lucky days were responsible for the non-Jew's ability to repay his debt. This too is in a sense participation in the festival—the Jew acknowledges that the festival is a fortuitous time to repay debts. Rava takes it one step further: The Jewish acceptance of the debt will cause the non-Jew to thank his god. Here we can see that the focus of the prohibition has moved entirely to a concern about the Jew's effect on the behavior of the non-Jew.

## "Lest He Go Thank His Gods": Tertullian, Rava, and the Stam

There is some similarity between Rava's statement and Tertullian's words in a different chapter (*On Idolatry* 22:2):

> If I give alms or confer a benefit on him, and that man prays that his gods or the guardian spirit of the colony may be propitious to me, my gift or benefit will therewith be an homage to the idols in whose name he returns to me blessing, which is his thanks.[20]

Tertullian posits that it is prohibited to give a gift to a pagan because the pagan will pray to his god on the Christian's behalf. Thus, the innocent Christian gift to the pagan will result in an homage paid to a foreign god. Both Rava and Tertullian fear that Jewish/Christian actions will serve as an occasion for pagan worship. Nevertheless, there are differences between Rava's statement and Tertullian's. First, Rava is not explaining why one should not give a gift to a pagan; he is explaining why a Jew must not collect a debt payment from the pagan on the festival. It is natural that someone would thank his god for receiving a gift or bless the gift-giver in the name of his god. Thanking a god for normal economic activity seems far less likely, especially since paying back money causes temporary distress. Furthermore, Tertullian is not referring to pagan festivals. He is simply noting that a Christian should never do something that causes the pagan to give homage to the idols. But the more general point is the same:

---

[20]  Translation by Waszink and van Winden, *De Idololatria*, 67.

A Christian/Jew should ensure that his acts do not bring the pagan to make statements or perform actions that constitute idolatrous worship.[21]

Rava's reasoning, "lest he thank [his god]" is expanded in multiple ways by the Babylonian editors. First, according to our reconstruction, the editors used this reason to explain not only the third line of the mishnah (prohibited to receive payment for a debt) but the other lines as well. In other words, these editors repeated Rava's statement with regard to the prohibition of a non-Jew lending a Jew money or objects. Rava's reasoning also underlies the stammaitic section that follows the thrice-repeated dispute (4a-4c); the phrase "lest he thank [his god]" appears four times in these lines.

Second, the explanation is used in a few other contexts as well:

| בבלי עבודה זרה לב ע"ב | Bavli Avodah Zarah 32b |
|---|---|
| ההולכין לתרפות - אסורין לשאת ולתת עמהם. | Those who participate in the idolatrous parade (*tarput*)—it is forbidden to engage in business with them. |
| אמר שמואל: גוי ההולך לתרפות - בהליכה אסור, דאזיל ומודי קמי עבודת כוכבים, בחזרה מותר, מאי דהוה הוה. | Shmuel said: A non-Jew who is participating in the idolatrous parade—on his way there it is prohibited [to engage in business with him]—for he will go and thank his god; on his return it is permitted [to engage in business with him]—that which happened, happened. |

Tannaitic Source — Amoraic Source — Stammaitic Source

This passage begins with a quote from Mishnah Avodah Zarah 2:3, which states that it is prohibited to engage in business with someone participating in the idolatrous parade. But the mishnah permits engaging in business with him on his return. The mishnah does not identify who this person is, although we can assume that it is a non-Jew. Shmuel, basing himself on Tosefta Avodah Zarah 1:15, clarifies that the mishnah refers to a non-Jew but adds (in a section we have not quoted) that the

---

21  Tosefta AZ 3:14-15 also prohibits giving gifts to non-Jews, but does not relate this to a fear that he will go thank his god, or relate it to the festival.

laws work differently if it is a Jew participating in the parade or returning therefrom. Shmuel is interested not in the reason for this prohibition, but to whom the mishnah refers. The stam adds an explanation to Shmuel's statement, using Aramaic phrases to explain why it is prohibited to engage in business with a non-Jew participating in the parade and permitted on his return. Engaging in business with the non-Jew on his way to the temple will lead him to thank his god for the business with the Jew. Here the stam echoes Rava's explanation of the mishnah. But by the time the non-Jew is returning, he has already offered his thanks, and therefore there is no prohibition on engaging in business with him.

Finally, the same concept appears in a story on Bavli Avodah Zarah 6b. We will begin with the earlier version of the story, which appears in Yerushalmi Avodah Zarah 1:1 (39b), in order to emphasize the late Babylonian reworking of the story to fit Rava's justification of the prohibition.

| **Yerushalmi Avodah Zarah 1:1, 39b** | **ירושלמי עבודה זרה א:א (לט, ב)** |
|---|---|
| A certain procurator sent a gift to R. Yudan Nesiah, a sack full of dinars. He [R. Yudan] took one of them and returned the rest. He asked R. Shimon b. Lakish [what he should do with it]. He [R. Shimon b. Lakish] said: Bring the benefit to the Dead Sea. | חד דוקינר אוקיר לר' יודן נשייא, חד דיסקוס מלא דינרין. נסב חד מינהון ושלח ליה שארא. שאל לר' שמעון בן לקיש. אמר: יוליך הנייה לים-המלח. |

A pagan sends R. Yudan (=Yehudah) Nesiah the gift of a sack of coins. From the context, we can assume that the gift was given in honor of a pagan festival. R. Yehudah Nesiah immediately sends back most of the money but holds on to one dinar and deliberates what to do in order to avoid benefiting from something given to him in honor of the festival. Resh Lakish rules strictly and instructs him to destroy the dinar—acceptance of any gift from the non-Jew on his festival is tacit participation in the festival, and even *ex post facto* the gift cannot be retained. Resh Lakish's ruling makes sense, even if the sugya is subsequently surprised by his stringency.

In contrast, in the Bavli's version, Resh Lakish is not concerned about the Jew benefiting from the gift but with how this will impact the non-Jew:

| בבלי עבודה זרה ו ע״ב | Bavli Avodah Zarah 6b |
|---|---|
| ההוא מינאה דשדר ליה דינרא קיסרנאה לרבי יהודה נשיאה ביום אידו, הוה יתיב ריש לקיש קמיה, | A certain heretic[22] sent a Caesarean dinar to R. Yehudah Nesiah on the day of his festival. Resh Lakish was sitting in front of him. |
| אמר: היכי אעביד? אשקליה, אזיל ומודה! לא אשקליה, הויא ליה איבה! | He said: What should I do? If I take it, he will go thank [his god]! If I do not take it, there will be enmity! |
| אמר ליה ריש לקיש: טול וזרוק אותו לבור בפניו. | Resh Lakish said to him: Pick it up and throw it into the pit in front of him. |
| אמר: כל שכן דהויא ליה איבה! | He said: All the more so there will be enmity! |
| כלאחר יד הוא דקאמינא. | [He said back]: I meant that he should do so in an unusual way. |

Sitting in front of Resh Lakish, R. Yehudah Nesiah deliberates over whether to accept the gift. If he accepts it, the pagan will go and thank his god. If he rejects it, he will provoke hostility. Resh Lakish rules stringently and demands that the rabbi throw the dinar away in front of the pagan who gave it to him in the first place. His primary concern seems to be to prevent the pagan from thanking his god, even at the expense of provoking his enmity.

The Bavli's version of events contains an awkward scene and a strained explanation. The Bavli must leave the pagan there to watch the entire exchange between Resh Lakish and R. Yehudah Nesiah (or else summon him back after Resh Lakish has issued his ruling). Resh Lakish instructs his colleague to throw the dinar into the pit **in front of the non-Jew**, for otherwise the non-Jew would think that his gift had been accepted and would go and thank his god. This leads to further complications, and the extremely awkward "rabbinic-style" conclusion that he should throw the

22 The Bavli uses the term heretic in this case to represent a non-Jewish idolator. See David Grossberg, *Heresy and the Formation of the Rabbinic Community* (Tübingen: Mohr Siebeck, 2017), 90-91; Michal Bar-Asher Siegal, *Jewish-Christian Dialogues on Scripture in Late Antiquity: Heretic Narratives of the Babylonian Talmud* (Cambridge: Cambridge University Press, 2019), 97.

money in such a way that the pagan would not notice that he was intentionally doing so.

The comparison between the Bavli and the Yerushalmi highlights the shift we have been noting throughout our analysis. The original story focuses on the problem of how to treat the material benefit that the Jew has gained in the wake of the festival. The secondary version found in the Bavli has adopted Rava's reading of the mishnah and has shifted the focus to the non-Jew's reaction to Jewish participation.

## Understanding Mishnah Avodah Zarah 1:1: The Stam

There is another sugya in the Bavli, this one purely stammaitic, that analyzes the prohibition of engaging in business with idolaters three days before their festivals.

| בבלי עבודה זרה ו ע"א | **Bavli Avodah Zarah 6a** |
|---|---|
| איבעיא להו: משום הרווחה, או דלמא משום ולפני עור לא תתן מכשול? | They asked: [Is it prohibited] because of profit, or perhaps it is because [of the prohibition] of putting a stumbling block before the blind? |
| למאי נפקא מינה? דאית ליה בהמה לדידיה. | What is the practical difference [between the two reasons]? If he has another animal. |
| אי אמרת משום הרווחה - הא קא מרווח ליה, אי אמרת משום עור לא תתן מכשול - הא אית ליה לדידיה. | If you say it is because of the profit he causes, he is still causing him a profit. If you say it is because of putting a stumbling block before the blind, he already has another [animal]. |

The Bavli enquires about the rationale for the mishnah's prohibition on engaging in business with idolators before their festivals. The suggestion that the concern is due to profit ties into the same concept used in the amoraic sugya we analyzed above. There, it was used by the stam to explain why it is prohibited to lend non-Jews goods or money. Here too it might explain only the facets of the mishnah where the Jew lends goods or money. Alternatively, Rashi suggests, using Rava's reasoning, that all aspects of the mishnah are prohibited because any economic engagement with the Jew will either economically or socially benefit the non-Jew and cause him to thank his god.

The second explanation of the mishnah suggests that a Jew who trades with a non-Jew during the three days before the festival places "a stumbling block before the blind," a prohibition based on Leviticus 19:14. The notion that a Jew who provides material with which an idolater may worship idols is considered a stumbling block is also found on Avodah Zarah 14a, where it is attributed to Abaye. There the Talmud quotes a mishnah that prohibits selling to idolaters specific items which are often used in idolatrous rituals. The author of our sugya, aware of how this principle was invoked by an amora elsewhere in relation to selling items to non-Jews, applies it to the first mishnah of the tractate. However, we should again note that the principle applies only to parts of the mishnah, and indeed the stam accepts this when it refers to selling an animal to a non-Jew. Selling an animal to a non-Jew before his festival may indeed be an infringement of placing a stumbling block before the blind. It is hard to imagine that borrowing an animal from him is also such an infringement.

The stammaitic comment on the halakhic difference between these two reasons is a good segue into the theme of the second part of this chapter: rabbinic leniencies. According to the stammaitic understanding, the prohibition seems to apply only to those objects which are actively used in worship.[23] The stam then proceeds to assert that according to this reasoning, the sale of such an object would be prohibited only if the non-Jew did not already own the product—thus extending the potential leniency even further. In other words, a Jew can sell whatever he wants to a non-Jew before the festival as long as he does not directly enable idol worship. And even if such a sale would directly enable idol worship, it would be prohibited only if the non-Jew would not have otherwise been able to worship his idol. Interpreting the halakhah strictly in accord with this line of reasoning would be the culmination of a sea change from the Mishnah's broad prohibition on all commerce and trade—what the Tosefta deems the "dust of idol worship"—to a dramatic leniency which practically eliminates the prohibition altogether.

---

[23] Note that Rabbenu Tam indeed attempts to limit the application of the mishnah solely to those objects used in idol worship. See Tosafot 2a s.v. אסור לשאת.

# Part 2: Categorizing Rabbinic Leniencies

The tendency towards leniency with regard to the prohibition of economic engagement with non-Jews during their festivals and fairs is not the innovation of the stam; it is clearly evident at all levels of the rabbinic material related to these mishnayot. Indeed, even a cursory glance at these rabbinic sources reveals how many exceptions there are or could to the general prohibitions. These leniencies may be divided into three genres: 1) historical, 2) scholastic, and 3) literary/fictional.

The first genre (what we called "historical") includes those instances where rabbis simply do not abide by the broad restrictions found in the sources. When challenged, rabbis explain that the prohibition they seem to have transgressed does not apply in the case at hand. These actions and their justifications are representative of actual rabbinic behavior (at least as far as we can determine) and demonstrate the extent to which many actual rabbis attempted to circumvent the prohibitions that they had inherited.

The second type of leniency ("scholastic") is initiated by a different process, one that occurs within the rabbinic academy. While studying these laws, rabbis categorize and characterize them, a process that often leads to a limitation of the application of the prohibition. While it is hard to know if these leniencies represent actual rabbinic practice, they certainly are a reflection of rabbinic thought.

The third type of leniency ("literary/fictional") is completely different and does not represent any attempt by an actual rabbi to change an existing law. Rather, these leniencies are formed by processes initiated by literary editors attempting to fashion the literary material they inherited. These leniencies are reactions to a world of text and not to the external world. There is no reason to assume that they reflect actual rabbinic behavior, although they may be used by the post-talmudic halakhic authorities as the basis for lenient rulings.

We believe that separating these leniencies into these three categories is a productive model for using rabbinic texts to answer historical questions. The first type of leniencies is reflected in stories that provide us with about as accurate of a view that we can achieve of how rabbis actually went about their lives. The historical significance of the second type of leniency is harder to assess, but used properly, it may provide us with a sense of rabbinic thought on the issue. The third type of leniency, we posit, has little to no value with regard to how we understand the history of the period, but is critical for understanding the literary process through which these sugyot were formed.

## Are You One of Those Who Buys at the Fair? Stories of Rabbis Acting Leniently

The first genre of leniencies ("historical") is best exemplified by the multiple stories of rabbis who simply ignore the prohibitions located in abstract rulings. Anyone who reads the legal narratives in these chapters of Avodah Zarah cannot help but notice how many rabbis ignore—or at least try to circumvent—the prohibitions of engaging in business with non-Jews at their fairs or festivals. We will begin with an example found on Yerushalmi Avodah Zarah 1:4 (and paralleled in Bavli 13b):

| ירושלמי עבודה זרה א:ד (לט, ד) | Yerushalmi Avodah Zarah 1:4, 39d |
|---|---|
| רבי חייא בר ווה שלח ליה מיזבון ליה סנדל מן ירידה דצור. | R. Hiyya b. Ba sent [a servant?] to buy a sandal from the fair in Tyre. |
| אמר ליה רבי יעקב בר אחא: ואת מלוקחי יריד? | R. Ya'akov b. Aha said to him: "Are you one of those who buys at the fair?" |
| אמר ליה: ואתה לא לקחת קלוסקין מימיך? | He replied: "And you, have you not bought [their] bread at some point in your life?" |
| אמר ליה: שנייא היא, דמר רבי יוחנן, לא אסרו דבר שהוא חיי נפש. | He responded: "That is different, for R. Yohanan said, 'They did not prohibit things that sustain life.'" |

Both rabbis make purchases at the fair, but Rabbi Ya'akov b. Aha questions R. Hiyya b. Ba's purchase. When challenged about his own practice, R. Ya'akov b. Aha defends himself by appealing to a statement issued by R. Yohanan, according to which the prohibition is waived when the Jew is purchasing something necessary for sustenance.[24] R. Hiyya b. Ba never has a chance to defend his purchase. This passage in the Yerushalmi continues with a group of rabbis asking whether they can attend fairs in particular cities such as Tyre and Acre. The passage is fairly

---

[24] The context to which R. Yohanan was referring is not clear. The phrase "sustaining life" appears with regard to the prohibition of buying bread from non-Jews as well (Yerushalmi Avodah Zarah 2:8, 41d). The same notion also appears in the Christian legal code examined above.

complicated and difficult to interpret.[25] But the very fact that the prohibition is not clear to the rabbi asking—or even to the rabbi being asked—is evidence of the erosion of the prohibition or perhaps that it was never practiced in the first place.

The following is another example of a rabbi considering a purchase at the pagan fair:

**Yerushalmi Avodah Zarah 1:3, 39c**

ירושלמי עבודה זרה א:ג (לט, ג)

רבי ביבי שלחיה רבי זעורא דיזבון ליה עזיל קטן מן סטרנלייה דביישן.

R. Bibi sent R. Ze'ora to buy him a small web of spun yarn from the [fair for the Roman festival of] Saturnalia at Bet Shean.

אתא גבי רבי יוסי סבר דמורה ליה בהדא דרבי יהושע בן לוי שרי, והורי ליה בהדא דרבי יוחנן אסיר.

He came to R. Yose, whom he thought would rule according to R. Yehoshua b. Levi, who permits; but he ruled according to R. Yohanan, who prohibits.

While the final ruling is stringent in this case, it is significant that R. Bibi sends R. Ze'ora to the fair at Bet Shean hoping that in the end he will receive a lenient ruling.

Another example of rabbis acting leniently can be found in a sugya about the relaxation of the prohibition in the Diaspora:

**Bavli Avodah Zarah 11b**

בבלי עבודה זרה יא ע"ב

אמר שמואל: בגולה אינו אסור אלא יום אידם בלבד.

Shmuel said: In the Diaspora only the day of the festival is prohibited.

ויום אידם נמי מי אסיר?

And is the day of the festival prohibited?

והא רב יהודה שרא ליה לרב ברונא לזבוני חמרא, ולרב גידל - לזבוני חיטין בחגתא דטייעי!

But did not R. Yehudah permit R. Beruna to sell wine and to R. Giddel to sell wheat at the festival of the Arabs!

שאני חגתא דטייעי, דלא קביעא.

The Arab festival is different because its date is not set.

---

25  See Saul Lieberman, *Texts and Studies* (New York: Ktav Publishing House, 1974), 4-10.

The source begins with a ruling which limits the prohibition to the festival itself. But even that ruling is further undermined by R. Yehudah's ruling to R. Beruna that he may sell wine and to R. Giddel that he may sell wheat on the day of the Arab festival. It is entirely expected that the Bavli would reconcile the rulings with the more stringent teaching of Shmuel, but this does not change the fact that R. Yehudah in practice ruled leniently.

Finally, on Bavli Avodah Zarah 64b-65a, we hear of rabbis sending gifts to non-Jews on their festivals!

| בבלי עבודה זרה דף סד ע"ב | Bavli Avodah Zarah 64b |
|---|---|
| רב יהודה שדר ליה קורבנא לאבידרנא ביום אידם. | R. Yehudah sent a gift to Avidarna on his festival. |
| אמר: ידענא ביה דלא פלח לעבודת כוכבים... | He [R. Yehudah] said: "I know he does not worship idols." |
| רבא אמטי ליה קורבנא לבר שישך ביום אידם. | Rava brought a gift to Bar Shishakh on his festival. |
| אמר: ידענא ביה דלא פלח לעבודת כוכבים. | He [Rava] said: "I know he does not worship idols." |

The fact that the rabbis justify their actions by noting that this particular non-Jew does not worship idols does not change the basic premise that these rabbis are sending gifts on the very day of the festival, an action explicitly prohibited in Tosefta 3:15-16.

In sum, there is overwhelming evidence that the trend in rabbinic circles was to circumvent—and at times ignore—the prohibitions of certain economic interactions with pagans. Rabbis limit the scope of earlier prohibitions and find multiple reasons to justify what seem to be transgressions of these prohibitions. These justifications often rely on social or economic concerns which demand interaction with their non-Jewish neighbors.

## Rabbinic Scholasticism and Halakhic Leniency

The second type of leniency (called "scholastic" above) is not a result of the external environment in which rabbis found themselves during this period, but of the internal dynamics through which rabbinic literature was composed. Rabbinic literature was intensely studied, debated, and modified within the collective atmosphere of the bet midrash. There, rabbis developed a mode of learning in which they scholastically analyzed earlier rabbinic traditions, including the prohibitions separating themselves from non-Jews. These scholastic analyses often lead to various leniencies, further opportunities to limit the scope of earlier traditions.

The process by which rabbinic scholastic analysis creates and innovates halakhic rulings has been demonstrated by David Friedenreich with regard to the related issue of the prohibited foods of non-Jews. Rabbis inherited food prohibitions from their Judean predecessors that were "preparer-related," meaning that the problem with such food was that it was prepared by a non-Jew and not that the ingredients were actually prohibited. For instance, the ingredients in bread are obviously permitted, but if it is baked by a non-Jew, the Mishnah prohibits it (Mishnah Avodah Zarah 2:7). Rabbis used processes of categorization and classification to limit many of these prohibitions. As stated, a Jew may not eat bread baked by a non-Jew. But the rabbis ask: What constitutes baking? Shmuel states that if both a non-Jew and a Jew participate in the process of cooking a piece of meat, the meat is permitted (Bavli Avodah Zarah 38a). Ravina then takes this to its extreme but still logical conclusion: Even if all the Jew does in the process of baking bread is throw a wood chip into the fire, the bread is permitted because this is considered "joint" participation. Ravina here is defining what Jewish participation means; he is not seeking a leniency to make it easier for Jews to eat bread cooked by non-Jews, even if this is the ultimate result of his statement. The leniency is a result of the scholastic process.[26]

An example of this process with the regard to the issue we examine in this chapter would be the prohibition of buying at the fair. A passage on Bavli Avodah Zarah 13a and 13b (analyzed below) posits that it is prohibited to buy at the fair because those who buy at the fair receive a tax exemption. Since the tax exemption applies only to buying from a merchant, one is allowed to buy from a householder, that is, a non-merchant. Again, the reason for the prohibition is defined, and this allows for a limiting of its scope. Thus, it is the rabbinic style of learning, whereby the rabbinic collective refines and understands the laws they

---

[26] See David Friedenreich, *Foreigners and Their Food: Constructing Otherness in Jewish, Christian, and Islamic Law* (Berkeley: University of California Press, 2011), 76-83.

inherited, which may have led to certain leniencies. As these examples demonstrate, rabbinic learning and halakhah must often be understood as a product of the rabbinic bet midrash and not always as a response to the external world.[27]

## Rabbinic Leniencies and Christian Stringencies: Explaining the Difference

Above, we examined some of the parallels between rabbinic literature and Tertullian in terms of the justification for the prohibition of engaging in business with pagans on their festivals. Here, we wish to contrast their opposing tendencies when it comes to the observance of the prohibition. Of course, it is important to note that it would be impossible, based on these sources alone, to compare how Jews/rabbis and Christians actually behaved. We can compare only the difference in attitude that rabbinic literature and Tertullian adopt towards the prohibition and towards countering their audience's behavior.

Stephanie Binder notes:

...the rabbis' general tendency is to permit business as much as possible within the framework of the Jewish religion. Tertullian, on the other hand, wants Christians to avoid a business nexus with gentiles as much as possible. In *De Idolatria* chapter 11, the principle expounded is the same as in Mishnah Avodah Zarah i: Christians, like Jews, must avoid any act that would benefit idolatry or one which would give themselves any benefit stemming from idolatry.... But while Tertullian is not ready to make life among the gentiles easier for Christians, the rabbis find ways of circumventing the biblical laws.[28]

Binder offers a lengthy explanation of this difference, at times focusing on different economic circumstances, differences in genre, and different points of focus. Missing from her analysis, though, is the significant category of intended audience.

---

[27] Indeed, large portions of Hayes's book, *Between the Babylonian and Palestinian Talmuds,* are dedicated to proving this point.

[28] Binder, *Tertullian, On Idolatry and Mishnah Avodah Zarah,* 153.

Tertullian and the rabbis are addressing very different audiences and they are using different genres to do so. Unlike rabbinic literature, which is a compendium of rabbinic law, discourse, and deed, Tertullian's work is a book of exhortations directed specifically at an external audience. The Christians Tertullian is addressing are genealogically of pagan descent. During his time, more and more pagans are joining the Christian fold, and Tertullian is therefore carving out Christian identity in a pagan world.[29] As such, Tertullian must draw a strict line separating Christians from pagans for fear of "backsliding." That he is facing an audience that in reality participates in pagan festivals is clear from chapter 14, which immediately follows the passage from chapter 13 we quoted above. He writes, "However, a great many have by this time ascribed to the notion that it is pardonable if they sometimes do what the heathens do, lest the name be blasphemed."[30] Christians are participating in pagan fairs and festivals claiming that their lack of participation will blaspheme the name of God. While Binder notes that Tertullian does relax some of the restrictions for private observances, in the public sphere a Christian needs to actively publicize his identity and beliefs.

In contrast, rabbis were almost all genealogical Jews. Their entire identity was firmly established within the fold of Judaism, and they seem to perceive little to no threat of a rabbi being seduced into paganism. Rabbis would have come from Jewish families, lived in Jewish homes where all members of the household were Jews, and their entire lives would have been identifiable as Jews. A rabbi who buys or sells something at the fair or during the pagan festival could hardly be mistaken for a pagan. At most, people (mostly other rabbis) would look askance at him for not observing a rabbinic prohibition—"you're one of the people who buy at the fair." Thus, rabbis in the talmudic period can relax their

---

[29] See Waszink and Van Winden, 10.
[30] Translation ibid., 49.

prohibitions of any contact with non-Jews for they have little fear of more problematic levels of assimilation.[31]

Furthermore, the internal setting in which rabbinic literature was formed helps explain why it deviates from patristic literature, which was mostly composed by individuals and not in the discursive world of the bet midrash. Rabbis sitting in the bet midrash endlessly debated these laws—not only through the lens of how they play out in the actual world, but scholastically through categorization and characterization. They created a world in which legal rulings can be discussed with little concern for the actual ramifications in the real world. The rabbis' intense and collective examination of their inherited traditions often lead to modifications of earlier rulings, and at times, certainly with regard to interactions with non-Jews, it led to limitations of earlier prohibitions. In sum, rabbinic literature is meant for other rabbis debating inside the four walls of the bet midrash; Tertullian is addressing a Christian going to live his life in a pagan world.

## A Literary Leniency: Resh Lakish and the Rose

In contrast to the categories described above, there are lenient positions with regard to participation in the festivals and fairs of non-Jews that are not representative of actual rabbinic law. In these cases, what looks to be the statement of a rabbi or a story concerning his behavior is in reality the editorial reworking of earlier material, a case where the editors of the Bavli ascribed to a sage a position that he likely he never held.

Determining which rabbinic statements were uttered by actual rabbis and which statements were created by later editors is one of the most important undertakings in critical study of rabbinic literature. Nearly every chapter in our two books contains one or more attempts to answer these types of questions. But in this chapter, the bearing that this literary detective work has on our historical understanding of the rabbinic world is

---

[31] This same process occurs later in Christian Europe. Jews did not fear assimilating, and thus were able to justify even further relaxation of the talmudic prohibitions. And even with those prohibitions they maintained, they did so out of tradition, not out of a genuine belief that such restrictions were necessary for the maintenance of Jewish identity. See for example Haym Soloveitchik, "Can Halakhic Texts Talk History?" in *Collected Essays* (Oxford: The Littman Library of Jewish Civilization), 169-223.

of special consequence. Avodah Zarah is a tractate with a high degree of practical significance for the lives of rabbis in the rabbinic period. How rabbis reacted to the idolatrous world in which they lived is a topic of intense interest to historians of the period; it is key to ascertaining rabbinic social and religious identity. But to determine how rabbis interacted with the surrounding culture, or even how they portrayed themselves as doing so, we must first isolate which dicta are purely the result of late literary processes and are not in any way reflective of pragmatic rabbinic rulings.

The case we examine is a statement attributed to Resh Lakish on Bavli Avodah Zarah 12b-13a, according to which a Jew can provide material benefit to stores participating in idolatrous festivals. From this statement, the stam extrapolates a remarkable rule: Jews may not benefit from idolatry, but they may provide benefit to idolatrous centers and those participating in them—a halakhah that would seem to blatantly contradict multiple talmudic sources.[32] We will trace the literary development of this statement and the sugya surrounding it and demonstrate that it was not in fact issued by Resh Lakish himself (or any other amora), but is rather the result of the redactional process. Following our reconstruction of Resh Lakish's statement, we will note how the stammaitic understanding of the amoraic material influences their understanding of the tannaitic material as well. When the original amoraic dispute is understood, we can also understand the original and more sensible meaning of the tannaitic material. As always, these two methodological approaches aid one another—strained interpretations are the sign of stammaitic, editorial intervention, and by analyzing the earlier appearances of the statements in the Tosefta and the Yerushalmi, we can reconstruct more original, credible readings.

The sugya to which we refer is based on the following mishnah from the first chapter of Avodah Zarah. The context is the idolatrous festival and accompanying fair:

---

[32] The best example is Mishnah Avodah Zarah 3:6, concerning a person whose house was adjacent to a place of idol worship. If the wall falls down, the person may not rebuild the wall in the place that it was because this would aid the idolatrous temple.

| משנה עבודה זרה א:ד | **Mishnah Avodah 1:4** |
|---|---|

עיר שיש בה עבודה זרה, והיו בה חנויות מעוטרות ושאינן מעוטרות, זה היה מעשה בבית שאן, ואמרו חכמים: מעוטרות אסורות, ושאינן מעוטרות מותרות.

A city in which there is idolatry, and some stores are decorated, and some stores are not decorated. This happened in Bet She'an and the Sages said: "The decorated ones are prohibited but the non-decorated ones are permitted."

The simple reading of the mishnah is that the decorations are a sign that a store is participating in the idolatrous festival, and thus a Jew should not do business there. We should note that the mishnah is already relatively lenient, even more so than other tannaitic sources. As we saw above, Tosefta Avodah Zarah 1:5 states that Jews should not even be seen going to the fair, and yet here, the rabbis rule that a Jew can go to a city holding a fair, just not to a store participating in it.

R. Yohanan in the Yerushalmi limits the prohibition even further:

| ירושלמי עבודה זרה א:ד (לט, ד) | **Yerushalmi Avodah Zarah 1:4, 39d** |
|---|---|

במה מעוטרות?

What were they decorated with?

רבי יוחנן אמר: בהדס.

R. Yohanan says: With myrtle.

רבי שמעון בן לקיש אמר: בשאר כל המינין

R. Shimon b. Lakish says: With any of the other species.

על דעתיה דר' יוחנן, הכל אסור.

According to the opinion of R. Yohanan, all is prohibited.

על דעתיה דר"ל, אינו אסור אלא התוספת.

According to the opinion of Resh Lakish, only the extra [produce] is prohibited.

היך עביד?

What should he do?

היה למוד להוציא חמש קופות והוציא עשר, אין תימר משם עיתור אסור. אין תימר משם פרקסים מותר.

If he was used to taking out five baskets, and he took out ten—if you say that this was due to decorations, it is prohibited; if due to business, it is permitted.

R. Yohanan contends that the only decorations that would prohibit a Jew from entering the store are those made of myrtle. Other decorations are not a sign that the store is participating in the festival. The anonymous voice in the Yerushalmi comments that if a non-Jew decorates his store with myrtle, the entire contents of the store are prohibited. Resh Lakish's opinion is a bit more difficult to interpret. On the one hand, he seems to be expansive, holding that all decorations are signs of participation in the festival. But the stam of the Yerushalmi recognizes the difficulty inherent in his position—how do we know these are decorations and not simply a display of wares? The answer is that Resh Lakish limits the prohibition to the additional produce that the storekeeper put out in in honor of the festival. Only such produce is prohibited. If he displays additional merchandise for the purpose of attracting customers, then a Jew may buy from the store. This, again, is an example of an analysis of a rabbinic statement that leads to a leniency.

The Bavli preserves the same dispute between Resh Lakish and R. Yohanan over this same mishnah and uses many of the same words. However, some subtle differences have completely changed the nature of the dispute, as we shall see.

| בבלי עבודה זרה יב ע״ב-יג ע״א | Bavli Avodah Zarah 12b-13a |
|---|---|
| אמר ר' שמעון בן לקיש: לא שנו אלא מעוטרות בוורד והדס, דקא מתהני מריחא, אבל מעוטרות בפירות - מותרות. | R. Shimon b. Lakish said: It was taught only with regard to those decorated with a rose or a myrtle, for he benefits from the smell. But those decorated with other produce are permitted. |
| מאי טעמא? דאמר קרא: *לא ידבק בידך מאומה מן החרם* (דברים יג:יח), נהנה הוא דאסור, אבל מהנה שרי. | What is the reasoning? Scripture says, *Nothing that is proscribed should stick to your hand* (Deuteronomy 13:18). Deriving benefit is prohibited, but providing benefit is permitted. |
| ורבי יוחנן אמר: אפילו מעוטרות בפירות נמי אסור, קל וחומר: נהנה אסור, מהנה לא כל שכן. | And R. Yohanan says: Even those decorated with other produce are forbidden. [This is based] on a *kal vahomer* argument: If deriving benefit is prohibited, all the more so is providing benefit. |

Tannaitic Source     Amoraic Source     Stammaitic Source

The debate between Resh Lakish and R. Yohanan in the Bavli is nearly identical to that in the Yerushalmi, although the positions have been reversed, a typical phenomenon in Bavli/Yerushalmi parallels. The only really significant difference is the inclusion of the rose in Resh Lakish's statement. However, despite the fact that this is only a one-word difference, it is an interpretive key to which we return below.

While the core amoraic dispute is phrased in nearly identical words, the stam's explanatory gloss is radically different. The stam explains that the rose and myrtle are prohibited "for he benefits from the smell," and appends a midrash to Resh Lakish's statement. The rose and myrtle are not signs that the store is participating in the festival—they are the problematic idolatrous objects a Jew must avoid. Other decorations do not have a pleasant smell and therefore stores decorate with other plants would not be prohibited, even if the decorations were clearly in honor of the festival. In order to understand the stammaitic reframing we need to uncover the steps that seem to have led to it. We are going to offer two possibilities for the processes that led to the creation of this remarkable statement. The first is interpretive—the stam has trouble interpreting an earlier statement. The second is conceptual—the stam wants to create a broader, more conceptual scope for the Resh Lakish/R. Yohanan dispute.

According to the first possibility, the stam is motivated by the interpretive need to explore the difference between the rose or myrtle and other produce. It seems the stam agrees with R. Yohanan—any decoration that is not simply the ordinary way in which a storekeeper displays his wares is a sign of participation in the fair. What then is the difference between the rose or myrtle and other produce such that a store decorated with the former is prohibited but one with the latter is not? The answer is smell. A Jew will derive benefit from smelling the rose or myrtle, but he will not derive direct benefit from merely being in the presence of the other produce. There is an extremely significant corollary to this. If only stores decorated with roses or myrtles are prohibited, then all other stores are permitted, **even if they are participating in the fair**. As long as the Jew is not directly benefiting from an idolatrous object, all interaction at the fair is permitted! But what about buying from non-Jews at their fairs? Won't such transactions provide them with benefit, a prohibition that seems to underlie much of the tractate's first chapter? And furthermore, when the Jew buys at the fair, does he not benefit as well, and thereby participate in idolatry?

The answer, so the stam concludes, is that Resh Lakish allows one to buy from non-Jews at the fair. And this particular ruling becomes even broader: Resh Lakish maintains that it is permitted to provide material benefit to idolatry! "Deriving benefit (smelling the myrtle and rose) is prohibited, but providing benefit (buying at stores without fragrant decorations) is permitted." As stated, this position is not hinted at anywhere else in the Talmud, and clearly contradicts other sources.[33] What began in the Mishnah (and was continued in the Yerushalmi) as an attempt to identify which stores are participating in the fair, and are thus prohibited to Jews, ends up as a comprehensive leniency allowing Jews to purchase items at the fair, so long as they do not derive ancillary benefit by smelling the roses (or myrtles).

According to the second possibility, the stam is motivated to transform a minor practical dispute into a broader conceptual one. The original dispute between Resh Lakish and R. Yohanan was over reality—are stores with decorations other than myrtle participating in the fair? There really is no broader significance to this dispute. It would bear importance only to the very specific question: Can a Jew enter a particular store? But the Bavli's version of the dispute goes far beyond the issue of determining which store is participating in the fair. In the Bavli, the amoraic dispute has morphed into a broad dispute over whether a Jew can confer material benefit on a place participating in idolatry. Indeed, the earlier dispute would not even be important to the Bavli's version of Resh Lakish: Once one permits conferring benefit on centers of idolatrous worship, it matters little how we determine whether a given store is indeed participating in such an idolatrous institution.

We should note that these two possible frameworks for the stammaitic intervention are completely emblematic of the stam's work throughout the Bavli. The Babylonian editors frequently intervene in earlier material to make it more intelligible. There is nothing at all surprising about such a process. Babylonian editors also often emend their sources and interpret them in order to broaden their significance. The creation of broad, usually diametrically opposed halakhic positions also allows for a wide variety of

---

[33] See Rasbha s.v. נהנה הוא דאסור for an example of a medieval commentator who struggles to reconcile the statement of Resh Lakish with the other rabbinic sources which explicitly prohibit economic interaction.

other sources, tannaitic and amoraic, to be brought into the discourse and examined each in light of the two opposing views.

Returning to the sugya, the stam interpolated material into this section in several other ways as well. First, the stam created a midrash ("Scripture says, *Nothing that is proscribed should stick to your hand*: Deriving benefit is prohibited, but providing benefit is permitted") to prove that it is permitted to provide benefit to idolatry. This midrash is not found anywhere else in rabbinic literature. Indeed, the midrash is completely counterintuitive—after all, the Torah prohibits interacting with anything that bears the taint of idolatry. Sifre Deuteronomy piska 96 reads this verse as prohibiting one from deriving benefit from even the smallest trace of idolatry. In complete contrast, the stam reads this very verse as the source of a comprehensive leniency—a Jew may provide benefit to idolatry!

Second, the stam intervened in R. Yohanan's statement as well, adding the *kal va-homer* section at the end to serve as a counterpart to Resh Lakish's refashioned statement.

Finally, in a subtle and telling sign of editorial intervention, the stam adds the rose to Resh Lakish's statement.[34] This hammers home a point that might not have been clear if the only example were the myrtle. In its original appearance in the statement, myrtle was a sign that the store was participating in the fair. But when coupled with the rose, the meaning of the myrtle is completely transformed. The problem with the rose and myrtle is that one is benefiting from their smell, and thus one cannot enter a store decorated with any type of fragrant foliage.

## Tannaitic Sources and Their Transformation

We will now turn our attention to the remainder of this sugya and examine the tannaitic sources and how they have been manipulated to match the stammaitic framing of the amoraic dispute. In order to ease understanding of this passage, we will first cite it in its entirety (absent some digressions not relevant to the Resh Lakish/R. Yohanan dispute). We will then offer a brief explanation which follows the traditional

---

[34] The myrtle and rose appear in juxtaposition as decorative wreaths in Bavli Sotah 49b.

understanding of the flow of the sugya. Finally, we will critically examine how the sources have been modified.

**בבלי עבודה זרה יג ע"א**

**Bavli Avodah Zarah 13a**

(1) מיתיבי, רבי נתן אומר: יום שעבודת כוכבים מנחת בו את המכס, מכריזין ואומרים: כל מי שנוטל עטרה וינח בראשו ובראש חמורו לכבוד עבודת כוכבים - יניח לו את המכס, ואם לאו אל יניח לו את המכס, יהודי שנמצא שם מה יעשה? יניח - נמצא נהנה! לא יניח - נמצא מהנה!

(1) They objected: R. Natan says: The day on which idolatry reduces the taxes, they announce, saying: "Anyone who takes this wreath and puts it on his head and on his donkey's head in honor of idolatry—they will reduce for him the taxes. And if not, they will not reduce for him the taxes." A Jew who is there, what should he do? If he puts it on, he derives benefit. If he does not put it on, he will provide benefit!

(2) מכאן אמרו: הנושא ונותן בשוק של עבודת כוכבים - בהמה תיעקר, פירות כסות וכלים ירקבו, מעות וכלי מתכות יוליכם לים המלח...

(2) From here they said: One who engages in business in the marketplace of the non-Jews—if it is an animal, it should be rendered useless; produce, clothing, and vessels should be left to rot; coins and metal vessels should be brought to the Dead Sea...

(3) קתני מיהת: יניח נמצא נהנה, לא יניח נמצא מהנה!

(3) In any case it was taught, "if he puts it on, it will turn out that he derives benefit; if he does not put it on, he will provide benefit!"

(4) אמר רב שישא בריה דרב אידי, קסבר רשב"ל: פליגי רבנן עליה דרבי נתן, ואנא דאמרי כרבנן דפליגי עליה, ור' יוחנן סבר: לא פליגי.

(4) R. Shisha[35] b. R. Idi said: R. Shimon b. Lakish holds: The [other] rabbis disagree with R. Natan, and I hold like those rabbis who disagree with him. And R. Yohanan holds: They do not disagree.

(5) ולא פליגי?

(5) And they do not disagree?

---

[35] This is the corrected reading found in all manuscripts. The printed editions mistakenly read R. Mesharshiya.

והא תניא: הולכין ליריד של עובדי כוכבים, ולוקחין מהם בהמה עבדים ושפחות, בתים ושדות וכרמים, וכותב ומעלה בערכאות שלהן, מפני שהוא כמציל מידם ...

Was it not taught: One may go to the fair of the non-Jews, and purchase from them animals, slaves and handmaidens, houses, fields and vineyards, and write [a sale document] and bring it to their courts, for this is like saving [them] from them...?

אלמא פליגי!

Therefore, they do disagree!

(6) אמר לך רבי יוחנן: לעולם לא פליגי, ולא קשיא: כאן בלוקח מן התגר דשקלי מיכסא מיניה, כאן בלוקח מבעל הבית דלא שקלי מיכסא מיניה...

(6) R. Yohanan could say to you: They do not disagree and there is no discrepancy [between the two baraitot]: This one refers to a case where he buys from a merchant from whom they take taxes; this one refers to a case where he buys from a non-professional from whom they do not take taxes...

(7) אשכחיה רבי יונה לרבי עילאי דקאי אפיתחא דצור, א"ל: קתני בהמה תיעקר, עבד מאי? עבד ישראל לא קא מיבעיא לי, כי קא מיבעיא לי - עבד עובד כוכבים, מאי?

(7) R. Yonah found R. Ilai at the gates of Tyre. He said to him: It is taught that an animal must be rendered useless. What about a slave?—I am not asking about a Jewish slave; rather, I am asking about a non-Jewish slave—what is the rule?

אמר ליה: מאי קא מיבעיא לך? תניא: העובדי כוכבים והרועי בהמה דקה - לא מעלין ולא מורידין.

He said to him: What are you asking? It was taught: Non-Jews and shepherds—one does not bring them up [from a pit] and one does not throw them down.

(8) אמר ליה ר' ירמיה לר' זירא: קתני לוקחין מהן בהמה עבדים ושפחות, עבד ישראל או דלמא אפי' עבד עובד כוכבים?

(8) R. Yirmiyah said to R. Zera: It is taught one may purchase from them animals, slaves, and handmaidens. Does this refer to a Jewish slave or perhaps even to a non-Jewish slave?

אמר ליה: מסתברא עבד ישראל, דאי עבד עובד כוכבים, למאי מיבעי ליה?

He said to him: It is reasonable that it refers to a Jewish slave, for if it referred to a non-Jewish slave, why even ask?

| | |
|---|---|
| כי אתא רבין אמר רבי שמעון בן לקיש: אפילו עבד עובד כוכבים, מפני שמכניסו תחת כנפי השכינה. | When Ravin came he said in the name of R. Shimon b. Lakish: Even a non-Jewish slave, for he brings him under the wings of the Divine Presence. |
| אמר רב אשי: אטו בהמה מאי מכניס תחת כנפי השכינה איכא? אלא משום מעוטייהו, והכא נמי דממעטי שרי. | R. Ashi said: When it comes to an animal, what "brings him under the wings of the Divine Presence" could there be? Rather, it is because it diminishes them. Here too, because it diminishes them, it is permitted. |

---

| Tannaitic Source | Amoraic Source | Stammaitic Source |
|---|---|---|

In sections 1-3 a baraita is raised as a difficulty on Resh Lakish—the baraita holds that providing benefit is prohibited. In section 4, R. Shishi b. R. Idi solves the objection by positing that, according to Resh Lakish, there is a tannaitic dispute on the issue and he accords with the opinion that disagrees with the baraita. R. Yohanan would maintain that there is no dispute and all sages rule that providing benefit to idolatry is forbidden. Section 5 cites a baraita as support for Resh Lakish. This baraita allows one to purchase items at the fair, which contradicts the first baraita and proves there is a tannaitic dispute on the issue. In section 6, R. Yohanan deflects the difficulty by contextualizing each baraita. Section 7 is an amoraic discussion about what to do with a slave purchased at the fair. The sugya concludes in section 8 with another question about slaves purchased at the fair.

## Providing Benefit to Idolaters: Rereading Tosefta Avodah Zarah 1:8

We will begin our analysis by examining the baraita brought in section 5. Formally speaking, the sugya cites this baraita as a difficulty on R. Yohanan, the amora who holds a Jew may not provide material benefit to idolatry. The sugya reads this baraita as if it posits that it is permitted to buy **any item** from non-Jews at the fair. This reading causes a significant problem with the words "for this is like saving them from them." To what do these words refer? These words cannot justify the very act of buying at the fair, because there is no need for any such justification, at least not according to Resh Lakish, R. Yohanan's disputant. According to Resh Lakish in the Bavli, with whom this baraita is supposed to accord, there is no problem whatsoever with a Jew buying at a fair, whether one is "saving from them" or not. To solve this problem, Rashi claims that the phrase refers only to the words that immediately precede it, "and bring it to their courts." Rashi subtly explains a line from the Talmud as if there were no difficulty, when in reality the line is not simple at all.

| רש"י עבודה זרה יג ע"א | Rashi Avodah Zarah 13a |
|---|---|
| ומעלה בערכאות שלהן - מקום גדוליהן ושופטיהן ומעלה שטרותיו לפניהם לחתום ואף על פי שכבוד ותפארת היא להם ואיכא למימר דאזיל ומודה. | And bring it to their courts—The place where their dignitaries and judges are found. And he may bring his documents in front of them to be signed. And even though this is an honor and glorification for them, and we could say that [the judge] will go and thank his god. |
| שהוא כמציל מידם - שמתוך כך יהיו לו עדים ומסייעין להציל מן העוררין. | For this is like saving them from them—For through this process there will be witnesses, and they will aid in saving the acquisition from protestors. |

Rashi begins by explaining why it would be problematic to bring documents to be verified at the non-Jewish court. He ties the issue into the concern raised by Rava in connection with the prohibition on engaging in business with non-Jews before the festival (6b). The pagan judges will thank their gods that the Jew brought a document to their court for them to verify! This point is critical because Rashi needs to explain why the baraita would need to justify bringing documents to non-Jewish courts. Next, Rashi explains that one may ignore any concern surrounding the non-Jewish court in order to save himself from future protests against his claims of ownership. This strained but brilliant interpretation by Rashi is a clear sign that the sugya reads the baraita against the grain to serve as a support for the invented position attributed to Resh Lakish.

The original meaning of the baraita is far clearer in the version preserved in the Tosefta:

| תוספתא עבודה זרה א:ח (כ"י וינה) | Tosefta Avodah Zarah 1:8 (MS Vienna) |
|---|---|
| הולכין ליריד של גוים... ולוקחין[36] מהם בתים שדות וכרמים עבדים ושפחות מפני שהוא כמציל מידם וכותב ומעלה בערכאים. | One may go to the fair of the non-Jews and buy from them houses, fields, vineyards, slaves, and handmaidens, for this is like saving [them] from them. And he may write [up a document] and bring it up in court. |

The Tosefta is abundantly clear because the clause "for this is like saving [them] from them" immediately follows the permission to buy these items and not the permission to bring the document to the court, as it does in the Bavli. A Jew may go to the fair to buy these **specific** items, for these are important items that Jews should desire to redeem from non-Jews. Buying a slave "brings him [the slave] under the wings of the Shekhinah" (Yerushalmi 1:1, 39c; Bavli 13b). Buying houses and other forms of land is permitted because this text refers to the Land of Israel, where Jewish ownership is desirable. Buying an animal is permitted because this prevents them from offering them as sacrifices. Finally, one may even write up an official document and bring it to their courts. We might have thought that such a document would be problematic because it serves to further publicize the acquisition, but the desire to bring these particular entities under Jewish ownership overrides other considerations. Most importantly, only these entities may be purchased; others remain prohibited.

---

[36] All three textual witnesses read "ואין," but this is a mistake. See Saul Lieberman, *Tosefet Rishonim II* (New York: Jewish Theological Seminary of America, 1999), 186. The correct reading is found in all textual witnesses of the parallel in Tosefta Moed Katan 1:8.

## Providing Benefit to Idolaters: Rereading a Contradiction Between Baraitot

The stam posits a tannaitic dispute that mirrors the same dispute ascribed to the amoraim—one baraita (section 2) holds that providing benefit, i.e. buying at the fair, is **always** prohibited, while the other baraita (section 5) holds that buying at the fair is **always** permitted. While the tension between the two baraitot was not entirely invented by the stam, it is only the late Babylonian stam that interprets these two baraitot as polar opposites, reflective of the stam's creation of the amoraic dispute. The Yerushalmi, on the other hand, resolves them in a far simpler fashion without ever creating an absolute antithesis between the two and without undermining the consensus prohibition on providing benefit to idolatry. In other words, while the skeletal structure of the sugyot is the same in both Talmuds—both contrast the two baraitot—the reasoning and explanation of the sources found in the two sugyot are vastly different, as is the outcome.

The Yerushalmi opens with the baraita that permits one to buy certain items at the fair:

| Yerushalmi Avodah Zarah 1:4, 39c | ירושלמי עבודה זרה א:ד (לט, ג) |
|---|---|
| (And does it not) teach: One may go to the fair and buy from there slaves, handmaidens, and animals. | והתני: הולכין ליריד ולוקחין משם עבדים ושפחות ובהמה. |
| Resh Lakish says: Not just Jewish slaves, but even non-Jewish slaves, for this draws them under the wings of the Divine Presence. | ריש לקיש אמר: לא סוף דבר עבדים ישראלים אלא אפילו עבדים גוים, שמקרבן תחת כנפי שכינה. |

Despite the fact that the term "והתני" looks as if it presenting a difficulty, it should be read as the beginning of the sugya, as if it says, "תני."[37] Resh Lakish's comments on this baraita underscore that he interprets it according to its original meaning: There is a specific leniency with regard to these items, and Resh Lakish wants to be sure that it includes all types of slaves. All other items remain prohibited. The Yerushalmi continues by

---

[37] See Ze'ev Wolf Rabinovitz, *Sha'are Torat Eretz Yisrael* (Jerusalem, 1939), 558.

contrasting this baraita with the more stringent source that prohibits buying animals:

(1) והתני: לקח משם כסות—תשרף, בהמה—תעקר תעקר, מעות—יוליכם לים המלח.

(1) But does it not teach: If he bought from there clothing—it must be burned; an animal—it must be rendered useless; coins—they must be brought to the Dead Sea.

(2) ניחא כסות—תישרף, מעות— יוליכם לים המלח, בהמה—תיעקר?

(2) Clothing, it must be burned; coins, they must be brought to the Dead Sea—this makes sense. But an animal must be rendered useless?

(3) והתני: הולכין ליריד ולוקחין מהן עבדים ושפחות ובהמה. רשב"ל אמר: לא סוף דבר עבדים ישראל אלא אפילו עבדים גוים שמקרבן תחת כנפות שמים.

(3) But does it not teach: One may go to the fair and buy from there slaves, handmaidens, and animals. Resh Lakish says: Not just Jewish slaves, but even non-Jewish slaves, for this draws them under the wings of the Divine Presence.

(4) תיפתר ישראל ישראל.

(4) Solve this by saying it refers to a Jew who purchases from a Jew.

(5) והתני: המוכר עבדו לגוים דמיו אסורין.

(5) But does it not teach: One who sells his slave to non-Jews, the proceeds are prohibited?

(6) עוד היא תיפתר ישראל ישראל.

(6) Solve this as well by saying it refers to a Jew who buys from a Jew.

(7) ישראל שהולך ליריד, לוקחין ממנו מפני שהוא כמציל מידן ובחזירה אסור שנהנה מחמת עבודה זרה. ובגוים—בין הולכין בין באין מותר.

(7) A Jew who is on his way to the fair, one may buy from him because this is like saving something from him. But on his return, it is prohibited because he has benefited on account of idolatry. And when it comes to non-Jews—whether coming or going, it is permitted.

This baraita in section 1, which requires disabling the animal, clearly contradicts the earlier baraita, which permitted buying animals from non-Jews at the fair, as is emphasized in section 2. For greater emphasis, the Yerushalmi repeats the contradictory baraita in section 3.

It is at this point that the two Talmuds diverge. To recall, the Bavli attributes the two baraitot to different tannaitic and amoraic opinions— one baraita is interpreted as holding that **all items** purchased from non-Jews at their fairs must be rendered useless, while the other baraita is interpreted as allowing the purchase of **any item**. The baraitot are thus diametrically opposed. In contrast, the Yerushalmi maintains a straightforward reading of the two baraitot, and reconciles the one actual discrepancy—the buying of an animal—by contextualizing the stringent baraita in section 1.[38] The baraita which mandates rendering the animal useless refers to buying **from a Jew** at the fair, and not from a non-Jew as we previously assumed. A Jew is allowed to buy an animal from non-Jews because this prevents the eventual idolatrous sacrifice of the animal. But one cannot buy anything from a Jew who is participating in the idolatrous fair. This is clearly not the simple reading of this baraita, but there is some logic behind the idea that the law is more stringent with regard to buying from a Jew at the fair than it is with regard to buying from a non-Jew. By the very act of going to the fair to sell an animal, the Jew is participating in a forbidden activity—the "dust of idol worship." Therefore, the rabbis' concern to prevent idol worship by buying the animal so it will not be sacrificed is overridden by the prohibition of interacting with Jews participating in the fair. But when it comes to interacting with non-Jews at the fair, the rabbis' overriding concern is to decrease idol worship. Thus, buying an animal is permitted, even though it would entail Jewish participation in the fair.

Section 5 of the Yerushalmi continues with an objection to this resolution. The text cites the beginning of Tosefta Avodah Zarah 3:19. In the Tosefta itself this text reads, "One who sells his slave at the fair of non-Jews." The context of the Tosefta clarifies the meaning of the difficulty— the baraita refers to selling a slave to a non-Jew at the non-Jewish fair, which is clearly prohibited. Here we must note that the baraita in section 1 is taken from the continuation of halakhah 3:19, and thus not surprisingly, the Yerushalmi pits these two sources against one another: How can the end of the baraita (section 1) refer to buying from a Jew, when the beginning of the baraita (section 5) refers to selling to a non-Jew? The Yerushalmi reiterates the same resolution from section 4: The

---

[38] Our reading is based on Rabinovitz, ibid.

context of the baraita is Jewish interaction.[39] Finally, the baraita in section 7 supports the notion that the law is more stringent with regard to interactions with Jews than with non-Jews.

We can now summarize the key difference between the Yerushalmi and the Bavli. The Yerushalmi maintains that in general it is prohibited to buy at the fair. Only certain items may be bought, particularly if there is a motivation to "save" the item from the idolaters. The one contradiction between the baraitot—the issue of buying animals from them—is resolved through a strained contextualization: It is permitted to buy animals from non-Jews, but not from Jews participating in the fair. In contrast, the stam of the Bavli creates the notion that these two baraitot represent diametrically opposed halakhic opinions, which correlate with two amoraic opinions. One baraita presents an absolute prohibition against buying at the fair, while the other baraita is read as permitting all such purchases. We should note, however, that this understanding of the baraitot is attributed only to Resh Lakish. The Bavli does attribute harmonizing contextualizations to R. Yohanan but does so in a unique Babylonian manner related to their understanding of the prohibition. We shall return to this topic below.[40]

---

[39]  The implication would be that it is permitted to sell a slave to a non-Jew. But this contradicts Mishnah Gittin 4:6. It is hard to know how far to take the implications of such resolutions—did the author of this resolution actively intend to imply that it is permitted to sell slaves to non-Jews? Highly unlikely.

[40]  There is one Babylonian amora who does participate in this early layer of the sugya: R. Shisha b. R. Idi (section 4 of the Bavli). In the context of the sugya, it would seem that R. Shisha reads the amoraic statements and the baraitot as does the stam—Resh Lakish holds that one may provide benefit to idolatry. However, it is possible that R. Shisha still refers to an earlier amoraic version of this sugya. This proto-sugya, similar to the version in the Yerushalmi, would open with Resh Lakish's limitation of the mishnah to stores decorated with myrtles. Only such stores, whose participation in the fair is explicitly idolatrous, are off limits. But R. Natan and the rest of his baraita seem to prohibit all participation in the fair. R. Shisha resolves this contradiction by inventing a group of sages who would rule against R. Natan. Those sages would allow participation in the fair, and restrict participation only at stores decorated with myrtles, as does Resh Lakish. The fact that this baraita is attributed only to R. Natan allows R. Shisha to posit the existence of this other opinion. In any case, according to this reconstruction, there is no evidence that R. Shisha read Resh Lakish as permitting Jews to always participate in the fair, as the stam reads him.

## "Because it Diminishes Them": A Late Amoraic Explanation

The Babylonian sugya concludes (after a digression about causing pain to animals) with two brief sections interpreting the baraita which mandates rendering useless any item bought at the fair. We wish to examine these sections (sections 7 and 8 in the numbering above) to see how they read these baraitot. Do they read them as complimentary as does the Yerushalmi—most items may not be bought at the fair, but one may buy land, slaves, and animals because this is saving them from pagan hands? Or do they read the baraitot as polar opposites, as does the stam in the opening section of the Bavli—the first baraita prohibits buying anything from non-Jews at the fair (it is prohibited to derive or provide benefit), and the second baraita allows one to buy anything (providing benefit is permitted)? We begin with a discussion between two fourth generation Eretz Yisraeli amoraim:

**Bavli Avodah Zarah 13b**

בבלי עבודה זרה דף יג ע"ב

אשכחיה רבי יונה לרבי עילאי דקאי
אפיתחא דצור, אמר ליה: קתני בהמה
תיעקר, עבד מאי? עבד ישראל לא קא
מיבעיא לי, כי קא מיבעיא לי - עבד גוי,
מאי?

אמר ליה: מאי קא מיבעיא לך? תניא:
הגוים והרועי בהמה דקה - לא מעלין
ולא מורידין.

R. Yonah found R. Ilai at the gates of Tyre. He said to him: It is taught that an animal must be rendered useless. What about a slave?—I am not asking about a Jewish slave; rather, I am asking about a non-Jewish slave—what is the rule?

He said to him: What are you asking? It was taught: Non-Jews and shepherds—one does not bring them up [from a pit] and one does not throw them down.

The first baraita brought in the Bavli stated that if a Jew buys an animal at the pagan fair, he must render the animal unusable. But R. Yonah asks what one must do with a slave bought at the fair. The problem with his question is that the first baraita does not mention anything about buying a slave and the second baraita assumes that **one can buy** a slave at a fair. Why would R. Yonah assume therefore that there is any problem with buying a slave at a pagan fair? There is no baraita that explicitly says that one cannot! The answer would seem to be that R. Yonah reads the baraitot the way the stam in the Bavli does—they categorically disagree with each other. If the second baraita allows a Jew to buy a slave at the fair, the first baraita (that attributed to R. Natan) would in turn demand that a slave bought at a fair be rendered unusable, a halakhah that is completely untenable. However, R. Yonah and R. Ilai are late Eretz-Yisraeli amoraim, and therefore it is unlikely that they would already interpret the baraitot in the same tenuous manner in which the stam does. So, if not from this baraita, why would R. Yonah assume it is prohibited to buy slaves at fairs?

We would like to suggest that instead of referring to the stammaitic reading of the baraita in the Bavli, R. Yonah is referring to the baraita which originated in Tosefta Avodah Zarah 3:19 and was interpreted in the Yerushalmi. This baraita reads:

| תוספתא עבודה זרה ג:יט | Tosefta Avodah Zarah 3:19 |
|---|---|
| המוכר עבדו ליריד של גוים דמיו אסורין, ויוליך לים המלח. וכופין את רבו שיפדנו, אפילו מאה בדמיו, ויוציאנו לחירות. | One who sells his slave at the non-Jewish fair, the proceeds are prohibited, and he should bring them to the Dead Sea. And we force his master to redeem him, even if this costs 100 times his value, and he goes free. |
| נמצאתה אומר, הנושא והנותן ביריד של גוים: בהמה תיעקר, כסות וכלים ירקבו, מעות וכלי מתכות יוליך הנאה לים המלח. | Thus you say: One who engages in business at a non-Jewish fair—[if he acquires] an animal, it must be rendered useless; clothing or vessels, they should be left to rot; coins or metal vessels, the equivalent in benefit must be thrown into the Dead Sea. |

According to the simple reading of the first section of the baraita, it is prohibited to sell slaves to non-Jews, because this removes them from their ability to perform commandments.[41] And the second section prohibits buying various items at the fair, a halakhah we examined above. However, as part of the resolution of a contradiction between baraitot concerning buying animals at the fair, the Yerushalmi (quoted above) read the baraita

---

41  See also Mishnah Gittin 4:6 and Tosefta Avodah Zarah 3:16.

417

as prohibiting **selling to a Jew** at the fair. This changes the reasoning lying behind the prohibition. The reasoning can no longer be because this removes them from their ability to perform commandments—it does not. Rather the reasoning would be more in line with the second half of the baraita: It is prohibited to engage in business with Jews at the fair. Applying the same logic, the second half of the baraita should prohibit **buying slaves from Jews at the fair** because one should not engage in business with Jews at the fair. It is this reading that caused R. Yonah to believe that buying slaves was prohibited. However, this section of the Tosefta does not actually mention buying slaves at the fair or what to do with those bought there, and therefore the amora needs to ask what is done with a slave that is bought at the fair. R. Ilai acts surprised at the very question and easily dismisses it, not because it is obvious to him that slaves may be bought at fairs, but because it is obvious that if a slave is bought, nothing can be done to him *ex post facto*. While it is somewhat tenuous to suggest that amoraic statements in the Bavli refer to anonymous resolutions in the Yerushalmi, such a reading seems methodologically preferable to positing that they refer to late and extremely tendentious stammaitic interpretations.

The final section of the Bavli is more complex in terms of whether the amoraic statements reflect the stammaitic understanding of the polarity of these baraitot. There is evidence that R. Ashi does not read the second baraita (section 5) as if it allows one to buy anything at the fair, the position the stam ascribes to Resh Lakish. However, his statement does represent a significant leniency when it comes to these laws, one that might almost coincide with that ascribed to Resh Lakish.

| בבלי עבודה זרה יג ע״ב | Bavli Avodah Zarah 13b |
|---|---|
| (1) אמר ליה ר' ירמיה לר' זירא: קתני לוקחין מהן בהמה עבדים ושפחות, עבד ישראל או דלמא אפילו עבד גוי? | (1) R. Yirmiyah said to R. Zera: It is taught one may purchase from them animals, slaves, and handmaidens. Does this refer to a Jewish slave or perhaps even to a non-Jewish slave? |
| (2) אמר ליה: מסתברא עבד ישראל, דאי עבד גוי, למאי מיבעי ליה? | (2) He said to him: It is reasonable that it refers to a Jewish slave, for if it referred to a non-Jewish slave, why even ask? |

(3) כי אתא רבין אמר רבי שמעון בן
לקיש: אפילו עבד גוי, מפני שמכניסו תחת
כנפי השכינה.

(4)אמר רב אשי: אטו בהמה מאי מכניס
תחת כנפי השכינה איכא? אלא משום
מעוטייהו, והכא נמי דממעטי שרי.

(3) When Ravin came he said in the name of R. Shimon b. Lakish: Even a non-Jewish slave, for he brings him under the wings of the Divine Presence.

(4) R. Ashi said: When it comes to an animal, what "brings him under the wings of the Divine Presence" could there be? Rather, it is because it diminishes them. Here too, because it diminishes them, it is permitted.

Sections 1 through 3 are a direct parallel to Resh Lakish's statement in the Yerushalmi but presented in a different format. For ease of reference, we replicate this here:

ירושלמי עבודה זרה א:ד (לט, ג)
והתני: הולכין ליריד ולוקחין מהן עבדים
ושפחות ובהמה.

רשב"ל אמר: לא סוף דבר עבדים ישראל
אלא אפילו עבדים גוים שמקרבן תחת
כנפות שמים.

**Yerushalmi Avodah Zarah 1:4, 39c**

But does it not teach: One may go to the fair and buy from there slaves, handmaidens, and animals?

Resh Lakish says: Not just Jewish slaves, but even non-Jewish slaves, for this draws them under the wings of the Divine Presence.

The Yerushalmi quotes the baraita that allows one to buy slaves, and then Resh Lakish comments. First he deflects an erroneous interpretation (only Jewish slaves) and then he justifies the correct interpretation: One may buy even non-Jewish slaves because this draws them under the wings of the Divine Presence. The Bavli presents the same conclusion in a question-and-answer format.

However, the sugya takes a turn with R. Ashi, who astutely notes that this reading does not explain why one may buy an animal. To return to the original baraita, it is easy to understand the dispensation for buying real estate—this restores Jewish control to the Land of Israel. It is similarly obvious that one may buy Jewish slaves—to restore them to Jewish ownership. And Resh Lakish provides a compelling reason why one can buy non-Jewish slaves. But why should a Jew have to "save the animals" from being used in idolatrous practice? This is the question that troubles

R. Ashi and leads him to suggest a far broader dispensation in terms of Jewish participation at the fair.

R. Ashi explains that buying animals at the fair "diminishes them." Rashi comments that taking an animal away from a non-Jew reduces the non-Jew's strength. The problem with this explanation is that it simply does not make economic sense—if the non-Jew's strength is reduced by selling his animal, then why would he sell it in the first place? While occasionally people sell under duress, this is for the most part not true and probably even less true of professional sellers participating in the fair. This leads to a number of other explanations among the medieval commentators.[42] What is important for us to note is that R. Ashi does not attribute this dispensation to a blanket prohibition, "it is permitted to provide benefit," the position the stam attributes to Resh Lakish. Even if we do not perfectly understand why R. Ashi thinks one may buy animals from non-Jew at the fair, he needs to find some way to justify granting this license. R. Ashi's understanding of the baraita may lead to a similar outcome as the position ascribed to Resh Lakish ("it is permitted to provide benefit"), but in principle it is completely different. R. Ashi maintains that it is prohibited to provide benefit to idolatry. But he also maintains that buying from non-Jews does the opposite. Thus R. Ashi, one of the last amoraim, still reads the baraita in a manner close to its original meaning—one may not buy at the fair unless there are extenuating circumstances.

Our comparison of the tannaitic and amoraic material highlights how a tremendous leniency was created in the laws of engaging in business with non-Jews at the idolatrous fair. We will trace this out step by step:

1) The Mishnah originally ruled that one may not go to any store participating in the fair. In the Yerushalmi, the amoraim Resh Lakish and R. Yohanan delineated which stores are considered to be participating in the fair based on the nature of the decorations.

---

[42] For example, Ramban 13a s.v. ויש מי שאומר states that it is forbidden to sell them property because selling to them at the fair adds to the glory of the idolatry. But buying from them will empty out their stores, thereby reducing the appearance of such adornments. Later in the same paragraph he suggests yet another meaning to R. Ashi's statement—at the fair the prices are lowered. Thus, buying at the fair limits the non-Jew's profit margin.

2) The Bavli modifies Resh Lakish's statement (similar to R. Yohanan's statement in the Yerushalmi). Instead of limiting which stores are considered to be participating in the fair, Resh Lakish is now understood as permitting all participation in the fair, as long as the Jew does not directly derive benefit by smelling the roses or myrtles used as decorations.

3) Both Talmuds cite two baraitot, one which rules that a Jew who benefits at the fair must ensure that any benefit he received is destroyed, and the other which allows a Jew to buy land, slaves, and animals. There is some genuine disagreement between these sources, particularly over animals. While the Yerushalmi solves the contradiction by limiting the prohibition, the Bavli reads the tannaim as reflecting the Babylonian version of the amoraim: Some rabbis prohibit any engagement with non-Jews at the fair, and some permit everything except for direct benefit. This final step anchors in tannaitic sources the enormous leniency ascribed to Resh Lakish. While this literary move makes it appear that the lenient opinion existed among the rabbis from the tannaitic period, it is almost certain that it is not reflective of the opinion of any talmudic sage. The stam creates this position for the interpretive and literary purposes described above and it should not be read as an historical opinion.

## R. Natan and the Reduction in Taxes: A Methodological Postscript

As a postscript to our analysis of this sugya, we return to the baraita attributed to R. Natan in section 1. The second half of the baraita has a parallel in Tosefta Avodah Zarah 3:19. In contrast, the first half of the baraita, which describes the tax relief at the non-Jewish fair, has no parallel in any other rabbinic text. It is not unusual to encounter baraitot that appear only in the Bavli, but such sources raise a thorny methodological issue—does material presented as tannaitic in the Bavli for which there are no parallels in tannaitic literature authentically reflect tannaitic thought?[43] We will consider this question with regard to the first half of our baraita.

| בבלי עבודה זרה יג ע״א | Bavli Avodah Zarah 13a |
|---|---|
| רבי נתן אומר: יום שעבודת כוכבים מנחת בו את המכס, מכריזין ואומרים: כל מי שנוטל עטרה ויניח בראשו ובראש חמורו לכבוד עבודת כוכבים - יניח לו את המכס, ואם לאו אל יניח לו את המכס, יהודי שנמצא שם מה יעשה? יניח - נמצא נהנה! לא יניח - נמצא מהנה! | R. Natan says: The day on which idolatry reduces the taxes, they announce, saying: "Anyone who takes this wreath and puts it on his head and on his donkey's head in honor of idolatry—they will reduce for him the taxes. And if not, they will not reduce for him the taxes." A Jew who is there, what should he do? If he puts it on, he derives benefit; if he does not put it on—he will provide benefit! |

There are multiple problems with the historical reliability of this source. First, as Zeev Safrai has noted, there is no external evidence of such a practice.[44] Second, the practice does not accord with the other sources concerning taxes at the fair. The earliest source to connect a tax reduction with the fair is Yerushalmi Avodah Zarah 1:4, 39c, which comments on the mishnah that prohibits going to an idolatrous city. Resh Lakish states that this mishnah refers to an idolatrous fair, and explains that Jews may not buy inside the city since they "benefit from the tax [exemption]." But outside the city in which the fair is taking the place, there is no tax benefit and, therefore, one may purchase from non-Jews there. The practice of obtaining a benefit by putting a wreath on one's head would completely disturb this distinction. Third, the practice seems almost impossible to implement in reality—every person would put this wreath on his head and/or on the head of his donkey? Even Safrai, who in the end does seem to accept the baraita as historical testimony, notes that such a practice would lead to bedlam in the marketplace.[45] Fourth, the baraita presents the Jew with a dilemma. If he puts the wreath on his head, he benefits

---

[43] See our discussion of the issue in the introduction to volume one of *Reconstructing the Talmud*.

[44] Zeev Safrai, "Fairs in the Land of Israel in the Mishna and Talmud Period," *Zion* 49 (1984), 142.

[45] Ibid. n. 14.

from an idolatrous practice.[46] But if he does not, he gives benefit to idolatry. But what is this benefit that he is giving to idolatry? Paying taxes to the government is not prohibited. This forces us to explain that if he does not put on the wreath, he pays the taxes to some sort of idolatrous authority and not to the usual tax collectors.[47] In other words, the Roman government tells the religious authorities that they may collect taxes at the fair, and the religious authorities in turn find a way for some fairgoers to avoid these taxes. Clearly, this is not reflective of any historical reality. Finally, the baraita uses some unusual terminology. Tannaitic literature almost never uses the word "יהודי" in reference to a Jew. Rather, the term "ישראל" is always used.

If the baraita is not an accurate reflection of the historical reality during the tannaitic period, then when and why was it created? While this exercise is always speculative, it is perhaps more than coincidental that the word "מעוטרות," decorated, is mentioned in the mishnah and the word "עטרה," from the same root, is found in R. Natan's statement. Perhaps the author of this baraita was attempting to understand what exactly these decorations were for. While we would assume that the mishnah refers to decorating the store with such a wreath, the author of the baraita combined the issue of tax reductions mentioned by Resh Lakish in the Yerushalmi with the decorations in the mishnah and concluded that the wreaths were not merely decorations used to denote which stores were participating in the fair. Rather, they refer to stores in which a wreath was put onto a person's head in order to symbolize his participation in the fair. This explanation concretizes the connection between idolatry and economic participation in the festival, which may have been less clear to late Babylonian rabbis.

This conclusion to this rather lengthy chapter brings us full circle: Why was it prohibited to have any economic engagement with non-Jews at their fairs or festivals? Having dismissed the R. Natan baraita as reliable historical evidence of a tax reduction for participating in the fair, we can conclude by considering the broader claim staked by some scholars that the entire prohibition on participating in the fair was due to the tax reductions for its participants. Such a tax reduction would mean that the Jew had received tangible benefit from idolatrous practice. There are

---

[46] See Tosafot s.v. יניח for a discussion of this issue.
[47] See Rashi.

indeed some texts that state or imply that those who participated in the fair did receive tax reductions (see Yerushalmi 1:4, 39c).[48] However, Yehudah Cohn rightfully rejects the historicity of this explanation.[49] Tannaitic texts never mention tax exemptions. And while the Yerushalmi does mention tax exemptions, it does not state that they are the reason for the prohibition; the tax deduction is simply a way to determine which stores participate in the fair, the same way decorations were used by the mishnah.

As we have underscored throughout this chapter, participating in the fair or in the economic interchanges around a festival is forbidden not for some other reason: because the Jew benefits from tax benefits, or because the non-Jew will thank his god, or because Jewish participation will enable the non-Jew to worship. Rather, participation in these institutions is in and of itself the "dust of idol worship"—close enough to idol worship that a Jew must avoid it.

---

[48]   See also section 6 in the sugya quoted above.

[49]   Yehudah Cohn, "The Graeco-Roman Trade Fair and the Rabbis," 187-193.

# AFTERWORD

"Let my teaching drop like rain, my saying flow like dew" (Deuteronomy 32:2). Moses' final song to his people likens his words, his Torah, to the nourishing force of rain and dew descending on a thirsty nation. In Sifre Devarim *piska* 306, R. Meir expands on this metaphor: Like rain, an abundance of Torah presents a challenge:

**ספרי דברים פ׳ שו**

*יערֹף כמטר לקחי* - היה ר׳ מאיר אומר: לעולם הוי אדם כונס דברי תורה כללים, שאם אתה כונסם פרטים - מייגעים אותו, ואי אתה יודע מה לעשות .

משל לאדם שהלך לקיסרי וצריך מאה זוז או מאתים זוז הוצאה: אם נוטלם פרט - מייגעים אותו, ואין יודע מה לעשות; אבל מצרפם, ועושה אותם סלעים ופורט ומוציא בכל מקום שירצה.

**Sifre Devarim piska 306**

*Let my teaching drop like rain*—R. Meir said: One should always gather words of Torah as (general) principles; for if he gathers them as details, they make him weary and he does not know what to do.

This is analogous to a man going to Caesarea, who needs one hundred or two hundred *zuzim* for expenses. If he takes them in *perutot*, they make him weary and he does not know what to do; but if he combines them into *sela'im*, he can make change and use them wherever he wishes.

R. Meir explains that if a person does not provide an organizational framework for the myriad of rabbinic teachings he has learned, his studies will quickly become burdensome to him. He will confuse his teachings, will not be able to recall them when needed, and may even forget them. The oral transmission of rabbinic sources demands a systematic method for memorizing the words of Torah. R. Meir explains that teachings should be grouped together according to general principles so that they may later be accessed when their particular details are relevant to a given situation. This is similar to carrying large denominations of currency and only breaking them into smaller amounts when necessary.

While R. Meir's teaching originally addressed the composition of the Mishnah, it is particularly suited for thinking about the work of the editors of the Bavli. These sages were faced with the tremendous task of **orally** preserving teachings from different genres, generations, and centers of learning in a single literary corpus. This monumental undertaking could be accomplished only with an organizational framework which allowed for the preservation of a tremendous number of sources. To accomplish this the stam worked on two planes: 1) uniting disparate traditions from different sources into long discourses on given subjects, and 2) expanding narrow fields of halakhic inquiry into broad conceptual categories. As we have seen, the creation of these passages and these rules often came at the expense of the original, nuanced meaning of the individual source, but their efforts were essential to the process of preserving, transmitting, and utilizing the words of the sages. It is our job as readers to appreciate this process of creating a coherent and consistent work, while still working to uncover the value of each individual source, each unique as a raindrop that makes up the entire nourishing rainfall.

# Acknowledgements

*Reconstructing the Talmud: Volume II* is the product of our teaching in the vibrant *batei midrash* of the Conservative Yeshiva and Jewish Theological Seminary. Each of us wishes to thank our organizations for the supportive and nourishing atmosphere they provide and our students and colleagues for the challenging questions they continually pose.

We want to thank our editor, Ilana Kurshan, for improving the content and style of our writing and Jeremy Tabick for his helpful remarks and copy editing.

Thanks to Dov Abramson and the Dov Abramson Studio for again designing the book and its cover.

Thanks to Elie Kaunfer and the Hadar Institute for again publishing and promoting our work. Hadar stands at the forefront of the rigorous and academic study of Judaism in a religiously meaningful setting. We are honored that such an institution shares our vision, and we look forward to continuing our work together in the future.

We would also like to thank the Rogoff family and the KG Foundation for their continued generous support in publishing our scholarship.

This book has been a joint effort between the two authors. While each chapter began with one of us, continual discussion of the material and subsequent revisions largely obscure the original authorship. We have found that each of us has talents that the other lacks, and while it may be a cliché, working together has created a sum that is certainly greater than the parts.

Finally, thanks to our families, here in Israel and abroad, for all their support and love and especially to our hard-working and talented wives, Dara Rogoff and Julie Zuckerman.

# About the Authors

**Dr. Joshua Kulp** is the Rosh Yeshiva of the Fuchsberg Jewish Center Conservative Yeshiva. Along with the two volumes of *Reconstructing the Talmud*, he is the author of *The Schechter Haggadah*.

**Dr. Jason Rogoff** is Academic Director of Israel Programs and Assistant Professor of Talmud and Rabbinics at the Jewish Theological Seminary of America. He is also a faculty member at the Rothberg International School of the Hebrew University of Jerusalem and the Schechter Institute of Jewish Studies.

Made in the USA
Monee, IL
13 September 2021